Radical Assimilation
in English Jewish History
1656–1945

The Modern Jewish Experience
Paula Hyman and Deborah Dash Moore, editors

Radical Assimilation in English Jewish History 1656–1945

TODD M. ENDELMAN

Indiana
University
Press
BLOOMINGTON AND INDIANAPOLIS

The paper used in this publication meets the minimum requirements of American
National Standard for Information Sciences—Permanence of Paper for Printed
Library Materials, ANSI Z39.48-1984.

Manufactured in the United States of America

Library of Congress Cataloging-in-Publication Data
Endelman, Todd M.
Radical assimilation in English Jewish history, 1656–1945 / Todd
M. Endelman.
p.   cm.— (The Modern Jewish experience)
Includes bibliographical references.
ISBN 0-253-31952-8 (alk. paper)
1. Jews—Great Britain—History.   2. Jews—Great Britain—Cultural
assimilation.   3. Judaism—Great Britain—History.   4. Great
Britain—Ethnic relations.   I. Title.   II. Series: Modern Jewish
experience (Bloomington, Ind.)
DS135.E5E49 1990
941'.004924—dc20   89-45475
                                                                       CIP

1   2   3   4   5   94   93   92   91   90

Contents

Illustrations follow page 57

For
Michael
and
Flora

Preface

This book is the outcome of a chance suggestion made to me in 1977 by Haym Soloveitchik, then Dean of the Bernard Revel Graduate School of Yeshiva University, where I was teaching at the time. He mentioned to me one day that the Memorial Foundation for Jewish Culture had awarded a grant several years earlier to a member of the Revel School faculty to study Jewish apostasy in medieval Europe and that the recipient of the award had never made use of the funds. Since the award had already been allocated, he thought that I might be able to claim it if I submitted a proposal to the Memorial Foundation on the merit of examining the phenomenon of Jewish conversion in the modern period. I was then in the midst of preparing my dissertation for publication and had not yet given much thought to what I would turn to next, so the suggestion was a welcome one, particularly since I viewed conversion as a radical form of the acculturation process, which, in its Anglo-Jewish context, had been the subject of my dissertation. In due time, the grant came through, and I was launched on a new project, one that proved to be richer and more complex than I at first imagined.

I had initially intended to write a book treating the phenomenon of conversion from the Enlightenment to the present in a comparative geographical context, but I soon realized, given the current state of research on the social history of European and American Jewish communities, that this would be impossible. So I decided to focus on forms of radical assimilation in English Jewish history (the field I knew best) and highlight in passing similarities and differences with Jewish communities elsewhere in the Western world. Although this book carries forward some of the themes I developed in *The Jews of Georgian England*, I have not reproduced materials presented at length there. For example, I have not treated in any extensive way the religious behavior of anglicized Jews in the eighteenth century, which was one of the central themes of *The Jews of Georgian England*. Instead, I have summarized the discussion presented there when necessary and referred readers to the relevant sections of that book for the evidence supporting my conclusions. On the other hand, because little has been written about the religious behavior and Jewish consciousness of the middle-class community during the Victorian era or the anglicized children of the immigrants in the interwar years, knowledge of which is essential to understanding drift and defection in those periods, I have gone into some detail in treating these topics.

A word about the evidence used in writing this book: For reasons that are explained in the introduction, it is impossible to measure statistically defection from the Anglo-Jewish community at any time in its history. Consequently, I have not been able to make the kinds of precise statements about trends in intermarriage and conversion that historians writing about other Jewish communities might be able to make. Moreover, as readers familiar with English Jewish history are well aware, Anglo-Jewry did not produce a stream of self-revelatory autobiographical literature—letters, diaries, memoirs, confessions—as did German Jewry, for example. Thus, it is frequently difficult, although not impossible, to assess the motives and emotional states of English Jews who merged into the mainstream. All of which is to say that there may be too much speculation here for historians accustomed to more abundant and precise evidence. Still, if one wants to write the social history of English Jewry, one must learn to make do with the limited evidence available or give up the enterprise altogether.

It would have been impossible for me to undertake this study without the financial assistance provided by the National Endowment for the Humanities; the Memorial Foundation for Jewish Culture; and the Office of Research and Graduate Development, Indiana University. I am very grateful to them for supporting my work in its early stages. In addition, I want to express my gratitude to the Oxford Centre for Postgraduate Hebrew Studies and its president, David Patterson, for the warm hospitality extended to me and my family while we were in England. When I was beginning my work there, I received many valuable suggestions from Harold Pollins and Bryan Cheyette. A stroke of good fortune later on brought me into contact with Aryeh Newman of the Hebrew University of Jerusalem, who went out of his way to share with me his own research on the Frankau family, for which I am particularly grateful. Archivists and librarians at research institutions in Israel and England kindly allowed me access to important materials in their care. In particular, I would like to single out the assistance given me by the staffs of the Mocatta Library and Anglo-Jewish Archives, University College, London; the Rothschild Archive, London; the Central Zionist Archives, Jerusalem; and the Central Archives for the History of the Jewish People, Jerusalem. I am also grateful to the editor of *Victorian Studies* for allowing me to reprint as parts of chapter 3 material that originally appeared in that journal in 1985.

I am particularly indebted to four friends who took time from their own busy schedules to read all or part of the manuscript: David Feldman, Paula Hyman, Jack Rakove, and Sheldon Rothblatt. I have learned much from them.

I have dedicated this book to my children, Michael and Flora, who will soon be old enough to read and profit from it. As always, I am grateful to Judy for her patience, good humor, and love.

Radical Assimilation
in English Jewish History
1656–1945

Introduction

Jewish emancipation in the West created a new world of opportunities for an ill-used people long accustomed to being buffeted to and fro. The bestowal of citizenship offered Jews unprecedented political and economic security, enabling them to pursue their livelihoods without arbitrary obstacles and harassment and thus escape the grinding poverty that was their common lot in previous centuries. In their own eyes and in the eyes of others, emancipation enhanced their social status and confirmed their worth as productive and respectable members of society. It also offered Jews novel possibilities for creative activity in the arts and sciences and in public life, allowing them to apply their intellectual faculties to materials and problems that had been outside the world of traditional concerns and to exercise their talents in new and diverse settings.

For most Jews in the West this was an exhilarating, heady experience. They abandoned their social and cultural ghettos with alacrity to embrace the opportunities rapidly unfolding before them. Ambitious, energetic, restless, they poured into new spheres of activity and, in startlingly short time, ceased to be a despised, impoverished minority on the periphery of gentile society and became instead active, if not always welcome, participants in its mainstream, contributing to its development and occasionally stamping it with their mark.

If, however, emancipation brought unambiguous benefits to Jews as individuals, the same cannot be said of its impact on Jews as a collectivity and Judaism as a culture and a religion. Before emancipation, when Jews lived in semiautonomous corporate communities and celebrated their distinctiveness and separation from gentiles, the hostility of the external world did not pose a threat to their continuity or cohesion, even if it took its toll in lives and property. Legal emancipation and social acceptance, however incomplete, changed all that. The acculturation and integration of Western Jews diluted old allegiances and thus weakened the fabric of communal solidarity. Spheres of activity outside the confines of their community beckoned acculturated youth, tempting them with excitements and pleasures unavailable to those who remained behind, immersed exclusively in Jewish social and business networks. New interests and loyalties jostled for primacy with old associations and concerns. At times, they coexisted, perhaps uneasily, but they coexisted nonetheless. But not infrequently the old gave way to the new completely. From the age of the En-

1

lightenment to the period of the Holocaust, several hundred thousand Jews separated themselves from the community of their origins. Some embraced Christianity outright; others drifted away in less definitive and abrupt ways.

That legal toleration and social acceptance could threaten the Jewish people was a possibility unforeseen by the leaders of Western Jewish communities in the age of emancipation. Insofar as it is possible to generalize, it can be said that the central focus of communal energies in the nineteenth and early twentieth centuries was the removal of legal obstacles to full integration into state and society and the defense of Jews and Judaism against manifest antisemitism, particularly after 1870. Western Jewish leaders displayed little sensitivity to the ways in which their efforts to promote integration also indirectly led to the dilution of Jewish identity and communal solidarity. Only slowly did they come to grasp how difficult the maintenance of a group identity would be in an age when the hold of religion was weakening and opportunities elsewhere were beckoning. Consequently, they devoted relatively little time to devising remedies to stem drift and defection.

The growth of Jewish nationalism after 1870 provoked the first serious discussion of the impact of emancipation on Jewish identity and solidarity. Zionist ideologues and publicists came to believe that assimilation posed as grave a threat to Jewish survival in post-emancipation societies as antisemitic demagoguery and violence did elsewhere. While the latter attacked Jewry from without, they argued, the former sapped its strength from within. This critique of the assimilationist faith in emancipation focused attention on how well Jewish cohesiveness was holding up in emancipated communities and engendered the first scholarly literature on conversion, intermarriage, and other forms of disaffiliation. Sociologists such as Arthur Ruppin (1876–1943) and Jacob Lestschinsky (1876–1966) produced important studies of Jewish economic and social life that emphasized the losses that Western Jewry had sustained through the absorption of assimilated Jews into the mainstream of society. In a more popular vein, the publicist Felix Theilhaber (1884–1956), in his provocatively titled *Der Untergang der deutschen Juden* (1911), predicted the demise of German Jewry through steady social leakage and a falling birthrate.[1]

The emphasis on the corrosive consequences of emancipation in these avowedly nationalist writers has not been echoed in recent historical writing on the Jewish communities of the West. In the mid-twentieth century, historians in both the Diaspora and the Land of Israel have concentrated on other items on the historiographical agenda—emancipation, *haskalah*, religious reform, *Wissenschaft des Judentums*, Zionism, antisemitism, and Jewish responses to antisemitism. When they have turned to the general topic of assimilation, they have tended to accentuate the perpetuation of Jewish identity rather than its rapid dissolution. While hardly denying the inroads made by intermarriage, conversion, and indifference, they nonetheless stress the balance Jews struck in reconciling conflicting demands. In response to hackneyed stereotypes about rampant assimilation, they rightly emphasize that the majority of Jews everywhere in the West at any particular moment remained loyal to their origins and that most did so by embracing forms of identity that were adapted to the radically new circumstances in which they now lived. Unlike earlier researchers, they celebrate the tenacity of Western Jews in preserving their Jewishness in the face of overwhelming pressures working to dissolve it. Although not overt, the implication of their work is that emancipation and toleration need not necessarily threaten Jewish survival and that an authentic and dynamic Jewish life is possible in the diaspora communities of the West.[2]

The history of the English Jewish community in the modern period (from the resettlement in the mid-seventeenth century to the end of World War II) offers particularly fruitful ground for exploring these questions about the maintenance of Jewish identity in tolerant circumstances. It does so precisely because English history is largely devoid of the active persecution and rampant discrimination so characteristic of the Jewish experience elsewhere. With the exception of the clamor over the Jew Bill of 1753—a minor event in English political history with no long-term implications—Jewish integration into the mainstream of society proceeded more smoothly, with less resistance on the part of the majority, than in other European states. Before emancipation legal obstacles to social and economic advancement were not onerous, certainly by comparison with the statutory inequality that was the rule in continental countries. In the mid-Victorian years, the campaign to achieve full political equality—primarily the right to sit in the House of Commons—failed to excite widespread interest among either Christians or Jews and never developed into a major political question. Antisemitism, while not uncommon in many social settings and in popular consciousness, remained largely outside the political arena. As an ideology of protest against modernity, it never captured the English imagination, except perhaps during the interwar period, and even in those desperate years it made relatively few converts.

Because English society was more flexible than others in accommodating Jews who wanted greater contact, if not fusion, with the majority society, the study of Jewish integration there takes on a paradigmatic quality. From the early eighteenth century, English Jews were able to move into gentile circles with an ease that became common in other communities only two centuries later. Those who were willing to give up the most distinctive marks of Jewish separatism and to embrace the code of behavior of the group they aspired to join found acceptance more often than not. By offering such opportunities for integration and absorption, England also presented Jews with an unprecedented challenge to the preservation of their religious and ethnic cohesiveness. Toleration and prosperity worked to dissolve ties of communal solidarity in much the same way that they have in the liberal societies of the West since the end of World War II. Then, as now, the accident of birth was no guarantee that a Jew would remain a Jew.

The majority of Jews in England at any time in the modern period struck a balance between the demands of group solidarity and religious tradition, on the one hand, and the lure of the majority culture, on the other. Before World War II, most were content with a limited degree of assimilation into the mainstream of the majority society, preferring to limit their closest social ties to persons from the community of their birth, regardless of the strength of their own attachment to Jewish religious observances. However, in every generation there were persons who abandoned the Jewish community altogether, either by converting to Christianity or by marrying a gentile (which in the Anglo-Jewish context was commonly regarded as an act of apostasy). Those who chose the path of radical assimilation, who sought total fusion with the majority, were usually indifferent to the practices and doctrines of Judaism well before their departure from the community. Judaism having become in their eyes an unnecessary burden or an embarrassing atavism, they ceased being nominal Jews at the time of their baptism or marriage and became nominal Christians instead. Their reasons for changing their religion were largely secular and opportunistic. Some sought to bolster their social standing by escaping the stigma attached to Jewishness, a stigma that persisted throughout modern English history despite a high level of public toleration. Others wished to participate in spheres of activity outside the range of usual Jewish occupations and interests and thought conversion would ease their way. Still others, having already mixed in non-Jewish social circles and grown estranged from traditional ritual and belief, drifted away from the community through indifference and intermarriage.

The number of Jews who merged completely into gentile society between the mid-seventeenth and mid-twentieth centuries was substantial, but unfortunately it is impossible to estimate how large a group it was. In Britain, the state did not oversee the affairs of religious bodies outside the Church of England or trouble itself about movement from one denomination or religion to another. Religious identity was a voluntary matter, outside the purview of the central government. Nor did the established church show any interest in gathering information from local parishes on the number of Jews who were baptized or who married Christians in church services without formally converting. Consequently, there are no official statistics for conversion or intermarriage. (In Central Europe, on the other hand, where religious affiliation was an aspect of a person's civil status, the state kept track of these matters.) For the nineteenth century, there are reports from missionary groups totaling the number of Jews baptized under their auspices, but these figures are untrustworthy, since, for obvious reasons, missionaries tended to inflate the number of Jewish souls they saved. Moreover, Jews converted by missionaries were not representative of the majority of Jews who cut their ties to the community. Missionaries worked largely in poor immigrant neighborhoods and had little contact with families in better circumstances, who, if they decided to embrace Christianity, did so largely for pragmatic reasons, without having been evangelized.

The one attempt to estimate the number of Jews baptized in England is seriously flawed. In 1899, the German conversionist J. F. A. de le Roi published a statistical survey of Jewish conversions in Europe and America during the nineteenth century. The absence of government or church records for Great Britain forced de le Roi to devise an indirect method of calculating the total number of Jewish conversions there. He reasoned that if, in Germany, the ratio of Jews converted under missionary auspices to those baptized in regular churches was 1:8 or 1:9, then it would be possible to calculate the number of Jews baptized in parish churches in England by using roughly the same ratio. In fact, so as not to overestimate the total number of converts, he used a ratio of 1:6. He thus estimated that there were 28,830 Jewish conversions in Great Britain in the nineteenth century. De le Roi's method, in addition to being flawed by its reliance on the questionable figures of missionary groups, also rested on the dubious methodological assumption that the circumstances affecting conversion in England were roughly the same as in Germany. De le Roi also ignored cases of intermarriage, which may have been as numerous as those of formal conversion and which in the English context almost always led to disaffiliation and thus functioned socially in much the same way as conversion.[3]

Despite the absence of statistical information on conversion and intermarriage in England, it is possible to study the decline of Jewish loyalties in the three centuries between the resettlement and World War II. Memoirs, correspondence, sermons, newspapers, genealogical tables, family histories, church records, missionary reports, novels, and other nonquantitative sources provide sufficient information both to gauge the broad contours of disaffiliation and to describe the motives of those who left and the circumstances in which they were absorbed into the larger society. Moreover, even if quantitative evidence regarding intermarriage and conversion were available, as they are for Germany, Austria, and Hungary, it alone would not be able to answer fundamental questions about the transmission of Jewish identity over several generations. This is because evidence of this sort can be used to calculate the rate of disaffiliation in any year in the aggregate but not to trace the Jewish loyalties of any group of particular families over several generations. Yet it is critical to do just this, since the decline of Jewish attachments is a cumulative multigenerational process. To be sure, there were instances of Jews emerging directly from the world of tradition and plunging headlong into the surrounding society, but they were hardly typical. More commonly Jews in each succeeding generation became progressively distant from the traditions and allegiances of their ancestors, so that the Jewishness (however defined) of the last generation to remain within the ancestral fold was in fact already enfeebled and diluted before any formal act of apostasy occurred.

The gradual, multigenerational character of the process of Jewish disaffiliation has worked to mask the extent of the phenomenon everywhere. For subtle and undramatic transformations, however great their cumulative impact, aroused less interest, both at the time and in historical retrospect, than dramatic and decisive ruptures. This obscuring of the extent of drift and defection has been particularly acute in the case of English Jewry, among whom dramatic bursts of outright apostasy—so characteristic of the Central European Jewish experience—were noticeably absent. In addition, succeeding waves of Jewish immigration from the Continent in the nineteenth and twentieth centuries periodically swelled the size of the community and thus masked the decline occurring among families long settled in the country. The number of newcomers easily outstripped the number of those lost through various forms of radical assimilation. Consequently, conversion, intermarriage, and disaffiliation never became burning issues of communal concern (except, perhaps, during the interwar period) in the way they did elsewhere.

Nevertheless, considerable leakage occurred, although without fanfare for the most part, if not in one generation, then in the next. It does not take a professional knowledge of Anglo-Jewish history to realize that scores of once-prominent Jewish families ceased to be Jewish between the mid-eighteenth century and World War II. Harts, Frankses, Goldsmids, Gompertzes, Montefiores, Cohens, Jessels, Franklins, Beddingtons, and Sassoons, to name only a few examples from the Georgian and Victorian periods, disappeared from the ranks of the communal notability, some over a century ago, others more recently. The departure of these families, once pillars of the Jewish establishment, indicates that radical assimilation was not an extraordinary event, a phenomenon on the periphery of Jewish life, but rather a common occurrence, eating away at the maintenance of group solidarity.

To study drift and defection, then, is to focus attention simultaneously on those forces that bound Jews to their ancestral community and those that worked to weaken traditional sympathies, pulling Jews into the larger society. Seen in this light, conversion and intermarriage appear not as deviant or marginal forms of behavior, of little concern to serious students of the modern Jewish experience, but as radical responses to pressures and attractions to which all Jews were exposed. On a spectrum of Jewish efforts to reconcile conflicting demands, disaffiliation in all its forms was clearly an extreme solution, but it would be foolish to ignore its relevance to the problem of Jewish integration into the modern world merely because it stands at the far end of that spectrum. After all, the same forces that led some Jews to sever their ethnic ties completely led, in other cases, to more moderate and conventional forms of assimilation, well within the pale of communal norms.

The central problem confronting the historian of drift and defection is to determine why some persons were more likely than others to cut their ties to Judaism and why disaffection occurred more frequently at certain times and less so in others. For although the severing of communal ties was a characteristic of the modern period in general, it was never uniform at all levels of society and in all periods. There were, rather, patterns of radical assimilation that emerged in the course of Anglo-Jewish history, bearing the impress of social and political conditions in the country at large and reflecting as well the origins of various groups within the community. During the Victorian years, for example, conversion and intermarriage were relatively rare among wealthy families that had been settled in England for some time, although a century earlier apostasy had been quite common among Sephardi families that were equally prosperous and equally anglicized. In short, the decline of English Jewry was not a steady, unremitting process, linked in a straightforward and unambiguous fashion to increasing acculturation and prosperity. Other factors, both internal and external to the Jewish community, intervened at times to slow, as well as advance, the pace of disaffection.

Although the weakening of Jewish solidarity runs as a persistent theme throughout Anglo-Jewish history, it has not attracted much historiographical attention, either from the amateur historians who dominated the writing of Anglo-Jewish history before the 1970s or from professional scholars, who in the last two decades have revitalized the field through the application of critical standards. The former, themselves more often than not active in communal life, approached the history of Anglo-Jewry in a spirit of uncritical admiration.[4] Their work celebrated the readmission of Jews to England, the organization of synagogues and charities, the founding of provincial communities, the rise of great merchant and banking dynasties, the triumph of toleration, and the personal achievements of distinguished Jews. Their version of Anglo-Jewish history was both whiggish and apologetic, emphasizing the harmony between Jewish life and English values and the contributions of Jews to the expansion of English society, while minimizing the discordant aspects of the processes of acculturation and integration. It is not surprising, then, that the theme of apostasy received little attention in their writing. The story of Jews who cut their ties to Judaism for pragmatic reasons was not a tale likely to inspire gentile respect or Jewish pride.

Academic historians who have written on Anglo-Jewry have also shown little interest in the subject. The topics that have attracted them have been the well-established themes in the historiography of the modern Jewish experience: the struggle for emancipation, antisemitism and Jewish responses, Jewish economic activity, Jewish political behavior, and religious schisms and communal politics. With the exception of Bill Williams's pioneering work on Manchester Jewry,[5] they have shown little interest in exploring the maintenance of group loyalties—or their dissolution—over the course of Anglo-Jewish history. To some extent, this may reflect what is in fact a trend characteristic of modern Jewish historiography in general— an absence of interest in the social history of Jewish identity and practice. There is another reason as well for neglect of this topic. The growth of non-white immigrant communities in Great Britain in recent decades and the accompanying explosion of racism have stimulated interest in the earlier Jewish immigration from Eastern Europe. As a consequence, historians have tended to pay more attention to "foreign" Jews than to "native" Jews. (The latter, of course, were more likely to cut their ties to Judaism, by virtue of their prior anglicization, than the former, who had only recently arrived from Poland or Russia.) Thus, we know more today about the social history of the Jews of Whitechapel than those of Maida Vale and Hampstead.[6]

The chapters that follow describe and explain the patterns of disaffiliation that developed in England from the second half of the seventeenth century, when Jewish settlement was renewed there, until World War II. By tracing the course of drift and defection among the Jews of England over several centuries, I seek to understand why Jewish attachments atrophied among some groups within the community more rapidly than among others. I pay particular attention to the fate of Jewishness within individual families over several generations in the belief that this is one of the most effective ways of gauging the transmission of Jewish consciousness over time. This may at initial glance appear to be an excessively anecdotal approach, one that takes too great a delight in the particular, but, given the absence of quantitative evidence, it is inescapable. Moreover, the family histories recounted here, however odd or amusing they might be in some of their particulars, are intended to represent larger social trends within the English Jewish community. I also seek to compare the advance of radical assimilation in Anglo-Jewish history with its spread in other Jewish communities. (Too few Jews lived in Scotland or Ireland to make comparisons with the communities there worthwhile.) Doing so will help identify what is unique in the interplay between English and Jewish history, the outcome of social structures, cultural values, and political forces peculiar to England, and what is common to the historical experience of Western Jews in general as they sought to reconcile their Jewishness with participation in the larger societies in which they lived.

1

Sephardim
1656–1837

Between the expulsion of 1290 and the readmission of 1656, Jews were not permitted to settle in England. This ban was not absolute, however, and persons of Jewish descent, including professing, observant Jews, trickled into the country from time to time. Most were physicians and merchants who left after completing their business; a handful were adventurers who were attracted by the endowments of the *Domus Conversorum* in London and accepted baptism after their arrival. The few professing Jews who came to England either received permission to observe their faith during their stay from the officials who sanctioned their visit or practiced their religion clandestinely. In any case, they were in no position to create a Jewish community. During the sixteenth century, the number of individuals of Jewish background arriving in England in this manner increased. Small groups of Marranos, crypto-Jewish refugees from Spain and Portugal whose ancestors had accepted Christianity under duress, settled in London and Bristol, avoiding persecution by living in the guise of Roman Catholics. Some observed Jewish rituals in secret and eventually returned to Jewish communities on the Continent, there discarding their Marrano masks; others ceased to profess Judaism (or, perhaps, already had before their arrival), remained in the country, and ultimately merged into the native population. Under the circumstances, the early Marrano colonies broke up and disappeared by the start of the seventeenth century.[1]

The modern Anglo-Jewish community begins with the settlement of a similar group of New Christian merchants during the Commonwealth. Before the mid-1650s, these foreign merchants lived as nominal Catholics, attending mass in the chapels of the French and Spanish ambassadors, apparently unwilling or unable to regularize their status in England. At the same time, but independent of the secret Jewish presence in London, millenarian interest in recalling the Jews to England, fueled by the religious ferment of the Civil War years, began to increase. Christians eager to hasten the arrival of the millennium believed that the return of the Jews was necessary to effect their conversion—English Protestantism would accomplish

9

what Roman Catholicism had repeatedly failed to do—and that this, in turn, was a prerequisite for the Second Coming. This intense interest in the spiritual fate of the Jews led Oliver Cromwell to convene the Whitehall Conference in December 1655 to consider their readmission. Although this assembly failed to endorse resettlement, Cromwell apparently assured the leaders of the tiny crypto-Jewish colony already in London that they might live there unmolested, worshipping freely as Jews. As a consequence, they were able to acknowledge their origins and establish a community, with a burial ground and a place for worship. However, neither Cromwell nor any government body ever issued an official document permitting Jews to return to England.[2]

In the half-century following the readmission, the Jewish community in London—few Jews settled in the provinces at the time—grew slowly. In 1660, there were thirty-five to forty families; in 1695, there were about 800 persons.[3] Most of these immigrants, like the Jews living in London at the time of the readmission, were Sephardim. (The few Ashkenazim who arrived in London in the early years of Jewish settlement there worshipped in the Sephardi synagogue; by 1690 they were sufficiently numerous to establish their own congregation.) Some came directly from the Iberian Peninsula, seeking refuge from the Inquisition. Others were the descendants of Jews who had fled Spain and Portugal a generation or two earlier and had settled in cities, such as Venice or Amsterdam, where they could live openly as Jews, or in European colonies in the Caribbean, where ecclesiastical surveillance was less rigorous than in the Old World. Still others were immigrants from Catholic countries, such as France and the Spanish Netherlands, where they and their ancestors had been compelled to continue living as Christians after having fled their Iberian homes.

Sephardim continued to migrate to London in the eighteenth century and even in the first decades of the nineteenth, but a shift in the sources of Sephardi immigration took place after 1760. Whereas in the first century of Jewish settlement, the chief motive for Sephardi migration was fear of the Inquisition, later poverty also became an important reason. From the 1760s, there was a fairly steady influx of Jews, mostly of Iberian origins, from impoverished communities in the Mediterranean—Gibraltar, Morocco, Italy, Turkey—and in Holland. Yet, significantly, there was relatively little increase in the size of the Spanish and Portuguese community in England. In 1720, the Sephardim numbered a little more than 1,000 persons; by mid-century, about 2,000 (out of a total Jewish population of 7,000 to 8,000). Then, over the next eighty years, the community failed to grow, despite the continual flow from abroad. On the eve of the Victorian period, when the total Jewish population stood at 25,000 to 30,000, the number of Sephardim was about what it had been in the mid-Georgian years. Dramatic evidence of the failure of the community to expand—indeed, of its propensity to shrink—may be seen in the fact that between 1740 and 1800 the annual number of marriages celebrated at the synagogue in Bevis

Marks fell by 43 percent.[4] Much, if not most, of the shrinkage in the size of the community was due to assimilation into the mainstream of English society and the severance of communal ties.

The adjustment of the Sephardim to English habits of thought and behavior and their entry into English society proceeded relatively smoothly. Unlike immigrants from Central and Eastern Europe, who generally arrived in England without prior exposure to the secular culture of the West, the Sephardim brought with them an openness to non-Jewish learning and mores that was a product of their particular historical experience. Neither before nor after the expulsion of 1492 had Iberian Jews or their descendants elsewhere in Europe lived in cultural isolation from the larger society. In matters of language, costume, deportment, and taste, the Sephardim of early-modern Europe were not markedly dissimilar from their neighbors. The social and cultural ghettoization of Ashkenazi Jewry, which was as much the outcome of the spiritual needs of Ashkenazi Jews themselves as of a policy of intolerance imposed from without, was foreign to the Sephardi experience. When those Sephardim who had been compelled to live as New Christians in Spain, Portugal, France, or the Netherlands settled in more tolerant countries, they did not face the crisis of acculturation that Ashkenazim experienced when they began to abandon their cultural and social isolation. As former Marranos or the descendants of Marranos, they or their parents had lived as Christians within Christian societies. They were, in Yosef Yerushalmi's words, "the first considerable group of European Jews to have had their most extensive and direct personal experiences completely outside the organic Jewish community and the spiritual universe of normative Jewish tradition." As nominal Catholics in Spain and Portugal, they had had "full access to the mainsprings of Western theological, philosophic, and scientific learning." Many were graduates of Iberian and French universities at a time when Jews elsewhere were generally barred from attending such institutions.[5]

The relative ease with which Sephardi Jews entered into the mainstream of English society was already evident by the first decades of the eighteenth century. Former Marranos or their descendants who grew rich in international trade and finance in the City of London copied the habits of Englishmen of property and invested some of their surplus wealth in country estates. Such purchases were not only prudent investments but also the means of acquiring social respectability, for the ideal of the English gentleman at this time was tied to the ownership of land and the cultivation of country pursuits. The earliest Anglo-Jewish country homes were quite close to London, since initially their owners remained active in the City and, thus, could not be too distant from their places of business. In the country, however, they and their families began to mix with their property-owning neighbors, eventually forging close social ties. (As stockbrokers, government loan contractors, and purveyors of precious stones, male members were already accustomed to mixing with elite landowners in London, to which the latter flocked in growing numbers in the eighteenth century to do business and to be seen. Contacts such as these probably made social integration in the countryside an easier process.) Growing intimacy between Sephardim and neighboring landowners and involvement in nonmercantile circles in general led in time to both intermarriage and conversion. By the end of the eighteenth century many families of Marrano origin whose fortunes had been made in the diamond trade or in government-loan contracting had ceased to have any active connection with either the Jewish community or the City of London.

The history of the Mendes da Costa family provides a good illustration of the process of radical assimilation among families of Marrano background.[6] Several members of the family who were born in Portugal arrived in England within fifteen years after the readmission. Like many other early Jewish settlers of Iberian background, they were not unskilled, penniless refugees but experienced merchants with resources and connections. They specialized in the diamond and coral trade with India, the Iberian and Latin American trade, and the trade in bills of exchange. By the early eighteenth century, they had acquired substantial fortunes and had become well-known figures in the London mercantile community. In 1675, Alvaro da Costa (1646–1716) purchased a house in Highgate, then a village on the northwestern fringe of London; not long after he added an additional wing, stretching into the back gardens, to house the families of his cousins Fernando Mendes (1647–1724) and John Mendes da Costa (1655–1726). There they lived the life of English gentlemen. Their children acquired a taste for beautiful objects and learned to love music. Fernando's daughter Catherine (1679–1756) studied painting at the home of the celebrated miniaturist Bernard Lens and herself became an accomplished portraitist. (Her portrait of her father, painted in 1721, now hangs in the vestry room of the synagogue in Bevis Marks.)

Other members of the family were also quick to establish themselves in the countryside around London. Anthony Mendes (d. 1739), Fernando's eldest son, bought a newly built terrace house in Highgate in 1715; his cousin Jacob Mendes da Costa purchased a splendid mansion, built for Chief Justice Pemberton in the 1670s, in the same vicinity in 1733. Anthony's brother James (d. 1748), a stockbroker with literary interests, was leasing a house at Mitcham in Surrey by 1724, to which the poet James Thomson was a frequent visitor. James's brother-in-law (and cousin) John Mendes da Costa (1674–1752) bought another property in Mitcham in 1721. The most impressive of the Mendes da Costa estates was Copped Hall at Totteridge in Hertfordshire (a few miles north of Highgate), which Joseph da Costa (1683–1753), a son of Alvaro, acquired in 1721 and which remained in the family until 1758. Daniel Defoe described it in his *Tour through the Whole Island of Great Britain* as "a very delicious seat, the house new built, and the gardens extremely fine."[7]

Wealthy Sephardim who acquired country homes behaved no differently from other *nouveaux riches* City men who sought confirmation of their social status in rural rather than urban settings. However, in the case of prosperous Jews, the purchase of a country property represented more than conformity to the social ideals of the landowning class. It also indicated a willingness to live, either permanently or temporarily, outside Jewish social circles and without access to synagogues and other religious institutions that are essential to Jewish observance. Those who moved away from the City of London expressed, by their very decision to do so, their distance from the values of traditional Judaism. Once settled in Surrey or Hertfordshire, they exposed themselves to a way of life that was bound to erode their Jewish loyalties even further. This was particularly true in regard to wives and children, since they did not remain in contact with other Jews to the extent that husbands and fathers did whose business interests kept them in the City.

An instructive parallel to the impact of country life on group solidarity may be found among the great Quaker business families of eighteenth-century London. Like Jews, Quakers were second-class citizens, barred from holding state or military office, practicing law, and attending the universities. Legal exclusion and popular prejudice, in tandem with their desire to perpetuate their own religious values, led them to create a viable network of institutions—especially schools and academies—as alternatives to those of the Anglican establishment. For most of the eighteenth century even the most prosperous Quakers resisted the allure of the social and cultural mainstream. For example, they tended to marry within their own community, creating in the process tightly knit economic and kinship networks similar to those of the Jewish *haute bourgeoisie*. Toward the end of the century, however, the wealthiest of the London families began acquiring country properties. Separated from the inward-looking Quaker milieu of London, they mixed with their Anglican neighbors and consequently absorbed a taste for country pleasures, like hunting and shooting, which normative Quakerism condemned as a waste of time. Eventually the assimilative pull of gentry culture weakened their sense of group loyalty. Sarah Hoare, daughter of the banker Samuel Hoare, Jr., recalled that when her family moved from Stoke Newington to then rural Hampstead in 1790 they entered a new world. "In separating from my grandfather and aunts, we were taken from under very powerful influence, from the constant society of Quakers, from long-established domestic habits—continued because no one had the courage to break them—and we were thrown upon new acquaintances, some of whom became friends, and we had new desires, both parents and children—to become more like our neighbours." Samuel Hoare subsequently sent his son to a boarding school in Buckinghamshire kept by an Anglican clergyman, "a step very dissatisfactory to Friends who then predicted what has since taken place, that he would quit their Society."[8]

In the case of the Mendes da Costas, it is clear that the Jewish loyalties of many members of the family were weak before they began to immerse themselves in county society. Alvaro da Costa, who was born and baptized in Lisbon and arrived in London as a child or teenager, showed little attachment to Judaism at any time in his life. He was not circumcised after fleeing from Portugal, as was the custom with former Marranos, nor did he ever formally join the Spanish and Portuguese congregation. He chose to become a naturalized citizen, although naturalization required taking a christological oath, rather than seek denization (as wealthy foreign-born Jews usually did). There is no evidence that he raised his children as Jews, or, for that matter, as Christians either. In his will, he expressed no desire to be buried in the Sephardi cemetery at Mile End (although, in fact, his body was interred there), and he left no money for the Jewish poor or for the recital of memorial prayers on the anniversary of his death. His cousin Fernando, who studied medicine at the University of Montpellier before settling in London, was even more distant from Judaism. As physician to Catherine of Braganza, the wife of Charles II, Fernando remained a Catholic, at least publicly, for several decades after his arrival. In 1689, after James's flight, he was expelled from the Royal College of Physicians as a Papist. He refused to be circumcised or to circumcise his sons, even when it meant that they would be disinherited by a wealthy uncle of his wife, who was a professing Jew. He never joined the Sephardi synagogue (although his portrait hangs there today), but in his will he left a bequest to the congregation's charity fund. He was buried in the cemetery at Mile End, as was his cousin Alvaro, though he too had not requested it.[9]

It is impossible to know what, in truth, Marranos like Fernando Mendes and Alvaro da Costa believed, if, in fact, they believed anything resembling the traditional doctrines of either faith. Perhaps living on the frontier between Christianity and Judaism had made them question the truths of both religions and prevented them from committing themselves fully to either. Or perhaps they had been influenced by heretical currents circulating in the Iberian Peninsula when they were students, as was the case with the former converso physician Juan de Prado, whom the Amsterdam community excommunicated at the same time as Baruch Spinoza. All that we can conclude with confidence is that they were not professing Jews in the conventional sense of the term. Nevertheless, they maintained ties with former Marranos who were, choosing their wives, business associates, and friends from persons with backgrounds similar to their own. As newcomers in English society, they found companionship among and forged economic ties with their fellow immigrants—even if their religious views were quite dissimilar. Ethnic identity, then, rather than religious practices and beliefs bound them to other former Marranos.

Alvaro's and Fernando's repudiation of communal allegiances was not typical of the early generation of Sephardi settlers. Their cousin John Mendes da Costa, with whom they shared a house on Highgate Hill, was a member of the congregation in Bevis Marks, serving on the *mahamad* (executive council) for the year 1712–1713. Moreover, at least some of Alvaro's children were professing Jews. His eldest son, Anthony da Costa (ca. 1667–1747), for example, was a member of the *mahamad* several times between 1721 and 1739. Unlike his father, who willingly swore a christological oath to obtain naturalization, the English-born Anthony publicly protested the Russia Company's refusal to admit him, as a Jew, to the freedom of the company; and in 1728 he took legal steps, which were unsuccessful, to force them to do so.[10] These demonstrations of Jewish identity, however, do not mean that members of the Mendes da Costa clan were observant Jews, regularly attending the synagogue, observing the dietary laws, keeping the various fasts and festivals. In fact, it is likely that they lived in a manner not too dissimilar from that of their gentile counterparts, particularly after they began to spend more time in the country than in London. In the 400 or so pages of testimony published in connection with a lawsuit between two members of the family in 1734—in which the family's daily comings and goings are described—there is little to indicate that Jewish practices or concerns played any important role in their lives.[11]

Among the first two generations of members of the Mendes da Costa family to be raised or born in England, family and ethnic ties were sufficiently strong to ensure that marriage partners would be chosen from families of similar background. In fact, in these early generations young people frequently took as husbands and wives their own cousins, a pattern that was to occur again and again in Anglo-Jewish history. Fernando Mendes's daughter Catherine, the portraitist, for example, was married to Alvaro da Costa's son Anthony, while his daughter Leonora (d. 1767) was married to another of Alvaro's sons, Joseph of Copped Hall, Totteridge. By the third generation, however, with increasing immersion in the larger society and, simultaneously, increasing distance from the Marrano experience, members of the family began to marry into elite circles outside the community of former Marranos. Moses Mendes (d. 1758), grandson of the physician Fernando and son of the stockbroker James of Mitcham, Surrey, was baptized at birth in the Church of England. At first he followed his father's profession, but having amassed a fortune, he retired to a fine estate, St. Andrew's, at Old Buckenham in Norfolk. Well known as a wit, bon vivant, poet, and dramatist, he wrote a number of musical entertainments that were successfully presented in London. In 1752, he married Anne Gabriella, daughter of the Rev. Sir Francis Head, Bart., and by her had two sons, who in 1770 both assumed the name of Head—undoubtedly to escape the stigma attached to the name Mendes at a time when Iberian names were popularly associated with rich Jewish bankers and brokers. Two of Mendes's grandchildren, the sons of James Roper Head, became prominent figures in public life in the first half of the nineteenth century. Sir George Head was commissary-general in the army, serving in Spain, Canada, and Ireland, a frequent contributor to quarterly journals, and deputy knight-marshal at the coronations of King William IV and Queen Victoria. His younger brother, Sir Francis Bond Head, Bart., served in the Royal Engineers from 1811 to 1825, was lieutenant-governor of Upper Canada from 1835 to 1837, and was a prolific author of books and articles on varied subjects.[12]

Joseph da Costa's daughter Catherine (1709–1747), who was known as Kitty, also formally cut her ties with the Jewish community and merged into the ruling elite. Her parents married her, at age nineteen, to Joseph da Costa Villareal (d. 1730), a wealthy Marrano, years her senior, who had fled Portugal in 1726. Two children were born—Sarah in 1728 and Abraham in 1729. Villareal died soon thereafter, leaving her, a beautiful woman of twenty-two, with a fortune of at least £ 100,000. Three weeks after her husband's death, she engaged herself, without her father's permission, to her first cousin Philip Mendes da Costa (1707–1780), a rake and a libertine. The outraged family persuaded the young couple to postpone their engagement until the end of the year of mourning. Before the year was over, however, Kitty repudiated her engagement to Philip. In an attempt to force her to comply—there was, after all, a great fortune at stake—he took her to the Arches Court of Canterbury, an Anglican ecclesiastical court, for breach of promise. By doing so, he demonstrated the extent to which his generation had broken with the values of the early Sephardi community in England (and traditional Jewries everywhere), which zealously guarded jurisdiction over matters of personal status and sought to keep intra-communal squabbles and scandals from the public eye. As Kitty's aunt Catherine, the wife of Anthony da Costa, wrote to Philip's mother in June 1731, "I cannot see there is any need of making a public business of it; especially, by a way so indecent, and till now, so unknown in our Nation."[13]

Philip's suit in the Arches Court of Canterbury failed, as did his civil suit seeking £ 100,000 damages in the King's Bench in early 1734. That summer he published the proceedings of the case, apparently hoping to embarrass Kitty and her family. Kitty, meanwhile, had moved to Nottinghamshire, where her husband had left her property. There she met William Mellish of Blyth, the younger son of a country family which had initially made its fortune in overseas trade. Her great wealth must have been particularly attractive to a younger son with no prospects. She married Mellish in 1735 and one month later was baptized at St. George's, Bloomsbury. There followed a lengthy court battle with her father over custody of the two children from her first marriage, whom she had earlier entrusted to him. She succeeded in regaining them, and, as her family feared, they were baptized soon thereafter, at St. Anne's, Soho, in 1738, Abraham becoming William and Sarah Elizabeth.[14] A few years later Kitty's money obtained a seat in Parliament for her husband, who represented Retford in Nottinghamshire from 1741 to 1751. Her fortune also obtained a well-connected husband, the heir of the first Viscount Galway, for her daughter, Elizabeth, who married in 1747 and became Viscountess Galway in 1751.

Other members of the third generation of Mendes da Costas in England also cut their ties to the Jewish community. Kitty's brother, Benjamin da Costa (1712–1759), left the community when he married a non-Jew. He became deputy receiver-general of the Post Office; his son, also named Benjamin (1739–1782), became accountant general in the Excise Office. Both Benjamins were buried in the churchyard of St. James's, Piccadilly.[15] Kitty's cousin, the naturalist and antiquary Emanuel Mendes da Costa (1717–1791), a brother of her would-be husband Philip, also distanced himself from the community. (It is unclear, however, if he ever formally abandoned Judaism, since he was buried in the Mile End cemetery.) One of the best mineralogists and conchologists of his time, he corresponded with the leading naturalists of Europe. Many of his friends were non-Jewish scientists, and in 1747 he was elected a fellow of the Royal Society. He served as librarian and secretary of the society from 1763 to 1767, when he was dismissed and prosecuted for embezzlement. (Mendes da Costa was either in debt or on the edge of it most of his adult life and constantly in need of funds.) His first wife, Leah del Prado—sister of the wealthy army contractor Abraham del Prado (d. 1782) of Twickenham—was also a cousin, but since they were wed at St. Benet's, Paul's Wharf (in 1747), it is possible she had been baptized. She died in 1763 without issue, and three years later Emanuel married Elizabeth Skillman, who was not Jewish. Emanuel's younger brother David (b. 1719), an unsuccessful army contractor who was agent for Abraham del Prado in Germany during the Seven Years' War, also married a Christian, Catherine Richmond Heide, at St. George's, Hyde Park Corner, in 1749, and had no ties to the Jewish community.[16]

Radical assimilation among the descendants of Marranos was not limited, of course, to the Mendes da Costa family—they simply moved more quickly than others to find a niche for themselves outside the Jewish community. Toward the end of the eighteenth century, with an increase in the number of prosperous Sephardi families and the expansion of their social and cultural horizons, intermarriage and conversion became less unusual in other families, appearing generally in the third or fourth anglicized generation. Indeed, by the early nineteenth century they were so common that there was scarcely a well-to-do Sephardi family settled in England for more than two generations in which drift and defection had not made significant progress.

The Ximenes family, for example, were established in England since the late seventeenth century. Their integration into English society took a sharp turn at the end of the eighteenth century. In 1784, David Ximenes (d. 1786), a stockbroker (whose wife, incidentally, was a Mendes da Costa), bought an estate, Bear Place, at Wargrave in Berkshire. When he died two years later, the estate passed to his eldest son, Moses (1762–1837), who soon thereafter, now a man of wealth, retired from the City. At his country home, he was on close terms with his neighbor Lord Barrymore. He acted in the elaborate amateur theatricals Barrymore staged, and after performances he hosted parties for the company that would frequently last until dawn. Acting aside, Ximenes's great passion was soldiering. He raised a troop of territorials and acquired for them a row of cottages originally put up by Barrymore for the guests at his theatricals. He also was one of the chief sponsors of an early imperial adventure (1792), now long forgotten, to establish a colony on the island of Bulama off the west coast of Africa.[17]

Though he was not a religious man, Ximenes maintained his membership in the Spanish and Portuguese synagogue for many years after leaving the City. However, in 1802, after being elected to a synagogue office and then fined for not accepting it (as was the custom), he refused to pay, quit Bevis Marks, became a Christian, and began styling himself Morris (or Maurice), rather than Moses, Ximenes. His departure was not a bitter affair. He paid what was due to the synagogue and wrote to the *mahamad* that he would always be amenable to contributing to "any of those charities that do so much honour to your heads and hearts, and in which no body of people are so praiseworthy as yourself."[18] Clearly the fine itself was not the motive for Ximenes's departure. It merely gave him the opportunity to do what he would have undoubtedly done at some time or another, seeing that he had already ceased to be a practicing Jew and had become an important figure in county society as well. His formal entry into the Church of England was obviously not the outcome of religious speculation but, rather, the pragmatic decision of a wealthy and ambitious man for whom Judaism had ceased to be important. In the end, his baptism paid off handsomely: he was knighted and became a magistrate and high sheriff of his county.

His younger brother David (1777–1848) also converted to Christianity and entered the mainstream of upper-class English life. He made a very successful career as a professional soldier, serving in Sicily, Egypt, America, Bermuda, and the East Indies, eventually rising to the rank of lieutenant-general. Like his older brother, he too received a knighthood. He also married well: his wife was the daughter of Admiral Fitzherbert Evans. Another brother, Daniel (d. 1829), also abandoned Judaism some time after 1800. His second wife, who was Jewish, died in 1797 and was buried in the Sephardi cemetery; two years later their fourteen-year-old daughter was also buried there. Not long thereafter, Daniel converted to Christianity, for his third wife, whom he married at St. George's, Hanover Square, in 1805, was the only daughter of a country vicar from Kent, who surely would not have permitted his child to marry an unconverted Jew. The Ximenes sisters, on the other hand, remained Jews. Rebecca married Emanuel Baruch Lousada (1744–1832) of Peak House, Sidmouth, Devon, the decendant of a prosperous West Indian family that came to England in the mid-eighteenth century. Her husband was a member of the Spanish and Portuguese congregation, serving on the *mahamad* for many years, despite Sidmouth's distance from London. Significantly, the Lousadas remained on friendly social terms with the Ximeneses and other relatives who had become Christians, frequently entertaining them at Peak House.

This suggests that whatever the Lousadas' attachment to their ethnic community their attachment to traditional religious values, which ban contact with apostates, was slight.[19] The other Ximenes sister, Abigail, married David Brandon of Hackney, who took an active role in synagogue affairs.

The history of the Salvadors also reflects the decline in Jewish attachments among wealthy Sephardim in the late-Georgian period. The preeminent figure in the family at mid-century was Joseph Salvador (1716–1786), a leading merchant in the diamond and coral trade and the Spanish and Portuguese trade, a frequent adviser to the government on public finance, and the prime force behind the introduction of the Jew Bill in 1753.[20] Salvador was born in England, inherited a fortune from his great-uncle (who had come from Holland to set up the family business in London in the 1670s), and shared the tastes of other wealthy Englishmen. He had a landed estate at Tooting in Surrey, where he lived in the grand manner, entertaining gentry and nobility, and was well known for his ties to fashionable courtesans. At the same time, though, he also remained attached to Judaism and to the network of wealthy Sephardi families that constituted the communal elite. He himself married a daughter of Isaac Lopes Suasso (1693–1775), the third baron d'Avernas le Gras (a title given to his Dutch grandfather by Charles II of Spain). His younger sister Rebecca married Moses Mendes da Costa (d. 1756), head of one of the most prominent Jewish firms in the City in the mid-eighteenth century; another sister married the diamond and coral merchant Moses Franco (d. 1756); and his daughter Judith (b. ca. 1739) became the wife of Joshua Mendes da Costa (d. 1815). Another daughter, Sarah (1749–1832), was married to his own nephew Francis (ca. 1747–1776), the son of his brother Jacob (d. 1749). (Joseph's two sons died in infancy.)

The next two generations of the Salvador family were less firmly rooted in the Jewish environment in which Joseph had grown to manhood, and they began to move into exclusively gentile circles. In 1773, following a series of business reverses, Francis sailed to South Carolina, where he and his father-in-law/uncle owned land, in an attempt to retrieve the family fortunes. There he became an enthusiast for American independence, and, while fighting for the cause in 1776, he was scalped by Indians. Four years later his widow, perhaps out of concern for her future (the family's financial position having declined further), had herself and her three young children baptized at the parish church at Twickenham, where they lived. Her son, John Lovell Salvador (1771–1836), later attended Christ Church, Oxford, and became a country vicar. One of her daughters married an Anglican clergyman, the other a resident of Twickenham. In his will, Joseph Salvador cut off his apostate daughter with a bequest of ten pounds—evidence that, unlike the Lousadas of Sidmouth, he still harbored the traditional Jewish animus against apostasy.[21]

Others in the family abandoned the Jewish community about the same time. Joseph Salvador's niece Sarah, a daughter of Moses Mendes da

Costa, brought with her a substantial dowry when she married Ephraim Lopes Pereira (1739–1802), the second Baron d'Aguilar (the title was Austrian, conferred on his father by Charles VI for financial services rendered the imperial family). (According to *The Gentleman's Magazine*, her dowry was £ 30,000; according to James Picciotto, writing in the 1870s, it was £ 150,000.) Sarah died in 1763, leaving several young children, who inherited the whole of her fortune and subsequently moved out of the Sephardi community. Her eldest daughter was married first to Admiral Keith Stewart, a great Scottish landowner, and then to Richard Fitzgerald, who came from an Irish landowning family. Her younger daughter, in Picciotto's words, "bestowed her charms and her fortune" on Dr. Ewart, physician-general to the British colony at Bengal. D'Aguilar himself took part in communal affairs in his younger years, but later he completely disregarded Jewish practices. After large business losses, he lived the life of an eccentric semi-recluse, separating from his second wife and withdrawing from respectable society and the Jewish community.[22]

The absorption of wealthy Sephardim into English society in the Georgian period was without parallel in the early-modern Jewish world (with the possible exception of British North America). Elsewhere in Europe intermarriage and conversion among well-to-do Jews, especially among the children of communal notables, began to occur frequently only in the early nineteenth century. Before this, the barriers between Jews and Christians were too firm to allow much social intercourse. Ancient prejudices and corporate privileges, on one side, and disinterest in the world beyond Jewry, on the other, limited contacts largely to instrumental exchanges in the marketplace. When Jews, whether rich or poor, did become Christians in pre-revolutionary Europe, they exchanged one identity for another and one network of social relationships for another. Their break with Judaism was absolute (except perhaps in the psychological sphere, where early loyalties and prior sentiments are not so easily abandoned). The movement from one faith to another, whatever the motives, was a dramatic leap, not a gradual evolution or blurred transition, for there was little neutral ground between the two cultures. Jews who became Christians in early-modern Italy or Germany were usually seeking to improve their living conditions and, perhaps less frequently, their social standing. Baptism rewarded them with relief from the restrictive statutes that embittered Jewish life before emancipation. It promised integration into spheres that previously had been impossible or difficult for them to enter.

When prosperous Sephardim in Georgian England cut their ties to Judaism, they did so in very different circumstances. Their abandonment of Judaism was the outcome of a prior process of partial integration into gentile society, rather than an initial attempt to gain access to new worlds or escape onerous restrictions. Sarah Salvador, for example, did not become a Christian in order to live as an Englishwoman outside the framework of Jewish society. She was already well on the road to integration into gentile circles at the time of her baptism. She joined the Church of England because she wanted to be fully identified with upper-class society and the dominant national culture. Similarly, when Moses Ximenes formally abandoned Judaism and became a Christian, he was already a prominent figure in country society. Baptism secured and improved his position and gave him access to honors—the county shrievalty and a knighthood—that would have been out of his reach had he remained a Jew, even nominally. Substantial integration, in other words, preceded baptism, paving the way for full and formal immersion into Christian society. As I. M. Jost, one of the pioneers of modern Jewish historiography, noted a century and a half ago, in Georgian England "the richest and most cultured Jews readily withdrew themselves from their co-religionists and mixed with the people of the country, *even before they changed their creed*."[23]

In general, the lines separating wealthy Jews from other propertied Englishmen were not rigidly drawn. Sephardi merchants and brokers who remained within the Jewish community, perhaps because they were less ambitious than friends and family who left, also had access to non-Jewish circles. In country houses and City coffeehouses, at charity dinners and meetings of learned societies, they socialized with their gentile counterparts to an extent not duplicated in other European states at the time. There were, to cite only one example, nine Jewish fellows of the Royal Society in the eighteenth century, the first having been elected in 1723.[24] Jews who wanted to broaden their cultural and social horizons without formally abandoning Judaism could do so because there was an openness and flexibility in social life that were absent in most other countries where Jews lived. Gentry and aristocratic circles were willing to tolerate the company of unbaptized Jews who were sufficiently wealthy and genteel. To be sure, prejudice and snobbery still operated to exclude Jews from exclusive circles and to deny them honors and places, and consequently those Jews who would brook no obstacles whatsoever to their ambition usually left the community. On the whole, however, the atmosphere was more tolerant and unbaptized Jews were more welcome than on the Continent.

In addition, Jews faced fewer legal impediments to their advancement in England than elsewhere. In most *ancien régime* countries Jews still constituted a corporate group, their activities subject to state regulation. In England their legal status was quite different.[25] No statutes restricted where they might live or what areas of trade they might enter. (They were, though, prevented from attending the ancient universities, entering the Inns of Court, or sitting in the House of Commons by the requirement of taking a christological oath before admission, but, it should be stressed, these oaths were not drafted initially to exclude Jews but various Christian minorities considered dangerous to the established order in church and state. In any case, there were not many Jews in the late-seventeenth and eighteenth centuries who were eager to take an Oxford degree or enter Parliament.) Similarly, they paid no taxes, tolls, or tariffs that Christian merchants and brokers did not pay. In short, their legal status was similar to that of other persons who were not members of the Church of England. Like Roman Catholics and nonconforming Protestants, they were second-class citizens, but it was a second-class citizenship that hardly resembled the truly degraded position of Jews in Central and Eastern Europe.

Nonetheless, wealthy Jews who desired full integration at this time were almost obliged to abandon Judaism because of the character of aristocratic and gentry society. In this stratum adherence to the Church of England was inseparable from being English and a member of the dominant class. Even if most landowners in Georgian England displayed little enthusiasm for churchgoing and other forms of Christian piety, they still regarded the Anglican church as one of the pillars of the established order, barring those citizens who were not communicants from taking any part in the governance of the nation. They looked to parish priests to play an active role in the administration of local government, while entrusting the education of their young to persons (private tutors, schoolmasters, and university dons) who for the most part were also clergymen. The physical proximity of the parish church to the great house of the local magnate and the frequent appearance of its incumbent at his table symbolized the close alliance between the established faith and aristocratic and gentry society. Wealthy Jews, like their Quaker counterparts, could participate in that world to some extent but could not become full members of it without embracing one of its essential pillars.

The willingness of the English upper class to mix with prosperous Jews created the preconditions for the radical assimilation of the Sephardi elite, but it alone was not sufficient to effect their alienation from Judaism. In general, no amount of toleration will induce members of a minority to renounce their group solidarity unless there has been some prior erosion of traditional loyalties. In the case of the Sephardim, their historical experience before their arrival in England—specifically, their exposure to Western secular culture and the necessity of having lived as crypto-Jews in Catholic societies—had contributed greatly to the weakening of their Jewish loyalties and consequently to their positive response to the openness of the host society. This heritage prepared Sephardi immigrants to accept English habits and tastes soon after their arrival. Their anglicization proceeded rapidly, without friction or misgivings—unlike the anglicization of later groups of Jewish immigrants—and thus they were prepared to look beyond their own community to satisfy their social and cultural needs.

One further element in the Sephardi experience contributed to the weakening of Jewish ties, and this was the fragmentary and unsettled character of Marrano Judaism and Jewish identity. Anglo-Jewish historians have treated the Jewishness of the Marranos and their descendants who settled in England as if it were no different from that of professing Jews who openly practiced their faith their entire lives. Captives of romantic myths about universal Marrano piety and steadfastness, they have been unable to assimilate historical evidence pointing to the contrary. Albert Hyamson, for example, author of the standard history of the Sephardim in England, expresses puzzlement that Fernando Mendes and Alvaro da Costa refused to be circumcised or join the synagogue. He finds it difficult to understand "why these and others who were buried among their brethren and were, at any rate socially, active among them, neglected formally to join the Community" and suggests that perhaps fear of the *mohel*'s knife kept them from membership. In any case, Hyamson does not consider their refusal especially noteworthy and ultimately dismisses it with the blithe comment: "These two outstanding men, although in their lives not fully members of the Jewish Community, were buried among their brethren in the Beth Haim in Mile End, and their children took a full part in the life of the Community." In his eyes, the Mendes da Costas were pillars of Anglo-Jewry, communal worthies faithful to Jewish ideals.[26]

The evidence, as we have seen, indicates otherwise. While there were, undoubtedly, pious persons, steadfast in their allegiance to Judaism, among the Sephardim who reached England in the seventeenth and eighteenth centuries, there were also those whose attachment to Jewish practice and belief was weak or confused because they or their immediate ancestors had lived as Catholics, not as Jews, for much of their lives. By the second half of the seventeenth century, when New Christian migration to England started, persons of Jewish origin in the Iberian Peninsula had been cut off from a full and open Judaism for more than a century and a half. The Judaism practiced there in the sixteenth and seventeenth centuries was a truncated, clandestine religion, without the supporting institutional framework of synagogues and study houses. Educated New Christians who yearned to hold on to their ancestral religion could gain some knowledge of Judaism indirectly through reading anti-Jewish polemical literature and works by Christian Hebraists or from hearing sermons preached at autos-da-fé. In some instances they even had direct access to a living Judaism through contact with professing Jews who made their way into Spain and Portugal for short periods or with Jews they met while traveling abroad on business.[27] Yet even if the Marranos were not sealed off from all Jewish influences, as some historians once believed, it is nonetheless true that the Judaism they observed atrophied from generation to generation, as inquisitorial scrutiny made it increasingly difficult to transmit a knowledge of Hebrew, liturgical practices, and ritual observances decade after decade. Marranos fleeing Catholic countries brought with them, in Yosef Yerushalmi's words, "a pastiche of fragments inherited from parents, gleaned haphazardly from books, disorganized, with significant gaps, sometimes distorted."[28] Moreover, not all New Christians who emigrated from Spain and Portugal brought even this minimal knowledge. Some came with only a vestigial attachment to Jewishness, their decision to flee

Spain having been made for them by the Inquisition, whose indiscriminate persecution of New Christians often extended to families that had given up all Jewish practices and sought full absorption into Iberian society.

Once abroad, a small number of New Christians failed to embrace Judaism and continued to live as Christians—out of reach now of the arms of the Inquisition. The great majority, though, entered Jewish communities and began a process of rejudaisation, whereby they learned how to live as Jews—ritually, emotionally, intellectually.[29] But occasionally the transition was not accomplished successfully. Throughout the Sephardi diaspora, there were former conversos who experienced difficulty in attuning themselves to Jewish beliefs and practices which they had known only haphazardly and from a distance, and some of them, like the well-known Amsterdam heretics Juan de Prado and Uriel d'Acosta, failed altogether to fit into Jewish society. An informer told the Inquisition in the Canary Islands in 1665 that a member of the Francia family in London stood up one day in the synagogue and announced, "Gentlemen, all this is suited either to very great fools or very wise men," whereupon he removed his *tallit*, threw down his prayer book, and walked out.[30] In some cases, former conversos moved uneasily between the Jewish and Christian communities, unable to settle comfortably into either. Confused, vacillating, hesitant, in Brian Pullan's words, "they faced both ways, neither conforming fully nor vowing themselves permanently to either creed."[31] Even when former New Christians succeeded in navigating their way back to membership in an open Jewish community, they could not forget the experience of having lived previously as crypto-Jews—that is, of having lived as full members of the majority society and having practiced a Judaism that was, by the late seventeenth century, as much a state of mind as a body of rituals. If they settled in a major Jewish community, like Amsterdam or Venice, with intellectual and other resources for reeducating them in the fundamentals of Judaism and integrating them into normative Jewish life, they were very likely to become observant Jews capable of transmitting their religion in turn to their children and grandchildren (although even in Amsterdam there was a group of Portuguese Jews "who lived on the fringes of the community and took no active part in its life" and whose connection to the community "was based on their origins and on family connections, but not necessarily on religious principles").[32] On the other hand, if former New Christians settled in a small Jewish community on the periphery of the Sephardi dispersion, there was a much greater chance that their return to Judaism would be less successful and their immersion in the larger society more extensive.

Despite its close links with the Amsterdam community, the Sephardi colony in London was very much on the frontier of settled Jewish life in Europe. It was small and culturally undistinguished, known for neither its piety nor its learning. It lacked both social cohesion and legal autonomy, and thus its religious leaders, such as they were, were ineffectual in imposing their authority on new arrivals. Moreover, the freewheeling commercial atmosphere of London and the lack of rigidity in English social arrangements encouraged the participation of Jews in spheres outside their own community. In short, the circumstances there were not conducive to reintegrating Marranos and their offspring into the world of traditional Judaism. It should not be surprising then that the very first conversos to settle in England tended not to embrace Judaism—only one-third of those resident in London before 1659 were buried in the Sephardi cemetery at Mile End.[33] Later arrivals usually affiliated with the congregation, but it is doubtful whether they became zealous guardians of the traditions of Israel and even more so that they were successful in passing them on to their prosperous English-born offspring. The latter—at home with English habits of thought and behavior, tolerated by their neighbors, casual in their observance of Judaism—frequently drifted away from the Jewish community altogether.

In a number of instances the failure of former New Christians to be successfully reeducated as Jews was not due primarily to the shortcomings of the London community but to their prior residence in the West Indies before their settlement in London. Sephardim who prospered in Barbados or Jamaica and then settled in England in order to enjoy their good fortune came from a climate even more indifferent to the perpetuation of Judaism than that in London. Not only were the West Indies on the outermost periphery of settled Jewish life—and thus ill equipped to instill traditional Jewish values in Marranos returning to Judaism—but the atmosphere in general in such raw, undisciplined trading colonies, where mortality was high, was hostile to religious and moral concerns. An insatiable hunger for profit and a willingness to use any means to attain it gripped planters and merchants, Jewish and Christian alike. Those who were successful sailed for England as soon as they were able, purchased country estates, made good marriages for their children, and sought to remove the marks of their origins in trade.[34]

A number of Sephardim who passed rapidly into the ranks of the English upper class were of West Indian origin. Beyond doubt their residence there helped to loosen their ties to the Jewish community once they were settled in the metropolis. The wealthiest and most prominent Jew in mid-eighteenth century London—Samson Gideon (1699–1762)—was of West Indian background.[35] His father, a merchant of modest wealth, had lived in Boston, St. Nevis, and Barbados before settling in London at the end of the seventeenth century. Samson did not follow him into the West Indian trade but turned his talents to more speculative ventures. He began as a dealer in lottery tickets, government securities, and stocks and eventually became the most prominent loan contractor of the period and one of the government's chief financial advisers. His father was a member in good standing of the Sephardi community, but Samson, one of the wealthiest men in the City, had larger ambitions and fewer Jewish attachments. He married a Protestant and had his children baptized a few days after their birth. Nevertheless, he remained a nominal member of the synagogue for many years after his marriage and the birth of his children. (The willingness of Bevis Marks to tolerate this arrangement testifies to the extraordinary decline of traditional values among the Jews of Georgian England.) He resigned in 1753 over the unauthorized use of his name by the Jewish promoters of the Jew Bill, being greatly annoyed in general by the frequency with which his name figured in the political agitation at the time. In effect, though, he had already ceased to be a Jew in any ritual or doctrinal sense of the term.

At the time Gideon formally left the Jewish community, he was already well on the way to establishing himself as a country gentleman and guaranteeing the future of his family in landed society. He purchased Belvedere House, a fine mansion with superb views over the Thames, in Erith, Kent, as well as properties in Lincolnshire and Buckinghamshire. In 1757, he married his daughter, Elizabeth, age eighteen, to the second Viscount Gage, age thirty-nine, with a portion of £ 40,000. The next year, after helping to raise a loan for George III in his capacity as Elector of Hanover, Gideon proposed to the Duke of Devonshire that he be rewarded with a baronetcy. The king would not risk the public furor that would have been created by making a Jewish broker a baronet, but in 1759 he was persuaded to bestow a baronetcy on Gideon's thirteen-year-old baptized heir, also called Sampson (but spelled with a *p*), then at Eton. In seeking a wife with noble connections for Sir Sampson, Gideon found that his own Jewish origins were "an insurmountable impediment, and the New Christian [Sir Sampson] was repeatedly rejected for no other reason than because his father was an Old Jew." In the end Gideon settled with "a learned law lord [Sir John Eardley Wilmot, Lord Chief Justice of the Court of Common Pleas] who, not possessing the same prejudices which had influenced the lay tribe of patricians, consented to a matrimonial connection between his daughter and our hero."[36] In 1770, after his father's death, Sir Sampson was elected to Parliament for Cambridgeshire and, in 1789, made Lord Eardley in the Irish peerage for political services. (The title became extinct at his death in 1824, since there were no surviving sons.)

Interestingly, although Gideon broke publicly with the synagogue and took measures to ensure that his offspring would have no connection with the Jewish community, part of him remained attached to his ancestral faith. After his death, it was learned that he had anonymously kept up his annual contribution to the synagogue. In addition, in his will, having commended his soul "to the gracious and merciful God of Israel," he bequeathed £ 1,000 to the congregation, as well as smaller legacies to the Sephardi orphanage and hospital, and requested that he be buried in their cemetery and that his name be commemorated annually on Yom Kippur as one of the benefactors of the synagogue. Initially there was some question whether the synagogue authorities would permit this, "as he had so much deviated from them in his life time," explained a contributor to *The Gentleman's Magazine* in 1795, "but a large legacy to charitable uses, which they must else have lost, at last conquered their scruples."[37] Why Gideon, a hard, ambitious man, wanted to be buried among Jews rather than Christians is something of a mystery. Perhaps, like some apostates, he was at heart ambivalent about breaking with the world of his fathers and at death sought reconciliation with those he had spurned while alive. A strange phenomenon, indeed, but not an uncommon one, as we shall see again and again.

The Lopes family, also of West Indian background, were equally successful in establishing themselves in English national life. Mordecai Rodriguez Lopez, having made his fortune in the West Indies, settled in England in the mid-eighteenth century and set himself up as a country gentleman at Clapham. He and his Jamaican-born son Menasseh Masseh Lopes (1755–1831) were members of the congregation in Bevis Marks, although by the end of the century they rarely attended services. In 1795, Menasseh married Charlotte Yeates, an Anglican, but did not formally withdraw from the community at the time. Three years later he purchased several manors in Devonshire, totaling some 32,000 acres. In 1802, just prior to a general election, father and son resigned from the Sephardi community and were baptized in the established faith, following which Menasseh was returned as member for New Romney. Their departure from the Jewish community, like that of the Ximenes family, was amicable. Mordecai wished his former coreligionists well, paid his debts, and presented the synagogue with £ 150 for the charity fund. Menasseh sat in the House of Commons until 1829, with the exception of two years that he spent in prison for electioneering bribery and corruption. In 1805 he was made a baronet, and in 1810 he served as high sheriff of the county. When he died, his title, lands, and fortune passed to his nephew Ralph Franco (1788–1854), who had become a Christian in 1801 and been elected to Parliament for Westbury (a borough in his uncle's gift) in 1814.[38]

Social ambition was the chief motive in the conversion of opulent Sephardim like Menasseh Masseh Lopes and Moses Ximenes. Questions of doctrine and faith, it appears, played little role in their decisions to become Christians. To be sure, their loyalty to Judaism and its observances weakened prior to their change of religion, but there is no evidence that this weakening was due to religious or philosophical objections to Jewish tenets. There were, however, a handful of instances in which ideological concerns, mostly deriving from Enlightenment ideals, influenced the decision to abandon Judaism. Such was the case with the physician and medical writer Jacob de Castro Sarmento (1691–1762), a native of Portugal who fled to England in 1720 or 1721. (He wrote on such diverse topics as the treatment of smallpox, springwater and its virtues, the movement of the tides, the properties of drugs, and the curative qualities of seawater for glandular problems.) De Castro Sarmento was very much a man of the Enlightenment and constantly proposing schemes for the more rational organization of the practice of medicine, particularly in his native Portugal, where he remained in close touch with leading medical figures. His less-than-orthodox religious views and his casual attitude toward Jewish law led him to clash several times with the authorities of the Sephardi synagogue before he finally withdrew. In 1724, for example, he was dismissed as doctor to the congregational poor for having written on the Sabbath and having ridden in a coach on the eighth day of Sukkot. In 1733 the *mahamad* fined him five shillings for taking legal action against the wife of a deceased Jewish patient—he had her arrested by the civil authorities for nonpayment of fees—rather than seeking redress within the synagogue. After de Castro Sarmento's second wife died in 1756, he severed his last links with Bevis Marks. In a letter to the synagogue elders, published in *The Annual Register* for 1758, he explained that he had entertained opinions and sentiments "entirely dissenting from those of the Synagogue" for some time and that now he no longer felt he could permit himself to appear to be a member of their institution. However, he added, "I do not renounce the intercourse I may have with you in the general society of men of honour and probity, of which character I know many among you, and whom, as such, I shall always esteem." About this time de Castro Sarmento married a Christian woman who had been his mistress for over a decade. The two sons she bore him were baptized in the Church of England. He, however, did not become a Christian, for, as is evident from his letter, he was not so much interested in cutting his ties to Jewish company and launching himself into gentile society as in disassociating himself from a religion whose tenets he no longer accepted.[39]

An even more clear-cut instance of the play of ideas in weaning Sephardim away from Judaism may be seen in the case of the literary historian Isaac D'Israeli (1766–1848), father of the famous Conservative prime minister. Isaac's father, Benjamin (1730–1816), arrived in England from Ferrara in 1748, commenced business as an importer of Italian goods, especially straw bonnets, began speculating in stocks and shares on the side, and eventually became a successful stockbroker. Isaac, who grew up at his father's country house at Enfield in Middlesex, was largely ignorant of traditional Jewish practice. While young, he formed a passionate attachment to the writings of the *philosophes* and in religious matters was not far from being a freethinker. His attitude to Judaism, in particular, showed the impress of the Voltairean school. In his view Judaism had preserved and cherished the prejudices of earlier, barbarous eras. The Talmud was a mass of superstitions, contradictory opinions, rambling oriental fancies, and casuistical glosses. The rabbis of old were dictators of the human intellect who tricked the Jews into accepting their decisions as divine law, thereby casting the people into a bondage of ridiculous customs. The system of dietary laws was the heaviest curse of all, for it estranged the Jews from sympathetic fellowship with other members of the human race, and, along with other particularistic customs, contributed to Christian prejudice against them.[40] (Isaac, who did not observe the dietary or any other Jewish laws, mixed largely in gentile company.) Isaac's son Benjamin recalled, in writing to Sarah Brydges Willyams, herself a descendant of the Mendes da Costas, "I, like you, was not bred among my race, and was nurtured in great prejudice against them."[41] Nevertheless, Isaac continued to pay his annual contribution to the synagogue. Perhaps he did so out of respect for his father or perhaps out of fear that he might be disinherited. Or perhaps he felt a sense of ethnic solidarity with family and friends who were professing Jews that transcended formal religous concerns.

The death of his father in 1816 and a financial dispute with the synagogue at the same time gave Isaac the opportunity to break formally with Judaism.[42] In October 1813, he had been elected a *parnas*, or warden, of Bevis Marks. The authorities assumed that, like other nonobservant Sephardim, he would refuse to serve and pay a fine. (This was a customary way of raising revenue.) D'Israeli replied that while he was willing to contribute to their annual subscription he had no interest in their "interior concerns." In the ensuing exchange, D'Israeli vented his alienation from Judaism and suggested why so many members were falling away from the community. He first explained that he did not attend religious services because as they were presently conducted they disturbed "instead of exciting religious emotions"—a frequent complaint at the time.[43] He then reminded the authorities that "the larger part of your society" had become "partly Jew and partly Gentile." "Many of your members are already lost; many you are losing! Even those whose tempers and feelings would still cling to you [like himself], are gradually seceding." If they wanted to stem the tide of defections, he told them, they would have to introduce more flexible and enlightened laws for the governance of the community. (Presumably he was referring to both administrative and religious matters.) He certainly was willing to continue a member if they acted in a less arbitrary manner, for he felt bound to them by friendship and "something like the domestic affections."

D'Israeli continued to make his annual contribution for the next few years but refused to pay the fine, for which he was repeatedly billed. Then, in November 1816, his father died, leaving him a fortune of £ 35,000. The following March, when he again received a notice about the fine, he sent in his resignation. A few months later, at the urging of his close friend Sharon Turner, a solicitor and antiquary, Isaac had his four children baptized. Benjamin noted in a letter to his lawyer dated 1847 that his own conversion would have been impossible while his grandfather was alive.[44] Isaac himself was content to remain outside any religion, but apparently Turner convinced him that his children would benefit socially from membership in the established church. If Benjamin's account is to be believed, Isaac was reluctant to take this step—his hesitation would certainly fit with his well-known dislike of revealed religion—and had to be persuaded to do so. However, there is some testimony indicating that he was not so resistant. Robert Southey wrote to a friend in 1830 that D'Israeli, having "slipt out of the synagogue, but thinking it necessary that his children should belong to some community, . . . got Sharon Turner to take them some years ago to St. Andrew's, in Holborn, and there the present Bishop of Barbadoes christened them." A childhood friend of Disraeli testified in 1887 that Isaac's father objected to his and the children's conversion and that "Isaac had to postpone it until the death of his father"—the implication being that this was something he had wanted to do for quite some time.[45] The former interpretation, however, is more consistent with Isaac's beliefs and character.

Isaac D'Israeli's decision to make his children Christians was motivated solely by concern for their worldly happiness and was typical of most defections from Judaism at the time, while his own break, which grew out of the Enlightenment critique of Judaism, owed as much to principle as to expediency and was, thus, exceptional. In this respect, the departure of his brother-in-law Joshua, or George, Basevi (1771–1851), a Lloyds underwriter, at the same time was more typical. Joshua's father, Naphtali (1738–1808), who had emigrated from Verona to London in 1762, had been active in communal affairs, serving as a *parnas* of the Spanish and Portuguese synagogue and president of the Board of Deputies. But George was more ambitious. After retiring from Lloyds, he moved to Brighton, where he was chairman of the magistrates bench from 1838 to 1843 and also a deputy lieutenant of the county. His eldest son, Nathaniel (1792–1869), became a barrister, his son George (1794–1845) a well-known architect.[46]

To describe conversions such as these as motivated by social considerations, while not incorrect, is not fully satisfactory either, for new considerations, absent earlier, entered into the process of radical assimilation in the first decades of the nineteenth century. When wealthy Sephardim in the previous century left Judaism, their goal was to complete their social integration into the landed elite that governed England. Conversions like these continued into the first part of the next century, but in addition Sephardim of more modest wealth whose ties to Judaism had weakened began to leave the community as well. Although prosperous, they were not sufficiently wealthy to aspire to membership in country society. Their object in leaving Judaism, rather, was to gain for themselves or their children unimpeded access to professional, bureaucratic, and artistic circles, primarily in London, that were playing an increasingly important role in British life. (There were few *legal* impediments to Jews pursuing careers outside commerce and finance, but for social and economic reasons few chose to do so before the mid-Victorian years.) James Picciotto, a pioneer historian of Anglo-Jewry, characterized apostates such as these as "men of keen feelings, of restless energy, of ambitious minds, and withal, of weak convictions." For them, "to remain on a dead level with those around them, hopeless of ever soaring higher in the social sphere must have proved gall and wormwood."

Their sights were set higher. "The mart, the exchange, the Synagogue, the domestic circle, did not suffice for their aspirations."[47]

Isaac D'Israeli's decision to have his children baptized was motivated by these kinds of concerns. He intended his son Benjamin to become a solicitor and paid a premium of 400 guineas to article him to a firm of solicitors in the City. (The humdrum nature of legal work did not agree with young Disraeli, and he left after two and a half years.) His younger sons, Ralph (1809–1898) and James (1813–1868), were educated at Winchester; later they became, in Robert Blake's words, "conscientious and dull public servants."[48]

The history of the Mendes Furtado family reveals a similar pattern of movement into new walks of life. Isaac Mendes Furtado (ca. 1729–1803), a native of Portugal who was brought to England as an infant, was a prosperous notary, annuity broker, and merchant. Never very strict in his observance of Judaism, Mendes Furtado resigned from the Sephardi synagogue in 1783 when the authorities called in constables to remove unruly congregants on Purim during the reading of the Book of Esther. (The *mahamad* had decided that the custom of drowning out the name of Haman during the reading was too indecorous.) For Furtado, who had quarreled with the synagogue on previous occasions, the Purim affair was merely an excuse to leave the community. He wrote to the *mahamad*, "I do renounce your Judaism and the inherent principals [*sic*] and sentiments and inheritance of your Land to come." His wife, who left the synagogue with him but was more sympathetic to Judaism than he, died in 1798 and was buried in the Sephardi cemetery. Four months later, in March 1799, three of his children, ages fifteen, seventeen, and twenty-three, were baptized at Stoke Newington, where Mendes Furtado was living at the time. He never converted but was buried in the Stoke Newington churchyard. His oldest son, Abraham (1765–1821), became a composer and songwriter under the name Charles Furtado; his youngest son, Jacob (1781–1830), who took the name John at baptism, became a musician.[49]

It is difficult to know whether prosperous Sephardim eager for worldly advancement were more likely to leave Judaism than their poorer brethren lower down the social ladder. In terms of career rewards and social honors, they certainly had more to gain from changing their religion than did Jews of modest or little means. Yet, scattered here and there among the evidence regarding conversion and intermarriage (the great bulk of which, not unexpectedly, concerns the rich and the famous) are indications that radical assimilation was not confined to those at the apex of the Sephardi community. For example, David Lindo, age sixteen, was married to Lucretia Hosier, age nineteen, by an Anglican clergyman at a public house near the Fleet Prison in 1729. They lived in the parish of St. Anne's, Westminister, and when David later deserted Lucretia, she sued him in the Consistory Court of London to compel him to return. Moses Suares (b. 1755) was baptized at St. Dunstan's, Stepney, in 1789. When a child of his was baptized in 1815 at St. Mary's, Whitechapel, he described himself as a salesman. Abraham Cortissos (1773–1811), a notary and descendant of a once-prosperous but now bankrupt family, married a Christian at St. Michael's, Cornhill, in 1806. The ceremony was witnessed by his cousin Samuel Cortissos and his wife, also a Christian. All his children were baptized at birth in the same church. Modena-born Judah Uzielli, also a notary, was baptized several years later, for in 1809 he became foreign secretary of the London Society for Promoting Christianity among the Jews. In 1829, David Alvarez (b. 1800), a clerk of Gun Street, Spitalfields, was baptized at the Catholic Apostolic Church (the Irvingite congregation) in Parliament Court, Bishopsgate. There is no record that his wife, who was Jewish by birth, also became a Christian, but all their children were baptized. In addition, a brother or cousin, Benjamin Thomas Alvarez (b. 1812), a painter and glazier, whose wife was not Jewish, was baptized there in 1835 and later his children as well. In 1829, to cite one last example, a gentile woman, Mary Denney, wrote to the *mahamad* to denounce Moses Delangy, a Sephardi, with whom she had been living for the past five years and by whom she was the mother of a three-week-old child. Delangy had been to see her only once since the birth of their child and had told her at that time that he was to be married to a young Jewish woman who had a dowry of £ 250 coming to her from a communal charity, but that he did not love this woman and intended to leave her after getting hold of her money. He had promised to return to Mary if she would move with him to the country. Mary blamed Moses for all her troubles, since she had held a good place as a servant until he had seduced her.[50]

The extent of radical assimilation among Sephardim who were not part of the wealthy elite is difficult to gauge. In general, information about shopkeepers, street vendors, clerks, and the like in the Sephardi community is limited. Thus, we can do no more than speculate about how pervasive conversion and intermarriage were at this end of the social scale. On first reflection, one might confidently assume that the incidence of apostasy would be less among the poor than the rich, since the rewards for becoming a Christian were not as great, for example, for a rhubarb vendor as they were for a West Indies merchant. The latter, having converted, could marry well, sit for Parliament, serve on the magistracy, enjoy honors, and educate his sons at public schools. A Christian rhubarb vendor, on the other hand, was not materially or socially in a much better position than a Jewish one. Yet it should not be forgotten that in a Christian society it is always easier to be a Christian than a Jew, regardless of social status. Moreover, informal social relationships between Jews and non-Jews, which could lead in time to intermarriage, were definitely more common at the lower end of the social scale than at the top.[51] Among the well-to-do, social intercourse was by invitation only, restricted by and large to set occasions and times. Casual encounters and chance meetings were infrequent. Lower down the social scale, daily life was not governed by such rigid conventions. Jewish street traders and shopkeepers lived on close physical terms with their non-Jewish counterparts, lodging in the same narrow streets and crowded courts, frequently in the same buildings, and mixing with them in the public houses, theatres, and open spaces where the common people of London went in search of entertainment and diversion. In circumstances like these, social intimacy between individual Jews and Christians developed. If the former's ties to Judaism were already weakened, intermarriage could result. Thus, it is possible that radical assimilation was as common, or nearly as common, among the poor and the lower middle class as among the very rich, and that the evidence for this has simply not survived because of the social obscurity of the persons concerned. The failure of the Sephardi community to grow between 1750 and 1850 could not have been due to the defection of prosperous members only. It may be that Sephardim of lesser rank left the community as easily and as frequently as merchants and brokers at the top.

The radical assimilation of scores of Sephardim in eighteenth- and early nineteenth-century England has no parallel in the Jewish communities of Europe at the time. Political and social conditions favorable to Jewish integration were not duplicated elsewhere until the nineteenth century, and in some reactionary states they never existed at all. The constellation of forces that encouraged the incorporation of Jews into the English mainstream would not have succeeded in effecting their integration, however, were they not already being propelled in that direction by their own historical experience as Marranos or the descendants of Marranos. Crypto-Judaism, while capable of stimulating heroism and steadfastness, could also breed indecision and weakness, religious confusion and philosophical uncertainty. The London Sephardi community was simply too weak in moral and political authority to counteract the negative impact of the Marrano experience and guide former Marranos and their families back into the bosom of traditional Jewish life. In these circumstances, drift and defection became common. Ashkenazim who arrived in England during the Georgian period encountered the same set of social and political conditions, but their response was not identical, for they came in greater numbers and, most importantly, they came as heirs of a very different historical and communal experience.

2

Ashkenazim
1690–1837

Although Spanish and Portuguese Jews pioneered Jewish resettlement in modern England, they ceased to be the numerically dominant element in the new community early in the eighteenth century. In 1695, they still constituted the overwhelming majority of the 800 or so Jews in London. However, within three decades they were overtaken demographically by Ashkenazim from Central Europe, who began to emigrate to England in the late seventeenth century. The Ashkenazi population continued to expand rapidly—by 1830, there were about 18,000—while the size of the older community remained fixed at about 2,000 persons. The enormous growth of the Ashkenazi community was due to an almost uninterrupted flow of immigrants from Holland, the German states, and even Poland. V. D. Lipman has calculated that about 6,000 Ashkenazim entered the country during the first half of the eighteenth century and 8,000 to 10,000 between 1750 and 1815.[1]

The Ashkenazim who settled in England in the Georgian period differed significantly from their Sephardi coreligionists in terms of their cultural outlook, commercial resources, and religious loyalties. The overwhelming majority of Ashkenazi immigrants were unskilled, propertyless persons seeking to escape the welter of discriminatory laws that embittered and impoverished the lives of Jews in most *ancien régime* countries. In England, where there were few restrictions hampering Jewish economic activity, they turned to various kinds of petty commerce—street trading, itinerant peddling, buying and selling old clothes and other second-hand merchandise, and, if they were successful, small-scale shopkeeping. Although most Sephardi immigrants were not wealthy merchants or brokers with international connections, it is clear that the percentage of Sephardim who arrived in England without property or a trade was far less than the percentage of Ashkenazim. Very few of the latter brought with them the resources to enter overseas trade, commodity or stock brokerage, or government-loan contracting.[2] The young Nathan Mayer Rothschild (1777–1836), who was sent by his father to Manchester in 1800—with £ 20,000 and his father's chief bookkeeper—to purchase English textiles and ship them to the family warehouse in Frankfurt (thereby circumventing English agents on the Continent), was altogether exceptional.[3]

Ashkenazi immigrants in the eighteenth century came from Jewish communities that were far more culturally and socially isolated from the surrounding world than those of the Sephardim. In Central and Eastern Europe, before the end of the eighteenth century, very few Jews had extensive social contacts with Christians or were exposed to Western literature and science. In fact, very few were able to read and write European languages: the language of everyday discourse in Jewish society was Yiddish, while the language of scholarship, which was wholly religious in character, was Hebrew. The great mass of Central and East European Jews lived largely within the parameters of traditional Jewish culture, neither seeking enlightenment outside their own religious tradition nor desiring broader social horizons (although this was beginning to change in some circles in Holland and northern Germany in the second half of the eighteenth century). Unlike their Sephardi brethren, Ashkenazi immigrants were not at home in gentile culture before their arrival in England. Similarly, their faith remained largely intact, challenged neither by new intellectual currents nor by the vicissitudes of a Marrano experience. This does not mean, of course, that the Ashkenazim who settled in England during the Georgian period were scrupulous in their observance of the Law and steeped in rabbinic learning. Indeed, the opposite was true. Most immigrants were poorly educated and rather careless in ritual matters, not because of prior contact with Western rationalism or previous social intercourse with Christians but because of the crushing poverty of most Jewish communities and the weakened authority of traditional communal leaders, both lay and rabbinic. Nevertheless, despite their ignorance and laxity, most Ashkenazim were not prepared to enter into non-Jewish circles in the way that the Sephardim were. In the majority of cases, their social and cultural isolation before emigration continued to act as a barrier to their rapid absorption into the non-Jewish world after their settlement in more tolerant circumstances.

There were, thus, few Ashkenazim in the eighteenth century who duplicated the economic and social ascent of the Sephardi families discussed in the previous chapter. Still, the notable exceptions to this rule merit attention—both because their radical assimilation proceeded in a remarkably similar way to that of their Sephardi predecessors and because this kind of social integration became more common among Ashkenazim toward the end of the eighteenth century and in the first decades of the nineteenth.

The Hart and Franks families were the first to move in and eventually merge with elite English circles. Moses Hart (1675–1756), founder of the family fortune in England, emigrated to London from Breslau about 1697 and, with the support of his cousin, the magnate Benjamin Levy (d. 1704), one of the twelve licensed "Jew brokers" on the Royal Exchange, grew wealthy as a stock and commodity broker. Hart himself was an observant Jew and a communal benefactor. He secured the appointment of his elder brother Aaron (1670–1756) as rabbi to the Ashkenazi synagogue, rebuilt the synagogue at his own expense in 1722, and dominated its affairs until his death. However, like his Sephardi counterparts, he was not immune to the attractions of the lifestyle of the English upper class. Contrary to traditional practice, he shaved his beard and did not cover his head; instead he wore a powdered wig in the fashion of the period—at least that was how he chose to present himself in a painting that hung in the board room of the Great Synagogue before its destruction.[4] As early as 1710 he leased a house in Richmond overlooking the Thames. Then, in 1718, he purchased a much larger home with several acres of grounds at Isleworth, across the river from Richmond; a few years he later rebuilt it extensively, adding extra wings. He hung the walls of his mansion with paintings by Van Dyck, Rubens, Brueghel, Poussin, Hals, and Holbein that included explicitly Christian subjects, such as St. Francis, the martyrdom of St. Lawrence, the inside of the Jesuit church at Antwerp, the passion of Jesus, and Jesus in the Temple driving out the money changers.[5]

In the country Hart and his family mixed socially with the local gentry, although it is difficult to know with what degree of intimacy. An unknown gentleman at Isleworth wrote at mid-century to a friend in London that Hart and his son-in-law Aaron Franks (1692–1777) "at the last vestry held here, mingled with the rest without opposition" though two clergymen and a justice of the peace were present. Several days earlier, he added, "no less than a coach-load" of Jews assembled at a clergyman's house to play cards.[6] However, such social contacts did not yet lead to intermarriage. Hart allied his daughters (his only son died young) to Jewish merchants and brokers of the same standing as himself. Simhah, or Frances (b. 1705), married Isaac Franks (d. 1736) in 1720, while her sister, Bilhah, married Isaac's brother, the above-mentioned Aaron, in 1743. (The Franks family was prominent in the diamond and coral trade and in the supply of provisions to the British army in the New World.) Judith (1706–1803) married her cousin Elias Levy (1702–1750), also a diamond merchant and army contractor, son of the "Jew broker" Benjamin Levy, the first really rich man in the Ashkenazi community.

The first generation of the Hart and Franks families to be born or raised in England nurtured broader social aspirations than did their German-born parents. They became extensive landowners and moved quite easily into the social life of the countryside. Isaac Franks, for example, in his will instructed his brother Aaron, the executor, to invest upwards of £ 90,000 in the purchase of freeholds for his two children. Aaron and his family also occupied a mansion in Isleworth, on a property adjoining his father-in-law's home. They entertained extensively and magnificently. Horace Walpole, who lived nearby at Strawberry Hill, Twickenham, was a frequent guest. Thus he recorded in 1774: "This morning indeed I was at a very fine concert at old Franks's at Isleworth, and heard Leoni, who pleased me more than anything I have heard these hundred years." Aaron's daughter Phila (d. 1802), a great beauty whom Joshua Reynolds painted in 1766 on her twenty-first birthday, married her first cousin, Moses Franks (1719–1789), the son of Aaron's and Isaac's brother Jacob (1688–1769) of New York, and they lived in nearby Teddington in a Palladian villa designed by Moses' friend Sir William Chambers. Moses and Phila were also on friendly terms with their neighbors. When Moses died at Teddington, Thomas Pitt, first Lord Camelford, wrote to a friend, "Poor General [Spencer] Cowper regrets extremely the loss of his neighbor Moses Franks, who was one of the few he cultivated."[7]

Moses' elder brother, Naphtali (1715–1796), also left New York for the greener pastures of English economic and social life. He too married, in 1742, a first cousin, another Phila, this one the daughter of Isaac and Simha Franks. Soon after their marriage they bought a house in Mortlake, close by their other Franks relatives. They also acquired an estate, Misterton Hall, in Leicestershire. Both there and at Mortlake, Naphtali lavished attention on the gardens. His mother, for example, sent him American plants and seeds with which to experiment. He also appears to have played the role of the country landowner: letters of his survive instructing his agent at Misterton to support the parliamentary candidate backed by Lord Denbigh, whose estate was a few miles from Misterton, in a county election, and soliciting Lord Denbigh to use his influence to obtain preferment for a friend in the navy.[8]

Although they were more integrated into country life than the generation of Moses Hart, the English-born Frankses and Harts who came of age in the first half of the eighteenth century still retained strong links to Anglo-Jewry. They married within the community, often within their own families. Aaron Franks and his nephews Naphtali and Moses served several times as wardens of the Great Synagogue and took an active role in directing its affairs. Aaron was very much a pillar of the Ashkenazi community. In 1744, he joined Moses Hart and Joseph Salvador in petitioning George II to use his influence with the Habsburg Empress Maria Theresa, urging her to rescind her recent banishment of Prague Jewry; later the three men were granted an audience by the king. When Aaron Franks died in 1777, at age ninety-two, he left the Great Synagogue a legacy of £ 1,000, a very considerable sum at the time. Two years earlier, when his nephew David (1720–1794) in Philadelphia, who had married a Christian, wrote to his brother Moses in England that he proposed to send his son Moses to London to study for the bar (a step that would have required him to take an oath on the true faith of a Christian), Moses replied that it was "highly imprudent to attempt it while Mr. A—— Franks is living. He never would admit a step of that sort in any of his family so avowedly, nor would any of us venture to countenance it, as it would highly insense him. Therefore, it is necessary to give up the thought at present." However, Moses added, "in its proper time"—that is, when their uncle Aaron was dead—"your son shall (if he chooses it) come here for the purpose aforesaid."[9]

Moses' response to his brother David is instructive: Moses urged him to abandon his project, not because it represented a break with Jewish practice and communal solidarity, but because the head of the family, a Jew of the old school, so to speak, would take offense. Clearly, by the second half of the eighteenth century, the commitment of the younger generations of Frankses to Judaism and the Jewish community had begun to diminish. Perhaps the clearest evidence of this was the willingness of Moses and Naphtali to marry their children to Christians. Naphtali's son Jacob Henry (1759–1840) became an Anglican, married a Miss Roper from Lutterworth in the neighborhood of Misterton Hall, took religious orders, and, with his father's assistance, secured a living in the locality. His two sisters remained spinsters, but also became Christians. On her death, the elder one, Abigail (1754–1814), left her fortune to a society for converting Jews. Moses' daughter Isabella married the Rev. William Henry Cooper, son of Sir Grey Cooper, Bart., in 1787. Both parties profited by the arrangement. Isabella Franks eventually became Lady Cooper, wife of George III's chaplain-in-ordinary; following the deaths of her parents, she inherited the Teddington property, while her husband received upwards of £ 170,000.[10]

The departure of the Frankses from the Jewish community was paralleled by that of their close relation, Moses Hart's daughter Judith. Judith Levy's husband, Elias, a warden and benefactor of the Ashkenazi community, died in 1750; and, there being no sons, Judith inherited his considerable wealth and then, six years later, that of her father. She thus came into possession of a fortune that gave her an annual income of £ 6,000 and allowed her to launch herself into fashionable society. She gave up her house in Wellclose Square, in the Jewish quarter, and moved to Albemarle Street, in fashionable Mayfair. She also bought a Queen Anne row house at Richmond. She came to prefer "the company of female Gentiles to that of the Hebrew ladies, merely on account of the superior elegances and politeness of the former." She spent her summers at different watering places, and "in the winter she visited masquerades, balls, etc. and introduced her daughter to the Duchess of N[orthumberlan]d's routes, then a noted match-maker, who delighted in procuring great fortunes for younger brothers of quality." Daughter Isabella's dowry snagged the third son of the Earl of Aboyne, the Hon. Lockhart Gordon, and the couple were married in April 1753 in the Church of England. Isabella, however, did not enjoy her good fortune, for she died, possibly in childbirth, eleven months later. Interestingly, despite her alienation from Jewish society, in 1787 Judith Levy contributed £ 4,000 toward the reconstruction of the Great Synagogue, although family sentiment—her father had paid for the first building—was more likely the motive than any lingering attachment to Jewish tradition.[11]

This kind of full assimilation into the English upper class was not in any sense representative of the experience of the Ashkenazi middle class at the time. For most of the eighteenth century there were few families as wealthy as the Frankses among the Ashkenazim, and thus few who could have qualified for admission into landed society. Toward the end of the century, however, the emergence of a new group of prosperous Ashkenazim created the material foundation for a renewal of that kind of radical assimilation, this time on a broader scale. The children and grandchildren of these merchants and brokers frequently followed in the footsteps of their Ashkenazi and Sephardi predecessors, employing the fortunes they inherited to purchase admission to gentile society. Yet, unlike earlier generations, the offspring of Jews who achieved financial prominence at this time were not universally lost to the Jewish community. Many did choose the path of full absorption into gentile society, but others clearly rejected this course. Indeed, within the same family it was not uncommon for siblings and first cousins to move in different directions, some casting their lot with the Jews, others with the larger world beyond the Jewish community. The longing for respectability and acceptance remained intense among most Jews, but countervailing trends came into play that made defection less inevitable. The very different histories of the descendants of the Goldsmid brothers, Asher (1751–1822), Benjamin (1755–1808), and Abraham (1756–1810), well illustrate the diverse ways in which prosperous Jews made their way in English society in the first decades of the nineteenth century.

Benjamin and Abraham Goldsmid were successful merchant bankers who grew fabulously rich when they became loan contractors to the government after the outbreak of war with revolutionary France. In 1783, before their meteoric rise, Abraham married a Miss Eliason from Amsterdam, a woman "of great fortune and extensive family connections"; and four years later Benjamin wed Jessie Salomons, daughter of Israel Levin Salomons (d. 1788) [known as Yehiel Prager within the Jewish community], a wealthy East India merchant—Jessie was reputedly the richest marriageable Jewess in England. Both brothers had far-reaching social aspirations, Benjamin especially. He and his wife set up house at Stamford Hill, where they gained "the friendship of all the gentlefolks for many miles round the spot and reciprocal visits were as frequent as the return of day, each being emulous to become more and more agreeable to the strangers, till the most complete union was formed in all the neighbouring villages of Tottenham, Edmonton, and several miles round with this family."

In 1792, Benjamin purchased a sixty-acre freehold at Roehampton and built a princely mansion, with a dining room sixty by forty feet, numerous drawing rooms, a ballroom, a library, and even a synagogue. He laid out extensive gardens and had an artificial lake constructed. When the local authorities would not permit him to divert a roadway that cut through his property, he built a tunnel under the road, in the style of an Italian grotto, so he and his family could reach the far parts of the gardens without having to cross the road. At Roehampton, he entertained distinguished guests lavishly and frequently. To celebrate Nelson's victory at the Battle of the Nile in 1798, he gave a fete that was, in the words of a contemporary, "in the most splendid style possible, beyond anything that was ever attempted anywhere else. . . . His Mansion was most splendidly illuminated with fireworks. Music and dancing prevailed in the house, with Masques &c. and intervals of refreshments which amused his visitants near 24 hours." His brother Abraham first had a country place at Morden, which the Rev. Edmund Nelson pronounced, after a visit in 1805, a "fine house" with gaudy, tasteless furnishings and poor grounds. A few years later Abraham acquired Merton Place, the country home of Emma, Lady Hamilton (Admiral Nelson's mistress). Four decades after the Goldsmid brothers' deaths, John Francis recalled in his *Chronicles and Characters of the Stock Exchange* that the newspapers "bore an almost daily testimony to their munificence," recording "entertainments to princes and ambassadors reviving the glory of the Arabian nights." They were for a while "Fortune's chief and most especial favorites."[12]

To further their quest for acceptance in English society, the Goldsmids also made generous contributions to non-Jewish charities. At the annual dinner of the Society for the Deaf and Dumb in 1810, for example, Abraham Goldsmid gave £ 700 out of a total of £ 3,000 subscribed that evening. Benjamin was particularly active in raising funds for the Naval Asylum at Paddington Green, an orphanage established amid much public fanfare in 1798 to maintain and educate the children of sailors fallen in battle. Benjamin contributed £ 2,000 personally and, by 1806, had raised another £ 2,600 within the Jewish community. Such generosity elicited from detractors of the Jews the warning that this liberality was merely an attempt on the part of the Goldsmids to buy popularity for themselves. In 1806, when the portraitist Richard Dighton drew Abraham with a list of his charitable donations—in the thousands of pounds—tucked under his left arm, the anonymous author of *The Commercial Habits of the Jews* declared his contempt and disgust excited by such "indelicacy" and warned that the portrait, which was then being exhibited in the windows of printshops, "was not the result of gratuitous adulation, but a wretched design and plot upon the admiration of the publick."[13]

Despite their eagerness to find acceptance outside Jewish society, Abraham and Benjamin retained strong links to the Jewish community. Although no evidence survives that they were especially attached to traditional practices, they did play a central role in the management of communal affairs—largely by virtue of their wealth—serving as synagogue officials and charity managers and patrons. In spite of their strong desire for gentile recognition, their origins were too close to the segregated world of early-modern Jewry to admit the possibility of severing their ties to Judaism altogether. This was not true of their children, who were raised in an entirely different social milieu. Although they were tutored in Hebrew and presumably learned the fundamentals of Jewish practice and worship, the parameters of their social experience were far broader than anything their parents had experienced in their youth. In the country, certainly, they lived completely outside the usual range of day-to-day routines characteristic of Jewish mercantile and financial families, and, as one contemporary noted, they were "by no means strict in their observance of the customs of their people."[14] In the end, their appetite for social experiences and companionship beyond the confines of Anglo-Jewry outweighed their attachments, both social and religious, to the community of their ancestors. After Benjamin died, in 1808—he hanged himself from a silk cord that he had used to lift his heavy, gout-ridden body from bed in the morning—his wife and seven children were baptized. An obituary in *The Monthly Repository* noted that "the deceased father once said, if common rumour be not fallacious, that he should be the last Jew of his family."[15]

Benjamin evidently sensed that his children did not share his own attachment to Judaism and the Jewish community. Whether he realized that his pursuit of gentile company and respect was in part responsible for their alienation we cannot know. However, it is clear that social ambition alone did not loosen his family's attachment to Judaism. Independent of any yearning for social integration, new, more-casual attitudes toward the observance of Jewish law were becoming common among well-to-do Jews in general in the last decades of the eighteenth century.[16] His wife, Jessie, whose attitudes undoubtedly influenced the behavior of her children, came from a family in which traditions were observed without fervor, rigor, or commitment to the world view that mandated their performance. Her father, Yehiel Prager, gave his children an essentially nonreligious education. When, for example, he sent his son Mark to spend some time with his two brothers in Amsterdam in 1780, he told them that he did not want Mark to spend too much time studying Talmud. Yehiel Prager and his brothers worried, to be sure, that the younger generation might identify too intensely with their gentile surroundings, but their argument against excessive acculturation was not that such behavior was inherently wrong but that it would give the family a bad reputation within the Jewish community, thus harming their commercial standing and making it difficult to arrange advantageous marriages for their children. (The three Prager brothers had about fifteen sons and ten daughters among them.) Raised in comfort and wealth and in a nontraditional, undemanding religious atmosphere, some of the Prager children, once grown, cut their links to the community altogether. Jessie and her children converted after her husband's death; her sister Louisa married George Elliot, a ship officer in the East India trade, in 1795 and raised her children as Christians. Her two youngest brothers, Mark and Lionel, became useless wastrels—they kept

bad company, spent lavishly, gambled and went in debt, and were inatten-
tive to business, causing great anguish to their mother and the whole family, who eventually dispatched them to India.[17]

At the time of Benjamin Goldsmid's death, his children were not married; once free of paternal control, they went their own way. On the other
hand, most of Abraham's children, who were older, were married before
his death in 1810—he too killed himself, with a bullet to the throat—and
for this reason, in part, remained within the Jewish community. His
daughter Isabel (1788–1860), for example, married her first cousin Isaac
Lyon (1778–1859) in 1804, and they and their descendants took an active
role in communal affairs until well into the twentieth century—as, in fact,
did most of Asher's children and their offspring. In Asher's case, his more-
modest financial success and correspondingly more-modest social ambitions were also important in keeping the family within the social parameters of Anglo-Jewry. Asher was a principal in the firm of Mocatta &
Goldsmid, brokers in bullion, diamonds, and pearls, and, while not a poor
man by any means, he never rose to the financial heights of his two
younger brothers and never strove to cut a figure in gentile society. Although no details survive, it is unlikely that his children received the kind
of upbringing that would lead them to desire entry into non-Jewish, landed
society. They were content with striving for social respect and, later, legal
equality—Isaac Lyon Goldsmid initiated the campaign for political emancipation in 1828—but they were not so desirous of admission to gentile society that they were willing to cut their ties to Judaism altogether.

In general, wealthy Ashkenazim in the first decades of the nineteenth
century were less likely to abandon Judaism than those who had amassed
great fortunes in the previous century. In part, this was due to an increase
in the size of the Ashkenazi upper middle class and hence the creation of
a broader network of potential friends and marriage partners. For most of
the eighteenth century, it should be remembered, there were very few
wealthy Ashkenazim; families like the Frankses were relatively isolated—
in terms of their wealth—within their own community, while Ashkenazim
and Sephardim remained socially apart, having little to do with each other.
Thus, it is not surprising that the Frankses looked beyond the Jewish community to satisfy their social needs and ambitions. By the early nineteenth
century, however, there were many more upper middle-class Ashkenazi
families; in addition, the social barriers between Ashkenazim and Sephardim were beginning to weaken. Rothschilds, Montefiores, Keysers,
Cohens, Mocattas, and Goldsmids married each other and created a dense
network of commercial and family alliances that persisted until after World
War I. There was also, at the same time, less pressure to abandon Judaism
because of intolerance and prejudice on the part of English society. While
it is difficult to measure such things, there is no question that there was
a greater willingness to tolerate Jews in a variety of spheres in 1830 than
there had been a half-century earlier. In 1827, for example, Isaac Lyon

Goldsmid's son, Francis Henry (1808–1878), was admitted as a student at Lincoln's Inn and six years later was permitted to take the oath before being called to the bar without swearing "upon the true faith of a Christian." At that time there also was considerable gentile support, among Whigs, Utilitarians, and some Evangelicals, for permitting Jews to sit in Parliament. (Tories in the House of Lords, however, blocked parliamentary emancipation until 1858, when Lionel de Rothschild was permitted to take his seat.)

The offspring of wealthy Jews who became Christians in the Georgian period were motivated chiefly by their inability to satisfy their yearning for social inclusion while remaining Jewish. Although England demonstrated greater toleration toward Jews than did other European states, there were limits to that toleration, particularly in the social sphere. Upper-class Englishmen were prepared to enjoy the hospitality of Jewish bankers and brokers and even to repay them with invitations to their own homes. This reciprocity, however, was not unambiguous. Jews were still considered slightly exotic, different in kind from other gentlefolk, and certainly socially inferior, whatever their wealth. Horace Walpole may have invited his Jewish neighbors to his home, but he did so with a feeling of condescension. As he wrote to a friend in 1778, "You may perhaps think that some of the company were not quite of a dignity adequate to such a high festival, but they were just the persons made the most happy by being invited; and as the haughtiest peers stoop to be civil to shopkeepers before an election, I did not see why I should not do, out of good nature, what the proudest so often do out of interest." In 1809 an anonymous writer observed that "the present *taste* for Judaic *fêtes* and *coteries*, in which our princes and nobles are not ashamed to participate" was a fashion of the moment, a fad, like styles in dress, subject to "the caprices of the . . . *beau monde.*"[18] Thus, a willingness to mix with unbaptized Jews was not an unambiguous endorsement of Jewish social acceptability. Moreover, although there were few legal disabilities that hampered Jewish economic pursuits, as long as Jews, like other non-Anglicans, were shut out of Parliament, the universities, local government, and the bar—elite institutions that were the preserve of those circles they sought to penetrate—they remained second-class citizens and thus were indirectly stigmatized as untrustworthy and dangerous. It might be said that wealthy Jews, both Sephardim and Ashkenazim, who converted acknowledged the limits to which Jews of even their standing were subject in their quest for social advancement.

Wealthy Jews who cut their ties to the community were also undoubtedly motivated by the desire to disassociate themselves from the unflattering image of the Jew in both high and popular culture. While English Jews who converted almost never recorded their reasons for doing so—unlike their counterparts in German-speaking lands—it is reasonable to assume that negative stereotypes about the group to which they belonged played some role in their decision. In literature, sermons, newspapers, journals, and private conversation and on the stage, Jews were portrayed as avaricious and crafty rogues, ceaselessly striving for gain, usually at the expense of Christians with whom they did business. One anonymous pamphlet reprinted several times during the course of the eighteenth century described them as "the subtlest and most artful people in the world, . . . so dextrous in bargaining that it is impossible for Christians to expect any advantage in their dealings with them." Even among the more-anglicized and respectable Sephardim, "the love of gain has obtained such an absolute empire in their souls that there is not the least remains, the least umbrage of candor or virtue." In the words of a figure in an imaginary dialogue from 1804, the Jews were a "knavish people, who will over-reach and cheat you if they can; a hard-dealing, hard-hearted people, taking all manner of advantage of the necessities of others." A Jewish pamphleteer complained in 1833 that the word "Jew" had become synonymous with "rogue": "'Don't Jew me,' says an Englishman to another whilst trafficking. . . ."[19] In addition, when Jews were featured in cartoons, popular songs, comic sketches, and plays in the late eighteenth and early nineteenth centuries, they almost always appeared in the guise of dirty peddlers and ragged old-clothes men. Prosperous Jews eager to find acceptance outside Jewish circles must have found these popular images embarrassing, however accurately they mirrored the occupational profile of the community.

Once baptized, though, former Jews faced little resistance to their social integration. Both ancient religious prejudices and more recent social stereotypes, however widely diffused, were not so powerfully entrenched that they prevented the incorporation of Jews willing to identify completely with the majority society. The English upper class was relatively open to outsiders—ex-dissenters and former Roman Catholics, anglicized Scotsmen and Huguenots, baptized Jews—who accepted its standards and values and qualified for admission by virtue of their wealth. By comparison with other early-modern societies, legal, cultural, and psychological obstacles to the assimilation of newcomers were weak or nonexistent. In Lawrence Stone's words, "The key concept of gentility was more dilute and ill-defined than on the Continent."[20] The children of a self-made man of obscure origin, provided they had acquired a genteel education—and the manners, graces, and values such an education bestowed—and provided they conducted themselves correctly, could achieve social respectability. Converted Jews were able to marry into gentry and noble families, serve in local government, enter Parliament, and mix freely in elite cultural and social circles. Many more Sephardim than Ashkenazim took this path in the Georgian period because their economic standing and cultural background predisposed them to radical assimilation to a much greater extent. But Jews from both groups found that once they shed their Jewishness a host of new opportunities opened up before them.

Yet, when converted Jews or their immediate descendants achieved exceptional prominence or notoriety, they sometimes found that their Jewish origins had not been completely obliterated at the baptismal font. The memoirist Sir Nathaniel Wraxall, in commenting on the generosity of Sir Sampson Gideon, the baptized son of the famous financier of the same name, wrote that he might have furnished the prototype of the virtuous Jew in an essay of Richard Cumberland. The *Annual Register* of 1806 referred to Sir Menasseh Masseh Lopes as "a Jew baronet," and when Lopes sold his pocket borough of Westbury to Sir Robert Peel in 1829 he was caricatured as a heavily accented Jewish peddler. When the barrister John Adolphus (1768–1845), whose father (a great-grandson of Moses Hart) had married a Christian and who himself had been raised a Christian, defended the Life Guard officers accused of murdering two men in a riot at the funeral of Queen Caroline in 1821, the caricaturist George Cruikshank depicted him with a brief inscribed "Jew v. Jury."[21]

The most famous example in English history of a converted Jew who was continually reminded of his origins is the case of Benjamin Disraeli.[22] Although Disraeli made his mark in Victorian political life, he launched his career—and first had to confront the legacy of his Jewish origins—in the years before Victoria's accession. His father, Isaac, was, to all appearances, content with his station in life—that of a minor literary figure who consorted with other writers and professional men of similar rank. Benjamin, who had been baptized at age thirteen, was more ambitious and sought to make his mark in fashionable society and politics. As a young man about London, he assiduously cultivated upper-class hostesses and companions. Possessing neither great wealth nor correct descent, he first attempted to penetrate these circles in the role of a dandy, resplendent in gorgeous waistcoats, velvet suits, and gold chains, with his hair in ringlets and lace at his wrists. Other parvenus before him, such as Beau Nash and Beau Brummel, had risen to prominence on the basis of their charm, wit, and originality in dress and deportment. Disraeli, too, pursued this strategy with considerable success. Exploiting the English aristocracy's taste for eccentric strays, he attached himself to patrons who could advance his career. But when he turned to parliamentary politics in the 1830s, he found that his Jewishness was a liability. His ancestry was an object of ridicule during each of the five election campaigns he fought between 1832 and 1837, when he finally won a seat in Parliament. On one occasion, when he faced the voters of Maidstone, he was greeted with cries of "Shylock!" and "Old Clothes!" Not surprisingly, then, he tried to play down his Jewish origins in the 1830s and only later, in the mid-1840s, when he realized that he could not avoid identification as a Jew—after all, his family name openly revealed his origins—did he publicly embrace his Jewishness, inventing a myth of racial chosenness with which to counter the caste pride of the landowning aristocracy.

Benjamin Disraeli's inability to leave his Jewishness behind was not typical of Jewish converts in either the Georgian or the Victorian period. Most converts, while motivated to leave the Jewish community for social reasons, were not so driven by ambition that they sought fame at the very center of national life. Their gentile friends and associates knew they came from Jewish families and undoubtedly remarked on their origins, but whatever was said or thought failed to block their successful integration into "Old Christian" society. Those who found their former Jewishness mentioned in public forums were those who gained widespread notoriety or fame, which, in the nature of things, few converts aspired to attain. Given the rough and tumble character of political life at the time, it is not surprising that Sir Menasseh Masseh Lopes, a corrupt borough-monger and former Jew, was pilloried as a shabby Jewish peddler. What is significant is that his background was not an insurmountable obstacle to his social and political ascent or that of his nephew and heir, Ralph Franco. Similarly, Disraeli also discovered that however much his critics ridiculed his origins they were not able to transform his Jewishness into a liability serious enought to derail his career.

The desire to escape legal disabilities and social prejudices was not confined to the very rich. Ashkenazim of more-modest means were also exposed to assimilatory currents, although not to the extent of their wealthier peers, since they continued to live in London and mix largely with other Jews. Still, there were sufficient social contacts between middle-class Jews and their immediate Christian neighbors, as well as suffcient religious indifference, that from time to time some of them left the Jewish community altogether. However, radical assimilation at this level of Ashkenazi Jewish society was not very common before the nineteenth century because most Ashkenazim before then were recent arrivals with little ability or desire to establish close personal ties to Christians. Most were not tormented by popular hostility toward Jews because their social horizons extended no further than friends and associates of similar origins. In addition, because they were content to remain brokers and traders, the legal disabilities that prevented Jews from pursuing professional and political careers were of little concern. The few middle-class Ashkenazim who left the community before the nineteenth century were almost without exception persons who pursued careers outside the world of commerce, that is, who entered fields outside the parameters of Jewish life and, thus, had more-intensive and more-intimate relations with Christians than did other Jews.

The famous tenor John Braham (1774–1856), for example, began singing as a choirboy at the Great Synagogue, but later, having embarked on an opera and concert career in England and abroad, he ceased to identify with Judaism and altered his family name, Abrahams, to the more English Braham. At Bath in 1795, he met and fell in love with Nancy Storace, an opera singer; they toured and lived together until 1816, though without marrying. Their son Spencer, who was born in 1801, became a successful Anglican clergyman: he was vicar of Willisborough in Kent, a minor canon of Canterbury Cathedral, and domestic chaplain to the Duke of Sussex. In 1816, Braham left his mistress and married a seventeen-year-old beauty,

Fanny Bolton, the daughter of a dancing academy proprietor. With the fortune he had made singing, Braham and his young wife lived well; they entertained musicians, dramatists, actors, poets, and critics, as well as the well-born and socially prominent. Their daughter Frances (1821–1879) made three advantageous marriages—her second husband was the seventh Earl Waldegrave—and became one of the great political hostesses of the mid-Victorian years, a remarkable triumph for the daughter of a Jew who hawked pencils as a young boy in the streets of London.[23]

The case of the otherwise obscure notary Bernard Van Sandau (d. 1848) also illustrates the possibility of occupation loosening Jewish ties. A native of Homburg, in Prussia, Van Sandau practiced as a notary in London from 1789, at several times in partnership with non-Jewish notaries who had previously been articled to him. His choice of occupation and partners created opportunities for social encounters outside the usual business and familial networks in which most Jews were enmeshed. He apparently married a Christian woman, for his son Lewis was baptized at St. Michael's, Bassishaw, in 1793, and he himself was buried at St. James's, Pentonville. Nevertheless, he remained in contact with members of the Jewish community, who continued to bring him work. In 1810, moreover, he subscribed for three copies of Shalom Cohen's *Shorshei emunah* [The Roots of Faith], a mildly unorthodox catechism for youth.[24] Whether this implies that he shared the outlook of the German *haskalah* and was motivated to abandon Judaism for ideological as well as personal reasons is impossible to know. It is equally probable that he subscribed because a Jewish client or business associate solicited him to do so.

In general, Ashkenazim who left the Jewish community, like their Sephardi counterparts, were not moved by either the Enlightenment critique of revealed religion or the *haskalah* attack on traditional Judaism. Material self-interest, social ambition, and religious indifference played the dominant roles in loosening Jewish loyalties, not any systematic, ideological program for the modernization of Judaism. Indeed, it is difficult to find instances of radical assimilation in Anglo-Jewish history where Enlightenment thinking figured prominently. The only unambiguous example of this within the Ashkenazi community, at any socioeconomic level, is the case of Meyer Loew Schomberg (1690–1761).[25] A native of Fetzberg, Germany, Schomberg studied medicine at the University of Giessen, practiced for a decade at Schweinsberg and Metz, and settled in London about 1720. Initially he was employed, at an annual salary of £ 30, to attend the poor of the Great Synagogue, but later he built up a large and profitable private practice. By 1740, he was receiving about 4,000 guineas a year in fees; according to one contemporary, he and John Fothergill, a celebrated Quaker physician, had the most extensive practices in London at the time. Schomberg's training and work set him apart from other Jews of German origin in Georgian England. He also gave his sons a much broader education than was common among Ashkenazim. The two oldest, the twins

Ralph [Raphael] (1714–1792) and Isaac (1714–1780), entered Merchant Taylor's School in 1726; Alexander (1720–1804) was sent to St. Paul's. But Schomberg also sought social companionship outside the Jewish community; for example, he and his two oldest sons were active Freemasons.

By the 1740s at the latest, Schomberg had cut his ties with the Jewish community. In 1742, Ralph married out of the Jewish faith; in 1743, Alexander obtained a commission in the Royal Navy, which would have been impossible while still professing Judaism; in 1746, Isaac entered Trinity College, Cambridge, and the following year was baptized at St. Mary's, Woolchurch. These steps were taken with their father's approval. Schomberg himself wrote a short tract in Hebrew in 1746—*Emunat omen* [The True Faith or The Faith of an Artist, i.e., Physician]—setting forth an Enlightenment-inspired view of Judaism that revealed the extent of his alienation from his ancestral faith. Here Schomberg defined Judaism as a religion of rational beliefs and ethical standards. He rejected the binding character of the ritual law, maintaining instead that Jews were obligated only to act virtuously. He accepted those traditional beliefs that were consistent with the faith of a deist—such as the unity and incorporeality of God—and rejected those that were not—such as resurrection of the dead, the coming of the Messiah, and the immutability of the Law. Schomberg's views were those of a man of the Enlightenment, not a Christian, and he remained outside the Church of England. In the will he drafted in 1759, he committed his soul to "that Eternal Being that gave me my Existence," although when he died he was given an Anglican burial. However, this may have been at the insistence of his children, now respectable members of the established church (with one exception), rather than the result of any death-bed recantation on his part. In any case, deistic beliefs such as Schomberg's were extremely rare among Ashkenazim who left the Jewish community in the eighteenth century. His children, who were raised initially as Jews, took the more-conventional path, identifying with the Church of England. (One of his six sons remained a Jew—the notary Moses [ca. 1720–1779], who was in partnership with two observant Sephardim.) Despite his own deistic faith, the father saw the social and professional advantages of identifying with the Church of England and either encouraged or did not object to his sons becoming Anglicans.

Leakage into the established church became more common among Ashkenazim in the first decades of the nineteenth century (except among the very wealthiest families) because of the growth of a native-born and thus fully anglicized generation and to the *embourgoisement* of more members of the community. Dozens of Ashkenazi families of modest fortune lost members to the Church of England at this time. Many members of the Gompertz family, for example, once prominent in the affairs of the Hambro Synagogue, left the Jewish community. All of the fifteen children of Barent (1771–1824) and Miriam Gompertz who lived to adulthood and married converted to Christianity and/or married outside the Jewish faith.

Henry (1796–1859), for example, a solicitor who lived in Kennington, was baptized on 22 January 1817 at St. Martin's, Outwich, and the next day was married to Elizabeth Wilks of Darenth, Kent, in the same church. His brother Solomon (1806–1883) was baptized in 1823 at Otterden, Devon; he later attended Peterhouse College, Cambridge, and took religious orders. He published a collection of his sermons in 1840 and six years later wrote an attack on Swedenborgianism. His brother Lewis (1797–1821) was also baptized as an adult, at age twenty-four, but died within a month of his conversion. Their parents remained professing Jews, but several of Barent's brothers left the community—after the death of their father, it should be noted. Isaac (1773–1836), a minor poet, married Florence Wattier in 1818 and baptized his children at birth; Ephraim (1776–1867), an authority on monetary and economic matters, married Adelaide Smith in 1811; Lewis (1784–1861), the eccentric champion of animal rights and one of the founders of the Society for the Prevention of Cruelty to Animals, married a Christian and was buried at Kennington Church next to his wife.[26]

As in the previous century, Jews with cultural interests or professional aspirations outside the usual range of Jewish occupations were more likely to abandon Judaism than those who continued to adhere to conventional patterns. Before the mid-Victorian years, however, few English Jews received an extensive secular or religious education. Merchants and brokers gave their sons the bare education required for the purpose of trade—a few years at a day school or with a private tutor were deemed sufficient. The care that Isaac Lyon Goldsmid lavished on the education of his eldest son, Francis Henry—he was tutored at home in classics, mathematics, political economy, modern languages, and Hebrew until he was eighteen—was rare. Francis Henry's mental training, noted his Victorian biographers, "was of a high order, superior by far to that of any other Anglo-Jewish family at that time."[27] Francis Henry grew up to become a pillar of the Anglo-Jewish establishment, but the few others in his and an earlier generation who received extensive exposure to English and European culture and sought careers of a decidedly un-Jewish character were likely to move beyond the pale of Anglo-Jewish life, especially if they harbored social ambitions as well.

This was certainly the case with the Ukrainian-born *maskil* Hirsch Baer Hurwitz (1785–1857), who settled in England in 1825.[28] His father, a wealthy timber merchant in Uman, gave him a European education—he spoke and wrote Russian, German, and French fluently—as well as a traditional Hebrew education. Hirsch Baer traveled to Leipzig frequently on business for his father and there encountered the German *haskalah*, whose outlook he embraced and began to champion at home. He developed a profound hatred for the Talmud, which he viewed as the chief cause of Jewish superstition and degradation, and urged Jews to return to the uncorrupted ordinances of the Pentateuch: "Destroy the first link—I mean the Talmud—and all the other follies will disappear of themselves. And only in this way will the fetters of our foolish prejudices, which bring us so much misfortune, be set aside."[29] Like other Russian *maskilim* he believed that the state should actively intervene in Jewish life—by banning traditional Jewish dress, for example—to force the Jews to be happy and virtuous. In 1822, he founded a modern school in Uman to propagate his ideas, but three years later he went bankrupt and fled with his family to England. He settled first in Lincoln, where there was no Jewish community, and then in 1830 found employment as a Hebrew tutor at Cambridge. Soon thereafter he was engaged by six distinguished members of the university, including the Regius Professor of Hebrew and the Professor of Arabic, to teach them Maimonides' code of Jewish law. In 1837, he received an official university appointment, as preceptor in Hebrew language, at a stipend of £ 30 a year.

Starting a new life in England provided Hurwitz, as it did many Jewish immigrants in the nineteenth century, with the opportunity to make a full break with his past. Some time prior to his arrival in Cambridge, he converted to Christianity and changed his name to Hermann Hedwig Bernard. His choice of career made the change imperative, as did his desire to mix in university circles. Moreover, his previous espousal of radical *haskalah* views had already loosened his ties to Jewish tradition and prepared him to look at other religious traditions with sympathy. According to a Polish nobleman who visited him in Uman, Hurwitz even then believed that Jews should read the New Testament, whether they believed in Jesus or not, for its superior ethical system. As a Christian, Bernard kept his Jewish past hidden. He remained aloof from the Jewish community in London; there were, for example, no Jewish subscribers to the selection of English translations of Maimonides, which he published in 1832. In the memoir he dictated a few months before his death, he stated—quite untruthfully—that his father was an Austrian Jew who had become a Christian before Bernard's birth. His daughter also insisted that Bernard had been brought up as a Christian. In addition, Hurwitz scrupulously avoided discussing all religious matters. A pupil of his who posthumously edited his translation of and commentary on Job noted that his teacher never spoke to him about his own or others' religious views.

The desire to participate in intellectual and professional activities outside the normal patterns of Jewish life also led Sir Francis Palgrave (1788–1861), barrister, historian, antiquarian, and first archivist of what is now the Public Record Office, to seek baptism in the Church of England.[30] Palgrave's father was Meyer Cohen (d. 1831), a wealthy stockbroker; his mother, Rachel (d. 1815), was a daughter of Gotchal Levien, one of the twelve licensed Jewish brokers on the Royal Exchange and an active supporter of Jewish charities and schools. Francis was educated at home by a private tutor and at any early age demonstrated a capacity for serious intellectual activity. His life of comfort and ease was shattered, however, when war with France and the threat of invasion caused a sharp slump on the stock exchange that ruined his father. At age sixteen, he was articled to a firm of solicitors and continued there for several years, becoming his parents' chief financial support until their deaths. Despite the extra burden he now carried, he continued to pursue his major scholarly interest, medieval history and literature. In 1814, he began contributing articles to the minor journals of the day and eventually became a regular contributor to the *Quarterly Review* and the *Edinburgh Review*. He came to frequent a circle of writers that included Sir Walter Scott. In 1821, he was elected a fellow of the Royal Society in recognition of his various publications, especially a collection of medieval *chansons* that appeared in 1818. These activities gradually drew Francis away from his family and the Jewish community, and sometime between 1815 and 1821 he was baptized in the Church of England.

Through his antiquarian interests, Cohen came to know Dawson Turner, a partner in Gurneys' Bank, a great bibliophile, and a devotee of the antiquities of Norfolk, where he had his country home. Invited there to help Dawson Turner complete his book *A Tour in Normandy*, Cohen fell in love with Turner's daughter Elizabeth and sought her hand in marriage. His Jewish origins, though, were a source of discomfort to the family. But when Cohen accepted the family's proposal that he change his name to Palgrave, Elizabeth's mother's maiden name, the stumbling block was removed. Turner gave him a marriage settlement of £ 3,000 and also reimbursed him for the legal expenses he incurred in changing his name, since, as he explained, it "was done on account of my family, & it is only right I should bear the expense."[31] Francis and Elizabeth were married in 1823, after a three-year courtship.

Two years earlier, in 1821, Francis Cohen had left the firm of solicitors in which he had been employed for many years and set up on his own. In 1827, he was called to the bar by the Inner Temple, and eventually he developed a successful practice specializing in peerage cases. He entered public life, serving on commissions investigating the state of England's archives and the reform of municipal corporations. In 1832 he was knighted for his service to reform and for his literary and antiquarian activity. In 1834 he was appointed Keeper of Records at the Chapter House, Westminster Abbey, and in 1838 was made the first Deputy Keeper of the Public Records, a post he held until his death, in 1861. During these years, he continued to publish a steady stream of articles, histories, and historical fiction. His published historical writings filled ten volumes, testimony to an impressive career. By virtue of his learning, intelligence, and determination—as well as his willingness to sever his links with the circles in which he had been raised—Palgrave was able to play an important role in the cultural and civic life of mid-nineteenth-century England.

While it is impossible to measure the extent of disaffiliation from the Jewish community during the first decades of the nineteenth century, there is no question that conversion and intermarriage increased within middle-class Ashkenazi Jewry. In the previous century, defection from Judaism was not a matter of concern to the leaders of the Ashkenazi community.

While there were occasional cries of alarm about religious laxity and indifference, intermarriage and conversion were sufficiently rare that they failed to spark public comment. If parents worried that their children might abandon Judaism, they did so in private and left no record of their concern. Henry Abrahams (d. 1779), who sought to discourage his children from leaving Judaism with a provision in his will disinheriting any who did so, was very much the exception. However, such provisions became far less unusual in wills drawn up in the early nineteenth century. Hannah Joseph, a spinster of Leman Street who died in 1827, left her estate to her niece "provided she keeps the Jewish religion." Samuel Hyman, a Plymouth pawnbroker who died in 1839, instructed in his will that children who married outside the Jewish community were to be disinherited. Myer Solomon (ca.1760–1840) of Pall Mall, a successful dealer in *objets d'art* and curios and a pillar of the Western Synagogue in St. Alban's Place, left legacies to several persons, with the proviso that they would be cancelled if his heirs left "the Mosaic Religion."[32] In addition, concern about the incidence of apostasy was first registered publicly at this time. When a small group of prosperous Sephardim and Ashkenazim joined together in 1841 to establish a reform congregation in London, they cited defection from Judaism as one of the evils besetting Anglo-Jewry that religious reform would cure. In a letter to the elders of the Spanish and Portuguese congregation, the seceding members argued that substantial improvements in public worship were essential to preserving Judaism: "Indeed, we are firmly convinced that their tendency will be to arrest and prevent secession from Judaism—an overwhelming evil, which has at various times so widely spread among many of the most respectable families of our communities [that is, Sephardi and Ashkenazi]." Improvements in the service, they felt, would "inspire a deeper interest and a stronger feeling towards our holy religion" and, by influencing the minds of the young, "restrain them from traversing in their faith or contemplating for a moment the fearful step of forsaking their religion."[33]

The conviction that improvements in Jewish worship would stem the tide of apostasy was not peculiar to the leaders of the nascent Reform movement in London. The rabbis and laymen who spearheaded the early Reform movement in Germany were equally convinced that adapting Judaism to contemporary conditions was the only alternative to its outright rejection by the younger generation.[34] Yet there is little reason to believe that in either Germany or England the character of Jewish worship played a critical role in driving Jews into the arms of the church. Those who became Christians were in flight from the burdens of Jewishness—from popular defamation, social contempt, and, especially in the case of Germany, legal discrimination—and not primarily in search of a more decorous and rational religion. To be sure, the nature of Jewish worship—its "undecorous" and "irreverent" character in the eyes of reformers—may have reinforced in a small way the image of Jews as unassimilable aliens with an insufficiently spiritual religion, but it was hardly responsible for the upswing in apostasy everywhere in Western Europe in the early nineteenth century. English Jews who became Christians were for the most part insensitive to the spiritual claims of either religion. They were concerned primarily with this-worldly rather than other-worldly salvation—a reflection of the religious indifference that characterized much of Anglo-Jewry at this time. As William Cooper, a supporter of missionary efforts to convert Jews, lamented in a sermon in 1814, "There is reason to fear that thousands of Jews have scarcely any faith at all. They, in fact, reject Moses equally with Christ, and the writings of the Old Testament they place as little dependence on as the writings of the New."[35] The leaders of the Reform movement argued, nonetheless, that enhancing the worship service would attract disaffected youth back to the synagogue, perhaps, in part, because they sensed the strategic and rhetorical value of such an argument within the community.

The increase in intermarriage and conversion in the late-Georgian period stemmed, in one sense, from the growth of the anglicized portion of the Ashkenazi community. The children and grandchildren of immigrants were better prepared, for linguistic and cultural reasons, to establish intimate social contacts with other Englishmen—and thus face exposure to the temptations of radical assimilation—than recent arrivals from Germany, Holland, and Poland. In a similar way, the modest increase in the number of Jews living outside London in the late Georgian period also multiplied the number of Jews who were exposed to intensive assimilatory pressures. In London, the center of Anglo-Jewish life since the resettlement, the very size of the Jewish population as well as its tendency to concentrate in certain neighborhoods acted as a counterweight to social forces promoting integration and helped to preserve group cohesion even when religious indifference became widespread. On the other hand, Jews who settled in small provincial towns, especially those that had no organized Jewish life, established more-extensive and more-intimate social ties with Christians than did those who remained in London.

Jews who settled outside London did so primarily for commercial reasons. Itinerant peddlers were roaming the countryside, especially the southern counties and the area around London, before the mid-eighteenth century; and by 1772 they were sufficiently numerous to justify the printing of an annual calendar, or almanac, in Yiddish, listing the dates of Jewish and English holidays, the dates of important local fairs, and the days on which coaches left London for the provinces. Most of these peddlers returned periodically to London to be with their families and to replenish their stock. However, some who made good opened shops in remote villages or port towns where they had done business previously. In other instances, Jewish shopkeepers transferred their businesses from London, where competition was intense, to provincial towns offering greater opportunities. During the Revolutionary and Napoleonic wars, in particular,

Jewish shopkeepers were attracted to the naval ports—Chatham, Portsmouth, and Plymouth, primarily—where they served the marine population as slopsellers, naval agents, pawnbrokers, and jewelers. In remote towns, there might be only one or two Jewish households and no semblance of organized religious life, while in some southern ports and market towns there were dozens of Jewish families and well-established congregations. But in both cases such Jews were exposed to more-sustained social contact with the gentile population than were their brethren in the metropolis, and thus they were likely to establish relationships that would lead them away from Judaism. The jeweler Samuel Levi (ca. 1730–1812) and his brother Moses emigrated from Germany to London as young men; they settled in Haverfordwest, in Wales, and later established a bank there and in nearby Milford Haven. Both brothers took the name Phillips—after a local citizen who had befriended them—were baptized in 1755, and merged into the general community. (The famous Welsh nonconformist preacher Hugh Price Hughes was a descendant of Samuel.) More common than overt conversion was intermarriage. The slopseller Moss Lyon married Sophia Thomason in Alverstoke, near Southampton, in 1810. He carried on business in Portsmouth, where his five children were born and baptized. German-born Simon Hyman from Devonport married Mary Corse of Plymouth in St. Andrew's Church, Plymouth, in 1813. One of their sons entered the navy as a midshipman in 1829 and died later of a snakebite; the other, Orlando, won a scholarship to Wadham College, Oxford, at age sixteen, took religious orders, and was a fellow of Wadham from 1835 to 1878. Hyms Jackson, a hawker, married Amelia Crabtree in Colne, Lancashire, in 1820. Both were presumably illiterate, since neither could sign the marriage record. Jacob Moses and Charlotte Green, who were married in the parish church of Claines, Worcestershire, in 1827 were also unable to sign their names at the time of their marriage. Isaac Bright (1763–1849), jeweler and watchmaker, came to Sheffield, which had no Jewish community, about 1786. He traveled to London to choose a Jewish wife—Anne, the daughter of Henry Micholls, later a prominent textile exporter in Manchester—but many of his ten children married local Christians. In Plymouth, intermarriages were sufficiently common that the congregation was provoked to denounce them as early as 1779.[36]

Jews who settled in provincial towns and villages with few or no Jewish households undoubtedly knew that it would be difficult to preserve Jewish tradition in such circumstances. Without the support of an organized community and a critical mass of co-religionists, village Jews faced almost insurmountable obstacles in fulfilling such religious obligations as worshipping in the company of other Jews on the Sabbath and festivals, observing the dietary laws, and providing their children with a Jewish education. Men who chose to live in Sheffield, Haverfordwest, or other towns that had no Jewish community implicitly put the pursuit of material success ahead of the preservation of their religious faith. Indeed, it is likely that only Jews whose links to tradition had already been loosened would have considered settling in a locale where there were no other Jews. What Naomi Cohen has remarked in regard to German Jewish emigration to the United States in the mid-nineteenth century applies equally to Jewish dispersion in the English countryside in the Georgian period: "The very act of emigration . . . indicated a readiness to break the hold of a rigid community which one did not choose but was born into. Emigration meant exchanging a traditional Jewish setting . . . for the unknown cultural deprivations of an alien environment. More important, it signified a reshuffling of priorities, which put individual freedom above control by the group or even above group survival."[37] Some may have viewed such a move as an explicit opportunity to leave Judaism behind altogether, that is, as an opportunity to cut all ties, social and religious, with their Jewish past. Most, however, were not so much in flight from their Jewishness as unconcerned with the difficulties provincial life put in the way of preserving Judaism. Exposed to intensive social contact with gentile society, they or their children frequently merged, without intentionally setting out to do so, into their new surroundings, in precisely the same way that Jewish peddlers and shopkeepers in rural America did a generation or two later.[38]

But in London, the heartland of English Jewry, the ease with which village and small-town Jews merged into local society was duplicated only among the very poorest strata of Jewish society. There, like their Sephardi counterparts, Ashkenazi street traders, old-clothes men, itinerant peddlers, porters, servants, beggars, criminals, and the like who were sufficiently anglicized mixed freely with their gentile neighbors.[39] Cohabitation or marriage was frequently the outcome of such intercourse. Many applications for admission to the charity school of the London Society for Promoting Christianity among the Jews, for example, came from intermarried couples eager to obtain free schooling for their children. One such couple, John Smith, a Jewish sailor turned shoemaker, and his illiterate Christian wife, Sarah Bellingham, were married at St. Mary's, Stratford Bow, in 1814. Interestingly, Smith, whose real name was Solomons, had changed his name when he first went to sea because he thought "they would not take him on board of ships in the name of *Solomons*, knowing that he was a Jew."[40] Among the numerous Jews who appeared at the Old Bailey, either as witnesses or as accused criminals, were a small minority who had ceased to practice Judaism and had drifted into largely gentile circles. A Mr. Jones, a "jeweller" (probably a pawnbroker) in Shire Lane, Temple Bar, who gave testimony in a highway robbery case in 1781, told the court, "I was a Jew, but have renounced Judaism"—that is, he had ceased to identify himself as a Jew but most likely had not been baptized. Two years later, John Watson, a butcher who was a Jew by birth, explained to the court that he called himself a Christian because "I am never among the Jews" and "I follow more the Christian ways than I do the Jews." In the 1780s, Joseph Levy, also known as Cocky Barber and Joe Barber, a former criminal turned thief-taker, claimed he was a Christian when he gave testimony, although he apparently had not been baptized. When Abraham Samuels testified in 1798 against a woman accused of passing counterfeit coins, he responded to the question of whether he was a Jew by stating, "I am not an Englishman," and then explained that while his mother was a Jewess he did not know what his father was. When Samuel Cohen appeared at the Old Bailey in 1824, he told the court that he and Susan Webb had been living together as husband and wife for four years.[41]

The most striking evidence of the dissolution of communal ties among the poor is the decline in Jewish criminality in the early years of the Victorian period. In the second half of the eighteenth century and in the early nineteeth, a very visible minority of the London community engaged in criminal activity, either on an occasional basis or as a full-time occupation.[42] Some of this criminal activity was linked to the concentration of Jews in the street trades and in the trade in secondhand merchandise, areas of commerce in which deceit and chicanery were a normal part of the conduct of business. Jewish pawnbrokers, for example, regularly purchased stolen goods; Jewish fruit sellers frequently passed counterfeit coins while making change. However, some criminal activity, such as burglary, shoplifting, and pickpocketing, was simply the outgrowth of poverty and in no way linked to the occupational structure of the community. Before the Victorian period, Jewish crime was regarded as an acute social problem by both critics of the Jews and the notables of the community; it elicited unfavorable and often vitriolic comments by journalists, reformers, travelers, and public officials. Then, in the 1830s and 1840s, Jewish criminal activity declined considerably, ceasing to attract much public attention. This decline was due, in part, to a remarkable improvement in the economic fortunes of the community, as increasing numbers moved up into the middle class and, in part, to the transportation to Australia of several hundred convicted criminals. Yet these two explanations alone do not account for the disappearance of Jewish crime as an acute social problem. An additional factor undoubtedly was the absorption of some of the Jewish *lumpenproletariat*, whose criminal behavior evoked public comment, into the surrounding gentile underclass in the decades before the 1830s and 1840s. Thus, if they or their offspring continued in their criminal ways in the Victorian period, they did so as "Christians," so to speak, their origins going unnoticed.

By the early nineteenth century, no stratum within the Ashkenazi community was untouched by radical assimilation. Rich and poor, stockbrokers, shopkeepers, and street traders alike, were among those who moved away from Judaism and the Jewish community. Some drifted into gentile society, perhaps by way of marriage, without intending to do so; others cut their links deliberately, formally converting to Christianity. Among the latter, some hoped to advance themselves professionally; some to improve their social standing; others, having drifted away from Jewish beliefs and practices, wanted to cement their social and psychological identification with the majority community and escape the popular stereotype of the Jew. In most cases, no one motive operated but several, working in tandem, came into play, the exact mixture being determined by the social context of the individual case. Obviously the absorption of the Frankses and the Goldsmids proceeded differently than that of the London shoemaker John Solomons Smith or the Portsmouth slopseller Moss Lyon. Yet, however different the social circumstances in which they lived, there was one element in the character of Anglo-Jewish life in the Georgian period that promoted communal disaffiliation equally at all levels of society, among both Sephardim and Ashkenazim—the absence of a strong communal structure with the authority either to impose discipline or to elicit voluntary conformity.[43]

The community in England was the first in Jewish history to be established on a purely voluntary basis. It was not an autonomous corporate body, like those on the Continent before the French Revolution, with legal and fiscal authority of its own. Indeed, one cannot speak of the Jewish community in England in the sense that one can in regard to its counterparts in the *ancien régime* states across the Channel, that is, a community whose formal membership was coterminous with all the Jewish residents in a locality. In England, membership in communal institutions was not compulsory; synagogues, charities, and schools survived on the voluntary contributions of those Jews who wished to affiliate with them and to enjoy the religious and social benefits they conferred. The rabbis and lay notables of the various congregations enjoyed no real powers of coercion. Their ability to enforce traditional norms and standards rested almost entirely on the willingness of individuals to defer to their rule. This meant, in practice, that their authority within the community was weak, for traditional beliefs, which sanctioned the authority of Jewish law and its interpreters, no longer commanded the unconditional loyalty of most Jews. There were, thus, no strong internal or external constraints to prevent Jews from doing as they pleased in matters of religion. Moreover, Anglo-Jewry lacked social cohesion: it was a relatively new community, without well-established, well-financed educational, charitable and religious institutions that might have served as a counterweight to the assimilatory pressures of living in an open society. It was a community of relatively recent newcomers, without extensive religious or secular education for the most part. The magnates who managed communal affairs were mostly restless and ambitious men, impious, secular-minded, eager to secure their fortunes and reputations. Intellectual leadership, either in the traditional rabbinic mold or in the new modern style, was altogether absent. These circumstances helped to loosen the ethnic and religious ties that had made premodern Jewish communities cohesive social units and thereby prepared the ground for radical assimilation into English society.

The Portuguese-born physician and medical writer Jacob de Castro Sarmento (1691–1762), in a mezzotint portrait of 1758, about to write a prescription for a patient. Influenced by Enlightenment ideas, de Castro Sarmento broke with the Sephardi community in 1758.

The literary historian and radical critic of Judaism Isaac D'Israeli (1766–1848), father of the famous Conservative prime minister. A man of moderate social ambitions, he was content to remain outside any religious body after quarreling with the authorities of the Sephardi synagogue.

Benjamin Disraeli (1804–1881). As a young man intent
on entering upper-class society, he cultivated the image
of an elegant dandy, as had other ambitious parvenus,
like Beau Nash and Beau Brummel, before him.

A soberer and more "semitic" portrait of Benjamin Disraeli from the pages of *Vanity Fair* (1869). Despite his baptism, Disraeli was continually reminded of his origins.

Jessie Goldsmid, wife of the merchant banker Benjamin Goldsmid, who converted to Christianity, along with her children, after her husband's death in 1808.

Judith Levy (1706–1803), daughter and wife of two early benefactors of the Ashkenazi community, used her inherited wealth to launch herself into fashionable society after the death of her husband and to snag a noble husband for her daughter Isabella.

The famous tenor John Braham (1774–1856) in the title role of Handel's opera *Orlando*. A former choir-boy at the Great Synagogue, Braham ceased to iden-tify with Judaism once he had embarked on an opera and concert career.

The Ukrainian-born *maskil* Hirsch Baer Hurwitz (1785–1857) settled in England in 1825, changed his religion and his name (to Hermann Hedwig Bernard), and became a teacher of Hebrew at Cambridge.

Nathan Mayer Rothschild (1777–1836), founder of the
English branch of the famous banking clan, in a characteristic pose by the pillar at the Exchange at which he
regularly stationed himself. Unlike his descendants, the
German-born Nathan was not greatly concerned with his
social position.

Charles Robinson's engraving of the civil marriage of Hannah de Rothschild (1851–1890) and the Earl of Rosebery (1847–1929), in *Illustrated London News*, 30 March 1878. This ceremony took place in the board room of the parish guardians of St. George's, Hanover Square; it was followed by a religious wedding one hour later at Christ Church, Down Street, Piccadilly.

Leopold de Rothschild (1845–1917), grandson of Nathan Mayer Rothschild, a well-known and popular figure in racing circles, as caricatured by Spy in *Vanity Fair* in 1884.

Spy's *Vanity Fair* portrait of the German-born financier Ernest Cassel (1852–1921), one of several Jews in the social set of the Prince of Wales. Although he was known as a Jew, Cassel secretly embraced Catholicism around 1881 at the request of his dying wife.

The socially prominent German-born laryngologist Felix
Semon (1849–1921), as caricatured by Spy in *Vanity Fair* in
1902. Semon refused to join any religious body but raised
his children in the Church of England.

The Rev. Michael Solomon Alexander (1799–1845), teacher, cantor, ritual slaughterer, and, after his baptism, missionary and first Anglican bishop in Jerusalem.

A 1905 cartoon by H. E. Bateman illustrative of the rising hostility to Jews after the turn of the century. The accompanying caption reads: "Schoolmaster—'What fault did Joseph's brothers commit in selling him?' Jewish Schoolboy—'They let 'im go too cheap.'"

3

Native Jews in the Victorian Age

The social composition of the native Jewish community of England changed markedly in the course of the nineteenth century. At the beginning of the century, the great mass of Jews were immigrants—or the children of immigrants—and thus cut off to a greater or lesser extent from social and cultural currents in the world around them. This began to change within a few decades, with the passing of foreign-born parents and grandparents and an increase in the number of Jews raised and educated in English surroundings. By the end of the century, the Jewish community in England had become overwhelmingly English in manners, speech, dress, deportment, and habits of thought and taste. The only exceptions were recent arrivals from Eastern Europe, whose religious loyalties and sense of Jewish identity largely insulated them from the pressures and temptations of radical assimilation, and small colonies of German Jews, in both London and the provinces, whose historical experience before emigration predisposed them to behave in precisely the opposite way, that is, to abandon the bonds of Jewish solidarity.

The economic profile of the native community was also transformed in the Victorian period. In 1800, most Jews were poor, dependent on itinerant peddling, petty trade, and street vending for their livelihoods. Then, in the course of the next half-century or so, there was a gradual improvement in the economic status of most of the community. Street vendors rose to keeping fixed stalls, stall-keepers acquired shops, small shopkeepers became proprietors of large emporiums or manufacturers or wholesalers, pawnbrokers and traders in secondhand merchandise were transformed into jewelers and antique dealers. At mid-century, according to V. D. Lipman's cautious estimates, 5 percent of London's 20,000 Jews were upper class and upper middle class in terms of income, 30 percent were middle class, 35 to 40 percent were lower class but not in receipt of relief, while 25 to 30 percent were poor and receiving occasional or regular aid from communal charities.[1] In other words, at least one-third of the community belonged to the servant-keeping strata of society by 1850. During the next three decades, an even larger proportion of Anglo-Jewry moved into the middle class. In the early 1870s, D. W. Marks (1811–1909), rabbi of the

Reform synagogue in London, noted that "the troops of Jewish boys, which, a quarter of a century ago, infested the highways as vendors of fruit and articles of small value, and the young men that assailed the ear with the incessant cry of 'old clothes' have almost disappeared, and have been succeeded by a generation that has taken to more legitimate pursuits either at home or in the British colonies." In 1882, Joseph Jacobs estimated that in London Jewry (whose population he calculated was 46,000) 14.6 percent were upper or upper middle class, 42.2 percent were middle class, 19.6 percent were lower class, and 29.6 percent were poor, that is, in receipt of casual relief or in institutions.[2] In fact, *embourgeoisement* among native English Jews was more extensive than Jacobs's statistics initially suggest, for recent immigrants from Eastern Europe inflated the proportion of the community falling into the least affluent categories. (Marks claimed that mendicity was confined almost entirely to foreign-born Jews.) Within the native community, the percentage of middle- and upper middle-class families was undoubtedly higher than the 56.8 percent he calculated for Anglo-Jewry as a whole.

The gradual *embourgeoisement* of native Jewry in the Victorian period was paralleled by an equally gradual dismantling of legal barriers that had prevented Jews from entering institutions of power and prestige within English society. Few Jews before this time aspired to sit in the House of Commons, study at Oxford or Cambridge, or enroll at the Inns of Court, and consequently there was no concerted movement to challenge the christological oaths that blocked the entry of Jews. (However, that was not the initial intention of the oaths; they had been designed to exclude Christians who were not members of the established church.) When the Anglo-Jewish elite campaigned for their removal or modification in the mid-Victorian decades, they met with success by and large. In 1830, Jews gained the right to become freemen of the City of London and members of the livery companies; in 1833, the right to be called to the bar; in 1835, the right to vote in parliamentary elections where otherwise qualified (although, in fact, Jews had been voting in many places since the previous century); in 1845, the right to hold municipal office; in 1858, the right to sit in the House of Commons; and in 1871, the right to take degrees and hold fellowships at Oxford and Cambridge (although, again, Jews had been attending certain colleges at the two ancient universities for several decades).

The removal of civil disabilities in the mid-Victorian period reflected a wider willingness on the part of the ruling class to admit professing Jews to positions of honor and prestige. Wealthy Jews with political aspirations faced no more difficulty by the end of the century in finding a seat in Parliament than did other aspirants. There were six unconverted Jews in the Commons as early as 1869 and sixteen by 1906. Nor, after passage of the Promissory Oaths Act of 1871, were Jews barred from holding ministerial office. That same year Sir George Jessel (1824–1883) was appointed Solicitor-General; in 1888, Henry de Worms (1840–1903) became Under-

Secretary of State for the Colonies. Honors and titles were also obtainable, more so in fact than political office. In 1885, on the recommendation of William Gladstone, Queen Victoria raised Nathaniel de Rothschild (1840–1915) to the peerage, although she had balked at so honoring his father sixteen years earlier. In 1895, Henry de Worms became Lord Pirbright and Sydney James Stern (1845–1912), Lord Wandsworth; in 1907, Samuel Montagu (1832–1911) became Lord Swaythling. Baronetcies and knighthoods came both more frequently and earlier than peerages. Isaac Lyon Goldsmid received a baronetcy as early as 1841; Moses Montefiore (1784–1885), who had been knighted in 1837 following his election as sheriff of London, became a baronet in 1846 in recognition of his diplomacy on behalf of persecuted Jews abroad. Anthony de Rothschild (1810–1876) was made a baronet the following year. David Salomons (1797–1873) received a knighthood in 1855, following his election as Lord Mayor of London, and a baronetcy in 1869. By the end of the century, more than a dozen Jews had been made either baronets or knights; in the years before the outbreak of World War I, another dozen or so were similarly honored.[3]

At the same time that wealthy Jews began to participate in public life, they also began to associate more intensively with non-Jews in social affairs and to take part in cultural and recreational activities heretofore outside the orbit of Jewish interests. The wealthiest families pursued the country pleasures of the landed upper class—racing and hunting—and a handful became well-known and popular figures in racing circles. In 1889, for example, *The Man of the World* remarked that there were "very few men better known and liked in Society, in the City, or on the Turf" than Leopold de Rothschild (1845–1917).[4] The Rothschilds, who were enthusiastic horsemen, were large landowners and great political magnates in Buckinghamshire, where, in 1839, they introduced staghunting to the Vale of Aylesbury. They entertained the political elite of the nation in a grand and opulent style in their country homes—and, aside from their numerous kinsmen, rarely included other Jews in their dinners, hunting parties, concerts, etc. Jewish bankers and professional men were accepted as members in the clubs of St. James's. Mayer de Rothschild (1818–1874) became a member of Brooks's in 1841; his brother Anthony in 1853. They and their older brother, Lionel, were also members of the Reform. When the barrister Arthur Cohen (1829–1914) was elected into the Oxford and Cambridge Club in the late 1860s, his cousin Leopold de Rothschild, then a Cambridge undergraduate, wrote home to his parents that "so popular is he amongst his own set that he obtained more white balls than have ever been given to any individual and only 4 black balls."[5] Indeed, London clubs were so willing to admit Jews that no Jewish city clubs developed in the metropolis, like those that became common in the United States, where city and country clubs began excluding Jews in the late 1870s.

By the last decades of the century, it was possible for rich Jews to gain admission to smart society without changing their religion. For thirty years, the Prince of Wales included a high proportion of Jews in his circle, a practice he continued as King Edward VII. Foremost among them were Nathaniel, Alfred (1842–1918), and Leopold de Rothschild; Arthur (1840–1912) and Reuben Sassoon (1835–1905); Baron Maurice de Hirsch (1831–1896); and Sir Ernest Cassel (1852–1921), who was known as a Jew, although he had secretly embraced Catholicism around 1881 at the request of his dying wife (herself a convert to the Roman faith), a fact not widely known until his own death, in 1921.[6] In the West End in general, T. H. S. Escott reported in 1886, Jews were "habitually to be seen in the drawing rooms or dining rooms of society," and "society, including the very *crème de la crème*, the possessors of the bluest of blue blood available" flocked to their entertainments in turn. The parties of Clarissa Bischoffsheim (ca.1837–1922) at Bute House, South Audley Street, for example, "were famous for the distinction of the guests." An obituary noted that she had "occupied a great place in Society," was "one of the inner circle," and would be "mourned in high places as well as in mean streets." An editorial writer in the *Jewish Chronicle* in the 1920s, in lamenting the apostasy of the children of Sir George Faudel-Phillips (1840–1922), recalled that neither Sir George nor his father, Sir Benjamin S. Phillips (1811–1889), had found "association with Jews and Judaism the least bar to the attainment of the highest honours, even at the hands of a body that gauges honour by the very strictest of standards, or to the most coveted social position or, indeed, to the gaining of the most alluring of life's material advantages."

Indeed, there were some very wealthy Jewish families, in addition to the Rothschilds, who socialized primarily with non-Jews and made "a very occasional entry" into Jewish circles only for "matrimonial necessities." Lady Monkswell, who was a frequent guest at magnificent banquets at the large Piccadilly house of Sir Julian Goldsmid (1838–1896), noted in her diary that few if any Jews were in attendance on these occasions. Claude Goldsmid Montefiore (1858–1939), the theologian of Liberal Judaism in Great Britain, recalled seeing few Jews other than relations in his house in Portman Square when he was growing up. His mother, a daughter of Sir Isaac Lyon Goldsmid, "liked to collect young people about her, a small, intimate set who dined or stayed with them regularly," most of whom were Christians. "Our environment was entirely uncosmopolitan and purely English," he later wrote.[7]

A number of contemporaries attributed the social "ascendency" of Jews, to borrow Escott's term, to the initiative of the Prince of Wales, who set the tone of smart society. "The innumerable host of his sattelites [*sic*]," Escott wrote, "follow his example, and bow the knee before the descendants of the tribes." A quarter-century later a Jewish observer, in noting that Jews found little difficulty in associating with gentiles as far as they themselves desired, claimed similarly that this was due "in no small measure to the fact that the late King [Edward VII] admitted Jews freely to his society, and in his own intimate circle entirely broke down the barrier between Jew and non-Jew." In the face of such an example, he asserted, "the English people as a whole cannot well refuse social equality to the Jews, as far as differences of tastes and customs will permit."[8]

Jewish integration was also made possible by an increasing openness of elite social circles to new wealth in general, particularly if the wealth came from the City rather than from the industrial Midlands or North. In the last decades of the century, upper-class society became less exclusive. Barriers were lowered; rules were relaxed. Merchant bankers mixed more freely and easily with government ministers and well-born landholders than they had in earlier periods. "New and alien faces appeared at Cowes, on the turf and at Covent Garden; new names among the birthday honours and in the list of those who rented grousemoors," the novelist Stephen McKenna remembered. The intense exclusivity that marked aristocratic society on the Continent in the late nineteenth century was generally absent; and to foreign visitors, Beatrice Webb recalled, London society "appeared all-embracing in its easy-going tolerance and superficial good nature."[9] Whatever the faults of the English aristocracy, the Duke of Argyll wrote in 1906, "it has never had any vulgar prejudice against 'new men.'" Nor, he added, "does there now exist in England any of that disgraceful antipathy to Jews which still prevails on the Continent of Europe." Lady Dorothy Nevill, daughter of Lord Orford, asserted that anyone willing to spend enough money could enter the highest social circles: "Birth to-day is of small account, whilst wealth wields an unquestioned sway."[10] Although observations like these certainly exaggerate both the absence of prejudice against Jews and the openness of upper-class society toward outsiders, they do testify to the existence of an extensive social arena in which Jews were welcome—extensive certainly by comparison with those in other European capitals.[11]

Jewish recruits to the higher reaches of Victorian society entered on the basis of wealth accumulated primarily in the City of London, and in this sense their social integration took the same path as that of their eighteenth-century predecessors. However, in the last decades of the century, Jewish attendance at public schools and, to a much lesser extent, at Oxford and Cambridge also began to play a role in taking Jews into privileged circles.[12] Before the 1870s, well-to-do Jewish families did not send their sons to public schools, partly because of the schools' unwillingness or constitutional inability to admit non-Anglicans and partly because of the parents' reluctance to educate their children in a Christian atmosphere. In such a school they would be unable to observe the dietary laws and celebrate the Jewish Sabbath and festivals and would be required to conform outwardly to established religious arrangements, such as attendance at chapel and house prayers, instruction in the New Testament, and observance of Christian holidays. Moreover, as long as Jewish social and occupational aspirations remained limited in scope, a public school education offered few advantages. Affluent Jewish parents educated their sons at home, sent them to

Jewish boarding schools (such as Leopold Neumegen's at Highgate and later Kew, or Louis Loewe's at Brighton and later Broadstairs in Kent) or day schools, or enrolled them in prestigious nonsectarian or church-affiliated day schools willing to accommodate Jews (such as St. Paul's and University College School in London, and Manchester Grammar School and Bradford Grammar School in the provinces).

This pattern began to change in the 1870s. Many Jewish parents now found the Christian character of public school education less objectionable, while many schools became willing to open their doors to Jewish students and to exempt them from chapel attendance and New Testament instruction. (Some parents preferred that their sons *not* be exempted; as Hermann Gollancz [1852–1930], rabbi of the Bayswater Synagogue, lamented in 1907, "Wealthy Jews and men of note among us send their sons to the public schools of the land and permit them to join hypocritically in the religious services held in church or chapel."[13]) At the same time, Jewish houses were opened at three public schools—Clifton (1878), Harrow (1880), and Cheltenham (1891)—in which the dietary laws were observed, religious and Hebrew instruction offered, and the Sabbath and festivals celebrated. From the 1870s, then, there was a steady increase in the number of youth from upper middle-class Jewish homes receiving their secondary education in the company of boys who were likely to occupy positions of status and power later in life.

At the same time Jews also began to study at Oxford and Cambridge. Before the 1870s, the colleges were not eager to admit Jews—some refused outright to do so—and placed various obstacles in their way, such as mandatory chapel attendance. Mayer de Rothschild (1818–1874), for example, entered Magdalene College, Cambridge, in October 1837, but later that academic year transferred to Trinity College, where the authorities were more understanding about his absence from chapel. A decade later his cousin Arthur Cohen, although recommended by the Dean of Ely, was refused admission by both Trinity College and Christ's College. Cohen's uncle Moses Montefiore and his cousin Mayer de Rothschild then wrote to the Prince Consort, Chancellor of the University, asking that he use his influence with the Master of Magadalene, who was also Dean of Windsor. Cohen entered Magdalene in the fall of 1849, but though he completed his work in 1853 (he was President of the Union as well as Third Wrangler), he did not take his degree until 1858, following passage of the Cambridge University Reform Act of 1856, which abolished the religious test for graduation. At Oxford, on the other hand, professing Jews were barred from even matriculating until passage of the Oxford University Reform Act of 1854, and even then they might encounter difficulties. Sackville Davis (1829–1913), the first unconverted Jew to graduate from Oxford, matriculated in July 1859, having been accepted by Worcester College on the assumption that he was a communicant of the Church of England. (He had a pleasantly ambiguous name and his association with the organized Jewish community was slight.) Once admitted, he apparently attended chapel. When the college authorities discovered he was Jewish and unbaptized, they tried to get rid of him. He threatened legal action, having, it seems, been promised support by prominent members of the London Jewish community. The college backed down and an agreement was reached: Davis would be permitted to take his degree if he did not attend chapel, hall, or lectures in the college.[14]

The scarcity of Jews at Oxford and Cambridge before the 1870s was not due entirely to barriers erected by the colleges; it also reflected a lack of strong interest on the part of Jews themselves in university education. This disinterest stemmed primarily from the absence of any significant benefits (intellectual ones aside) to be gained from attendance at university. An English university degree did not confer the status that a degree in Germany did, where Jews sought to win social acceptance and political emancipation by demonstrating their devotion to and mastery of German culture and science. Similarly it did little to advance their career opportunities, for the universities were not training grounds for occupations Jews were like to enter. For the first three-quarters of the nineteenth century, Oxford and Cambridge were "educators, first and foremost, of the clergy of the Establishment." Over 70 percent of Oxbridge graduates in the period 1834–1853 became Anglican clergymen; over 60 percent in the period 1854–1863; and over 50 percent in the period 1864–1873.[15] Also, as was the case with the public schools, Jewish parents resisted sending their sons to institutions that were suffused with Christian symbols and sentiments, regardless of the concessions they might make to Jewish undergraduates. Even Hannah Rothschild (1783–1850), who sent her son Mayer to Cambridge, found Oxford "too orthodox to be an agreeable residence for any other sect beside Protestant." Her grandson Leopold, who was at Trinity College, Cambridge, in the mid-1860s, wrote home of his discomforture at a dinner party where most of the guests were fellows of different colleges and thus clergymen: "naturally their conversation was very 'shoppy' and they wandered into the mysteries of theology and of various doxies until at last I was so mystified that I did not dare open my lips." A friend who was present "was afraid that they might forget my presence and make some attack upon the Jews!"[16]

After 1870, the number of Jewish students at Oxford and Cambridge increased as a result of several factors: a greater willingness among college authorities to admit non-Anglicans of various stripes, the increasing prestige of the universities in national life, and a weakening of Jewish sensitivity to their Christian character. Yet the number of Jews who attended before World War I was never large. When the future geneticist Redcliffe Salaman (1874–1955) was an undergraduate at Cambridge in the mid-1890s, he later recalled, there were at most a dozen Jewish students, all sons of well-to-do and generally long-established families. In 1906, the head of Christ Church, Oxford, estimated that there had not been more than half a dozen

Jews at the college in the previous ten years. And six years later, according to Sir Basil Henriques (1890–1961), there were only thirty Jewish undergraduates in all the Oxford colleges. In all, the number of identifying Jewish students in either university at any one time before 1914 probably never exceeded twenty-five or thirty and often was less.[17] The few Jews who received an Oxbridge education, however, frequently established friendships that later in life gained them access to spheres of social and political influence. "In a country and an age where power was still remarkably concentrated, friendships counted for much. Those made during, and growing out of, the [Oxbridge] years would be of lasting importance."[18] This was true for the first Lord Rothschild, who joined the circle of the Prince of Wales while at Cambridge in the early 1860s. And it was equally true four decades later for Leonard Woolf (1880–1969), who as an undergraduate at Trinity College, Cambridge, established the close ties that took him to Bloomsbury and beyond.

The willingness of elite social and political circles in the Victorian age to admit and even befriend unconverted Jews had a profound impact on the incidence of apostasy in upper middle-class Jewish society and, to a lesser extent, among less-wealthy strata as well. In earlier periods dozens of once-prominent Jewish families ceased to be Jewish because Jewishness was perceived as an obstacle to careers, honors, and status. The removal of civil disabilities and the relaxation of social barriers undercut the primacy of these motives for abandoning Judaism. As Oswald John Simon (1855–1932) told a missionary in 1887, while some Jews had been baptized before emancipation in order to attend university or enter Parliament, now, when being a Jew involved "no inconvenience to anybody," this no longer occurred: "the most pious, the most learned, the most cultivated, and the most enlightened remain honourably by the Covenant." Conversion had ceased to be as useful to English Jews as it was to German or Hungarian or Russian Jews, for whom it continued to serve as an entry ticket into the larger society. Among wealthy families long settled in England, defection became extremely rare in the course of the nineteenth century. In fact, conversion and intermarriage were so unusual in the upper reaches of Anglo-Jewry that when they began to occur more frequently early in the twentieth century, they evoked considerable comment. Lily Montagu (1873–1963), one of the founders of Liberal Judaism (that is, radical Reform) in Britain and herself a well-connected member of the communal notability, described the beginnings of widespread intermarriage among leading families at that time as "a terrible and ominous novelty." When Eva Spielmann (1886–1949) became engaged to a gentile, William Hubback, who taught classics at University College, Cardiff, in 1910, there was considerable distress in her family. No member had ever married a non-Jew, although both sides had been settled in England for at least three generations. (Her mother's family, the Raphaels, had been in England since the eighteenth century.) Once her engagement was announced, several relatives canceled invitations already issued to her, while others with marriageable daughters forbade her to visit their homes in case she might, in her words, "contaminate them."[19]

The paucity of instances of conversion and intermarriage among the native Anglo-Jewish notability reflected a sense of communal solidarity that was unusual in the Western Jewish world at the time. In Paris, Berlin, Vienna, New York, and other urban centers, between 1815 and 1914 material prosperity and Jewish loyalty usually proved incompatible over several generations. In Victorian London, though, the great Anglo-Jewish families tended to retain a more than nominal association with Judaism and the Jewish community. The men routinely accepted positions of responsibility in the management of charities, synagogues, schools, and other communal bodies. Sons succeeded fathers in positions of communal leadership for three or even four generations—in contrast to the pattern that prevailed before 1830 or so in England, when wealthy families tended to be absorbed into Christian society after a generation or two. In a mood of self-congratulation and with some hyperbole, Cecil Roth highlighted the contrast thusly: "On the whole, the highly distinguished 'Jew' of the continental countries during the nineteenth century was a Jew in name only, and not by creed, having at the best only a nominal connexion with the Synagogue. In England, with the one formidable exception of Benjamin Disraeli, this was not the case, and the Jews who figured most prominently in the public eye were at the same time closely asssociated with every aspect of Jewish activity. . . . " The *Jewish World* noted in 1892, for example, that most of the seven Jews returned to the House of Commons in a recent election attended seriously to their communal responsibilities.[20]

The nature of the Jewish notability's attachment to Judaism and the Jewish community was complex. Most were not Orthodox Jews by the standards of Central or East European Orthodoxy at the time or the standards of British and American Orthodoxy today, but they were respectful of religious tradition and far more observant than wealthy Jews elsewhere in the West. They were not in any sense Jews in name only, nor was their Jewish identity merely a lingering ethnic allegiance. They observed the major Jewish holidays, kept the Sabbath, and adhered to the dietary laws, although their manner of doing so did not always agree with Jewish tradition and was considerably influenced by contemporary Christian practice.

When the Anthony de Rothschilds were in the country, for example, they marked the Sabbath with a short family service in their home after breakfast, following which Louisa de Rothschild (1821–1910) gave her daughters, Constance (1843–1931) and Annie (1844–1926), Bible lessons. Ordinary pleasures and duties were put aside: carriages and horses were not taken out, lessons were not done, letters were not written. Louisa de Rothschild would spend part of the day reading Jewish devotional literature as well as other religious writings, including works by Theodore Parker, James Martineau, and F. W. Robertson. The fast of Yom Kippur (the

Day of Atonement) was observed strictly. Constance, then eighteen, noted in her diary in 1861: "The evening of the Fast. A terrible evening always, we sat and talked and then read prayers. I prayed for strength for the great day. . . . The Fast day. A day of penance and tribulation, indeed, I felt it so. I tried not to think of hunger, dinners, and teas, but I tried to question myself carefully on my sins and my faults." On Yom Kippur only her father attended synagogue; the rest of the family generally remained at home since it was a long walk to the synagogue and Louisa could not follow the Hebrew.[21]

Some form of Sabbath observance was, in general, characteristic of most families in the Anglo-Jewish elite during the Victorian years. The Liberal politician Herbert Samuel (1870–1963), whose parents were quite traditional, went regularly to Sabbath services as a child. Later, while at Balliol College, he experienced a religious crisis. He rejected a number of fundamental tenets of Judaism and wrote to his mother early in 1892 that he felt obliged to give up "the profession of Jewish beliefs." To pretend to hold them would be "the grossest hypocrisy" and would destroy his self-respect. However, his wife, Beatrice Franklin (1871–1959), whom he married in 1897, came from an even more observant family than his own, and, partly to accommodate her, Samuel agreed to compromise his principles, although not without an initial struggle. In January 1898, when he and Beatrice were wrangling over some aspect of Jewish practice, his mother-in-law (who was also his aunt) wrote to him: "Your upbringing has unfortunately been faulty. You are a man of rare intelligence and laws without reason cannot appeal to you. You have been goaded to declare that you would not enter a synagogue. Well, circumstances compelled you to go twice." She reminded him that, having married, he had become a man with great responsibilities. "Therefore, my dear boy, brave everything. I do not suggest belief, but occasionally accompany your good wife [to synagogue] as you would to any other building." Since he had crossed the synagogue threshold once, she counseled, he would find it easier to accustom himself to attending occasionally at present than he would be able to do later. Samuel did not accompany his wife and children every Sabbath to the New West End Synagogue, to which they belonged, but he did attend on the High Holidays. In addition, he never worked or traveled on the Sabbath, but remained at home and read or went for a walk. He also maintained some form of the dietary laws both in and out of his home, although the manner in which he and his wife did so was easygoing by traditional standards. Their son Edwin (1898–1978), second Viscount Samuel, recalled that as a day-boy at Westminster School in the years just before World War I he followed his mother's "own peculiar version of the Jewish dietary laws by picking the pieces of ham out of the beef rissoles served at school lunches."[22]

Observance of the Sabbath among the Anglo-Jewish elite frequently took unconventional forms. As a child, Leonard Montefiore (1853–1879) regularly attended the Reform synagogue in Berkeley Street with his mother. (His father was more casual in religious matters.) When he attended Balliol College in the mid-1870s, he never worked on the Sabbath, but since he did not want to pass the day in mere idleness, he visited the Oxford workhouse to talk with and entertain the old people there. The banker Samuel Montagu was more strict in his observance than most of his contemporaries; however he permitted his children to play tennis on the Sabbath—but not croquet. He reasoned that there was nothing prohibited, strictly speaking, about the former, but the children could chip the mallets when they played croquet. (Breaking or damaging an object is regarded as a form of work according to the laws of Sabbath rest.) Similarly, when the family went to Brighton, he permitted them to ride in a bath chair, pushed by a man, on the Sabbath, but not in an open victoria, drawn by a horse. Here he reasoned that as the Christian pushing the chair was a rational being, he could observe his day of rest on Sunday, while the horse had no choice in the matter and might be forced to take another party for a drive on the following day as well. In some very observant homes, a gentile servant was employed on the Sabbath to wind the family's watches and tear the toilet paper into small pieces.[23]

The parents of Sir Basil Henriques each observed the Sabbath in his and her own fashion. David Henriques (1851–1912) never missed a Sabbath service at the Reform synagogue, of which his father was a founder and president. Basil's mother Agnes, being slightly lame, seldom attended because the flight of stairs to the women's gallery was steep. (Men and women continued to sit separately in most Reform congregations in Europe.) In any case, she did not like synagogue ritual or, for that matter, home ceremonies either. But she was, according to her son's testimony, a deeply religious person. She taught her children to pray, kneeling at her feet—a most un-Jewish posture for prayer—so that they might learn to feel humble before God, and Basil continued to pray on his knees all his life. Following dinner on Friday evenings, at the commencement of the Sabbath, the family would read prayers together. Then each child in turn would recite the Ten Commandments and kneel before her while she placed her hands on his head and blessed him with the priestly benediction (Numbers 6: 24–26). Agnes taught her children a highly spiritualized, almost Protestant-like version of Judaism, a faith rather than a body of observances, so that they grew up largely ignorant of the ceremonies known to most Jews. Nevertheless, Judaism, however colorless it became in her hands, remained an important ingredient in her relations with her children. She gave them "little talks" before they said their prayers; she wrote sermons, prayers, homilies, and pious quotations in little black notebooks that she sent with her children when they went away to school; above all, Basil wrote, "she taught us to love God."[24]

The Judaism of the Henriques family, like that of most of the Anglo-Jewish plutocracy, was a religion without sharply defined doctrines. Issues of belief and faith did not trouble the Victorian Jewish elite, most of whom were indifferent to or ignorant of philosophical and theological distinctions and quite content to observe traditions that did not overly inconvenience them. (This was not always true, however, of their children who came of age toward the end of the century and later.) David Henriques, according to his son, could not have defined what he believed, but he derived great happiness from the synagogue service anyway. When he discovered that Basil, then at University College, Oxford, was becoming seriously interested in religious questions, he became concerned and urged him not to give so much thought to spiritual matters: "dear Basil, you were not sent up to Oxford to think so much, as you seem to be doing, of the 'salvation of souls.' It would appear . . . that your set discuss these matters far too much and they are neither satisfactory nor conclusive." David Henriques and other wealthy Jews did not admire religious virtuosity or spiritual sensitivity. Their Judaism stressed reasonable behavior, fraternal responsibility, ethnic loyalty, intellectual courtesy, and communal charity. It lacked intellectual rigor and spiritual enthusiasm. Louisa Cohen (1850–1931), wife of the stockbroker and banker Sir Benjamin Cohen (1844–1909), described her contemporaries at the turn of the century as having "le talent mais non le génie de la religion; leur état d'âme est à peu près, s'il n'est pas exactement celui de Protestant anglais."[25] (She was in the habit of corresponding with close relations in French.)

The wives and daughters of communal magnates appear to have been more concerned with spiritual matters—a dramatic reversal of traditional gender roles within Jewish family life and a clear indication of the impact of Protestant habits on Anglo-Judaism. Some read inspirational and devotional works, although not usually of a specifically Jewish character. Like their husbands and fathers, they ignored the doctrinal or religious content of Judaism and concerned themselves, in a vague sort of way, with the role of religion in fostering personal morality, spiritual health, and social harmony. Louisa Cohen rejected the Orthodox views in which she had been educated, but, in her daughter Hannah's words, "always retained sympathy for the religious point of view" because she felt "that for many people a religious sanction for morals was indispensable." Thus she told her children to do whatever their father wished with regard to religious observance. Agnes Henriques taught her children that in either ethical or religious questions they must look to their conscience—"the indwelling Spirit of God"—for guidance. The inward law, not the outward written one, was to be the final arbiter of all actions—an antinomian position at variance with both liberal and traditional Judaism. The young Constance de Rothschild longed for "true, pure, bright, simple-eyed faith" and was constantly depressed to discover that the doctrines of different religions clashed and that "no two people, of whatever faith they may be, can worship together." Synagogue services disappointed her because the singing and sermons were bad. The services at Westminster Abbey were more satisfying, as she noted in her diary: "Went to Westminster Abbey which I enjoyed immensely. The place, the service, the singing, the sermon—all were so full of the true and real dignity of religion. It was most stirring, and yet, most soothing. I should like to go weekly to hear such a service. It is truly ennobling."[26]

Despite the absence of doctrinal and ritual rigor in the Judaism of communal notables, they did not as a group show any enthusiasm for a liberalization of worship and belief. Most were members of Orthodox congregations, whose services, while doctrinally unreformed, were nevertheless decorous and dignified. Many served as officers of the United Synagogue, the union of anglicized Orthodox congregations in London, established in 1870. Few were attracted to Reform Judaism, which, in any case, in Britain was not very radical, in either doctrine or practice, by comparison with the Reform movements in Germany and the United States. (In the nineteenth century, there were only three Reform congregations in the country—in London [1841], Manchester [1856], and Bradford [1873].) The innovations introduced in London and copied in Manchester aimed largely at making the worship service more refined and less wearisome, not at reducing the particularism of Jewish customs and beliefs, which was a major goal of Reform elsewhere. (The Bradford congregation was founded by recent immigrants from Germany and hewed closer to the German Reform pattern.) Prayer in the Hebrew language and separate seating for men and women were retained, as were specific prayers for the coming of the Messiah, the return to Zion, and the restoration of the sacrificial cult in Jerusalem. Perhaps the most radical break with tradition was the elimination of the second day of festivals.[27] Although some members of the communal elite joined the Reform congregation in London, most were satisfied to remain within the genteel Orthodoxy of the United Synagogue.

The failure of Reform Judaism to make headway in Victorian England was not due to the personal religiosity of the communal elite, who, in other circumstances, might have been its warmest supporters. The notables were not traditional Jews outside the synagogue. While content to incorporate some aspects of traditional practice in their lives, they were hardly inclined to observe the full regimen of orthodoxy. At the same time, however, they felt no compelling need to alter the public face of Judaism, that is, its theology and worship service. The political pressures that induced the Jews of nineteenth-century Germany to attempt to make Judaism acceptable to the Christian majority in the hope of gaining full emancipation—and that led many talented, wealthy, and ambitious Jews to renounce Judaism altogether—were absent in England. There was no widespread clamor that Jews renounce their particularist ways in order to receive the rights of citizenship, rights that English Jews already enjoyed in the eighteenth century. Thus, unlike their counterparts in Germany, English Jews did not feel that their religion itself was on trial or that they had to prove their own loyalty to the state by abandoning their group solidarity.

Yet the positive attitude of the elite toward religious tradition reflected something more than the absence of political pressures for reform. Perhaps equally important in engendering this attitude was the centrality of religious practice in upper middle-class English society as a whole in the Victorian period. The irreverence and indifference of the previous century were no longer characteristic of the propertied classes. Family prayers, regular church attendance, and a distinctive pattern of behavior on Sunday were hallmarks of respectability at the upper end of the social hierarchy. T. H. S. Escott described London as "the only European capital entirely given over to the rule of sabbatarianism." On Sundays, he observed, "most of the smart people go to church, to the Chapel Royal, or to St. Margaret's, Westminster, if they belong to the political set; and many other shrines are specifically set apart for society's elect." Even in the 1880s and 1890s, when much of the pietistic veneer of Victorian religiosity was beginning to crack, Sunday was still a major ritual, "a convention that anyone with claims to respectability defied at his peril," in Hugh McLeod's words. Whatever their private doubts and hesitations, most middle-class and upper-class Englishmen still observed the public forms of Christian practice, for the routines of Christianity were still recognized proprieties of life—they were simply an essential part of what was "done." They were matters of "good taste" and "correct behavior" as much as anything else.[28]

The outlook of prosperous native Jews bore the impress of these patterns of Victorian religiosity. Well-to-do Jews, as members of a minority group eager to secure social acceptance, took their cues from respectable society, especially Anglican upper middle-class society, and, just as they adopted the fashions of those circles in matters of costume, entertainment, display and decoration, and recreation and leisure, so too they conformed in the area of religion. Religious observance being a necessary part of respectability, they adhered to the established conventions of the faith in which they had been raised. When Adelaide Franklin urged her son-in-law Herbert Samuel to accompany his wife to synagogue, she asked him only to fulfil his obligations as a husband, not to subscribe to any items of religious belief. Refusal to accept the theological tenets of Judaism was not a cause for disaffiliation from the Jewish community or even neglect of certain basic observances, as it was elsewhere in Europe where ideological lines were more sharply drawn and the pressures to abandon Judaism were more intense. Hugh McLeod's description of upper middle-class Anglican religiosity in late Victorian London applies with equal force to the religiosity of the Anglo-Jewish notability: "All this was a matter of 'decency' and betokened a regard for propriety rather than exceptionally strong religious convictions."[29]

As a consequence, positions of leadership within the community were frequently occupied by persons who did not fully accept the outlook of the institutions they directed. Arthur Cohen, for example, an agnostic who considered the ceremonies and customs of Judaism inessential to true religion, served as vice-president of the Council of Jews' College, a seminary for training Orthodox rabbis, for twenty-six years! Cohen had ceased to observe most Jewish practices when he left his parents' home, but had remained, in his daughter's words, "a very loyal Jew." He retained "a sentimental feeling" for old customs that he himself had repudiated as too restrictive and admired "the old people who had not adopted modern ways." Still, he observed in some manner or other the Passover holiday and Yom Kippur, when he often fasted and attended synagogue. In general, despite his religious views, he took an active part in a range of communal affairs: he spoke at charity dinners, gave away prizes at Jewish schools, subscribed to welfare schemes, and served on the boards of communal organizations, including the Board of Deputies, which he also headed for fifteen years.[30]

The art critic Marion Spielmann (1858–1948) rejected Jewish beliefs as a young man but, like Arthur Cohen, did not sever his communal ties. When he went to see Chief Rabbi Hermann Adler (1839–1911) to obtain the license necessary for his marriage (to his first cousin, a sister of Herbert Samuel), Adler expressed his regret at what he had heard about Spielmann's attitude toward Judaism. Spielmann explained to him at length his disenchantment with Jewish practice—"the dull routine dietary laws," "the irksome customs roped in by 'thou shalt' and 'thou shalt not'," "the rapid prayers and praises reeled off in the Synagogue in a race between the Minister and the Congregants"—and his inability to accept fundamental tenets of the faith, such as the efficacy of prayer, divine providence and intervention in human affairs, the eternality of the soul, and the authenticity of the biblical narratives. In astonishment, Adler asked Spielmann why, given his views of God and his relations to the Jews, he continued to remain interested in the Jewish people. His answer is instructive: "Because they are my people; I am of them, and I hold on to my heritage of race."[31] For Spielmann—and for Arthur Cohen and many other prosperous Jews—the bonds of ethnicity were stronger than those of religious conviction. The practice of Judaism was irksome and superfluous in their eyes, but they still remained members of the community, respecting religious conventions and, in many cases, playing a leading role in the management of communal affairs.[32]

The willingness of wealthy Jews to continue giving time and money to Jewish organizations over several generations also derived from feelings of family solidarity and tradition. The families who constituted the Anglo-Jewish elite in the nineteenth century were closely linked through marriage and business ties. Men of property and broad secular interests continued to take part in communal affairs because doing so had become a family habit and duty over several generations; not doing so would constitute an act of disloyalty to relatives near and distant. Personal religious beliefs and practices simply did not enter into the picture. In 1913, Albert Henry Jessel (1864–1917), a vice-president of the United Synagogue and a nephew of its principal founder, Lionel Louis Cohen (1832–1887), invited his kinsman Robert Waley Cohen (1877–1952), also a nephew of Lionel Louis Cohen, to become treasurer of the United Synagogue, an office previously held by Waley Cohen's father-in-law, Henry Beddington (1850–1926). Waley Cohen was not an observant Jew and had not previously served on the Council of the United Synagogue, from which the officers were expected to be recruited, but he was part of the sprawling Cohen clan, one of the pillars of the Anglo-Jewish establishment. And, like many of his relations, he valued religious tradition—even if he himself did not follow it—precisely because it was venerable and established.[33] In his invitation Jessel reminded Waley Cohen of "the family ties which bind you to the Institution," and after an initial demurral Waley Cohen accepted, although he did not subscribe to the religious doctrines and practices of the organization he was to serve.[34] For him and many other Jews, family loyalties and communal obligations were too closely linked to maintain one and sever the other.

In those rare instances when the offspring of Victorian Jewish notables broke the bonds of communal cohesion—usually through intermarriage rather than outright conversion—Jewish opinion strongly condemned the defections. When Arthur Cohen's daughter Margaret (1864–1931) married a gentile in 1895, becoming the first in the family to do so, Cohen felt compelled to resign as president of the Board of Deputies, a post he had held for fifteen years. He believed that the marriage would deprive him of the authority and influence that the head of the Board ought to have in the community.[35] In this instance, Cohen acted on his own initiative; no other pressure was necessary. In another case, after Henry de Worms sanctioned the marriage of his daughter Alice in 1886 to a member of the Church of England and himself took part in the church service, he was asked to resign the presidency of the Anglo-Jewish Association, which he had held since 1872. The *Jewish Chronicle* observed that, while de Worms could not have absolutely forbidden his daughter to become a Christian, he could have at least visibly expressed his disapproval by absenting himself from the marriage ceremony. Angered and embittered by criticism such as this, de Worms severed his connections to other Jewish institutions and quit the Central Synagogue. At the same time, his brother George (1829–1912) resigned the vice-presidency of the Anglo-Jewish Association, although he remained active in other communal bodies. A coolness developed between de Worms and his former associates, and more and more he sought companionship in upper-class, non-Jewish circles. (He became Lord Pirbright in 1895.) When he was not invited to join the Jewish deputation that congratulated Edward VII on his accession, de Worms apparently decided to cut himself off altogether from English Jewry. When he died, in 1903, he was buried in the churchyard of Wyke St. Mark, near Guildford, to the great shock of the community. No members of his family attended the funeral save for a few relatives of his widow, who became, or had already become, a member of the established church.[36]

Only among the Rothschilds, the most prominent and most prosperous clan in the Jewish cousinhood, were there several intermarriages during this period, all of them involving daughters who married into the landed elite. In 1838, Hannah Mayer de Rothschild (1815–1864), daughter of the founder of the English branch of the family, fell desperately in love with Henry FitzRoy, younger son of the second Lord Southampton. She wanted to marry FitzRoy, but her mother violently opposed the idea. (Had her father been living—he had died the previous year—it is doubtful whether she would have fallen in love with FitzRoy in the first place.) The family asked FitzRoy to leave England for six months with the understanding that if he and Hannah then remained determined to marry, the matter would be reviewed. Six months later, their love still burned bright. The family could neither reconcile itself to the marriage nor prevent it. But they marked their disapproval by withholding a dowry from Hannah and absenting themselves from the wedding ceremony, which took place at St. George's, Hanover Square, on 29 April 1839. In all, there were not more than a dozen people there, and of Hannah's family only her brother Nathaniel (1812–1870) attended. Her mother drove her to the church in a common four-wheeler, dropped her at the door, and returned home immediately. Jews whom Hannah did not know, as well as cousins from abroad, sent her withering letters of condemnation. When her brother Anthony visited his relatives in Frankfurt and Paris shortly thereafter, he found them extremely agitated about Hannah's marriage. He wrote home to his brothers in London, "I spent two days in Frankfurt and never was I more uncomfortable in my life. Uncle Amschel was a regular bother, asking me about getting married and writing to Uncle Salomon [in Vienna] that I only waited till his death to marry a Christian." Prodded by his uncle and aunt in Paris, who feared that Hannah's defiance of family discipline might encourage their own daughter to act similarly, Anthony urged his brothers not to receive Hannah and her husband for the present. Later, he added, "when it is all forgotten . . . you will be able to do what you like."[37]

In the 1870s, three of Hannah's nieces followed in her footsteps, marrying into the English ruling class, but they did so without breaking their ties to the Jewish community or suffering the abuse their aunt had known. In 1873, Annie de Rothschild married Elliot Yorke, third son of Lord Hardwicke, over the initial opposition of her father, Anthony, and his brothers. Yorke's family hoped that Annie would convert, but she felt that conversion was "impossible." According to her sister, Constance, "she could not begin her married life with a falsehood." Four years later, Constance in turn married Cyril Flower, the future Liberal politician and, after 1892, first Lord Battersea. Although both sisters were married in church, they continued to adhere, at least nominally, to Judaism. Their religious views, however, were actually closer to Unitarianism than to their inherited faith. In 1873, Constance wrote that she felt "only Jewish by race, not by religion or by doctrine": "My mind is not in the least impregnated with Jewish doctrine, I have not the feeling of pride of isolation. . . . My Church is a universal one, my God, the Father of all mankind, my creed charity, toleration, and morality. I can worship the great Creator under any name." Constance and Annie both attended church frequently and in later years the former came close to embracing Christianity. On New Year's Eve 1890, she noted in her diary: "It is not true that Christ is the son of God, but it is true that Christ is the most divine character in history." She felt cut off from Judaism—"so limited, so narrow, so racial"—but "only at the very outer gates of Christianity," which she could not enter, however attractive she found the Christian religion. Late in life, she felt that she might be "acting a lie" because she had not become a Christian although she loved Christian worship—"the day of rest, the pause in the week, the time to think, to put away worldly things, to deny oneself some amusement."[38]

Constance de Rothschild's inability to become a Christian had little to do with theological scruples. The established church was certainly broad enough to accommodate her own hazy views. Rather, her unwillingness to convert derived from her loyalty to her family and sensitivity to their position within Anglo-Jewry. Or, in the words of the novelist Chaim Bermant, "The God of Abraham, Isaac, and Jacob was also the God of the Rothschilds and to have formally embraced Christianity would have been an affront to the memory of their fathers"[39]—and, perhaps more critically, an insult to cousins and uncles then serving the community in a variety of positions. Both Constance and Annie knew of the scandal created by the apostasy of their aunt several decades earlier, and this alone may have restrained them from converting. In any case, neither of them had children—Yorke died five years after their marriage, while Flower was probably a homosexual[40]—and thus they were spared the potential embarrassment of having to raise their children as Christians. (It is highly unlikely, indeed, inconceivable, that they would have been raised as Jews. Flower, for one thing, was not very fond of Jews and voiced his distaste for them quite openly.[41])

Constance and Annie de Rothschild's cousin Hannah (1851–1890), the only child of Mayer Amschel de Rothschild, also married into the aristocracy, but unlike her cousins she retained a more than nominal attachment to Judaism. She met her future husband, the Earl of Rosebery, in the late 1860s, perhaps at Newmarket, for her father, a highly successful racehorse owner, and Rosebery moved in the same racing circles. Her father died in 1874, but by then Rosebery had become an intimate friend of the Rothschild clan and a frequent guest at their country homes. Hannah and Rosebery announced their engagement in early 1878, despite Hannah's own misgivings about marrying a Christian and her undoubted awareness that her father would never have approved such a match.[42] She did not want to give up her religion, however, and Rosebery respected her resolution. Had he insisted that she convert, she probably would not have married him. The fiercest opposition to the match came from Rosebery's mother, the Duchess of Cleveland, who harbored a strong dislike for Jews and whose house, in the words of Rosebery's younger brother, "alone stood out against an infusion of Jewish society." Six days after Rosebery proposed, his mother wrote to express her unhappiness that he had chosen as his wife and the mother of his children "one who has not the faith & hope of Christ." Rosebery himself was not indifferent to religious matters and took a great interest in church affairs, but he was also a tolerant man and honored his wife's devotion to Judaism. She continued to observe Jewish tradition by kindling candles at sundown on Fridays, attending synagogue on the anniversaries of her parents' deaths and at other times, and fasting and praying on the Day of Atonement. She allowed her children to be raised as Christians, however.[43]

The marriages of Constance, Annie, and Hannah de Rothschild were in some respects unique. By virtue of their extraordinary wealth and influence, their family mixed socially with members of the ruling class far more than other wealthy Jewish families did. That these women found husbands from outside their own religious community is hardly surprising given the constant presence in Rothschild homes of eligible young gentile men, most of whom had been at Cambridge with the girls' first cousins, Lionel's sons, in the 1860s. However, it is worth noting that none of their five male first cousins married out of the community, nor did any of these male cousins' male offspring, although they mixed in non-Jewish circles as much as their female cousins did, if not more so. In fact, in every known instance of intermarriage involving a family from the Victorian Jewish notability, the partner marrying out was a woman. Perhaps there was less pressure on daughters to choose Jews as marriage partners. Sons, after all, were responsible for the continuity of family firms—banking and brokerage houses whose successes were built on the intimate bonds of family and ethnic community—and marriage outside these networks would have been disruptive in more than one way. In the case of the Rothschilds, sons frequently married their own cousins, other Rothschilds in particular, an effective strategy for preserving and concentrating family wealth over several generations (as was the practice of not admitting sons-in-law, Jewish or gentile, as partners).

However atypical the upbringing of Rothschild women, they did share the aversion of the Anglo-Jewish elite to conversion. On the face of it, to have adopted their husbands' religion would have been the most natural and straightforward course. When the daughters of Jewish bankers married noble landowners elsewhere in Europe, they discarded their Judaism with alacrity, in part because their husbands would not have wed them otherwise; also, their object in marrying into the aristocracy may well have been a social advancement that required the abandonment of Judaism.

Hannah de Rothschild's refusal to be baptized and Rosebery's willingness to support her decision testify to the differences between the social status of Jews in Victorian England and their standing elsewhere in Europe, as well as to the shifts that had occurred in England since the early part of the century. For however maligned Jews were on the stage or in the press, polite opinion did not consider marriage to an unconverted Jew an unspeakable fall from aristocratic grace or a threat to the gentility of the gentile partner. Jewishness, then, was not an insurmountable obstacle to social advancement. Nor was this true solely in respect to the Rothschilds. Both daughters of the Amsterdam-born banker Henry Bischoffsheim married into landed society and yet remained members of the Reform congregation in London and supporters of Jewish charities. In 1881, Ellen (1857–1933) married an Irish peer, the fourth Earl of Desart, and though she lived much of the year at the family seat in Kilkenny, she still devoted considerable time to charities concerned with Jewish women and children. The following year her sister, Amelia (1858–1947), married Sir Maurice FitzGerald, Bart. She later became an active supporter of the Jewish National Fund, the land purchase and development agency of the World Zionist Organization.[44] It is doubtful whether conversion would have substantially enhanced the social position of the Bischoffsheim sisters or of any of the Rothschild women who married out of the community in the 1870s.

Drift and defection also became rare during the Victorian period among less-prosperous Jews as well, again a reversal, or at least a slowing, of previous trends. In this period the Jewish lower middle and middle classes in London, Manchester, and Birmingham displayed a strong sense of ethnic conhesiveness and communal loyalty. They lived, largely of their own choosing, socially apart from their Christian neighbors, in quarters with disproportionate numbers of Jewish families, such as Maida Vale in London and Cheetham Hill in Manchester.[45] Although they enjoyed full civil and political rights and were highly acculturated, for social purposes they preferred to associate primarily with other Jews. "They did not mix freely with their Christian neighbours," Benjamin Lewis observed in 1912; though Jew and Gentile met in business, "outside that sphere they passed like ships in the night." Julia Frankau (1859–1916), a bitter critic of middle-class Jewish parochialism, emphasized in her novel of Maida Vale Jewry, *Dr. Phillips* (1887), that these people were not "ambitious"; they preferred to live apart "in an inviolable seclusion, which they at once cultivate, boast of, and are ashamed at." "The world was nothing to them beyond 'their people.'" In London, she noted, there were "houses upon houses in the West Central district, in Maida Vale, in the City, which are barred to Christians, in which the very name of Jew is an open sesame."[46]

The cultural and intellectual horizons of middle-class Jews were limited, and hence they rarely ventured into the larger world to find enlightenment or drink at the fountains of high culture. Indeed, by comparison with other Western Jewish communities, Anglo-Jewry was remarkably ill-educated and philistine, taking little interest in literary and artistic matters of a general nature, as well as failing to support Jewish scholarship and education. John Mills, in surveying British Jewry in 1862, attributed Jewish indifference to literature to the commercial spirit of the country—that is, the Jews were just like everyone else, except more so—and to their previous exclusion from "civil and literary posts," as a consequence of which they had become accustomed to living as a community entirely within themselves and exercising their talent largely in "mammon-seeking." Yet the opening of previously closed doors failed to alter the overall complexion of the community in regard to cultural and intellectual matters. Middle-class Jews, unlike their peers in Berlin, Vienna, and Paris, remained overwhelmingly uninterested in the life of the mind and the spirit. "All the burning questions of the hour are to them a dead letter; art, literature, and politics exist not for them," wrote Julia Frankau. "They have but one aim, the acquisition of wealth." Two decades later Chaim Weizmann (1874–1952), newly arrived in Manchester, made the same assessment: "Materialist, commercial England has succeeded in burning out everything exalted in our Jews, so that the creation of a Jewish intelligentsia here has become an impossible task." English Jewry, he felt, had assimilated the spiritual penury, intellectual apathy, and pitiless materialism of the host society. "Only the very rich, or the very gifted, are allowed to do anything besides unmitigated bread-winning."[47]

Communal critics—novelists, journalists, preachers—particularly deplored the enthusiasm of middle-class Jews for cardplaying, which, in their judgment, had come to constitute the major leisure-time activity of much of Anglo-Jewry in the late-Victorian period. Israel Zangwill (1864–1926), writing in the *Jewish Standard* in 1888, expressed regret that "in too many Jewish households not one evening comes round without cards, to the complete exclusion of every other form of recreation." Simeon Singer (1848–1906), rabbi of the Bayswater Synagogue, thought Anglo-Jewry was "far too much addicted to card-playing as the one unfailing resource to kill the demon of ennui." Critics saw incessant cardplaying as the curse of the community, not because it was inherently evil, but because it prevented its devotees from developing broader cultural interests. "Playing cards at each other's houses is their sole experience of the charms of social intercourse; their interests are bounded by their homes and those of their neighbouring brethren," Julia Frankau observed. Leonard Merrick (1864–1939), in his novel of Maida Vale Jewry, *Violet Moses* (1891), claimed that the cardplayers of that milieu found it incomprehensible that "ladies and gentlemen [of the Anglo-Jewish elite] meet, and dance, and listen to music, and manage to amuse themselves without gambling." To them, such behavior was eccentric; the phrase "music and conversation" was "a funny allusion amongst them, an expression not to be taken literally, but merely a phrase full of humour by which they imply that a visit paid to some house proved dull."[48]

Although such criticism perhaps exaggerated the centrality of card-playing in Anglo-Jewish life, its emphasis on the inward-looking character of the middle class was not far from the mark. Cardplayers or not, the Jews of Maida Vale and other middle-class neighborhoods were not inclined to look beyond their own set for companionship or recreation. Nor did they seek to push their children into new worlds outside their own social networks. Indeed, the opposite was true. They feared that mixing with gentiles would lead to intermarriage, which, along with conversion, they condemned outright. In their eyes, Benjamin Lewis noted, a renegade was "the most contemptible thing on earth," not so much because he changed his religion, although that was difficult to accept at face value, but more because he or she committed "the unpardonable crime of betraying the race." Amy Levy (1861–1889), in her novel *Reuben Sachs* (1888), captured this sense of ethnic exclusivity in her description of a Maida Vale Jewish mother's attitude to intermarriage: "Mrs. Samuel Sachs indeed had been heard more than once to observe pleasantly that she would sooner see her daughters lying dead than married to Christians." Several characters in Julia Frankau's novel *Dr. Phillips*, which appeared a year earlier, express similar sentiments: "Mrs. Collings said she would rather see one of her children dead than married to a Christian. Mrs. Detmar would not go quite as far as that; only she would, certainly, rather see her married to the poorest Jew that ever walked, even to an absolute pauper." Interestingly, the only mother to express a more liberal opinion on intermarriage, Mrs. Jeddington, is described as "socially ambitious." Her husband has made a fortune selling ready-made and secondhand clothing to the colonies and changed his name from Moses to Jeddington (an obvious swipe at the Beddington family, whose name was initially Moses). The Jeddingtons are already looking beyond the pale of Maida Vale Jewry; "they belonged to that class of Jews who see in every Christian a probable 'swell,' in every Jew a direct descendant of an old clothesman or hawker." Mrs. Jeddington prefers that her daughter marry "one of their people" but thinks her husband does not care one way or the other.[49]

The social cohesion of the middle strata of Anglo-Jewry was not matched by any corresponding loyalty to religious practice. Over the course of the nineteenth century, there was a continual decline in synagogue attendance, home observance, Hebrew literacy, and other fundamental hallmarks of Jewish knowledge and practice. Already at mid-century regular synagogue attendance on the Sabbath was uncommon within Anglo-Jewry in general. The government census of religious worshippers in 1851 found that the ratio of attendants to sittings in places of worship was lower among Jews than among any other denomination, with the exception of Quakers. For a nationwide Jewish population of 35,000, there were 8,000 seats in regular synagogues, only 3,000 of which were occupied on the Sabbath morning of the census, a turnout of about ten percent. (In assessing the meaning of this figure, it is necessary to remember that women were not expected to attend synagogue on a regular basis.) While perhaps the majority of middle-class Jewish householders stayed away from their businesses on Saturdays, they did not otherwise observe the laws of Sabbath rest. As Charlotte Montefiore (1818–1854) noted in 1853, although "the warehouse is closed and the exchange is deserted," among many Jews "nothing holy or solemn take the place of their weekly avocations . . . open shops, galleries, exhibitions, public places of resort, are constant allurements, and help to fill up the weariness of an empty day." Ask a London Jew how he spent the Sabbath, an observant Jew wrote in 1855, and "he will tell you that he took his wife and daughters to the theatre, because, poor things, he cannot go out with them all week, and it is the only evening on which they can go to a place of amusement." Only on the Day of Atonement was synagogue attendance the norm; then "every Jew who has the least feeling of Judaism attends," John Mills observed in 1853. "Hundreds on that day join the service who are never seen there on any other occasion throughout the year."[50]

At the end of the century, middle-class native-born Jews were less likely to be regular synagogue-goers than the wealthiest members of the community. The *Daily News* religious census of 1903, which found low rates of attendance in London synagogues in general, revealed that attendance was better at synagogues in upper middle-class neighborhoods than in ordinary middle-class neighborhoods. On the first day of Passover (which coincided that year with Easter Sunday), the number of male worshippers at the New West End Synagogue, whose membership was the wealthiest in Anglo-Jewry, exceeded the number of permanent seatholders in the congregation; but that was not the case at the Borough Synagogue, the Hammersmith Synagogue, the Hampstead Synagogue, and the two synagogues in the Highbury/Canonbury area, for example. At the Borough Synagogue, the ratio of male attendants to seatholders at the Passover morning service was 62 percent; at the Hammersmith Synagogue, 58 percent; at the Hampstead Synagogue, 77 percent; and at the two synagogues in the Highbury/Canonbury area, 79 and 89 percent.[51] Regular attendance was clearly not among the recognized proprieties of life for the middlemost strata of Anglo-Jewry. On Sabbaths and minor festivals even fewer of them were to be found at services. For example, when Norman Bentwich (1883–1971) attempted to attend services at the Hampstead Synagogue two consecutive times during the intermediate days of Passover in 1897, the necessary quorum of ten men failed to materialize.[52]

In general, standards of observance and knowledge of Judaism and Hebrew were markedly lower than they had been in the previous two generations. In a sermon at the Dalston Synagogue in 1890, Hermann Gollancz lamented that the dietary laws were daily losing ground: "Whereas, comparatively few years ago, one would have enquired where one has to *abstain* from partaking of food in a Jewish family, the enquiry to-day would be, in what Jewish house one could venture to join the dinner table without doing violence to one's religious convictions." (Gollancz thought that commercial travelers especially were inclined to eat pork and shellfish.) *Jewish Society*, a short-lived London weekly, reported in 1890 that forbidden dishes like oyster patties and lobster salads were "by no means novelties at Jewish tables" and were highly appreciated by persons who were nominally adherents of Orthodox Judaism. To be sure, in the majority of homes pork remained taboo, less for religious than for psychological and social reasons, but otherwise the dietary laws were not strictly observed. The religious system of which they were a part had lost its meaning for most middle-class Jews, and so they were quietly and slowly abandoned.[53]

Much of the native-born middle class also neglected to give their offspring a Jewish education. Some parents, probably a minority, engaged a teacher to instruct their children one or two hours a week and, having done this, an editorial in the *Jewish Chronicle* in 1884 noted, "go about their business or pleasure with the conscientious peace which springs from a sense of fulfilled obligations." Many more neglected their children's Jewish education altogether. When Herbert Bentwich tried, unsuccesfully, to establish a fee-paying Jewish day school for middle-class children in North London (the area served by the Dalston and North London synagogues) in the early 1880s, he found that very few inhabitants of the area took an interest in the project. Instruction in Jewish studies and Hebrew was not an important consideration to the "trading and commercial classes" of the community—they sent their children to schools where they would receive the best English education. Bentwich estimated that there were more than 1,000 Jewish families in the district, with a minimum of 3,000 children among them, in which no provision was made for the religious and Hebrew education of the young. This pattern was repeated in other middle-class districts as well. Most of the congregations in London belonging to the United Synagogue did not offer Hebrew and religious classes for their members' children until the end of the nineteenth century. The Anglo-Jewish leadership assumed that while they should provide for the Jewish and secular education of the communal poor the religious instruction of middle-class children was a matter for parents themselves to arrange. Wealthy families, by and large, did provide some instruction for their sons and daughters; middle-class families, on the whole, were more indifferent. As a consequence, many native-born middle-class Jewish men, especially the younger generation, were ignorant of Jewish history and literature and unfamiliar with the range of traditional observances and customs. They were also incapable of reading or understanding the Hebrew prayer book and thus could not follow the synagogue service and the reading of the Torah.[54]

Among contemporary observers alarmed by the growth of religious indifference, there was a strong feeling at the end of the century that middle-class Judaism was in radical decline. An increasing number of persons who were born Jews were drifting further and further from any religious observance, while for many, if not most, Judaism had become, in the words of Simeon Singer, "a thing of rare times and irregular occasions," set apart from other spheres of life. It had ceased to be what it had been to earlier generations, "an ever-flowing, ever-spreading, all-embracing, all-enriching stream." Even those who attended synagogue perhaps half a dozen times a year were no longer motivated by a sense of religious obligation, it was argued. An editorial in the *Jewish Standard* in 1888 lamented that middle-class Jews who were drawn to the synagogue came out of habit, pulled by "the lingering ties of old associations." A writer in the *Jewish Chronicle* in 1901 termed the Judaism of much of the community "a mixture of family sentiment, recollections of childhood, unsatisfied doubt, and unmistakable superstition." Attachments like these, of course, could not be passed on to the younger generation. Fathers and mothers might continue to perform certain ceremonies that had been realities to them in their youth, but their sons and daughters, far removed from the domestic atmosphere in which their parents had grown up, were much less likely to find meaning in them. The old associations that moved one generation had a weaker hold on the next, so Judaism became more and more shadowy, disappearing altogether for some, thinning down almost to the vanishing point for others.[55]

The decline of Judaism within the native middle class owed little, if nothing, to any increasing attraction to Christian beliefs or worship—few middle-class Jews, after all, changed their religion. It proceeded, rather, from a more general disinclination to consider religion of any kind to be a critical element in the routine of daily life. Communal leaders sensed that secularization—rather than assimilation to Christianity—was the source of the religious neglect that so troubled them, although they did not employ this term to describe what was happening. However, they said essentially the same thing when they denounced, in sermons and editorials, rampant materialism as the main cause of spiritual decay. For example, Chief Rabbi Hermann Adler, in a sermon at the North London Synagogue in 1897, attributed the scanty attendance of worshippers on the Sabbath to a love of ease. Too many Jews, he felt, were entirely absorbed by "low, selfish, materialistic tendencies." They talked, thought, and cared for nothing but money; they sought wealth in order to live in luxury, indulge their expensive tastes, and satisfy their every caprice and folly; "their whole mental horizon is bounded by the money-market and the card-table." Simeon Singer came to the same conclusion: few Jews could "endure prosperity and carry their Judaism with them unscathed from the ordeal." Adler attributed the materialism of the community to "the struggle for existence" that characterized British society as a whole and to the "feeble and flaccid" resistance of Jews to the temptations it presented, while Singer emphasized social ambition as the culprit: "The notion that happiness is only to be found in a state above that in which we find ourselves is nowhere exerting so corrupting an influence as among our middle classes."[56] Neither Adler

nor Singer nor any other contemporary critic of Jewish apathy attributed
the crisis to the spiritual attractions of rival creeds.

Still, on occasion, here and there, native middle-class Jews formally cut
their ties to Judaism and became Christians. As was true in the Georgian
period, the spread of indifference to ritual and worship prepared the
ground for conversion (in almost all cases to the Church of England), but
apathy was not the chief factor in loosening communal ties. For in the second half of the nineteenth century much of the community was indifferent
to the practice of Judaism—yet quite content to remain within the social
borders of the Jewish community. The chief dissolvent of communal ties
was something else: the few native middle-class Jews who left the community were persons who were temperamentally uncomfortable with the ambiguous status of Jews in Victorian society and wished to avoid any unpleasantness in their efforts to achieve social recognition outside the
community of their birth.

During the mid-Victorian years, as we have seen, Jews gained access to
positions of status and prestige within English society. Nevertheless, there
still lingered—in the popular imagination and in high culture and at all
levels of society—doubts about the assimilability of Jews and their fitness
to play a role in polite society and public life. At a formal, institutional
level, English society was open to Jews—perhaps more so than any other
society in Europe—but this does not mean that Englishmen always
thought well of Jews. The negative image of the Jew—the outcome of many
centuries of religious bigotry—was too deeply embedded in Western consciousness to be erased in a few decades, even in the relatively benign atmosphere of Victorian England. While there was no Jewish Question on
the public agenda, no organized antisemitic movement seeking to undo
emancipation, as was the case in Germany and Austria from the late 1870s,
there were clear expressions of hostility and suspicion. Caricaturists, novelists, and dramatists frequently employed unflattering—and hoary—
stereotypes of Jews in their works. (Charles Dickens's Fagin and most of
Anthony Trollope's Jewish characters are obvious examples.[57]) In speeches,
sermons, and debates, Judaism was disparaged and Jews were portrayed
as aliens and outsiders, sharpers and cheats, the traditional blaspheming
enemies of Christianity. As a Jewish apologist, writing at mid-century, explained, "the very name of Jew conveys implicitly the ideas of fraud, deception and superstition." In the streets of Birmingham in the 1870s, Christians occasionally taunted Jews with unpleasant street cries and hand
gestures, such as forming a cross with their fingers and spitting over them
at passing Jews.[58] There is no question that actions like these and the sentiments underlying them troubled those who were seeking admittance to
gentile institutions and social networks and were thus sensitive about their
group image.

Jewish boys at public schools, for example, were made aware that they
were not the same as everyone else. Jawaharlal Nehru, who entered Har-

row in 1905, recalled that although the Jews there "got on fairly well . . . there was always a background of anti-Semitic feeling." They were "the damned Jews." Charles de Rothschild (1877–1923), who was at Harrow a decade earlier, looked back on his years there with much unhappiness. As he later told a friend, "If I ever have a son he will be instructed in boxing and jiu-jitsu before he enters school, as Jew hunts such as I experienced are a very one-sided amusement, and there is apt to be a lack of sympathy between the hunters and hunted." Even if Jewish students did not experience outright hostility, they were made conscious of being different from most of their schoolmates. Ivy Litvinov (1889–1977), daughter of a non-observant Jewish father and a Christian mother, had a difficult time at a private boarding school (although nothing overtly antisemitic occurred), and when she later transferred to Maida Vale High School, the presence of so many Jewish girls there caused her to wonder whether "it had been something mysteriously Jewish in my own face, and in myself, that had set me apart from my school friends [at the boarding school she had attended previously]." Her mother agreed with her that being Jewish handicapped a girl from the start if she intended to live outside Jewish society: "A man might not notice a girl being dark, with striking features, unless the address [one in a Jewish neighborhood] put ideas into his head. After all a pretty girl who's *not* Jewish does start with an advantage. Other things being equal."[59]

Young men moving into gentile social circles encountered subtle expressions of prejudice that suggested to them that their Jewishness was, if not an absolute impediment to their integration, at least something of a liability. A young Jewish journalist in Leonard Merrick's novel *Violet Moses* confesses he is reluctant to admit he is a Jew because "one is always afraid the genial faces will harden, and the cheery smiles grow chilly, and fade away—we have seen it so often." Christians might aver that their prejudice had disappeared and Jews might try to persuade themselves that indeed it had, but, in the view of Merrick's journalist, "it is all rubbish." For him, "the very name [Jew] is ugly . . . it is a jerk, the word itself sounds like a gibe."

In Leonard Woolf's *The Wise Virgins* (1914), a *roman à clef* based on his courtship of Virginia Stephen, the gentile Garlands befriend the Jewish Davises (i.e., the Woolfs) soon after they move into their new suburban home in Richstead (i.e., Putney), but when daughter Gwen realizes that the Davises "don't seem to go to church" she experiences "a cold little douche of disappointment." The Davises become very friendly with the Garlands but do not know many other people in the neighborhood, although under ordinary circumstances, Woolf tells us, their friendship with the Garlands would have brought them a very wide acquaintance. However, he explains, "even Mrs. Garland could not be entirely a passport to a family no member of which had ever been seen either in the church or on the tennis court." It was not overt antisemitism that prevented the inclusion of the Davises in suburban society, for, in Woolf's words, "everyone is open-minded nowadays, and liberal-minded too," but rather "a very natural feeling that people should, like decent Christians, sometimes have a racket in their hands on weekdays and a prayer-book on Sundays." To otherwise tolerant Englishmen, Jews could seem, no matter how thoroughly steeped in Englishness, disquietingly different and even alien. Leonard Woolf and his family struck Virginia Stephen that way, although she eventually agreed to marry him. She told him directly, after his proposal of marriage, that she hesitated to accept because he was a Jew and seemed so foreign. (His family had been in England for several generations, and he himself had been educated at St. Paul's School and Trinity College, Cambridge.) Later in life she recalled her initial reaction: "How I hated marrying a Jew—how I hated their nasal voices, and their oriental jewellery, and their noses and their wattles—what a snob I was."[60]

Striking testimony to the social stigma that still clung to Jewishness in the Victorian period can be seen in the reluctance of recent converts and families with Jewish ancestors to air their origins. The family of the economist David Ricardo (1772–1823) seemed to have been particularly sensitive about their Jewish roots. When his brother Moses proposed writing a biography of David a few years after his death, the rest of the family prevailed on Moses to give up the matter because, according to a contemporary, "they are now people of fortune and of some consequence, and landed gentry, [and] they do not like that the public should be reminded of their Jewish and mercantile origin." Some of the family professed to believe that their ancestors were originally Christians and became Jews only in the seventeenth century, the suggestion being that the one-time Jewishness of the Ricardos was only a temporary aberration. In 1895, Joseph L. Ricardo unfolded before his cousin Horace Wilkinson a fantastic tale of Ricardo origins. He explained that in the middle of the seventeenth century an Andalusian grandee by the name of Ricardo married a Jewess, and that three of their five sons converted to Judaism and shortly thereafter settled at Amsterdam, where they joined the Sephardi community. Sir Francis Palgrave also was eager to have his origins forgotten. When Sir Antonio Panizzi, who had feuded with Palgrave, catalogued the library of the British Museum, he listed all of Palgrave's books under his original name of Cohen in order to annoy him. A sister-in-law of Palgrave recalled after his death that "to us, and for upwards of 30 years of his married life he never alluded to his own previous name or religion." She remembered very clearly "the first time of his withdrawing the curtain which hid that part from our view, his speaking of that elderly cousin (Miss Levien) and of his father and his own name (which signified Priest) and of his being of the tribe of Levi." At the turn of the century, when Lucien Wolf was considering publishing a history of important Anglo-Jewish families, he approached the descendants of Meyer Schomberg, who had died in 1761, for their assistance, but they refused to give any information for publication in such a work.[61]

Unpleasant sentiments about Jews were widely diffused in English society throughout the nineteenth and early twentieth centuries, but they were more an irritant than a cancerous growth. Alongside the strident ideological forms of antisemitism that flourished in Germany, Austria, and France—which demanded the exclusion of Jews from public life and the revocation of emancipation—the prejudices of Englishmen were tepid and benign. In most cases, their major impact was psychological. They were a source of inner turmoil and tension, causing some acculturated, native-born Jews to feel uncomfortable about their Jewishness and occasionally generating mild feelings of self-contempt. The Selmans, for example, in V. R. Emanuel's novel of the same name, view their origins as "a sort of unfortunate accident, just as they might have happened to have had wens on their noses." In their eyes, being Jewish "was simply bad luck for which they were in no way responsible."[62] Popular stereotypes and snobbish prejudices may have led to self-hatred such as this, but they rarely caused substantial setbacks in the careers or social ascent of Jews eager to enter the larger world. For example, they were not sufficiently virulent to prevent Leonard Woolf from marrying into the Victorian intellectual aristocracy.

Still, there were some circles where hostility to Jews was pronounced and Jews encountered rebuffs on account of their origins. At the top of society, for example, alongside the "smart set," who acknowledged the Prince of Wales as their leader and admitted Jews into their midst, there were also old aristocratic families, solidly rooted in country life, who, in Victoria Sackville-West's words, "took no account of 'sets' or upstarts, jargon or crazes," and were far from enthusiastic about the entry of Jews into upper-class society. "They had genealogical tables at their fingers' ends; they thought more of a small old family than of a large new fortune; they were profoundly and genuinely shocked by the admission of Jews into society; they regarded the fast set, in so far as it comprised some people who by birth were entitled to inclusion in their own faction, as a real betrayal of the traditions of *esprit de corps*." Many aristocrats condemned the Prince of Wales for his friendship with wealthy Jews, as did his mother—she considered his genuine liking for Nathaniel de Rothschild most unfortunate. Lady Warwick described in her memoirs how she and her friends resented the introduction of Jews into the Prince's social set. They did not dislike individual Jews but were hostile to them as a group because "they had brains and understood finance," while her clique, she admitted, "did not like brains" and knew only how to spend money, not make it.[63] However, because fashionable society in the Victorian period was too large and diverse to be dictated to by one set, wealthy Jews, as well as other *nouveaux riches*, had no difficulty in finding their way into upper-class circles.

In the last decade before the outbreak of World War I, some of the easygoing toleration of the previous century gave way to a hardening of attitudes.[64] In both social and public life, antipathy toward Jews became more common. External challenges to Britain's worldwide economic and political power punctured the buoyant optimism of earlier decades, shaking national confidence and causing uneasiness about the country's future. Against this background of national self-doubt, antisemitism assumed a sharper, more ideological focus than in the past and entered the arena of public discourse. Antisemites attacked the influence of Jewish economic interests on foreign policy, questioned the capacity of Jews to assimilate fully to English standards, and denounced Jewish tribalism as a threat to national health, prosperity, and morality. In addition, the growth of compact East European immigrant neighborhoods in London, Manchester, Liverpool, and Leeds reawakened English concerns about the foreignness of Jews in general and fueled fears about the unwholesome character of Jewish habits.

While in retrospect it is clear that this upsurge in antisemitism was never as widespread or as virulent as in Central or Eastern Europe, this was not always obvious to contemporaries. After 1900, there was considerable concern within the Jewish community that Britain was suffering from the same anti-Jewish malady as continental countries. The political agitation leading to passage of the Aliens Act of 1906 unsettled communal leaders and led them to take new measures to hasten the anglicization of the foreign-born community, whose un-English ways, they feared, were threatening their own status. Following anti-Jewish riots in South Wales in 1911, "Mentor" in the *Jewish Chronicle* warned his readers to disabuse themselves of the illusion that the position of Jews in England was better than that of Jews elsewhere, even if there were three Jewish ministers in the present government. Two years later Morris Joseph (1848–1930), rabbi of the Reform synagogue in London, spoke to the annual meeting of the Anglo-Jewish Association on the theme "Anti-Semitic Tendencies in England." Such a choice of subject would have been impossible a decade earlier. In the discussion following his lecture, several persons in the audience charged that he exaggerated the extent of antisemitism in the country, but Claude Montefiore, hardly an alarmist, seconded Joseph's assertion that there had been an increase in anti-Jewish feeling. He pointed out, for example, that it was less easy for Jews to get into certain clubs than it had been six or seven years earlier.[65]

The persistence of unflattering stereotypes about Jews throughout the Victorian period and the upswing in various forms of antisemitism after 1900 influenced a small number of native Jews who had already drifted away from religious practices to abandon their community altogether and embrace Christianity. For them, it would appear, Jewishness was an inconvenient burden—rather than an absolute impediment—in seeking fuller integration into gentile society. Those who took this path were few, at least before the end of the century. Indeed, they were so few that their departure aroused virtually no public comment, so that it is difficult to examine their flight in detail. Still, enough examples have come to light to illustrate its general character.

The eminent shipbuilder Joseph d'Aguilar Samuda (1813–1885) converted to Christianity in 1856, along with his wife and children, in order to advance his social position. As a young man, Samuda had taken an active role in the affairs of the synagogue in Bevis Marks, serving in almost every office at some time. He also joined, at least temporarily, the ranks of those attempting to set up a Reform congregation, but in middle age he set his sights higher. From 1868 to 1880, he sat in Parliament as Liberal MP for Tower Hamlets. His unmarried sister, Abigail (1810–1907), whose allegiance to Judaism was more typical of wealthy Jews in the Victorian period, never forgave him and refused to speak to him the rest of his life. Once, when leaving a public function at which they happened to meet, she said to him, "This building is not large enough to hold us both."

The journalist Samuel Phillips (1814–1854), an exact contemporary of Samuda, left Judaism as a young man. The son of a successful London tradesman, he studied first at the University of London and then at the University of Göttingen. Some time before September 1836, he was baptized, for in that month he entered Sidney Sussex College, Cambridge, intending to take orders in the Church of England. However, the failure of his father's business forced him to leave Cambridge after only one term. After an unsuccessful attempt to revive the business and then a stint as a private tutor in an aristocratic family, he settled in London and made a successful career writing for *The Times* and other London newspapers. He also published a popular novel, *Caleb Stukeley* (1841), in which stereotyped Jewish characters—shabby, dirt-encrusted, dark-complexioned, grasping tradesmen—play a minor role. Phillips's use of such stereotypes suggests that he was eager to show his emotional and social distance from his origins.

The newspaper proprietor Julius Salter Elias (1873–1946), Viscount Southwood, also abandoned Judaism in his youth, although it is not clear whether he was ever formally baptized. In the 1860s, his father was a rising manufacturer in Whitby of jet buttons, bugles, and brooches, but women's fashion changed and the family fortunes fell. The family moved nomadically through the North and the Midlands and eventually came to London, where the father had a small news agent's and confectioner's shop in Hammersmith. Julius attended a number of schools around London, the last a Church of England school in Clerkenwell. By this time he was already estranged from Judaism. He left school at age thirteen, worked at various jobs, and finally joined Odhams Brothers, where he worked his way up from office boy to head of the firm.[66]

Toward the end of the century disaffiliation from the Jewish community became more common, although it never took on epidemic proportions, even among the very wealthy, as happened in Germany and Austria at this time. Nevertheless, after 1900, religious leaders began to lament publicly not only religious neglect but communal disaffection as well. In a sermon at the New West End Synagogue in November 1905, Simeon Singer condemned those Jews "who measure their success in life by the distance to which they are able to withdraw themselves from all Jewish associations, and by the force with which they can attach themselves to those who are not of their own people." Their highest ambition, he charged, was to be able to say that "they have rid themselves of all Jewish consciousness, and are merged body and soul among the Gentiles, by whom they are surrounded." In March 1908, Hermann Gollancz told his Bayswater congregation that wealthy Jews who achieved prominence in English society were deliberately withdrawing from the community in order to allow themselves to rise even higher in the social scale "by throwing off what they regard as the weight of their former surroundings that keeps them down." Discussing the same subject in another sermon three years later, Gollancz emphasized the social and psychological roots of the flight from Jewishness. Those who left the community, in his view, felt a sense of shame about the accident of their Jewish birth, as if it were a condition for which they needed to apologize to their gentile friends. Nor did those seeking to hide their origins come even largely from the wealthiest strata. F. L. Cohen, the first Jewish military chaplain, in surveying the number of Jews in the army in 1903—there were forty-one officers and 185 noncommissioned officers and privates—commented that the proportion of the rank and file who disguised their Jewish origins was not as excessive as formerly, but that such men were more numerous than those who voluntarily classified themselves as Jews. He estimated that 200 or more Jews still preferred to avoid revealing their identity. The situation in the navy was similar. Alderman Emanuel of Portsmouth told the Law and Parliamentary Committee of the Board of Deputies in 1900 that "there was a considerable number of Jews in the Navy, but in the majority of cases they did not disclose the fact that they were Jews."[67]

The commonest form of disaffiliation from the Jewish community at this time was not conversion but intermarriage. The gradual integration of Jews, especially young men, into social and cultural spheres outside the Jewish community—along with the spread of religious apathy among both Jews and gentiles—led, in the nature of things, to romantic encounters and marriage. In Leonard Merrick's novel of Maida Vale Jewry, *Violet Moses*, the stockbroker Leopold Moses falls in love with the daughter of a non-Jewish business acquaintance and proposes marriage. "Religious scruples did not weigh with him an atom, nor social ones," Merrick observes. "Maida Vale was growing used to mixed marriages." When Violet initially refuses his offer, her father urges her to reconsider, arguing that her husband's Jewishness is no obstacle: "The Jews are everywhere to-day, and we and they are intermarrying more every year. You can easily meet one and get quite thick with him without suspecting him to be a Jew at all." Intermarriage also figures prominently in Julia Frankau's Maida Vale Jewish novel, *Dr. Phillips*. Here young Florie Collings, whose parents show little interest in the world beyond their own community, falls in love with a well-bred young man from a county family, Alec Murphy. They meet secretly in Eastbourne in August, where her family is vacationing, and she is swept off her feet. Communal bonds and religious scruples melt before her passion for Alec: "The spirit of separation that had rolled heavy between her love and herself seemed uplifted. She could see no Judaism and feel no Christianity. . . . It was love, love, nothing but love, and the whole world must be love, now she was of that world of love."[68]

Within native-born Anglo-Jewry, the increase in intermarriage was not confined, of course, to the residents of Maida Vale, but occurred at all levels of the community, in both London and the provinces. Among the very wealthiest families, which had been relatively immune to intermarriage for most of the Victorian period, such unions became less novel after the turn of the century. When Arthur Cohen's daughter Margaret married a Christian in 1895, it was the first such marriage in his immediate family, but within the next two decades two other daughters of his also married outside the community. In 1895, Hermann Gollancz deplored the fact that mixed marriages "occur much too frequently in our own times." Almost twenty years later, in a Passover sermon in 1914, he denounced, in far harsher tones, the recent marriage in an Anglican church of a woman whose father was a former president of the Anglo-Jewish Association and whose great-uncle was one of the mid-nineteenth-century champions of Jewish emancipation. "Can hypocrisy go much further?" he thundered. "Can such infidelity to one's Faith, and such base ingratitude to the pioneers of civil and religious liberty, be exceeded?"[69]

Walter Yates, son of a prominent Liverpool family closely related to the Samuels and the Montagus, married the daughter of an Anglican clergyman in 1896. Yates wrote his first cousin Herbert Samuel in January 1896 to announce his decision to marry outside the community and to justify this radical break with family tradition. He explained that he had not followed "the Jewish creed" for some years because it ran counter to human reason, but that he had continued to conform outwardly because he lived at home and because there were younger children in the house who were not yet old enough to think for themselves. Now, having fallen in love, he was resolved "to at once declare myself in my true colours" and be done with the hypocrisy of pretending to adhere to Judaism. However, to spare his family's feelings, he arranged to be married quietly in the country, in a village where his in-laws spent their summers. The left-wing political theorist Harold Laski (1893–1950), son of the acknowledged leader of the Manchester community, secretly married a gentile woman eight years his senior in the summer of 1911, just before entering New College, Oxford. To his father, Harold's apostasy was a staggering blow that sent him to bed, ill and in shock; he became reconciled with his son only in 1920, when his gentile daughter-in-law decided that the family feud had lasted long enough and promised to convert and to raise their only child as a Jew.[70]

In order to dissuade their offspring from taking gentile partners, some well-to-do Jews made provisions to disinherit those who did. Frederick Halford (1836–1919), son of the founder of the wholesale clothiers B. Hyam and Son, stipulated in his will that if any of his daughters married a non-Jew she was to be considered as having died in his lifetime without issue—that is, she would be completely disinherited. Sir Charles S. Henry (1860–1919), a wealthy London metal merchant who took an active part in communal affairs, directed in his will that any child, nephew, or niece converting or marrying out would forfeit all interest in his property. Sir Philip Magnus (1842–1933), minister of the Reform congregation, educator, and member of Parliament for the University of London from 1906 to 1922, took an even more severe stance: he threatened to disinherit and break personal relations with a son who was merely becoming estranged from Judaism, let alone proposing intermarriage. In 1898, while on holiday in Rome, he wrote to his married daughter in London, Lucy Franklin (b. 1871), asking whether his son Leonard (1879–1924) had attended synagogue on the previous Sabbath. He told her that those who voluntarily put themselves outside Judaism "put themselves at the same time outside of all the privileges and advantages of the family to which they belong." If Leonard refused to carry on the traditions of his people—and by this Magnus referred to Reform, not Orthodox, practices—then he would thereby give up all his claims to his father's fortune and love. "If a son of mine decides to put himself outside my camp," he wrote, "refusing to help forward the cause which is dear to me, and which I inherited from my ancestors, he must go his own way unaided by me, without sharing my confidence or friendship. . . ."[71]

When Samuel Montagu, an ardent supporter of traditional Judaism, died in 1911, a disinheritance clause in his will provoked unfavorable comment in the national press, but it succeeded, nonetheless, in preventing his son Edwin (1879–1924), the Liberal politician, from leaving the communal fold. Edwin had opposed his father's Orthodoxy from boyhood and had clashed with him repeatedly. (Many years later he remarked to Lord Morley that he had been trying to get out of the ghetto all his life.) At Cambridge, his opposition blossomed into full-scale rebellion. He wrote his father in November 1898 that he considered himself an Englishman by race and believed that his "interests" were mainly in England. Still, he reassured him that he would always be a "a good Jew"—but "according to my lights, my definition of a good Jew differing from yours." However, he declared his unwillingness to compromise on basic principles, even if it meant losing his father's love and giving up certain "temporal or temporary advantages." In fact, though, he did compromise himself repeatedly. In 1901, he reluctantly agreed to attend synagogue with the family on Rosh Ha-Shanah, Yom Kippur, and Passover, and the following year agreed not to be away from home during the major holidays without his father's consent. His feelings, however, remained unchanged. As he told his mother in April 1902, he could not take an interest in his sister Lily's club work with Jewish girls because she was working for "sectarian purposes" and thus strengthening "barriers" while he wanted to abolish them. Yet he could not break with his father, for he depended on him for the allowance that permitted him to remain in politics. In fact, after his entry into politics, he quarreled with his father not only over his religious duties but also over the size of his allowance. "Why do I put up with it?" the twenty-eight-year-old Edwin asked his father in 1907. "Because I am at present too great a coward to throw up everything and leave 'home' to make my own life."[72]

When Samuel Montagu died in January 1911, Edwin inherited a life interest in a portion of the estate that provided him with about £10,000 a year—as long as he remained a Jew and did not intermarry. Soon thereafter he fell in love with Venetia Stanley, daughter of the fourth Lord Sheffield. When, in February 1912, his mother, who was unaware of the relationship, urged him to marry, he answered that it was out of the question: "It is not only that I don't as a rule like Jewesses. It is also that I firmly believe to look for a wife in one set of people is as wrong as it would be to say you must look for a wife among blue-eyed women." Later that year he proposed to Venetia but insisted that were she to accept she would have to convert to Judaism, for he had no intention of forfeiting his inheritance, however much he opposed Jewish solidarity. She initially accepted but then changed her mind, chiefly because of the obstacle of having to change her religion. He proposed again in 1915, suggesting comfortingly that her becoming a Jewess was no different than "a woman who marries a Frenchman [becoming] a Frenchwoman." He also tried to reassure her that her new faith would ask little of her: "As to the religion, it seems always to me the easiest of religions and makes no demands of me save a very rare visit to synagogue and Passover at my mother's. You have no use for formulated religion, nor have I, still less for ceremonial masquerading as religion." This time she agreed. However, she told him forthrightly that the conversion would be purely a nominal one. In her words, "Were I to be washed 1000 times in the water of Jordan and to go through every rite and ceremony that the strictest Jewish creed involves, I should not feel I had changed my race or nationality." She made it perfectly clear to him that she would convert solely to please his mother and secure his inheritance, for, as she told him, "one is happier rich than poor."[73]

Toward the end of the century there was also increasing concern about mixed marriages among middle-class Jews. In 1890, a debate on the causes of intermarriage erupted in the pages of the short-lived London weekly *Jewish Society* and continued for several months. The exchange was initiated when the newspaper commented in its inaugural issue of 31 January that parents were so terrified about their daughters marrying out that they were offering prospective Jewish husbands enormous dowries. The paper added that some young men excused intermarriage on the grounds that Jewish women were too extravagant in their material demands, but it then rejected this claim as baseless: men who justified themselves in this way were only seeking an excuse for their folly, for very few mixed marriages resulted in happiness. In the months that followed, none of the correspondents who joined the fray denied the assertion that mixed marriages were on the rise; on the contrary, they confirmed that fact. The debate focused, rather, on the role of female "extravagance" in thrusting eligible men into the arms of gentile women. Several letter writers maintained that as long as Jewish women displayed what one of them called "an affinity for vulgar and extravagant display" intermarriages would continue. A prospective bride with a dowry of £1,000 or £2,000, the argument went, overvalued herself, put no limits to her vanity, whatever her native charms and virtues, and consequently expected her husband to provide her with luxuries superior to those she had previously enjoyed. Christian women, on the other hand, were seen to be more moderate in their demands and not so given to "vulgar display." Opponents of this interpretation were unable to provide an alternative explanation and were content largely to label the accusation of "extravagance" nothing more than a feeble apology. The only alternative put forward for the increase was the assertion by the newspaper itself several weeks into the debate that the behavior of the notables was having a deleterious effect on the community as a whole: "When wealthy and educated Hebrews separate themselves from the community by marrying Gentiles, it is no wonder that the middle and lower classes follow suit." Interestingly, no writer suggested the more obvious explanations: the increase in social contacts of an informal and intimate character between Jews and non-Jews and the decay of traditional practices and religious scruples.[74]

It is clear that the entry of unprecedented numbers of young men and women into occupations and institutions previously outside the range of Anglo-Jewish experience created the social foundations and cultural preconditions for the rise in mixed marriages. In the Georgian period and for much of the Victorian period as well, few employment opportunities existed for Jews outside the world of commerce. The removal of certain social and legal barriers in the mid-Victorian years and a revolution in the economic structure of English society began to change this, encouraging the entry of outward-looking Jews into new fields. In particular, the shift from an economy based on agriculture to one based on commerce and industry created a world of new opportunities for city dwellers. The growing complexity of urban life stimulated the expansion of high-status, nonmercantile white-collar occupations that either had not existed before or had offered few opportunities for outsiders. From the end of the century, Jewish parents eager to see their children move in broader circles sent them in increasing numbers to grammar and public schools that would prepare them to do so. Some of these young men and women then went on to study at one of the ancient or new universities. For the first time a substantial group of Jews began pursuing careers—in the liberal professions, literature, journalism, theatre, science, the civil service, the arts, education, politics—that took them away from exclusively Jewish social settings. In clubs and galleries, at professional gatherings, in common rooms and lecture halls, and in countless other predominantly gentile surroundings, they encountered values and outlooks that undermined their faith and forged personal relationships that eroded their communal allegiances.

Jewish youth who attended university, for example, met head on a broader world of learning and socializing than their parents were accustomed to and thus faced the possibility of estrangement from the Jewish community. Simeon Singer recognized this danger when he mentioned to a group of Jewish students at Cambridge in 1893 that university life constantly reminded them "how learning and culture and many of the highest gifts of the intellect and the spirit are to be met with outside the limits of Judaism." Speaking to the same student congregation in 1910, Morris Joseph also underlined the difficulties besetting the Jewish undergraduate. He pointed out how even the physical setting in which the student was placed—the Gothic architecture of many university buildings and the prominence of college chapels among them—constituted a danger. "He is set in an intensely Christian atmosphere, all the more potent because of the historic associations that go to the making of it; and the simple services of the plain brick structure that does duty for a synagogue present a glaring contrast to the impressive form and environment of the public worship of the University churches."[75]

Rabbis Singer and Joseph were justified in their concern. At university, some Jewish youth so absorbed the reigning ethos that they broke completely with the Jewish community. Sir Sidney Lee (1859–1926), Shakespeare scholar and co-editor of the *Dictionary of National Biography*, matriculated at Balliol in 1878 as Solomon Lazarus Lee but soon became Sidney Lee. (His father and uncle, who were associated with the North London Synagogue, had earlier changed the family name from Lazarus to Lee.) After Oxford, Lee turned his back on the Jewish community, though without ever formally converting to Christianity. For those young persons already alienated to some extent from Jewish practice and belief, university life encouraged further estrangement. This was certainly the case with the cousins Edwin Montagu and Herbert Samuel, although the latter, as we have seen, remained within the Jewish fold despite his loss of faith. This was also true of the distinguished electrical researcher Hertha Ayrton (1854–1923), born Sarah Marks. While still a schoolgirl, she began to subject the orthodoxy of her home to scrutiny. Then, through her Cambridge-educated cousin, Marcus Hartog (1850–1924), she came into contact with a set of free-thinking gentile graduates whose conversation and companionship helped to unsettle her Judaism further and expose her to wider intellectual horizons. In 1873, she met the feminist Barbara Bodichon, who befriended her and enabled her to enter Girton College, Cambridge, in 1876, where she became known for her advanced views. She subsequently changed her name to Hertha and in 1885 married the physicist W. E. Ayrton, with whom she studied at the Technical College, Finsbury, after leaving Cambridge.[76]

The importance of the university in weakening Jewish loyalties is also clear in the stormy rebellion of Hugh Franklin (1889–1962).[77] Hugh's father, Arthur Ellis Franklin (1859–1938), a senior partner in the investment banking firm A. Keyser & Co., was a strictly Orthodox Jew, a pillar of the New West End Synagogue, and an active communal worker. Educated at Clifton College, Hugh went up to Caius College, Cambridge, in 1907, intending to study engineering. Even before he arrived there, he had broken, at least intellectually, if not in practice, with his father's Orthodox faith. The next spring he joined a small group of Reform Jewish students who seceded from the Cambridge synagogue, but over the summer he apparently lost faith in Judaism of any kind. Just before the High Holidays he wrote to his father from Switzerland, where he was working in an electrical plant, to declare his lack of religious belief and his desire to tour Italy instead of returning to London for the High Holidays. He was summarily called home, but this was only the beginning of a bitter family controversy.

For the next two years, while at university, religious issues, *inter alia*, continued to plague Hugh Franklin's relations with his father. Half a year after his return from the Continent, in February 1909, he set down in writing his views on religion, perhaps to clarify for himself what he actually believed or perhaps to prepare himself for the struggle with his father. From this sketch, it is clear that Franklin had become a thoroughgoing materialist. In his view, human beings invented God to explain phenomena they could not understand and mistakenly attributed human powers—such as the ability to distinguish between right and wrong and the ability to think—to him rather than viewing them as the outcome of an evolutionary process. As a substitute for traditional religion, Franklin proposed a new creed he called "Moral Theism." In his words, "The one ideal to aim at and accomplish is for the good and betterment of the world as a whole, and for that end all should work." In place of prayers and rituals, he envisioned "a review of our doings and thought and character, the events of the world and their effect and how to improve matters generally." He thought that "a 'sermon' might be a reminder or a help to accomplish this in the form of showing things in their proper light and helping others see them so." Yet, despite such views, he did not break with family tradition immediately. As late as May 1910, he attended Passover services with his parents and only the following autumn refused to join them at the synagogue at the New Year holiday. Following the morning service, he chanced to meet them on the street, and as he was dressed in a light flannel suit, which they considered shockingly disrespectful attire for a religious festival, they turned him out of the house, and he had to spend the night at a hotel in Charing Cross. He returned home after they left for the country at the conclusion of the holiday but then moved out again when the family came to town for Yom Kippur, considering this the tactful thing to do.

Hugh Franklin's rebellion against family tradition was not limited to the sphere of religion; it developed in tandem with a growing absorption in radical politics in general and the suffragette movement in particular. During his last year at Cambridge, he was already devoting much of his energy to organizing profeminist meetings and demonstrations. In the years before the war he became a prominent activist in the suffragette campaign and was imprisoned for his militancy three times: once for attempting to strike Winston Churchill with a dog whip in the corridor of a railway car, once for throwing a stone at Churchill's house in Eccleston Square, and once for setting fire to a railway car at Harrow. His father was sufficiently distraught about his participation in the suffragette campaign that in January 1911—after Hugh's first arrest—he offered a substantial payment to Victor Duval, a colleague of Hugh's, to influence his son to leave the movement. For Arthur Franklin, however, worse was still to come. Hugh's absorption into radical politics plunged him into almost exclusively gentile social circles and, not surprisingly, he fell in love with a woman who was not Jewish, Elsie Duval, Victor's sister and a militant suffragette. She converted to Judaism, although apparently not under Orthodox auspices, for she and Hugh were married at the Reform synagogue in 1915. This did not satisfy Arthur Franklin, however: he never saw Hugh again and cut him out of his will. Elsie Franklin died of influenza in 1919, and when Hugh remarried in 1923, to Elsie Tuke, the daughter of a printer's machine mender, the ceremony took place in a registrar's office. Hugh's brother Jacob (b. 1884) also married outside the community—in 1931, when his father was in his seventies—but since he was a partner in the family banking firm, his father saw him daily. However, he had as little as possible to do with him, never met his wife, and disinherited him as well. Arthur Franklin's wife, on the other hand, saw her wayward sons occasionally, although without her husband's knowledge.

Jews were not the only minority at the ancient universities to feel the seductive pull of the dominant culture. The experience of Nonconformists paralleled that of Jews. They, like the Jews, fought throughout the nineteenth century to have the ancient universities open their doors to non-Anglicans. Having succeeded, they too discovered that there was a price to be paid for their success. The children of prosperous Nonconformists who received a public school education and then went on to study at Oxford or Cambridge were exposed to influences that were difficult to resist and that made the insular subculture of Nonconformity appear dull and lifeless. One Nonconformist undergraduate recalled the attractions of Oxford as "that atmosphere of culture, that centre of vivid interests, that open vista to the highest honours in church and state . . . the sunshine of social recognition." Many Nonconformist students became Anglicans in order to shed their sense of marginality and exclusion and to embrace the world of culture, influence, and privilege that the universities represented. The establishment of the Nonconformist colleges at Oxford—Mansfield, Manchester, and Regents Park—were belated recognition of this and an attempt, not notably successful, to stem the tide.[78] Interestingly, Catholics were much more alert than either Jews or Nonconformists to the threat university attendance posed to traditional loyalties. They mounted no campaign to open the universities to Catholic students, and some actually celebrated their exclusion. One writer in *The Rambler* exclaimed in 1851, "Thanks be to God, the Protestantism of England has shut out Catholics from Oxford, and with few exceptions indeed, from Cambridge also." Even the proposal to establish Catholic halls at the universities met with much opposition. Critics felt that after three years at a Protestant university Catholic students would emerge less obedient, orthodox, devout, and pure—an assessment that was undoubtedly correct in light of the experience of Jews and Nonconformists. Indeed, even after religious barriers to admission were abolished, relatively few Catholics attended. In 1897, there were only twenty-eight Catholic undergraduates at Oxford and thirty at Cambridge.[79]

The increase in the number of Jewish professional men and university graduates whose activities in the greater world were undermining communal attachments was sufficiently great by the last decade of the century that a small group of professionals launched a scheme to strengthen "the bonds of race" among their colleagues. Herman Cohen, a barrister, approached the portraitist Solomon J. Solomon (1860–1927) in the summer of 1891 with a proposal to create an association of Jewish professional men whose pursuits in the broader life of English society might potentially endanger their identity and heritage. Solomon, who had been raised in a moderately Orthodox family and remained strongly attached to the Jewish community despite his success, was persuaded, and the two of them, together with Israel Zangwill, the best-known Anglo-Jewish writer of the period, and Elkan Adler (1861–1946), a solicitor, famous bibliophile, and half-brother of Chief Rabbi Hermann Adler, founded the Maccabaeans in September 1891. The initial idea was to create a society that would meet several times a year to consider questions affecting the Jewish people and, at the same time, would unite Jews of talent and education who earned their livelihood outside the world of commerce. As it turned out, the ardor of the founders for fostering Jewish solidarity was not sustained, and the group evolved into a polite dining society whose periodic meetings were addressed by Jews who achieved prominence outside the Jewish community. Indeed, some of its members, like the painter William Rothenstein (1872–1945), had no contact with communal life aside from their membership in the Maccabaeans.[80]

The attempt of Cohen and his associates to stem the tide of drift and defection matters less for what it accomplished—or, rather, failed to accomplish—than for what it represented: awareness of the threat to Jewish cohesion posed by successful integration into the mainstream of society. In earlier periods, communal leaders had been preoccupied with legal and social arrangements that had confined Jews to the world of commerce, but by the end of the century these barriers to occupational diversification no longer operated for the most part. The acculturation and secularization of native-born Jews, on the one hand, and the relaxation of exclusionary practices by the majority society, on the other, prepared the ground for the emergence of new kinds of Jews—soldiers, artists, men of letters, journalists, scientists, educators, physicians, barristers, solicitors, civil servants, politicians. And these Jews, in part because their professional activities and educational background accustomed them to mixing in gentile circles, were no longer content to identify themselves primarily with a community that now appeared to them parochial and intolerant. Moreover, as they moved increasingly closer to non-Jewish circles, they became more sensitive to and disturbed by the stereotypical ways in which Jews were perceived in English society. Hence they felt even more impelled to distance themselves from the community of their origins—to belittle its practices, to bemoan its insularity, to ignore its demands for solidarity and loyalty. Such Jews—and thousands more like them in the interwar period—cut their ties in one way or another to Jewry and merged heart and soul into the main currents of English life. As a prescient observer noted in 1912, "What centuries of persecution had been powerless to do, has been effected in a score of years by friendly intercourse."[81]

4

German Immigrants in the Victorian Age

The native Jewish community of the nineteenth century was largely descended from families that had migrated from Central Europe during the Georgian period in order to escape the poverty and degradation that characterized Jewish life there. This exodus continued in the nineteenth century, even after the first tentative steps toward legal emancipation were taken—perhaps as many as 200,000 Jews left Central Europe between 1830 and 1910—but now the vast majority of emigrants crossed the Atlantic to the United States, where opportunities for material advancement were greater.[1] A very small minority, however, settled in England, although it is impossible to know how many, since the British census, while recording country of origin of persons of foreign birth, failed to distinguish between Jews and Christians at a time when there was a substantial German colony in England. In addition, because this immigration stretched over many decades and disrupted neither native Jewry nor the larger society, as the later East European wave did, it attracted little attention at the time. At best, one can say that several thousand—but certainly no more than 10,000—Jews moved to Britain during this period.[2]

The new arrivals differed from their eighteenth-century predecessors in a number of critical ways. Unlike earlier immigrants, they were not destitute and unskilled and thus forced into low-status street trades to earn a living. They tended rather to be middle class in their background—a reflection, in part, of the rapid social and economic transformation of German Jewry that occurred in the nineteenth century. They came with greater resources—a secular education, prior experience in large-scale commerce, access to capital—and a broader cultural outlook than their predecessors, and thus they were better positioned from the start to make their way into the English middle class.

Most of the new arrivals were merchants and commercial clerks with current links to or previous experience in large-scale trading ventures, attracted to England by its unrivaled mercantile and industrial preeminence. A number of immigrants who rose to prominence in the textile trade in the Midlands, like Moritz Rothenstein (b. 1836) and Jacob Moser (b. 1839) in Bradford, had served apprenticeships in Jewish merchant houses in Germany before settling in England. Others, like Emanuel and Philip Freud in Manchester (half-brothers of Sigmund Freud) and Jacob Behrens (1806–1889) in Bradford, had gained experience in family firms before their emigration. Some were sent to England for the specific purpose of establishing branches of already flourishing ventures. The story of Jacob Behrens is typical (though the extent of his success was not). His father, Nathan, headed a merchant house in Hamburg that imported woolen and cotton goods from England, then the center of world textile production, and in turn distributed them in northern Germany. Jacob visited England a number of times during the years 1832–1834 to buy textile goods in Leeds for the family firm. His inability each time to persuade local manufacturers to make up goods to his exact specifications convinced him of the advantage of setting up a permanent branch in England. In 1834, he rented a small factory and warehouse in Leeds; at first he manufactured and shipped woolen goods for the firm in Hamburg but later he set up as a manufacturer and exporter on his own, eventually becoming one of the great textile magnates of the region.[3]

Unlike earlier arrivals, most immigrants from Germany in the Victorian period had received some secular education before their departure. At a minimum, they could read and write German; in many instances, they were literate in other European languages as well. A very small number had attended university and acquired professional training. The laryngologist Felix Semon (1849–1921) had completed his medical studies in Berlin; the industrialist Ludwig Mond (1839–1909) had studied chemistry at Marburg and Heidelberg; the journalist Karl Marx (1818–1883) had studied history and philosophy at Bonn, Berlin, and Jena.[4] One indicator of the cultural status of the immigrants, whatever the level of their formal education, was their ability to take part in musical, literary, artistic, and political activities outside the Jewish community—in the company of either gentile German merchants or native English merchants and professionals. In Manchester, for example, the prosperous calico printer Salis Schwabe (1801–1853) moved easily in middle-class philanthropic and political circles. He took an active role in the anti-corn law campaign, became a close friend of Richard Cobden and Elizabeth and William Gaskell, entertained them and other middle-class notables at his country home in Wales, served as Chopin's host when the composer visited Manchester, chaired a meeting of German residents at the time of the 1848 revolution to demonstrate their sympathy with the Frankfurt Assembly, and in general made his mark on liberal philanthropic activity in the city.[5] In Bradford, Birmingham, and Manchester, German Jews and German gentiles banded together to establish social and cultural clubs where they could eat heavy, multi-course, two-hour meals in the German fashion, read German periodicals, gossip about politics and business in their native tongue, nap, and play cards.

The first two chairmen of the Schiller Anstalt in Manchester, a library, newspaper reading room, and dining club, were Jews, as was much of the membership—a fact that led Friedrich Engels to refer derisively to the institution as "the Jerusalem Club." In London, the merchant banker Isidore Gerstenberg (1821–1876) and the orientalist Emanuel Deutsch (1829–1873) were members of the German Association for Science and Art, founded in 1864 by the political exile Gottfried Kinkel.[6]

Immigrants to England in the Victorian period also differed from earlier arrivals in their pattern of settlement. In the eighteenth and early nineteenth centuries, almost all newcomers settled in London, where the great bulk of the Jewish population was concentrated, although some, after a stay in London and a stint peddling in the countryside, set up as shopkeepers in ports on the south and east coasts, such as Chatham, Portsmouth, Plymouth, and Yarmouth, or in preindustrial county towns, such as Exeter, Canterbury, Oxford, and Ipswich. However, in the Victorian period, substantial numbers of immigrants settled immediately in the industrial heartland of the country, in such manufacturing centers as Manchester, Leeds, Bradford, and Nottingham. Representatives of Jewish trading houses in Germany that imported and distributed English textiles and other manufactured goods came to establish permanent branch offices that would allow them to circumvent local brokers and ensure a steady flow of goods at favorable prices. The Behrens family came to the Midlands under such circumstances, as did scores of others. To cite only two examples: Jacob Weinberg arrived in Nottingham at age twenty to establish a branch of the well-known Hamburg firm of Simon, May and Co. and succeeded in making it one of the most flourishing in the city. Isidore Gerstenberg came to Manchester, also at age twenty, to represent the Hamburg textile merchant Abraham Bauer, though he moved to London several months later, where he continued to work for Bauer until setting up on his own four years later.[7] Young men without capital or connections also migrated to the Midlands with the intention of working as clerks and managers in the offices, warehouses, and factories of their fellow immigrants. After a number of years they frequently went into business on their own.

Immigrants continued to settle in London as well, certainly in numbers equal to those who went to the Midlands, for it remained a major center of small-scale manufacturing and a dynamic commercial and financial capital, despite the concentration of heavy industry elsewhere. Thus, it continued to attract persons with entrepreneurial drive, capital, and business experience—cigar importers, antique dealers, toy manufacturers, wool brokers, grain brokers, lumber merchants, leather merchants, fancy goods merchants, stockbrokers, investment bankers. Several Jewish banking families in Germany sent their sons to London (and Paris and New York as well) to take advantage of rapidly expanding opportunities in government loans, international trade, and railroad, mining, and industrial securities.

Jakob Stern of Frankfurt, a brother-in-law of Nathan Rothschild, sent two of his eight sons—David (d. 1877) and Herman (1815–1887)—to London; while another Frankfurt brother-in-law, Benedikt Moses Worms, sent all three of his. When Ralph von Erlanger, a Frankfurt agent of the Rothschilds in the period after the Napoleonic wars, launched his own concern, he too sent one of his sons to London. Speyer Brothers, Bischoffsheim & Goldschmidt, and Schuster, Son & Co.—likewise offshoots of Frankfurt family concerns—also began in the same way.[8]

Although the immigrants of the Victorian period came to England chiefly for economic reasons, they were also uprooted to some extent by the pervasive anti-Jewish hostility of their homeland. Some were in flight from discriminatory statutes that limited freedom of settlement and occupation; a handful were refugees from the political repression that followed the abortive revolutions of 1848 (but they were no more representative of the migratory stream as a whole than their counterparts who fled to America). But most were not so much attempting to escape this or that obstacle to advancement as seeking to flee a milieu in which Jews were routinely treated with contempt and derision. In his memoirs Jacob Behrens repeatedly recalled the indignities he suffered while growing up in Hamburg. He described, for example, how he and his father would be refused lodging when traveling to fairs because they were Jews. He also related how his friendship with Ferdinand David (1810–1873), a young Jewish pupil of the Cassel orchestra conductor, was abruptly terminated when the latter insisted that David convert and sever all relations with Jews in order to advance his career. "This was typical of the times and such experiences fixed an indelible impression in my mind," Behrens wrote. Felix Semon, who grew up in Berlin several decades later, also cited the intolerance of German society as a motive for emigrating to England. In his autobiography he recalled the difficulty of choosing a profession when he was a *Gymnasium* student in the 1860s. All the careers he was most inclined toward—the diplomatic corps, the army, the civil service—were closed to Jews. Commerce held no interest for him; history and natural science did, but a university career without baptism was also an impossibility. Thus he was led by a process of elimination to medicine. When he completed his training, he chose to leave Germany, in part because of the widespread dislike of Jews there. Sigmund Freud (1856–1939) considered settling in England several times for similar reasons and never ceased to envy his half-brothers in Manchester, whom he visited in 1875, for being able to raise their children far from the daily persecutions to which Viennese Jews were subject. A few months after becoming engaged to Martha Bernays, he recalled for her "the ineffaceable impressions" of his trip to England and asked, "Must we stay here, Martha? If we possibly can, let us seek a home where human worth is more respected."[9]

Immigrants in the Victorian period differed from their predecessors in one other important respect as well: they did not grow up in a traditional

Jewish milieu, segregated socially and culturally from the surrounding society. Although legal emancipation was incomplete before 1871, the corporate and national character of Jewish life was well on the way to dissolution before then. German Jews were embracing gentile patterns of thought and behavior and abandoning traditional religious customs. Old loyalties and allegiances were weakening, and new identities were being forged. Thus the new immigrants from Central Europe, unlike those who emigrated earlier, were accustomed to participating in spheres of activity outside the confines of Jewish social and business networks. Few had received a traditional Jewish education or had grown up in homes in which regular synagogue attendance and observance of the dietary laws were the norm. Jacob Behrens, for example, who grew up in Hamburg in the 1810s, received no Jewish education except for some last-minute preparation for his bar mitzvah at the Reform synagogue. Ludwig Mond's upbringing in Cassel in the 1840s and 1850s was not too different. He was educated at non-Jewish schools, learned only enough Hebrew to go through the bar mitzvah ceremony, and as he grew to maturity gave up all religious observances, declaring himself an agnostic. For him, a man of science and thus a positivist, there was no such thing as a reasonable religion; indeed, to follow a religion was in itself unreasonable; the only sensible course was to believe nothing of which one was not certain.[10]

Even immigrants who had been raised in consciously Jewish homes were exposed to cultural and intellectual influences that worked to diffuse Jewish loyalties. By the second half of the nineteenth century, it was not unusual for Jews in Germany to celebrate Christmas, and many of those who emigrated to England brought the practice with them. The German Jews of London's northern suburbs, according to Cecily Sidgwick, celebrated Christmas in the German fashion "because they had been brought up to do so, and because the memories and customs of their German homes were dear to them." Although "they grumbled a good deal at the annual cost of it . . . every year there was a large and elaborate interchange of presents, and a family gathering in each household; and on Christmas Eve, for the pleasure of the family and relatives only, a Christmas tree." Such Jews were not alienated from Judaism completely, but they were, in Sidgwick's words, "quite unorthodox," their profession being limited largely to being married and buried according to Jewish rites.[11]

The immigrants' prior acculturation to gentile standards and habits and complete or partial estrangement from Jewish beliefs and customs, as well as their exposure to the pervasive antisemitism of Central Europe, profoundly influenced their communal and religious behavior after settlement in England. Many held aloof from any formal identification with Judaism, while those who affiliated with synagogues remained for the most part haphazard in their attendance at services and lukewarm in their observance of domestic rituals. (Because the German immigrants were few in number in relation to the native Jewish community and synagogues already existed in the cities where they settled—with the exception of Bradford—they did not form congregations of their own, as did their coun-terparts who emigrated to the United States at this time.) Most either passed out of the Jewish community altogether—through conversion or intermarriage—or established such a weak connection to it that their chil-dren or grandchildren eventually did so. To be sure, none of this can be established with statistical certainty, but contemporary testimony and other nonquantifiable evidence make it clear that the majority of immi-grants from Central Europe in the Victorian period took advantage of their new surroundings to shed or fatally dilute their Jewishness.

Contemporaries commented frequently on the disinclination of German immigrants to identify themselves publicly as Jews. When the newly ap-pointed chief rabbi, Nathan Adler (1803–1890), surveyed the congrega-tions under his authority in 1845, the New Synagogue in Glasgow replied that many "respectable" German Jews lived in the city who did not be-long to or attend the synagogue. The *Jewish Chronicle* noted in April 1859 that there were hundreds of foreign-born, prosperous Jews in the country, especially in London, Liverpool, and Manchester, who studiously es-tranged themselves from the community, neither belonging to synagogues nor subscribing to communal charities. In Manchester, in particular, there were many German Jews who were not even known as Jews. When Chaim Weizmann arrived there in 1904, he recalled in his memoirs, "The great majority of German Jews . . . were disassociated from their people, and many of them were converts to Christianity." In August 1865 the *Jewish Chronicle* reported that there were many prosperous German Jews in Brad-ford but no congregation, not even a burial ground. These German Jews, according to the newspaper, did not want to be known as Jews (although apparently everyone knew they were). They failed to circumcise their sons or educate them in any way as Jews. They buried their dead in a Christian cemetery and married their children to gentiles in church ceremonies. Ef-forts by the Leeds congregation to stimulate the formation of a synagogue in Bradford in the early 1860s failed. When the chief rabbi himself visited the city in 1865, six Jews showed up at the meeting he called and told him that he was wasting his time in attempting to create a congregation. Five years later, when there were 200–300 German Jews in the city, the one ser-vice held that year—on Yom Kippur—attracted only fifteen people. The following year, when services were held on both Rosh Ha-Shanah and Yom Kippur, thirty to forty persons attended on the latter day. When the community's first rabbi, Joseph Strauss (1844–1922)—German-born, German-educated, and Reform in outlook—arrived in 1873, he found the older and wealthier Jewish residents "indifferent to Judaism." Chief Rabbi Adler charged him with bringing these families back into the fold, dubbing him a "missionary for Judaism."[12]

Some of those who distanced themselves from Judaism remained equally aloof from Christianity out of contempt for revealed religion of any kind. Jacob Behrens, who failed to establish even nominal links with the Anglo-Jewish community (despite his marriage to a Jewish woman, like himself a native of Germany), resembled an eighteenth-century deist in his religious outlook. His exposure to religious bigotry in his youth in Germany made membership in any religious body impossible for him. "All forms of service conducted on lines strictly laid down and according to dogma find no response in me, even if they do not repel me. When either Christian minister or Jewish rabbi calls on the inscrutable God with the audacity and familiarity of an old acquaintance, I can see nothing but a hollow lie or an unfathomable depth of stupidity." Reasonable men, he felt, could not believe in the personal God of organized religion. Thus he refused to give his children any religious training, being convinced that it was hypocritical to educate children in a faith in which one did not believe.[13] However, his descendants and those of his brothers, Louis and Rudolf, drifted contentedly into the established church. For them and other English-born offspring of German Jews, freethinking anticlericalism was neither attractive nor relevant to their own experience. They were eager to get on in polite English society, and principled opposition to institutional religion was simply not socially respectable.

The religious outlook of Ludwig Mond was as sharply deistic as that of Behrens. For him there was no such thing as a reasonable religion. He and his German-born Jewish wife were completely alienated from Jewish practices. They did not celebrate Jewish holidays in their home. They failed to circumcise their sons, Robert (1867–1938) and Alfred (1868–1930), or make any effort to raise them as Jews—or, for that matter, as Christians. For Mond's alienation from Judaism was fueled by a principled objection to revealed religion, not by social ambition, as evidenced by his unwillingness to acclimatize himself to English ways. He preferred to speak German at home, and his sons grew up speaking that language better than English. In addition, despite his wealth, he never acquired the trappings that would have eased his way into upper-class society, such as a fashionable London address, a country estate (his home, Winnington Hall, Cheshire, adjoined his chemical factory), a racing stable, a hunting pack, or a yacht. He even declined a peerage when it was informally offered to him. He also did not seek to make socially advantageous matches for his sons. Alfred married Violet Goetze, daughter of a London coffee merchant, in 1892—the officiating clergyman almost refused to perform the ceremony when he discovered that the bridegroom was neither a professing Jew nor a Christian— and Robert married Edith Levis, daughter of a wealthy Manchester rubber importer of German Jewish origin, in 1898. Her family, including aunts, uncles, and cousins, had drifted away from the Jewish community earlier in the century, and she had converted to Christianity following her parents' deaths. The third generation of Monds in England, not surprisingly, were raised as members of the established church, although two of Alfred's children, much to their mother's distress, later embraced both Judaism and Zionism. Their grandfather Ludwig also experienced some uneasiness late in life about his earlier rejection of his ancestral faith, and on his deathbed he sent for a rabbi and made arrangements for a Jewish burial.[14]

Felix Semon also espoused views similar to those of Mond and Behrens. While believing in "divine government" and claiming to be "by nature of a religious turn," Semon refused to join any religious body, for he thought that all religions, each alone claiming to possess the truth, were too exclusive. Like the deists of the previous century, he cited the suffering and bloodshed engendered by religious differences throughout history as an obstacle to faith and affiliation. Yet he raised his children in the Church of England, partly because his wife was a Christian (although he did not cite this as a reason) and partly because he did not want "to close many careers open to them, by mere obstinate adherence to the old tradition." Whether adherence to Judaism in fact was a serious obstacle to career advancement in early twentieth-century England is doubtful. Perhaps Semon was led to believe that this was so by his upbringing in Germany, where, indeed, being Jewish was frequently an absolute barrier to occupational mobility. In any case, his children merged into the English mainstream— so much so that when his son Henry, a dermatologist, was asked in 1926 to supply biographical information for an entry in the *Jewish Year Book*, he indignantly replied, "I cannot imagine where you could have read that I am a member of the Jewish community—much as I respect both it & many of its members, who are my friends."[15]

A principled refusal to join any religious body was not characteristic of German Jews who failed to affiliate with Anglo-Jewish institutions. More common, at least in provincial cities, was membership in a local Unitarian chapel. As S. M. Schiller-Szinessy (1820–1890), rabbi of the Reform congregation in Manchester, explained in 1859, in justifying his decision to preach on the differences between Judaism and Unitarianism, "our attention is due to Unitarianism on account of the fortuitous circumstance that it is *that* form of Christianity to which such Jews as feel themselves induced to abandon their brethren and to turn their backs on the religion of their fathers are in the first instances chiefly attracted." Most of the German Jewish merchants who arrived in Manchester between 1790 and the mid-1830s abandoned Judaism, and most of them became Unitarians. The most prominent in the group, Salis Schwabe, apparently took his new faith seriously. According to an obituary in the *Christian Reformer*, "sincere and deliberate conviction" had led him to Unitarianism, not the hope of "worldly advantages," which were available only to members of the Church of England. Unlike most Jewish apostates in the nineteenth century, whose attachment to their new faith was nominal, "he adhered with quiet and honourable firmness to the forms of worship of Unitarian Christianity." At home, for example, he would lead the servants, assembled in the library, in prayer and read to them from the Bible and from sermons by Unitarian divines. His children remained active in the Cross Street Chapel after his death, serving as trustees for many years.[16]

In Nottingham the majority of the German immigrants, most of whom were active in the city's hosiery and lace trade, became Unitarians. The most prominent was Lewis Heymann (1802–1869), a native of Teterow in Mecklenburg-Schwerin, who settled in Nottingham about 1834. He commenced business as a lace manufacturer but later became primarily a shipper. He and his German-born Jewish wife joined the High Pavement Chapel not too long after their arrival, for their two oldest children, who were born in November 1835 and January 1837 respectively, were baptized there in June 1837. Like Salis Schwabe in Manchester, his attachment to his new faith was not a matter of mere convenience. Heymann and his family attended worship regularly, and he served as a warden of the congregation several times. He also occupied a prominent place in local politics, serving as alderman and, in 1857, becoming the town's first foreign-born mayor. His fellow Unitarian, the silk merchant and brewer Edward Goldschmidt (ca. 1827–1903), who emigrated from Hamburg to Nottingham in 1851, was active in politics a generation later. Goldschmidt was elected a member of the town council in 1870, served as alderman from 1876 until his retirement in 1895, and was nominated as Liberal candidate for Parliament in 1890 but refused to accept.[17]

The tendency of newcomers who settled in the provinces and then abandoned Judaism to affiliate with Unitarianism was a departure from the usual pattern of apostasy in Anglo-Jewish history. In general, when Jews in England embraced Christianity, they joined the Church of England—for obvious reasons. Their motives for becoming Christians were almost always pragmatic. They were seeking to escape the stigma attached to Jewishness and complete their absorption into the mainstream, to improve their social fortunes, and, before emancipation, to gain entry to institutions, like Parliament, that were closed to professing Jews. In these circumstances, Jews in flight from their Jewishness naturally joined the high-status established church rather than low-status Nonconformist chapels, whose members were themselves often objects of scorn and were also barred from certain offices and honors. If the object of conversion was social advancement rather than spiritual salvation, it hardly made sense for Jews to become Baptists or Methodists.

However, in the manufacturing cities of the Midlands and the North, the reference group for upwardly mobile Jews was not the same as it was in London or in the countryside. The elite to whom the recent arrivals looked for guidance in matters of deportment and style and with whom they sought to merge was Unitarian and industrial-mercantile, not Anglican and landed (as it was for Jews who made their fortunes in finance and overseas trade in the City of London). In Manchester, for example, the membership of the Cross Street Chapel included opulent merchants (many

with country estates purchased out of the profits of trade), affluent professional men, and bankers. Its members played a key role in establishing the
major educational and cultural institutions of the new liberal order in the
city, such as the Literary and Philosophical Society and the Mechanics Institute. They were well-educated and culturally sophisticated men and
women, not dour philistines, as literary caricatures of dissenters frequently
suggest. To the contrary, they subscribed to the substantial quarterly re-
views, spent considerable sums of money on oil paintings, and ardently
read the latest poetry. The Unitarians in Manchester were, in the words
of a contemporary observer, "as a body, far away superior to any other
in intellect, culture, and refinement of manners, and certainly did not come
behind any other in active philanthropy and earnest efforts for the social
improvement of those around them."[18]

Yet the attraction of Unitarianism to German Jewish immigrants in the
provinces was not entirely social. Although rooted in Calvinist Presbyteri-
anism, Unitarianism had become by the early nineteenth century relatively
broad-minded. It was theologically relaxed, spiritually undemanding, and
politely rationalistic. Its ministers were frequently men of wide secular
learning, intellectually sophisticated, and tolerant of diverse opinions.
Most importantly, the denomination's antitrinitarian stance removed what
was to Jews the most baffling and objectionable aspect of Christianity and
made sincere acceptance of the faith possible. To immigrants critical of traditional religion whatever its form, this was an immense advantage. They
could enjoy the social benefits of belonging to a religious body whose
members were wealthy, dynamic, and influential without having to accept
supernatural theological doctrines repugnant to their own outlook.

In London, where Unitarians did not occupy the same position they did
in Manchester and other industrial cities, German Jewish immigrants did
not join Unitarian chapels in substantial numbers. The records of the
Rosslyn Hill Chapel in Hampstead, which drew its upper middle-class
membership from neighborhoods throughout northwest London (a major
area of German Jewish settlement), indicate that only four or five families
of German Jewish origin belonged to the congregation in the 1860s and
1870s and only eight or nine families at any one time from the 1880s to
the start of World War I. If German Jews in London formally abandoned
Judaism, they were more likely to be baptized—or have their children
baptized—in the Church of England, which was the religious affiliation of
the dominant strata of society there. Thus, David Ullman, father of the
novelist Cecily Sidgwick, married outside the Jewish community after settling in London in 1848 and raised his children as members of the established church, as did the laryngologist Felix Semon. Louis Heinemann, father of the publisher William Heinemann (1863–1920), married within the
community, but he and his Manchester-born wife, Jane Lavino, abandoned
Judaism for the Church of England.[19]

An even smaller number of Central European Jews in London chose yet another religious alternative to membership in the established church—affiliation with a universalist ethical society or ethical church. Hungarian-born Maximilian Loewe (ca. 1830–1905), a follower of Lajos Kossuth, settled in London following the collapse of the 1848 revolution. Loewe was an enthusiastic supporter and close friend of Charles Annesley Voysey, the heretical Anglican priest who established his own congregation, the Theistic Church, in London in 1871. Loewe (or Low, as he eventually spelled his name) and his wife, the daughter of an Austrian rabbi, discarded all Jewish practices soon after their marriage. At some point they were attracted to Voysey's antisupernatural theism, which rejected such fundamental pillars of Christian belief as the divinity of Jesus and the divinely revealed character of scripture. When Voysey launched his own church, Low was one of the wealthy Londoners who backed him financially. The publisher William Swan Sonnenschein (1855–1931) and his wife, a descendant of an old Huguenot family, were members of the London Ethical Society, the first to be established in England; and Sonnenschein's firm issued its literature, including many volumes in the Ethical Library series, mostly at a financial loss. His father Albert, a native of Moravia, had emigrated to England at mid-century, opened a school in Highbury, and married the daughter of the Rev. Edward Stallybrass, a missionary for many years in Siberia. The educator Samuel Sigmund Fechheimer (1867–1916) joined an ethical society at age sixteen and helped to found the Ethical Church in Queen's Road, Bayswater, in 1909. Since he was an honored founder, his ashes were kept in a funeral urn in a niche in the wall of the church. Of the various ethical churches and societies in London, the Hampstead Ethical Institute, which was established at the turn of the century, drew the largest group of Jews of Central European origin. In later years it attracted Jews from other backgrounds as well; and after World War I it became predominantly Jewish in its makeup. One sociologist has even suggested that its largely Jewish membership in this century endowed it with longer life and greater cohesion than other ethical societies enjoyed.[20]

In general, though, the ethical movement in Britain, unlike its counterpart in the United States, attracted relatively few Jews, native or immigrant. At first, this may seem surprising, for the ethical movement offered Jews who were alienated from Jewish tradition the possiblity of religious affiliation without the acceptance of supernatural doctrine. It spared them the hypocrisy of endorsing, even nominally, Christian beliefs that were as irrational and fantastic as those they were rejecting. Felix Adler's Ethical Culture Society attracted widespread support from German Jews in New York and other American cities precisely because it forged a progressive, high-minded middle path between Judaism and Christianity. It allowed its adherents to escape the ritualism and supernaturalism of existing religious bodies and yet proclaim, at the same time, their commitment to universal religious ideals.[21]

In England the ethical movement did not have the same appeal to Jews, largely because of its historical associations with radical political culture. There secularism was part and parcel of a broader stream of causes that threatened the established order in state and society: attacks on private property, republicanism, anticlericalism. The secularist movement brought to mind the sight of atheists haranguing large, unruly crowds in parks; it suggested working-class infidelity and moral laxity. Secularists were, in Susan Budd's phrase, "perpetual outsiders," frequently suffering social ostracism and occupational discrimination. Genteel men and women, whatever their true religious views, did not go in for this sort of thing, as Felix Adler himself discovered when he toured England in 1892. After failing to obtain a hearing for his ideas at Oxford, he wrote home to his wife that the atmosphere there was suffused with conservativism: "Even the scientific men are more or less pledged to conventionalism, and are constrained to all sorts of subtle compromises."[22] It is not surprising, then, that few German Jews in England—or native Jews for that matter—cast their lot with the ethical movement. Only those with strong personal convictions and equally strong personalities were likely to become members. Most who wanted to escape the stigma of Jewishness but felt uncomfortable with supernatural religion swallowed their reservations and settled comfortably into nominal conformity with the established church or, in some provincial cities, a Unitarian chapel. Others, generally those who were not eager to better their social standing in gentile circles, remained quietly outside any religious body.

The tendency of German Jews to shed their Judaism after settling in England contrasts sharply with the religious behavior of their native-born middle-class counterparts, who did not disaffiliate with the community in great numbers in the Victorian period. To a limited extent, the high rate of defection can be explained by the fact that the newcomers were leaving a Jewish environment in which religious observance and knowledge had already declined precipitously. In other words, they came to England without a strong prior attachment to home observance and synagogue attendance and once there simply carried their disengagement one step further. On the other hand, native middle-class Jews, while perhaps more diligent in some matters of observance than Jews elsewhere in the West, were not on the whole pious practitioners of their ancestral faith. Yet most were content to remain within the boundaries of the community of their birth, even if they felt little attachment to traditional rituals and beliefs. In other words, alienation from Judaism as a system of doctrines and practices need not necessarily lead to estrangement from the Jewish group—as should be abundantly clear from the history of the Jewish community in the United States in the twentieth century.

The German environment shaped the behavior of Jewish immigrants to Victorian England in another, more profound way, however. The new arrivals carried with them attitudes toward Jewishness that bore the impress of conditions quite different from those in their new home. In German-speaking lands, Jews had remained second-class citizens until the last third of the century, and even after emancipation they still faced widespread social and occupational discrimination. In addition, ideological antisemitism was virulent, deep-rooted, and far from being a marginal element in high culture or respectable society. As a consequence, Germans Jews who identified strongly with the majority society frequently experienced their Jewishness as a misfortune or a burden; in some instances, bitterness and resentment at the accident of Jewish birth developed into pathological self-hatred. (It is no coincidence that studies of Jewish self-hatred utilize materials from German-speaking lands almost exclusively.[23]) Those who emigrated to England at this time often behaved in regard to their Jewish identification as if they were still living in their homeland, where conversion was a common response to discrimination and denigration. Once settled, they took advantage of their new surroundings to jettison that part of their past with which they were uncomfortable. Emigration became for them not only a means of improving themselves materially but also an opportunity for refashioning their identity. To be sure, it is possible that they found integration into their new surroundings blocked by their Jewishness—although there is little evidence that this happened—and that they remained apart from the Anglo-Jewish community in order to expedite their acceptance. However, we know that prosperous native-born Jews were able to break into gentile circles and institutions without rejecting communal bonds. This suggests that it was not antisemitism in England that encouraged their flight but the formative impact of conditions in their homeland in the period before their emigration. The experiences of their early years made it difficult for them to assess Jewish status in England dispassionately, and thus they failed to realize that worldly success and advancement were attainable there without abandoning the Jewish community.

In the case of those immigrants who settled in the provinces, the small size of some communities and the absence of well-developed communal institutions—synagogues, charities, schools—may also have contributed to the tendency to choose a different religious affiliation. Bradford, for example, had no Jewish institutions of any kind when German Jewish merchants began settling there in the 1830s. In nearby Leeds there were a mere handful of Jewish families in the first half of the century—seventy persons at most by 1850; a cemetery was acquired only in 1840 and a synagogue (a converted room) was established only in 1846. There the presence of a disproportionate number of single men and the absence of a substantial Jewish middle class encouraged intermarriage and a falling away from Judaism among both native and immigrant residents. Still, the Jews of Leeds were more numerous and better provided than those in Bradford, and thus by the 1860s Jewish merchants from Germany who settled there were more likely to establish a Jewish affiliation than those who went to Bradford.[24] On balance, however, the underdeveloped character of Jewish life in the provinces, while contributing to drift and defection, was not the decisive element; for German Jews in London were no more steadfast in their allegiance to Judaism, and yet the London community was more numerous and better organized by far than any other in the country.

In regard to the Manchester community, Bill Williams suggests that the absence of a Reform synagogue (before 1856)—with its decorous worship, enlightened preaching, and progressive ideas—contributed to the apostasy of German Jewish merchants who arrived there in the first half of the century. He points out that the Reform congregation was established at a time when many Manchester Jews were hesitating between Unitarianism and Judaism; while it failed to recapture families whose assimilation was far advanced, it did succeed in keeping the allegiance of those whose distaste for orthodoxy would otherwise have led them to depart. It became, in his words, "a religious safety-net for the future." The argument Williams advances is not novel. The founders of the London Reform congregation, it should be recalled, like enthusiasts for Reform everywhere in the West, argued that the creation of an up-to-date Judaism would stem the tide of apostasy by offering young men and women a way of remaining Jewish that was in harmony with the modern world. The German-born American Reform rabbi David Einhorn termed the Reform movement "the liberation of Judaism for the sake of preventing an estrangement from Judaism," while his German contemporary Samuel Holdheim called the radical Reform congregation in Berlin that he headed "an alliance against apostasy."[25] Their assumption—one that Williams apparently shares—was that Jews who became Christians in the nineteenth century were fleeing Judaism— that is, primitive rituals, lengthy and disorderly services, unenlightened doctrines. In truth, while these aspects of Judaism repelled increasingly secularized and acculturated Jews, those who left the community altogether were more in flight from the social and psychological stigma attached to being Jewish, as well as concrete obstacles to occupational mobility, than from Judaism *per se*. No amount of reform, no matter how radical, would have kept such men and women within the community.

Not all immigrants from Germany in this period deserted Judaism, of course. Most of the religious functionaries of the Victorian community were German-born and German-educated—a reflection of the intellectual poverty of the native community. The most notable were Nathan Adler (1803–1890), chief rabbi from 1845 to his death; Gustav Gottheil (1827–1903), rabbi in Manchester for thirteen years before his departure for New York City in 1873; Michael Friedlander (1833–1910), principal of Jews' College for more than forty years; and Samuel Marcus Gollancz (1820–1900), reader at the Hambro Synagogue in London and progenitor of an intellectually distinguished Anglo-Jewish family. There were also, here and there, lay persons who were loyal to traditional practices before their emigration and remained so afterward. The Nottingham lace shipper Jacob Weinberg, for example, was meticulously observant. He shut his office on the Sabbath and festivals and maintained a private synagogue in his home. He took no active part in political or civic life but devoted his leisure hours to Jewish learning. In Highbury, Canonbury, and Stoke Newington, a small community of strictly Orthodox Central European immigrants—followers of S. R. Hirsch's so-called neo-Orthodoxy—coalesced around the North London Beth Hamedrash in the last decades of the century.[26]

But such immigrants were clearly exceptional. Most of those who chose to identify themselves with Anglo-Jewish institutions did not perpetuate traditional practices and beliefs. Their attachment to Judaism was lukewarm, limited in some instances to being married and buried according to Jewish rites. Their homes were largely devoid of Jewish ritual and their attendance at synagogue rare and unusual. Their efforts to provide the next generation with the learning that would allow them to live as Jews were half-hearted and minimal, if not altogether absent. Their children, who were educated in English schools, grew up feeling far more English than German or Jewish. They mixed with non-Jews in a variety of formal and informal settings and participated in spheres of activity outside the social boundaries of English Jewry. Yet, however attenuated their sense of Jewish identity, to the larger society they remained somehow different, not quite English. Thus many found their Jewishness to be a burden that was not worth bearing and ceased to have any contact with Jewish institutions or social circles after they entered the adult world.

In two volumes of memoirs published in the 1930s, the poet and critic Humbert Wolfe (1886–1940) recorded with great sensitivity the anguish of growing up Jewish in such circumstances in Bradford.[27] Wolfe's father, a native of Germany who had been in business in Milan before settling in Bradford, was a prosperous wool merchant. The family maintained a loose attachment to Judaism. They visited the synagogue, which was Reform, on Rosh Ha-Shanah and Yom Kippur, and Humbert attended religious school classes there on Sunday mornings for a number of years, but nothing in his upbringing fostered warm feelings toward Judaism. Attendance at High Holiday services left him emotionally unmoved. The rabbi (Joseph Strauss) had no message to impart; the Hebrew hymns made no impression. "There was nothing here to inspire or excite the young worshipper." Strauss's position in the community brought home to Wolfe how little his parents and their friends valued religion, for the wealthy merchants who managed the synagogue treated Strauss like a clerk in one of their warehouses, bullying him into "a state of sullen stupidity." They brooked no interference with their consciences by someone they considered their paid servant. His business was "to interpret the ways of God to man in general, but to avoid the particular at all costs." Their contempt for Strauss was infectious; Wolfe learned from his elders to sneer at him.

Although Wolfe felt unmoved by Judaism, he could not forget he was Jewish. At school and university he was acutely sensitive about being set apart from his fellow students by his origins. Regularly taunted by a group of urchins as he made his way to the synagogue school on Sunday mornings, he felt bitterly ashamed of being different, envying the church- and chapel-goers on their way to worship. As he wrote of himself, "Each Sunday the boy ran this gauntlet, hating not his persecutors but the object of their persecution." Overt attacks such as these, however, were rare and less destructive of his confidence than were a myriad of small signs, not always conscious, reminding him that he belonged to a minority, "edged on the one side, excluded, different." That the English were too "easygoing and good-humoured" to carry their antisemitism to extremes only made matters worse, for "when the taint of Jewry means only exclusion from garden-parties, refusal of certain cherished intimacies, and occasional light-hearted sneers, it is difficult to maintain an attitude of racial pride." Had he been secure in his faith or taken pride in his Jewishness, he later realized, he would have been better able to withstand the sense of being different.

In his last years at school, Wolfe developed strong literary interests and simultaneously began to think seriously about religious questions. The "faint shamefaced Judaism of Bradford" offered him no answers or solace, and so he turned to Christianity. He discussed the desirability of being baptized with a friend, George Falkenstein, who had himself become a Unitarian. Falkenstein admitted that Unitarianism was a compromise, "a sort of half-way house." To Wolfe, the budding poet and prospective Oxford man, this choice seemed "well enough for unadventurous or doubtful spirits" but "a little too mild" for himself. Yet he could not bring himself to embrace Christianity. He repeatedly slunk in to evening services at St. Jude's and found himself pleased with the eloquence of the preacher and the light streaming in through the stained glass windows. He realized that it would be "comfortable" to feel himself "numbered among those to whom these spiritual elegances belonged" and "advantageous" to the career he envisioned. "But something—probably no more than a mixture of shyness and apathy—had held him back." He arrived at Wadham College, Oxford, still concerned about the fate of his soul—and his career—but unsure about what religion he was committed to. He had no doubt that Judaism was unsatisfactory but still could not take the plunge into the Church of England—"a step which a desire to be like other men tempted him to take"—for he was concerned about what his mother would think (his father was dead) and restrained by "something stubborn in his blood, which remembered Zion." When Wolfe left Oxford, he passed by examination into the civil service and went on to a distinguished career in a number of departments, in addition to writing and editing over forty books. In 1910, he married a gentile, the daughter of an Edinburgh schoolmaster; and as an adult he took no part in Jewish affairs other than joining a small dining club of Christians and Jews who were interested in intellectual and spiritual revival in Palestine.

The painter William Rothenstein grew up in a German Jewish home in Bradford similar in its Jewish loyalties to Wolfe's. His father, who arrived in Bradford in 1859 at age twenty-two, was a rationalist in religious matters and attended the Unitarian chapel in Chapel Lane—though he also subscribed generously to the needs of the Jewish community. However, his mother, also a native of Germany, remained faithful to Judaism. Before a synagogue was erected, she attended High Holiday services conducted by a visiting rabbi in a rented hall; later, when a building and a rabbi were acquired, she took the children with her. They greatly disliked the experience and irreverently mocked the Hebrew prayers when they returned home.

The Judaism of the Rothenstein home did not reach very deep. One summer, when the family was on holiday at Scarborough, a handsome evangelist from Oxford holding children's services on the sands captivated young William and baptized him. William took his new faith seriously, solemnly discussing with the family maids the almost certain damnation of his parents. With the approach of his thirteenth birthday, he faced a personal religious crisis, for his mother insisted that he celebrate his bar mitzvah, while he believed in the saving grace of Jesus of Nazareth. He refused to learn how to read the Hebrew blessings, so they were transliterated for him. In the end he went ahead with the ceremony, convinced that Jesus would not allow him to utter blasphemy and would appear in person to save him from wrongdoing. As he waited to be called to the Torah, he thought he saw the shadow cast by the *ner tamid* (eternal light) sway a little and took this as a sign that Jesus was coming to his rescue. But when he went forward to recite the blessings, nothing happened. He experienced intense disappointment and afterward came to the conviction that no one religious system was better than another.[28]

As an adult, Rothenstein held to this conviction; neither he nor his wife, a lapsed Roman Catholic, affiliated with any religious community, although they were not opposed to religion on principle. Yet, when their son, John, was born in 1901, they had him baptized in the parish church of the Norfolk village where they were spending the summer. Clearly they felt that even if they found no solace in organized religion their son might; and, at the very least, he should be able to enjoy the benefits of membership in the established faith. When he was five or six, they asked a close friend, the Rev. Henry Woods of Temple Church, London, to come to the house to explain God to John because they were constitutionally incapable of doing so; that is, they simply could not express whatever religious sentiments they felt in dogmatic terms. In time, as can happen with the children of irreligious parents, John moved dramatically in the opposite direction, becoming a fervent Catholic. However, he postponed his formal conversion for many years because his father, the lapsed Jew, objected. William Rothenstein was not troubled by the supernatural doctrines of the Roman Church, for religious dogmas of any sort meant little to him, but by the minority status of the religious community John proposed to join. "What he intensely disliked," John recalled in his autobiography, "was the propensity of English Catholics—far more pronounced then than it is today [1965]—to form a closed world within a world; the idea of my becoming a member of a society that might make me sectarian, cut off from the mainstream of national life, and above all from . . . upper-middle-class Liberal tradition. . . ." Having himself emerged from a "sectarian" group "cut off from the mainstream of national life," William did not want his son to join a similarly marginalized group. John waited until he was financially independent and then, in 1926, was received into the Catholic Church. Toward the end of his life, William was also drawn to Roman Catholicism. During World War II he attended mass with his son and daughter-in-law, but since he could not accept the necessity of dogma, he remained unbaptized. He died in 1945 and was buried in the parish churchyard near his Gloucestershire country home.[29]

The assimilation experience of Jews whose parents had emigrated from Germany was in some respects similar to that of their contemporaries from the older community who were beginning to venture outside familiar social and occupational paths. Young men and women from both groups came to feel that their parents' way of life was narrow and unexciting and began to look for new opportunities in the larger gentile world, beyond the narrow sphere of family businesses, Friday night gatherings, charity dinners, and ethnically exclusive card parties and dances. However, there were some critical differences. The children of German immigrants plunged into the mainstream more rapidly and extensively than did the descendants of other immigrants. The kind of thoroughgoing assimilation that led to the disintegration of an identifiable German Jewish community in England by the end of World War I was not typical of the descendants of immigrants from Holland, Poland, and Germany who arrived in the Georgian period or of immigrants from Eastern Europe who came in the period 1870–1914. Among the first native-born generation of these groups full assimilation was rather atypical. For most Jewish families in England, the movement away from religious and communal loyalties was a cumulative process stretching over many decades, gaining momentum in each successive generation, while for immigrants from Germany in the Victorian period it was radically foreshortened.

Between "new" and "old" families there was little close social contact. Few marriage alliances took place between recent arrivals from Germany and native English Jews. Similarly, offspring from both groups who were breaking away from family and communal restraints tended to go their own way, merging into the mainstream independently, their paths rarely intersecting. Children of German immigrants as well as those from well-established Anglo-Jewish families found marital partners either outside the Jewish community or among equally deracinated families of similar origin. Only occasionally did assimilatory trajectories of "old" and "new" families

cross through marriage. An instructive example of the coming together of
these two patterns is the case of the Frankau and Davis families of London.

The Frankau family came originally from the Bavarian village of Diespak.
Like thousands of other Bavarian Jews, Adolph Frankau (1821–1856) sailed
for the United States as a young man, becoming a naturalized citizen in
Connecticut in 1844. But in 1847 he recrossed the Atlantic and settled permanently in London. He carried on a successful business in the City as
an importer of meerschaum pipes and smoking accessories and lived in
Hampstead until his early death in 1856. His wife, Rosetta Neuberg (ca.
1822–1880), was also of German Jewish origin. It seems unlikely that they
had any ties to Jewish life, for she made no effort to raise their children
as Jews. Their son, Frederick Joseph Frankau (1855–1933), was educated
at Rugby School in the 1860s, when professing Jews would not have been
welcome there. He did not enter the family business, which continued to
prosper after Adolph's death under the management of Louis Blumfeld,
a former employee. Frederick went on to Gonville and Caius College, Cambridge, became a barrister, and married an Englishwoman. Neither he nor
his descendants had any connection to the Jewish community. His only
sister, Gertrude (1858–1913), never married, continued to live in Hampstead, and was a member of the Rosslyn Hill Unitarian chapel. Rosetta's
brother, Joseph Neuberg (1806–1867), also left the Jewish community. A
native of Wurzburg, Bavaria, he was in business first in Hamburg and later
in Nottingham. About 1840, having amassed a fortune, he left business
and some time thereafter moved to Hampstead, where his relations lived.
After unsuccessfully courting Barbara Leigh Smith (later Bodichon), a
leader in the women's movement, he married Mary Ann Stirland, a woman
of Scottish descent. A man of broad cultural interests, he served informally
for almost twenty years as German secretary to Thomas Carlyle, accompanying him to Germany on two occasions.[30]

Adolph Frankau's brother Joseph (1813–1857) also left Diespak as a
young man, settling first in Frankfurt on Main and then moving on to London, where in 1837 he went into business importing leeches, sponges, and
cigars. He married Frankfurt-born Amelia Geiger (1813–1863), a first cousin
of the Reform leader Abraham Geiger, at the Western Synagogue in London in 1843. They were sufficiently attached to Judaism to send their
English-born son, Arthur (ca. 1845–1904), to be educated at the Realschule
der israelitischen Gemeinde in Frankfurt, a well-known secondary school
that combined secular and Jewish studies. Arthur entered his father's business and in 1883 married Julia Davis (1859–1916), who was without money
and fifteen years his junior. Her father, Hyman Davis (1824–1875), came
from a well-established Anglo-Jewish family, some branches of which were
quite prosperous. He had hoped for a career as a painter but had been
forced by the demands of supporting a family to make a living in more-
mundane ways. He practiced dentistry in Dublin from 1849 to 1863 and
then returned to London, where he made a tenuous living as a photogra-

pher. He and his wife, Bella (ca. 1825–1900), brought up their nine children in an ambiguously Jewish atmosphere. The children recited early morning prayers every day without fail and faithfully attended the Reform synagogue on the Sabbath. Julia and several of her siblings were educated at an elementary school kept by a Miss Belisario, "a Jewess of the most rigid kind," who maintained a strictly Orthodox establishment. A stern disciplinarian, she would enter the classroom during a thunderstorm, her wig awry, and upbraid her charges for tittering instead of pronouncing the traditional Hebrew benediction on hearing thunder. After leaving Miss Belisario's school, Julia and her younger sister Eliza (1866–1931) received further instruction at home from tutors, one of whom was Karl Marx's daughter, Laura Lafargue.[31]

From the start, Julia and Arthur Frankau began to distance themselves from their parents' Judaism. They were married in the Reform synagogue in Upper Berkeley Street in 1883 but resigned their membership two years later after refusing to have their son Gilbert (1884–1952) circumcised. Gilbert and his younger siblings were raised in the Church of England, though he was not baptized until 1897—that is, at age thirteen!—when he was "old enough to understand things for himself." Indeed, he claimed that he did not know of his Jewish ancestry until he was past sixteen, although this is difficult to believe.[32]

Arthur Frankau was, by occupation, a typical representative of the prosperous Jewish merchant class of London, but he and his wife were not content to remain part of the social milieu into which they were born. They lived in the grand manner and sent their children to upper-class public schools—Gilbert and Ronald (1894–1951) to Eton and Joan (1896–1986) to Wycombe Abbey—so that they would acquire the outlook and demeanor of their well-bred schoolmates. Julia was a prolific contributor to the periodical press, a novelist, a short-story writer, and the author of three works on eighteenth-century English engravings. She was also an active, energetic hostess. Her guests, however, were not drawn from the Jewish *haute bourgeoisie* of Mayfair, Bayswater, and Kensington but from the largely gentile milieus of journalism, literature, theatre, and the arts. Whatever social aspirations she nourished, her cultural interests alone were guaranteed to carry her into circles where Jews were distinctly a minority. For in London, in contrast to Berlin or Vienna, Jews played little role in artistic, literary, or intellectual life, either as creators, patrons, or mediators. In conversation with friends and in her writing, she distanced herself and her husband from their origins, frequently by portraying Jews in a highly charged negative light. She boasted to Marie Belloc Lowndes, an intimate friend of hers from about 1900 and the sister of one of the best-known antisemites of the day, Hilaire Belloc, that her husband's fine qualities were due to the German Lutheran stock from which he came and to the absence of any Jewish blood! (Lowndes was convinced that Julia was being entirely truthful.) She also enjoyed gossiping to Lowndes about "unpleasing traits" in the characters of popular and famous Jews of the day, as if to demonstrate by her willingness to betray the flaws of the Jews that she was not one of them heart and soul.[33]

Above all, it was in her fiction—especially in her 1887 novel of Maida Vale Jewry, *Dr. Phillips*—that Julia Frankau gave vent to her very strong desire to escape identification with the common run of London Jews. The central figure in the novel, the charming Jewish physician Benjamin Phillips, "the pet of Maida Vale drawing rooms," has built up an extensive, almost exclusively Jewish practice. He is greedy, as are all the Jews in the novel, and sensual. He lives well, buys a carriage for his unattractive but wealthy wife, and keeps a gentile mistress. Suddenly he faces ruin when his stock market speculations turn sour. To save himself from financial disaster, he murders his wife, who is recovering from surgery for an ovarian tumor, with an overdose of morphine, thus enabling him to inherit her money and marry his mistress. The latter, however, rejects him for a younger, well-born, Christian gentleman, and, when the Jews of Maida Vale learn of his extramarital affair, they abandon him as well.

Julia Frankau's Benjamin Phillips is thoroughly repugnant, but it is not so much in her overwrought delineation of his character that Frankau revealed her discomforture about her origins as in her portrayal of the milieu in which he moves. Frankau's Maida Vale Jews are almost without exception uneducated, narrow, clannish, materialistic, and tasteless. They live in large overfurnished homes filled "with floating suggestions of a Bond Street showroom." They are ignorant of politics, literature, and art; indeed, they take no interest in the world beyond their families and friends, businesses and homes. They stick together, admitting few non-Jews into their company. "Playing cards at each other's houses is their sole experience of the charms of social intercourse." The root of their corruption is, as self-hating Jews and antisemites always maintained, their inordinate love of money. "The great single Deity, the 'I am the Lord thy God, and thou shalt have no other,' that binds Judaism together, is as invincible now as it was when Moses had to destroy the Golden Calf on Mount Horeb. And that Deity is Gain." And that deity is never more ardently worshipped than at the card table. "The red light played on the money, on the cards, on the diamonds, on eager faces and grasping fingers. The play went on almost in silence; no light jest or merry quip, no sacrilegious sound of laughter disturbed the devotion of Judaism to its living God."[34]

Frankau's condemnation of Maida Vale Jewry reveals how anxious she was to distance herself from the great mass of middle-class Jews. The Jews she created in her writing embodied all the negative qualities that she feared could be attributed to her by virtue of her Jewish origins. By assigning these flaws and blemishes to other Jews, she was trying to tell the gentile world, as well as reassure herself, that she was different, that she had escaped from the tribal milieu of graceless *nouveaux riches* Jews. Indeed, she made it quite clear in *Dr. Phillips* that exceptional Jews could transcend the narrowness of that world if they exerted themselves. "Sections of [middle-class Jewry] are trying very hard to struggle against this race-barrier, and with a modicum of success. But they have much to contend against." In her last novel about Jews, *The Sphinx's Lawyer* (1906), she made the same point. Here the charming, cultured solicitor, Errington Welch-Kennard, teaches Lillian Henry, daughter of a self-made, unmannered Jewish businessman, how to behave in genteel company, entertain guests, dress herself, and decorate her home. Lillian, Frankau emphasized, learns quickly: "She gathered so soon, on so slight a hint, that it was unnecessary to intrude her race and religion constantly upon the attention of her chance acquaintances. She might be proud of both, but, if she were proud of her hair, or her teeth, or her complexion, she would still behave modestly in not mentioning them."[35] Frankau did not object to Jews qua Jews, but only to those who were less modest and discrete in their Jewishness than she. In fact, in a preface that appeared in the second edition of *Dr. Phillips*, she specifically denied that her work was an attack on Jews. It was, rather, "a picture of a small and little known section of society before it yields to the influence of advanced civilization and education," a section that, to her regret, "owns Judaism as a religion."[36]

Julia Frankau's brother James Davis (1853–1907) and her sister Eliza also moved away from conventional middle-class Jewish circles. James was a well-known man-about-town and popular figure in bohemian society. Educated at University College, London, he built up a lucrative practice as a solicitor from 1874 to 1886; eventually he gave up the law and turned to journalism and the theatre. He owned and edited a number of society journals, including *The Bat*, *The Cuckoo*, and *The Phoenix*, wrote drama criticism and reported on horse racing for *The Sporting Times*, and from 1893 wrote the librettos for several enormously successful comic operas. However, his primary interest—one might say obsession—was the race track: most of the money he earned from his writing was gambled away or went to purchase and train racehorses. In addition, he entertained lavishly and was overly generous to friends and hangers-on in the racing world and journalism. As a consequence, he was perpetually in debt. In fact, his pseudonym, "Owen Hall," was said to have been derived from his usual financial predicament, for he was continually "owing all." Davis married within the Jewish community, but his vocational and avocational interests took him into largely non-Jewish circles. His sister Eliza recalled that he gathered around him "the brightest wits of the gay Press and the gayer broads . . ., pretty ladies of high and low degree, fine gentlemen with fine mortgages, famous heroes of the oar, trainers and distrainers, lords and their honourable brothers, and dramatists with and without poetry to their equipment." The novelist George Moore, who first met Davis in the early 1880s, was struck by his "cosmopolitanism" and "Hellenism" and became a regular visitor to his house, "a house of champagne, late hours, and evening clothes, of literature and art, of passionate discussions." At his death,

Davis was sufficiently alienated from the Jewish community that he was buried in a Christian cemetery.[37]

Eliza also made her mark as a writer. At age eighteen, eager to marry after her sister Julia had wed and left home, she made a disastrous marriage to David Aria (d. 1913), a man she did not love. He was a poor businessman and gambler; after five years of marriage, they separated and he sailed for South Africa, leaving her with a young daughter to support. She turned to journalism and within a few years became well known as a writer on fashion. With financial backing from Harry H. Marks (1855–1916), editor of *The Financial News*, she eventually launched her own fashion monthly, *The World of Dress*, which she edited for many years. She continued to identify herself as a Jew and became a member of the radical Reform congregation established in 1911, but, like Julia and James, she moved in literary, artistic, and theatrical circles in which Jews were a minority. Her only child, Nita (d. 1923), married a government official in Burma who was not Jewish.[38]

The children of Arthur and Julia Frankau, who were not raised as Jews in any sense, pursued careers that took them even further away from contact with Jewish circles. Ronald, who attended Eton and then studied for a short time at the Guildhall School of Music, became a comedian, first in musical comedies and revues, then, from the late 1920s, on radio. Joan was educated at Wycombe Abbey, in Hamburg and Paris, and then at Girton College, Cambridge. In 1920, she married Stanley Bennett, a fellow of Emmanuel College, and was herself later a fellow of Girton and lecturer in English. A student at Cambridge in the 1940s recalled that for Joan Jewishness was "not even a memory, but simply a genealogical fact, a documentation that she had been born of Jewish parents." She made no effort to hide her antecedents; in fact, she took some pride in them, but she was totally ignorant of all things Jewish, having been raised outside of any Jewish context.[39]

Gilbert, the eldest, had a far more tortuous relationship with his Jewish origins and could never completely erase from his consciousness what was for him the burden of his descent. He was educated at Eton but, unlike most public school graduates, went into trade, entering the family cigar firm in 1904, the year his father died. With the outbreak of war ten years later, he wound up the business and was commissioned an officer in the army. Several years earlier he had begun to write seriously, and in the interwar period he enjoyed great success as a novelist and short-story writer in both Great Britain and the United States. He adopted an outward pose and a political outlook that, consciously intended or not, distanced himself from the mass of English Jews. He lived extravagantly, married three times (in each case a gentile), put on insufferably arrogant aristocratic airs, took up hunting and fishing, and acted dashing and tough like the heroes in his novels. But much of this was a pose—he confessed to his closest friends that he was terrified of riding, that he was haunted by the fear that at bottom he was really a coward. In politics, he actively championed right-wing causes, enthusiastically supporting Italian fascism in the 1920s and even defending Nazi persecution of Jews in the early years of Hitler's rule. In an article in the *Daily Express* in May 1933 with the provocative title "As a Jew I Am Not against Hitler," he asserted that the outcry against the German leader was overdone and that his attempts to rid Germany of Jews who were not "good" Germans were justified. Writing as an Englishman "of Jewish blood, though not of the Jewish faith," Frankau maintained that there was a "substratum of truth" to the Nazi cry that Jews were not Germans. "Many German Jews," he wrote, "are entirely out of sympathy with the aspirations of the Nordic tribes among which they have made their homes." And, as evidence, he asserted that the communist movement there was largely fomented by Jews. Such Jews were perils to every country they inhabited, and Hitler was certainly correct in kicking them out. Fortunately, he added, British Jews were patriotic, proud of their country, loyal to its flag, free of the "ghetto-spirit" still found in their co-religionists in Germany.[40] Here, like his mother, he made the distinction between "good" Jews—like himself—and "bad" Jews—like those in Germany who supported left-wing political parties and thereby invited persecution.

Frankau's bravado and swagger suggest that he was uncomfortable about his origins—Jewish, middle class, foreign—and that he may have tried to compensate for them by emphasizing habits of thought and behavior believed to be quintessentially English and upper class. Unlike his brother and sister—indeed, unlike most converts in Anglo-Jewish history—he could not simply put aside his family background and allow himself to be absorbed without fuss into the larger society. Instead, he insisted on parading his Englishness in public in a way that was thoroughly untypical of Jews who were raised as Christians. In this sense, he was as uncharacteristic as Benjamin Disraeli, who in his own way could not remain indifferent to his origins.

For Gilbert Frankau, the passage of years did not make the question of his Jewish origins any less burdensome. In the interwar period Jewish problems were very much headline news. Arab-Jewish conflict in Palestine, Nazi persecution of Jews in Germany, and Blackshirt violence in the East End renewed public interest in the Jews and their fate. The extraordinary views Frankau expounded in the *Daily Express* reflect his deep discomforture at this turn of events. When his daughter Pamela (1908–1967), also a writer, published a novel about the persecution of Jews in Germany and became active in rescuing Jewish refugees, he expressed anger at her identifying herself with the Jewish people, particularly, as he told her, when he had taken the trouble to provide her with a genuine Christian mother. He preferred not to trumpet his ties to the Jewish people. When an English admiral in Malta during the war said to him, "You'll agree with me, Frankau, about these damn Jews," he replied with a loud laugh. On hearing this story, Pamela asked her father whether he told the admiral that he was a Jew. He replied that he certainly had not, that it was none of his business.[41] Pamela, who was raised as an Anglican but converted to Catholicism during the war, was not at all uncomfortable about her Jewish antecedents. But then she always lived as a Christian—her religious and national identities were fixed and unambiguous from birth—while her father's experience was very different.

Gilbert Frankau grew up in a milieu that was neither unambiguously Jewish nor unambiguously Christian. His parents remained Jews—from inertia primarily—but made their children Christians in order to ease their way in the world. For Ronald and Joan, this was not apparently a problem. They were of a different mettle than their older brother and resilient enough to live comfortably with the contradictions in their upbringing. However, for Gilbert and for other German Jewish offspring of similar temperament and upbringing, this kind of indeterminacy was troublesome. The ambiguous religious and ethnic character of their home life left them without a firm sense of who they were, and thus they were unable to cope with even low levels of contempt and exclusion. Moreover, because they closely resembled their gentile neighbors in all the external details of life and did not follow a recognizably Jewish regimen or affirm distinctively Jewish beliefs, they were acutely sensitive to accusations that they were different, that is, somehow less English. Humbert Wolfe, it should be recalled, felt that he had been especially vulnerable to the taunts of other children because he had been brought up in a lukewarm Jewish atmosphere and lacked the pride that would have allowed him to withstand their contempt. He concluded that a Polish Jew, secure in his faith, was better able to withstand virulent antisemitism than a deracinated English Jew, ever alert to the least suggestion of being different, the occasional social sneer or jibe.

The poet E. H. W. Meyerstein (1889–1952), who was raised in circumstances similar to those in the Frankau home, felt that he became the target of wounding schoolboy taunts precisely because he was neither fully Jewish nor fully Christian. His father, Sir Edward William Meyerstein (1863–1942), was a wealthy London stockbroker whose parents had emigrated from Germany in the mid-nineteenth century. Sir Edward and his wife practiced no religion at any time in their lives, but brought up their children from an early age in the Church of England, presumably for pragmatic reasons. According to Meyerstein, his father, "if he believed in a deity, never mentioned the fact," while his mother "often mentioned God, as a being, apparently immaterial, in whose sight she was justified in whatever she did." Although the children attended Church of England services, they were not formally baptized until 1903, just prior to Meyerstein's departure for Harrow. There he suffered greatly as a newly minted Christian of German Jewish origin. Boys would shout at him in the streets of Harrow; athletes would roar out behind him a musical comedy song of the time about a Mr. Rosenstein. The music master told another boy that Meyerstein liked Mendelssohn's piano music because the composer was a Jew; when Meyerstein won the school music prize, the music master refused to post the announcement on the school board. As Meyerstein later recalled, a boy from a well-established Jewish family who was proud of his religion and believed he was as good as anyone else got through school just fine, but a boy of Jewish or partly Jewish antecedents who had been baptized and also had a German name was "due for hell." He felt he would have been much happier had he been able to boast "I am proud of my race!" and then bashed his tormenters with his fists. His father tried to assure him that there was no prejudice against Jews in England, but, as Meyerstein realized, his father's experience and his own were entirely different, since his father had been educated at a day school (University College School) with few social pretensions and a sizable Jewish enrollment and had passed most of his life among bankers and brokers.[42]

Meyerstein's experience at Harrow haunted him his entire life, influencing both his self-confidence (rather, his lack of it) and his attitudes toward Jews. At Oxford, he participated enthusiastically in chapel (primarily for aesthetic rather than spiritual reasons), but later he ceased to identify himself in any way with the Church of England. Indeed, he felt that he did not fall within any denominational pale. Yet he realized, however reluctantly, that he would always be viewed as a Jew, regardless of his formal religious status. His reputation as a poet, he believed, had suffered because the English would not tolerate "a bloody German Jew" in their poetic pantheon. Had he been a pianist, an impresario, or a financier—or had his name been different—there would have been a place for him, or so he claimed. Yet he protested, in vain, that he was not a Jew and not particularly proud of the race that had persecuted Spinoza and crucified Jesus. He did not like Jews or "the Jewish genius" (he made exceptions for Felix Mendelssohn and Heinrich Heine) and was never at ease in their company, believing that they were always expecting "some sort of display or exhibitionism" that he could not give them.[43]

The reactions of a Meyerstein or a Frankau were not typical, however. For most offspring of German Jewish immigrants who abandoned or drifted from their ancestral origins, entry into gentile society was a less troublesome experience. Anguish and anxiety were not the usual accompaniments of radical assimilation in England. In some cases, the break with Judaism was not even the outcome of a premeditated scheme for social advancement but the unintended consequence of prior social integration and religious secularization. In families with few Jewish commitments, the choice of a spouse—itself subject to the vagaries of sexual attraction and financial calculation—frequently determined the Jewish fate of the next generation. If a young Jew from a home that was only nominally Jewish

took a partner from a similar background, they might remain attached to
the Jewish community, though in a tenuous way. But if this young person
happened to chose a spouse from a Christian family, the couple and their
descendants would almost certainly have no contact with the Jewish community. In either case, the Jewish fate of the family would depend not on
any previous commitment to or strategy for radical assimilation but on
chance circumstances and, of course, prior indifference to traditional religious practices.

The way this worked out in practice can be seen in the Jewish affiliations
of the London branch of the Warburg banking clan. Fredric Elias Warburg
(1832–1899) emigrated from Sweden to London around 1860. (The Swedish
Warburgs were not, strictly speaking, German Jews but in the context of
this discussion can be considered as such, for they had only recently settled in Sweden and were similar in their religious habits to family members
who remained in Germany.) The founder of the English branch made a
fortune in the City, largely through financing, in association with Ernest
Cassel, London's first subways. He and his wife never attended synagogue
or in any way practiced Judaism. Two of their three sons married Christian
women and ceased to be even nominal Jews on their marriage, raising their
children in the Church of England. A third son, John Cimon Warburg
(1867–1931), by chance married a woman of German Jewish origin, Violet
Amalia Sichel, and consequently he remained a Jew, i.e., he was married
in a synagogue service and buried in a Jewish cemetery. His Judaism did
not go much further than that. His son, the publisher Fredric John Warburg
(1898–1981), explained that the family's Jewishness was largely a matter of
inertia. The Warburgs, he wrote, were Jews "because they were born of
Jewish parents and believed themselves to be Jews," but "their religious
feeling was slight and their racial exclusiveness negligible." They were
both too proud and too lethargic to disaffiliate themselves formally from
the Jewish group through conversion; thus they remained Jews until something unintended occurred to make them leave their Jewishness behind.
"They then changed with as little fuss as a man changing from one lounge
suit to another of a slightly different colour. So they remained basically the
same, substituting for the practice of not going to synagogue the rather
similar practice of not going to church."[44]

Unlike her husband, Violet Amalia Warburg felt that religion was important. In the view of her son, Fredric, she turned to Judaism because she
was unhappy and lonely—her husband ignored her and her in-laws bul-
lied her. Whatever the reason, she found some relief in the consolations
of religion. She gave her children religious instruction, hiring a tutor to
come to the house to teach them Judaism. There were also periods when
she and the children attended Sabbath services with some regularity. But
her approach to Judaism was decidedly nontraditional. For example, she
never fasted or had her children fast on Yom Kippur (a practice common

even among otherwise lax Jews) because her "fondness" for her children would not allow "the smallest degree of religious fanaticism," and thus they ate substantial meals that day without qualm.[45]

Her son, Fredric, did not share her interest in Judaism, however easy-going its character. As a boy, his main concern was to be so like his schoolmates as to be indistinguishable from them. At Westminster School, where he was enrolled at age thirteen, he gladly would have attended chapel (actually divine service at Westminster Abbey), but his mother was adamant that he, like the other Jewish boys, be excused. Nonattendance marked him out as a Jew, so "to the horrors of being a new boy at a public school was added the horror of being known as a Jew." The "substantial if superficial" antisemitism of his schoolmates caused him to suffer, in his words, "profoundly."[46] The source of his suffering, however, was not entirely—or perhaps even mainly—persecution from without. Herbert Samuel's son Edwin started Westminster School at the same time as Warburg, but apparently he did not suffer greatly from anti-Jewish taunts and jibes during his years there, for he makes no mention of antisemitism at school in his memoirs. This is not to say that he never heard unpleasant remarks about his origins. To claim so would be patently absurd. But for Samuel, who came from a family whose Jewish commitments were firm and unambiguous, the level of antisemitism he encountered at school was not sufficiently powerful to disturb his equilibrium or subsequently merit inclusion in his memoirs. Warburg, on the other hand, was in a situation similar to that of a Humbert Wolfe or an E. H. W. Meyerstein: he was not prepared, by virtue of his background, to withstand even moderate levels of anti-Jewish sentiment. Thus, precisely because he was eager to flee his Jewishness, he was unable to brush off remarks that reminded him of it. Not surprisingly, as an adult he had no contact with Judaism or Jewish communal affairs. He married twice, both times to non-Jews, and effectively left the community.

The absorption of German Jews and their offspring into English society progressed steadily in the years before World War I. Although it is impossible to gauge their incorporation into gentile society in any quantitative way, the available evidence seems to indicate that with every year increasing numbers of these Jews ceased to be identifiable as such. Their departure was not a dramatic affair for the most part because their numbers were not great in comparison with the size of the native-born community. Further, their presence was overshadowed by the new East European immigrant community, which became the focus of widespread public attention from the 1880s. Their absorption also failed to attract public notice because the host society, which, after all, determined the pace of integration, put few obstacles in their way and for the most part welcomed them with open arms, thus obviating the necessity to wage a public campaign to secure access to new circles and institutions. Moreover, those who left their Jewishness behind them were already so indifferent to Jewish concerns that they seem to have experienced little remorse or inner discomfort; if so, they left few records of it.

During World War I, the pace of assimilation among families of German Jewish origin received an unexpected boost. The anti-German hysteria of the war years caused hundreds of families to anglicize their names in order to avoid suspicion of disloyalty to Britain. Ansbachers became Ansleys; Auerbachs, Arbours; Meyers, Merricks; Rothensteins, Rutherstons; Schlosses, Castles; Waldsteins, Walstons; and so on. Although the immediate motive for name changing was the desire to obscure German, rather than specifically Jewish, origins, the effect was the same. Stripped of their German names, the children and grandchildren of Jewish immigrants from Central Europe could disappear even more easily into the larger society. As Albert Rutherston explained in urging his brother William Rothenstein to join the rest of the family in changing his name: "A German name will be a hindrance and an inconvenience so long as we live. It is not giving the children a fair chance because the bitterness will never go." Moreover, he emphasized, the Rothensteins—or Rutherstons—were "a new family." Changing the family name would help the family sink its roots in the country. "Why not whilst we can make them [the children] as strongly planted as we can?"[47]

The wholesale name changing of the war years made possible the virtual disappearance of the German Jewish group in the 1920s and 1930s. Individual families here and there continued to identify as Jews, of course, but they were the exceptions. When J. B. Priestley returned home to Bradford in 1933, he discovered to his regret that there was "hardly a trace now of that German-Jewish invasion" of the previous century. That same year, when Jewish refugees from Nazi Germany began arriving in Great Britain, they found no circles or associations of Jews of German origin to help them in their resettlement. Indeed, the rise in anti-Jewish agitation and discrimination in Great Britain at the time discouraged persons of Jewish origin who felt no strong Jewish commitments—regardless of when their ancestors arrived in England—from asserting their links with Jewry. Stephen Spender, whose maternal grandfather, Ernest Joseph Schuster (1850–1924), came from a Frankfurt Jewish banking clan, recalled that when he was growing up in the teens and twenties both his Jewish and German origins were "passed over in silence or with slight embarrassment" by his family. As a child, he had no idea that he was "a quarter Jewish." From the conversation of nurses and governesses, he had gathered the impression that Jews were "a strange race with hooked noses" and "avaricious manners" with whom he had no reason to imagine that he had any connection.[48]

The assimilation of the descendents of the German immigration of the Victorian era was complete by the outbreak of World War II. Their disappearance from the stage of Anglo-Jewish history was rapid, occurring within one or two generations after the arrival of their forebears in England, and quiet, attracting almost no attention from friendly or hostile observers. Communal officials and thinkers certainly failed to notice their absence, but in general they were not quick to bemoan leakage that resulted from drift and alienation that developed gradually over several generations. Their major preoccupation before 1945 was protecting Jews, at home and abroad, from threats from without, and for the most part they were insensitive to equally destructive forces, like indifference and ignorance, eating away at Anglo-Jewry from within. When defections from Judaism did catch their attention, they were usually the more dramatic cases of conversions of professing Jews effected by missionary endeavors. But the damage done to Jewish cohesion by these acts of apostasy, as we shall see, was insignificant by comparison with the gradual erosion of loyalties that resulted from more casual efforts to integrate into the mainstream of English society.

5

The Fruits of Missionary Labors

English Jews who abandoned their ancestral religion were motivated on the whole by this-worldly rather than other-worldly concerns. Christian doctrine and faith played little role in loosening their attachments. Most remained ignorant of centuries-old supersessionist claims about the theological bankruptcy of Judaism, and very few experienced spiritual ferment before their conversion or emerged from the experience fundamentally transformed and renewed. In the great majority of cases, clerical intervention and assistance were also singularly absent. Apostasy in Anglo-Jewry owed little to the scriptural exegesis or spiritual guidance of conversion-minded clergymen. This was not due, however, to any lack of effort. Indeed, both established and dissenting churches were tireless in their attempts to effect the conversion of the Jews, devoting more money and energy to this task than did religious bodies elsewhere in Europe.

Christian mission to the Jews grew out of the well-established belief that the Jews, despite their initial rejection of Jesus, would one day acknowledge their mistake and convert. Of course, spreading the good news to all peoples was a critical element in Christian thinking from the start, but because of the intimate character of the initial relationship between the two religions there was particular emphasis on stripping away the veil from Jewish eyes. The gospel had been preached to the Jews before other peoples, and their own scriptures, it was believed, contained evidence of the messiahship of Jesus. In this light, the persistent refusal of the Jews to admit their error was a particular affront, while their ultimate conversion was especially desirable. As a missionary in Edwardian Manchester wrote in a public appeal for funds, "The Jews, in their corporate capacity, stand forth conspicuously in this city . . . as a silent protest and an organized negation of Christianity . . . if only as a measure of self-defense, Christ should be preached to them."[1] Similar sentiments over the centuries led Christians to devote an inordinate amount of attention to bringing Jews to the baptismal font.

The missionary impulse was not equally strong at all times and in all places, however. In the first centuries of Christianity, preachers of the new faith actively sought converts within the Jewish communities of the Hellenistic world and frequently met with considerable success, particularly among recent pagan converts to Judaism and their descendants. In the early medieval period, on the other hand, the church hierarchy did not actively seek to evangelize the Jews, although conversionist activity of an informal character was carried out by the lower clergy. But from the thirteenth century, when the attitude of the church toward the Jews in general hardened, it pursued their proselytization aggressively and systematically, employing public disputations and involuntary sermons to weaken their faith, a policy that bore fruit in Spain even before the great expulsion of 1492. When the West became more tolerant toward religious diversity in general in the late seventeenth and eighteenth centuries—and toward Jews in particular—the Christian churches could no longer rely on the state to supply the atmosphere of intimidation that had underwritten previous proselytizing activity. The Protestant churches in particular repudiated the use of state coercion to assist the conversion of the Jews. For them, conversion, whether of Jews or gentiles, was the outcome of an intensive individual process of spiritual self-examination and scriptural exploration. Accordingly, the missionary movements that developed within Protestantism from the seventeenth century on devised new, noncoercive techniques for attracting Jews to Christianity. They sought to win Jewish souls with sympathy and goodwill, through gentle persuasion and with assurances of brotherly love rather than with fiery polemic and ominous threats. Indeed, they attributed the failure of Roman Catholic missionizing over the centuries to the church's persecutory policy.

The first Protestant missions devoted exclusively to winning Jewish souls were founded in Germany—in Hamburg in 1667 by Esdras Edzard, a disciple of Johannes Buxtorf, and in Halle in 1728 by Johann Heinrich Callenberg—but the idea of *Judenmission* never aroused widespread interest. In England there was far greater enthusiasm. In the decades before the Civil War (that is, even before the reestablishment of a professing Jewish community), the growth of millenarian thinking focused attention on the ultimate fate of the Jews in relation to the Second Coming. Most of those who believed both that the Millennium would be realized in the near future and that Protestant England would play an active role in its realization also believed that the national conversion of the Jews had to precede any final scheme of redemption. The religious turmoil of the Civil War years further fueled expectations about the final days, stimulating some millenarians to call for the readmission of the Jews precisely so they might be exposed to the properly professed Christianity of the English and thus led to salvation. The widespread dissemination of such ideas, as well as his own millenarian convictions, led Oliver Cromwell to convene the so-called Whitehall Conference in December 1655 to pave the way for readmission.[2] But hostility to the scheme from both merchants fearful of Jewish competition and old-fashioned theological Judeophobes was greater than Cromwell expected, and the conference was dissolved without any decision having been reached. (Jewish resettlement ultimately proceeded along other lines.)

Although conversionist millenarianism declined after the restoration of the monarchy in 1660, interest in the ultimate conversion of the Jews—whether in England or in the Land of Israel after their ingathering—remained strong. Pamphlets, tracts, sermons, and treatises on chiliastic themes circulated widely in the late seventeenth and eighteenth centuries and continued to stimulate expectations about the fate of the Jews. The excitement created by the messianic movement around Shabbetai Zevi in 1665 and 1666, for example, revived interest in the restoration of the Jews to Zion and their conversion there, either as a prelude to or in consequence of the Second Coming. In the controversy following passage of the so-called Jew Bill in 1753, the ministerial party defended the measure by arguing that the easing of naturalization requirements for Jews would promote their conversion. Extending the privileges of Englishmen to the Jews and treating them with compassion, it was predicted, would encourage their conformity to English manners and sentiments, permit their assimilation into Christian society, and thus prepare the ground for their ultimate conversion. Even after the clamor over Jewish naturalization died down, conversionist hopes continued to be expressed in a variety of forums—in studies on prophecy, for example, and in polemics against deism. When news about the prospective conversion of thousands of Polish Jews (followers of Jacob Frank) to Catholicism reached England in 1759, one anonymous correspondent to the *Gentleman's Magazine* expressed horror that Jews were abandoning their faith to embrace the idolatry of popery, with its "false traditions and wicked inventions," and urged them to hold out a little longer for Protestantism, "that true Christianity."[3]

Despite the persistence of conversionist hopes after the Resettlement, the emergence of a community of professing Jews in London failed to elicit any organized efforts to win Jewish souls at any time in the seventeenth or eighteenth centuries. However, individuals, lay and clerical, acting on their own initiative, occasionally exerted themselves to proselytize Jews. In the 1750s, for example, Edward Goldney, a wealthy merchant, urged the Archbishop of Canterbury to host a series of sumptuous banquets for leading English Jews in the hope that such benevolence would incline their hearts toward Christianity. (Not surprisingly, the archbishop did not respond to the suggestion.) Goldney also met with Rabbi Aaron Hart of the Great Synagogue on more than one occasion in order to urge him to change his religion. Hart had no desire to engage in a religious debate with Goldney and tried to put him off with the observation that as his father, grandfather, and great-grandfather had been Jews he intended to remain one as well.[4] Enthusiastic efforts such as these were episodic, not very successful, and, on the whole, insufficiently threatening to elicit any response on the part of the Jewish community.

Public interest in the conversion of the Jews became more intense after the French Revolution. The overthrow of the old order in France, the spread of French authority to Germany, Holland, and Italy, Napoleon's adventures in the Near East, and his convening of the Parisian Sanhedrin, all contributed to reawakening millenarian speculation and again fueling hopes that some momentous change in the condition of the Jews was imminent.[5] These hopes intersected in the first decade of the nineteenth century with a widespread evangelical campaign to revitalize English religious life in general and bring the message of Christianity to persons and places without knowledge of it. This missionary impulse gave birth to a number of voluntary societies dedicated to evangelizing activity at home and abroad, including the London Missionary Society (1795), the Religious Tract Society (1799), the British and Foreign Bible Society (1804), and the London Society for Promoting Christianity among the Jews (1809) [hereafter referred to as the London Society], the first institution devoted to direct missionary work among English Jews.

The earliest proposal to establish an independent missionary society dedicated solely to Jews was made by a small group of evangelical millenarians in 1796. At the time most evangelicals believed that the heathens, not the Jews, should be given priority in any missionary work. When the former were converted, they maintained, the latter would follow as a matter of course. A small group of evangelicals dissented, arguing that before the infidel peoples would be brought into the Christian fold a remnant of the Jewish nation would have to be converted. They were not able to sway the majority, and no independent society emerged at the time. Then the fortuitous arrival in London several years later of Joseph Frey, an erratic and ambitious convert from Judaism, offered them an opportunity to bring their plan to fruition. Born in Franconia in 1771, Frey had received a traditional Jewish education and as a young man earned his living as a private tutor, ritual slaughterer, and cantor. He was baptized in 1798 and then entered a seminary in Berlin that was sponsored, in part, by the London Missionary Society and the Church Missionary Society. In July 1801, having completed his studies, he sailed for London with the intention of joining a group sponsored by the London Missionary Society that was to travel to South Africa to do missionary work. The Missionary Society decided that Frey would be more effective among the Jews of London than among the native peoples of Africa, so it sent him to study at a seminary at Gosport, where he remained until May 1805, when he commenced "his regular labours" among his brethren in the metropolis.[6]

Frey's missionary activities included composing Hebrew tracts, preaching in the Jewish neighborhoods of London, and directing a charity school for the children of the Jewish poor that opened in January 1807. As the chief object of his sponsors was the conversion of the heathen in Africa and the Indies, they did not lavish much money or attention on his labors in London. This was a source of frustration for Frey, who was personally ambitious and eager to expand the scope of his work. He pointed out to the directors of the Missionary Society that his efforts were being crippled by two major problems. First, he was unable to provide financial support for recently converted Jews, who were almost always destitute and were cut off from future employment within the Jewish community by virtue of their apostasy. Second, he could not exercise any control over the charity school students after they returned to the "anti-Christian" influences of their homes at the end of the day. Frey wanted the Missionary Society to establish a house of industry to train and employ recent converts until they could find employment elsewhere and a boarding school to keep Jewish children away from their parents and other relatives while they were being given a Christian education.[7]

The Missionary Society was unwilling to fund these proposals; it did not want to detract from projects in the foreign mission field that it considered more important, and it believed the house of industry and boarding school schemes were tantamount to bribing Jews to become Christians. Frey, however, persisted in his attempts to enlarge his Jewish operations. How "can you be satisfied with 12 children in the school whilst at least 50 or 100 might share the same unspeakable blessings?" he asked the committee that supervised his work in October 1807. "God forbid!"[8] The Missionary Society's continual refusal to give Frey more funds or autonomy led him and a number of supporters to separate from the parent body and establish the London Society for Promoting Christianity among the Jews in 1809.

From its inception, the London Society grew rapidly. It enjoyed the support and patronage of both evangelical churchmen and Nonconformists (until 1815, when it came under the sole auspices of the Church of England), and by means of nationwide collection sermons and annual membership dues it was able to finance an ever-expanding program of missionary activity. (Between 1810 and 1858, the London Society spent over £850,000 on its work.[9]) In 1809, it took a long lease on a former Huguenot chapel in Brick Lane, Spitalfields; four years later it began constructing a complex of buildings at Bethnal Green—known as Palestine Place—in order to have a permanent center for its work in the Jewish quarter. Lectures were delivered to "inquiring" Jews and recent converts, at first by Frey and, after his dismissal in 1816 for adultery and other sexual irregularities, by other converts. Tracts, pamphlets, and copies of the New Testament were distributed—at coffeehouses, in hospital sick wards, at funerals, outside synagogues and shops, and in public markets. A free school with the capacity to enroll 300–400 Jewish and Christian children was opened, as was a boarding school where Jewish children were isolated from family and friends until their education was completed, at which time they were bound as apprentices to Christian artisans and merchants. The Society also established a number of enterprises to provide training and employment for its clients who were out of work as a result of their change of faith. Recent converts were taught candlewick making, basketmaking, shoemaking, bookbinding, printing, and lithography. The Society also provided direct financial aid—for food, clothing, housing, and medical care—to prospective and recent converts, most of whom were destitute and without marketable skills.[10]

The London Society was the dominant force in Jewish missionary work in England until the great influx of East European Jews in the last decades of the century. The dissenters who withdrew from the Society in 1815, after cooperation with the Anglicans proved impossible, did not establish a missionary organization of their own at the time. A kindred Nonconformist organization—the British Society for Propagating the Gospel among the Jews—was created only in 1842. Although it never rivaled the London Society in the scope of its work, it operated in a similar fashion, offering lectures, distributing tracts, and providing material relief.

Both Anglican and Nonconformist conversionists aimed at gathering the entire Jewish nation, not just random individuals, into the Christian fold, for the final unfolding of salvation, they believed, required the collective return of the Jews to the faith they had long ago scorned. Thus both the London Society and the British Society eventually established extensive networks of missionary stations abroad—in Central and Eastern Europe, North Africa, and the Near East—that in time consumed more of their resources than those at home. Representatives were even sent to convert the Jews of India, Ethiopia, and China. In theory, conversionist groups should have sought recruits as well from all ranks of the English Jewish community—rich, middling, and poor—since their goal was the *national* redemption of the Jews. But, in practice, organized missionary activity was confined almost exclusively to the humblest stratum. Frey himself noted at the outset of the enterprise that it was "chiefly" among "the poor and the ignorant" that "we must look for success at first"—although, he continued, "there is no doubt but afterwards, some of the rich, the wise and the mighty will listen to the joyous sound."[11] Despite Frey's optimism, "the rich, the wise and the mighty" remained outside the scope of conversionist activity, largely because missionaries had no access to them. Their material well-being isolated them to a considerable extent from missionary overtures, which were confined, by necessity, to public places like streets and markets. They could not be visited in their homes or offices, nor could they be induced to attend lectures in a church or mission hall in a lower-class neighborhood.

Most Jews converted in England by missionaries were thus drawn from the poorest and least respectable strata of the community. A Jewish critic of Frey publicly challenged him in 1810 to produce "one respectable Jew, one honest man" among the converts he had made. Indeed, quite a few of the London Society's early converts greatly embarrassed its supporters. Jacob Josephson was caught stealing silver plate from the country home of the chief benefactor of the London Society; his wife was discovered to be committing adultery with Frey. William Leigh (né Benjamin Levy) was tried in 1816 for scheming to defraud a group of merchants of goods worth more than £ 50,000. A home for female converts set up in 1813 had to be shut down three years later because the women were too rowdy and dissolute. Jerusalem-born Judah Catarevus, a "rabbi" employed to do missionary work in London, was found visiting a whorehouse in Houndsditch and was dismissed from his post. The Rev. Charles Simeon, a prominent supporter of the London Society from its start, suggested to a friend in 1830 "that as little as possible be said of our early converts." Jews converted by the London Society in the middle decades of the century appear to have been less dissolute but equally impoverished. The 1,300 Jews baptized at the Jews' Episcopal Chapel in Spitalfields between 1831 and 1880 came from the same economic stratum as those Jews applying for relief to the Jewish Board of Guardians.[12]

Jewish poverty was the essential backdrop to successful missionary activity. It created opportunities for establishing contacts that in other circumstances would have been rejected. For Jews who were unable to feed, clothe, and house themselves adequately were more likely to respond to comforting offers of spiritual and material aid than those who were not in distress. Of the first three converts made by Frey, one was deeply in debt, one had no food to eat or bed to lie on and had sent his children into the streets to beg, and one was experiencing business difficulties.[13] The story of Abraham Joseph Levi (b. 1817) captures the vulnerability of such persons. Levi left his home in Wiesbaden, Germany, at age twenty-five, when his parents attempted to marry him to someone of their rather than his choosing. He settled in Paris, but after failing to make a living he moved to London in 1844 to try his luck there. He was no more successful than before and returned to Paris, where another venture failed when he was duped by a person who pretended to be his best friend. In 1848, he again tried his luck in London and again suffered more business disappointments. One day he accepted a tract from a missionary and, after reading it, was moved to get in touch with agents of the London Society, who arranged employment for him and effected his eventual conversion.[14] Isaac Edward Salkinson (1820–1883), later famous as a translator of Milton and Shakespeare into Hebrew, was brought to espouse Christianity under similar circumstances. Salkinson grew up in Shklov, in Belorussia, in an atmosphere of traditional piety, abject poverty, and family tensions. He left home at seventeen and wandered for several years in the Pale of Settlement, living hand to mouth, avoiding conscription, and acquiring along the way a *haskalah* education. In 1849, he arrived in London, without possessions, friends, or means of earning a living. He was befriended by missionaries of the British Society, who fed and sheltered him and arranged lessons for him in English and other secular subjects, without revealing at first their true identity. He tried several times to escape his benefactors and make it on his own, but he could not find work and had no friends to whom he could turn for advice or help; in the end, overcome by hunger and despair, he returned to them. Eventually he was baptized, sent to study at a Presbyterian seminary in Edinburgh, ordained a minister, and despatched to British Society stations in Pressburg and later Vienna.[15]

Critics of conversionist activity, both Jewish and Christian, repeatedly charged that the material relief offered to potential converts was little more than a bribe to conform to the outward forms of Christianity. B. R. Goakman, who headed the printing office of the London Society in the early 1810s and afterward wrote a stinging attack on its conduct, recalled that one potential convert placed under his direction said that "he cared nothing about Jesus Christ so long as he could get a good belly-full of victuals, and that he believed all the boys [in the printing office] were of his opinion!" An anonymous Jewish critic of the London Society reported the case of a young man who was bribed with £ 2 to attend Frey's lectures and was told by Frey, "Never mind your father, come to hear me, bring with you as many Jewish boys as you can procure, and I'll make a man of you." Another Jewish critic, M. Sailman, a Hebrew teacher in Southampton, claimed that Frey and his associates ingratiated themselves with Jewish boys who were hawking things in the streets by purchasing some small article worth a few pennies and leaving five or six shillings for it. They would repeat the same benevolent act until they had gained the confidence of the lads, who would then be told that if they came to hear Frey they would receive a new suit of clothing.[16]

It is impossible to verify the truth of specific accusations such as these. Nonetheless, it is clear that material relief was critical in bringing Jews into contact with conversionist activities, even if it did not eventually cause them to change their religion. The log book kept at mid-century by a relief worker for the London Society, a Mr. Cadman, reveals that the hope of receiving aid and of being apprenticed attracted many young men to its doors. Most of those who turned to Cadman for help were unemployed and had no marketable skills; some were ill; some had already applied to their parishes for relief. Quite a few were recent immigrants who had lived in England for six months or less. All were desperate. James Goldsmith, a hairdresser in Spitalfields, applied to Cadman for temporal relief in June 1851, after he was unable to find employment in his trade or in any other. Goldsmith told Cadman that "he did not know what to do, he was at present in a destitute condition . . . he had only a piece of dry bread to eat on Saturday and nothing yesterday, he had no means of procuring either food or lodging. . . ."[17]

A minority of those who responded favorably to missionary overtures did so with the calculated intent of exploiting Christian enthusiasm for the conversionist enterprise in order to make a living. In September 1845, the *Sunday Times* cautioned clergymen against a young Polish Jew who was representing himself as a recent convert seeking money to go abroad but was in fact still in England. Moses, or Morris, Lissack, a Hebrew teacher and jewelry dealer in Bedford, recounted in his autobiography the story of an insincere convert by the name of Herschell, whom he met in the mid-1840s. When Herschell first came to Bedford, the Jews there received him warmly, frequently inviting him to meals since Hershell appeared to be an observant Jew and it was difficult for a single person to obtain kosher food in a small provincial town. When it was learned that he was taking instruction in Christianity from a clergyman in nearby Biddenham, he defended himself by saying that he made a living by repeatedly being baptized and that the deception he employed was no worse than the untruths a tradesman used to make a sale. It was, he conceded, a lucrative business, not just for himself but for others as well: "If Christians are such fools as to pay Jews for being baptized, let them do it. We all know that there is not a Jew baptized, either in this country or in any other, but he makes some profit out of it. Either they are actually paid for it, or they are made missionaries, or they marry rich ladies, or they receive some other kind of support from the Christians." Lissack, who condemned such deceit and hypocrisy, in part because it reinforced the popular association of Jews with trickery and deception, warned Christian friends about the fraud Herschell was perpetrating, but they indignantly replied that Lissack was simply angry that a Jew was converting. The baptism took place in Bedford on 29 March 1846 amid great fanfare—bills were posted about the town announcing the ceremony and notes were sent to local Jews inviting them to attend. When Lissack persisted in calling the new Christian an imposter, the clergyman who had baptized Herschell threatened to bring Lissack before a court of law for damaging his reputation. Lissack also claimed that converted Jewish peddlers carried letters of recommendation from well-meaning Christians attesting to their baptism and that they showed these letters as they hawked door to door in order to boost sales.[18]

Charlatans like Herschell were not typical of Jews who turned to the missionary societies or to benevolent Christians for material aid. More common were persons in genuine need who, once they had been succored and had changed their religion, came to look upon the societies as all-embracing welfare agencies to which they could turn for support in later years. Long after having embraced Christianity, such persons continued to turn to them for help with rent, employment, medical care, and education; for loans to set themselves up in business; and even for passage money to lands of new opportunities. Two examples from mid-century should suffice: John Englander, age thirty-seven, who had been baptized in Cracow by an agent of the London Society and had been taught bookbinding there, asked for help in paying his rent after having been in London only six weeks; Alexander Cohen, a native of Poland who had been in England for three years and was unable to find employment as a Hebrew teacher, requested money for himself to return to Poland (he intended to leave his wife in London to work as a dressmaker but did not plan to send her any money). The basis for such requests was the feeling that conversion was a kind of contractual agreement, the converts bartering their Judaism in exchange for temporal aid. When their requests were refused, they felt they had been cheated and responded angrily, at times employing violence against the societies' representatives. In 1851, Lewis Nathan demanded that the director of the Episcopal Jews' Chapel in London, the Rev. Cartwright, give him either regular employment or a regular allowance. When his request was denied, Nathan threatened to stand up in the chapel and denounce Cartwright for condemning him to live on four shillings a week. After several weeks of threatening and harassing Cartwright and Cadman, Nathan assaulted Cadman and was arrested by the police. Six months later Solomon Morris, also a convert, appeared at the chapel with a stick to denounce the missionaries' refusal to give him sufficient funds to set himself up in business. He did not want to appear week after week begging for a small handout and demanded to know why they did not give him the £ 5 he needed. He then pulled off one of his boots, whose soles were almost worn through, and asked, "Was it not a disgrace to the London Society that a converted Israelite should be obliged to wear a boot like that?"[19]

The willingness of unbaptized Jews to seek aid from the missionary societies was largely a consequence of their inability to find help within the Jewish community. Although Jewish poverty declined between the early nineteenth century and the start of the mass migration from Eastern Europe, there was no time at which communal charities were able to meet all the demands made on them. Before the establishment of the Jewish Board of Guardians in London in 1859, synagogues, independent voluntary societies, and wealthy individuals dispensed charity in a variety of forms without any centralized planning or direction. At one time there were seven charities dispensing clothing.[20] (The situation in the provinces was similar although the number and variety of charities were much smaller.) The creation of the Board of Guardians, while satisfying the desire of its founders for systematized, efficient relief, still did not provide sufficiently for the needs of the Jewish poor. Consequently, there were Jews both before and after 1859 who turned to the conversionists for help when their requests to Jewish groups were turned down. For example, in the 1810s, B. A. Cohen, a Sephardi Jew in London, married and with four children, found himself in serious trouble after his business failed. He applied to the Spanish and Portuguese Jews Congregation for relief, as well as to a number of individual Sephardim privately, but without success. He and his family were literally without bread for several weeks; he was forced to pawn most of their clothes; and he, his wife, and one of his children became seriously ill. He then applied to the London Society for assistance and was given a job in its printing office, although he had no interest in leaving Judaism. When, however, Jews who had previously refused him aid became aware of the help he was receiving and realized that he might convert, they came to his assistance and eventually obtained for him a teaching post in the Sephardi charity school.[21]

Jewish leaders and groups in London were particularly negligent in establishing schools for children of the poor, and from the start missionary groups exploited this weakness for their own purposes. As an early critic of the London Society wrote, "they know the power of money, and there-fore . . . they TEMPT the Jews, by the offer of gratis maintenance and edu-cation, to do violence to their consciences by delivering up their children to them, to be fed the food forbidden by the Jewish nation, and educated Christians."[22] Frey's first school, established in early 1807, when he was still employed by the London Missionary Society, never enrolled more than a dozen children in its first two years but still raised fears that Jewish parents without means to educate their children would take advantage of the free schooling being offered. In January 1807, Solomon Hirschell (1761–1842), rabbi of the Great Synagogue, warned the community in two successive Sabbath sermons about the dangers posed by the missionary school and declared that any Jew who sent his children there would be con-sidered as if he himself had been baptized and ceased to be a Jew. The appearance of the school also spurred the creation of a trade school for poor Jewish youth in June of that year as part of the Jews' Hospital com-plex. The schools of the London Society were more successful in attracting Jewish students; by 1859, 736 Jewish children had passed through them. And they too acted as a spur to the creation of further Jewish charity schools, most notably the Jews' Free School, established in 1817.[23]

Before 1880 the majority of students at the schools of the London Society were not the offspring of unbaptized Jews but came from homes in which at least one of the parents was either a baptized Jew or a gentile; that is, they came from families that were already estranged from the Jewish com-munity, had not themselves received a Jewish upbringing, and would have become Christians even if they had not been enrolled in missionary schools.[24] But a minority came from families that were still nominally com-mitted to Judaism but were beset by problems that caused them to seek free schooling, which included room and board, for their children. For ex-ample, in 1837 Alexander Gompertz, an ironmonger and former member of the Hambro Synagogue, having fallen on hard times, asked the London Society to take his three children. Two years later, Alice Abrahams of Bris-tol wrote to the London Society seeking admission for her children. She and her husband, Harris, had kept a jewelry and silver shop in Bristol for twenty years; but now that her husband was dead, she had no means to support the children. In 1870, Leah Benheim asked to have her daughter Rachel admitted, her husband, Solomon, a slipper maker, having deserted them three years earlier.[25]

Poverty was not the only characteristic shared by Jews converted by mis-sionary societies. Most were also strangers in new surroundings, having recently emigrated from Central and Eastern Europe. Lissak noted at mid-century that of those Jews baptized by the London Society since its found-ing, fewer than a dozen were born in England. His impressionistic com-ment is confirmed by an analysis of the baptismal records of the Episcopal

Jews' Chapel in Spitalfields. Between 1831 and 1880, 583 men (age seventeen and over) were baptized there, almost all of them foreign-born. In the 1830s, 85 percent were immigrants; in the 1840s, 77 percent; in the 1850s, 90 percent; in the 1860s, 90 percent; and in the 1870s, 93 percent. During this same period, a far smaller number of women—only eighty-nine, less than 10 percent of the total—were baptized there. Unlike their male counterparts, most of them were born in England and were already married at the time of their conversion, either to Christians or to Jews who were converting at the same time or who had converted previously. They were also, on the whole, older than the men who were converted during this period; 36 percent were thirty-five or older, while less than 20 percent of the men had reached that age. For the women, baptism was the outcome of prior alienation from the Jewish community through intermarriage or marriage to a convert.[26]

The paucity of native English Jews among male converts was a reflection of the more extensive resources, material and otherwise, on which they could draw if they found themselves in distress. Jews with well-established roots in a community could more easily obtain help—from family, friends, charities, and, if they were members, friendly societies—than those who were fresh off the boat. Most male converts were young immigrants without access to these resources. Far from home, without money or friends, unable to find their bearings in an inhospitable and foreign environment, they were prepared—unlike their native counterparts—to be befriended by missionary agents offering psychological support, spiritual hope, and temporal care.

Joseph Philip Cohen, for example, a native of Prussia, arrived in London at the urging of a cousin who had already emigrated, only to discover that the cousin had gone on to the United States. Like so many immigrants before him, he took to hawking, but he met with considerable disappointment, in part because he knew no English. He eventually took a partner, who after an initially amicable relationship absconded, robbing him of everything he had. He then met a missionary of Jewish birth who befriended him and helped him find his way to Christianity. Cohen was baptized in 1845 and later served as a missionary, at various stations both at home and abroad, for the Nonconformist British Society for the Propagation of the Gospel among the Jews. The immigration experience also served as the background to the conversion of Moses Margoliouth (1818–1881), a native of Suwalki, Poland. He received a traditional *yeshivah* education in Poland but also learned German and Russian. In July 1837, age nineteen, he left home (for reasons never made clear) and sailed to England, landing at Hull in August. After two months, he later recalled, "I began to feel very miserable and wished myself back again in Poland." He failed to make friends among the Jews of Hull—"semi-infidels" whose company he did not enjoy—and decided to return home. He traveled to Liverpool in order to write his parents for money for the trip. In Liverpool he met a converted

Jew who conversed with him about Jesus and the New Testament, initiating thereby a train of events that ended with his baptism in April of the following year.

Henry Aaron Stern (1820–1885) also came to profess Christianity after experiencing want and loneliness as a recent immigrant. He grew up in a small village in Hesse-Cassel but was sent at age twelve to a modern Jewish school in Frankfurt, the Philanthropin, which was affiliated with the nascent Reform movement. Five years later he moved to Hamburg to pursue a career in commerce. In 1839, he was offered a good position with a firm in London, but on arrival in England he found that the firm had failed. Pride prevented him from returning to Germany, although he had little on which to survive. One Sunday afternoon a fellow lodger invited him to the London Society's chapel at Palestine Place. Stern was impressed by the service and returned to his room, resolved to read the New Testament. A period of mental anguish then set in, bringing him to what he described as "the brink of despair." At the same time his slender funds were slowly disappearing, forcing him to pawn his possessions. Eventually he entered the Operative Jewish Converts' Institution at Palestine Place, where printing and bookbinding were being taught, and in March 1840 he was baptized.[27]

Poverty and immigration together defined those Jews who were most susceptible to missionary overtures. Few immigrants, however, responded favorably to these overtures—very few indeed if we exclude those who did so with the cynical intention of obtaining relief without sacrificing their loyalty to Judaism. Those who did relinquish their previous religious identity were very likely predisposed by personality traits that were neither socially nor historically determined. Those who actually converted were selected, so to speak, from the pool of potential apostates by psychological factors, although, given the nature of the surviving evidence, it is impossible to say in any particular case what these were. In other words, we can never know why one impoverished immigrant responded positively to offers of missionary assistance while another one in equally dire straits did not, in the same way that we can never know why one of their upwardly mobile well-to-do co-religionists drifted from the community while another, equally wealthy and equally ambitious, remained a pillar of the communal establishment.

The most difficult question to answer about the conversions made by missionaries is to what extent they were sincere. Were these new Christians devout believers or cynical scoundrels, indifferent pragmatists or distraught and desperate souls? A handful, clearly, were altogether unscrupulous, like the Jew Morris Lissack encountered in Bedford who made a living from regularly changing his religion. There were also some who, while not making a habit of multiple conversions, returned to Judaism after receiving assistance and publicly expressed their remorse at having left the community. Solomon Harris, a cabinetmaker in Manchester, was baptized in 1846, but two years later, having regretted his action, he received 10s 6d from the Old Hebrew Congregation there to help him return to his native country. In 1848, Reuben Robinson of Manchester wrote to the *Jewish Chronicle* to confess his error in being baptized. A letter to the editor commenting on the case held want and misery responsible for his conversion: "He had no shelter, no food, and was on the brink of starvation when a kind missionary from 'pure love of Israel' fed him, sheltered him and clothed him." In these circumstances, the correspondent explained, "Mr. Robinson would have believed anything and have been converted to anything, not to die in the streets."[28] Undoubtedly there was a strong element of pragmatism in conversions such as these.

Jewish observers at the time tended to view all conversions made under missionary auspices as religiously insincere and materially motivated. Lissack's attitude was typical, and his words bear repeating: "We all know that there is not a Jew baptized, either in this country or in any other, but he makes some profit out of it." The *Jewish Chronicle* and the *Voice of Jacob* consistently portrayed converts as rapacious swindlers who exploited Christian benevolence, or as irresponsible slackers who preferred to eat and drink without having to toil, or as cunning atheists who lacked any religion to begin with and were thus only nominally Jewish. As the convert Moses Margoliouth noted in 1843, English Jews were fond of asserting that no Jew could become a real Christian and that all converts were therefore imposters.[29] It is understandable why Jews viewed apostates in this light. First, they found it difficult, if not impossible, to believe that a Jew could honestly accept supernatural doctrines like the trinitarian nature of God that were so contrary to Jewish teaching and human reason. Second, from their perspective, admitting the sincerity of these conversions was tantamount to acknowledging the spiritual appeal of Christianity and, correspondingly, the inadequacy of Judaism. Thus they tended to dismiss converts as charlatans and rogues.

In truth, the reality of apostate motives was more complex than contemporary Jewish discussions would suggest. There is no question that the great bulk of conversions claimed by missionary groups would never have occurred had there been no immigrant poverty. The initial point of contact between the missionary and the potential convert was, without doubt, the offer of material relief. However, once contact was made and help was extended, some recipients undoubtedly came to accept the religious viewpoint of those who befriended and cared for them, whatever their motives were when they first sought assistance. It certainly made it easier psychologically to continue to accept help if they did so. To do otherwise would have meant acknowledging, to themselves, that they were carrying on a charade, behaving deceitfully, pretending to the world that they were one thing when they were actually another—something few persons are prepared to do. In fact, the longer Jews remained under the protection of the societies, the more they came to see their motives as disinterested and their profession of Christianity as sincere. In the end, their material and religious concerns became hopelessly entangled, so much so that it is almost impossible to separate the two. To Jewish spokesmen, however, missionary relief was a case of bribery pure and simple.

Conversions that occurred in small provincial communities, where missionary groups were not generally active, were much more likely to be motivated by nonmaterial concerns than those that took place in London, Manchester, or Liverpool. Representatives of the London-based societies toured the provinces regularly, largely to address Christian gatherings and raise funds for missionary work in London and abroad rather than to proselytize local Jews. For a time, in the 1820s and 1830s, missionaries (most of whom were former Jews) occasionally visited small communities to pass out tracts and, if possible, engage local leaders in public disputations, but this activity did not continue into the second half of the century. The most prominent of these traveling missionaries was the Rev. Joseph Wolff (1795–1862), son of a Bavarian rabbi and from 1821 a leading agent of the London Society in England, the Near East, and Central Asia. Wolff once visited Plymouth during Passover and placarded the walls of buildings with signs defying the Jews to debate the evidences of Christianity. "Our community, ever timid," L. Hyman later recalled, "declined the challenge, until being urged strongly, at last a meeting was appointed on Sunday during Pesach at the house of Mr Lazarus Solomon." Jews and Christians, including members of the clergy, were present. After a number of arguments were made on both sides, Abraham Joseph, one of the disputants, produced an issue of the *Asiatic Journal* from 1833 in which Wolff had described a messianic vision of his: with Abraham, Isaac, Jacob, Jesus, and the Apostles present, Paul told him, Wolff, that he had a crown on his head. The vision embarrassed the Christians present, and the chairman, a Christian physician, hastily adjourned the meeting. Wolff left Plymouth and skipped the lectures he had scheduled for Exeter.[30]

Visits like these, even when less dramatic, produced almost no converts. Local clergymen, on the other hand, without recourse to the material resources of the societies in London, were occasionally able to convince individual Jews with whom they came in contact of the truth of Christianity. (It should be remembered that Jews living in small towns had much greater contact with non-Jews than those living in London.) This was not by any means a frequent event, but when it occurred it tended to leave an impression on contemporaries. The most prominent convert to be won in this manner was Michael Solomon Alexander (1799–1845), first Anglican bishop in Jerusalem. Born and raised in Posen, Alexander taught in a traditional Jewish elementary school from 1815 to 1819. He emigrated to England the next year, following the death of his father and a quarrel with an older brother. He hoped to obtain a position as a ritual slaughterer in London but was disappointed. With the help of Solomon Hirschell, he obtained work as tutor to a Jewish family in Colchester. While there he apparently read the New Testament for the first time. (He later claimed that he had never even heard of it before this.) He next served as cantor and ritual slaughterer to the small communities in Norwich (1820–1821), Nottingham (1821–1823), and Plymouth (1823–1825). To supplement his meager income, he also gave Hebrew and German lessons, to both Jewish and Christian students. At Plymouth, one of the latter was the Rev. B. Golding, curate of Stonehouse, who aroused Alexander's interest in Christianity and eventually effected his conversion. His baptism was a cause for great celebration, for here was a learned "rabbi" (as Alexander was popularly described), not a starving unemployed misfit, witnessing the truth of Christian claims. More than 1,000 people attended his baptism at St. Andrew's Church, Plymouth, on 22 June 1825. His own conversion accomplished, he took up missionary work for the London Society for a short time in southwest England and within a few months converted his wife, Deborah Levy, whom he had met and married in Plymouth less than a year earlier, and two Jews from Exeter.[31]

In Bedford, whose Jewish community at this time consisted of four or five families, another religious functionary was converted to Christianity, again in circumstances where material relief played no role at all. Nathan Joseph, son of Michael Joseph, founder of the local synagogue, acted as cantor and ritual slaughterer for the small community. He came in contact with the Rev. T. S. Grimshawe and, after several disputes on the evidences of Christianity, declared to him his intention of joining the Church of England. When news of his impending conversion got out, Solomon Hirschell revoked his authorization to act as ritual slaughterer and banned Nathan from officiating at services. Nathan hesitated for a time, reconsidered and even did public penance in the synagogue, but then determined to go ahead with his conversion. He traveled to Norwich, where he received further instruction in Christianity, and was baptized there in 1830 as Henry Samuel Joseph. Soon after he published a pamphlet, directed to his former Jewish brethren, defending himself against the accusation that he had been influenced by worldly motives. So common was the perception that Jews converted solely for opportunistic reasons that he felt it necessary to show that he had been moved by what he called "a sense of duty." From Norwich he went to Liverpool, where he worked as a missionary, eventually being ordained a clergyman in the established church.[32]

Whatever their motives, Jews who embraced Christianity as a result of conversionist activity faced difficulties following baptism that those who converted on their own initiative did not. The latter became Christians in the wake of their alienation from Judaism and their social integration into gentile circles, baptism for them being the final step in a process of radical assimilation that had started much earlier in their lives or even during the lives of their parents. They usually became Christians after their friends and acquaintances had ceased to be exclusively Jewish. New Christians who were the products of missionary endeavors were in a different—and

difficult—situation. They were not integrated into any rank of English society at the time of their baptism; most were recent immigrants who previously had associated with and were employed by Jews. Baptism cut them
off from their former associates. It frequently prevented them from gaining
employment in Jewish firms or shops or from obtaining credit from the Jewish wholesale merchants who supplied street traders. Thus, the missionary
societies argued, it was necessary to continue to provide material assistance to the converts after their baptism.

Baptism also exposed converts to harassment and occasionally violence
from Jews who viewed conversion as a species of treason. As Moses
Margoliouth remarked in 1843, the converted Jew could expect only "hatred and calumny" from his "unbelieving brethren." For example, in 1809,
after Barnard Jacobs of Petticoat Lane visited the Jews' Chapel in
Spitalfields, his neighbors broke his windows, smashed his furniture, and
swore they would murder him. For a time the London Society felt compelled to furnish him with the protection of a constable, but one day when
he went out into the street alone he was soundly thrashed. Frey himself
was more than once "endangered" by rowdy crowds of several hundred
Jews "of the lower order" who packed the Jews' Chapel to mock and bait
him. At times the directors of the London Society feared for his life. Jonas
Davis (b. 1812), who was kicked out of his home and disinherited by his
merchant father after he was baptized at a Baptist chapel in London in December 1831, felt that he was in danger of being physically attacked by
Jews—"many of whom who knew me were hot against me"—and sailed
to the United States the following July. Margoliouth cited, in a later work,
an incident in Liverpool in the 1840s concerning a Jew who was errone-
ously suspected of flirting with Christianity. The man entered a Jewish shop
on the eve of Passover, was accosted by another Jew, who accused him of
being "an accursed M'shoomad" [apostate], and was given a tremendous
blow to the face that almost broke his nose.[33] Although missionaries grossly
exaggerated the persecution converts suffered at Jewish hands—there
being a tendency to cast them, in imitation of Jesus's suffering, as virtuous
martyrs tortured and mocked by vicious Jews—they were correct in under-
scoring the gap that opened up between converts and the community to
which they had formerly belonged.

Most Jews who were baptized under missionary auspices found themselves marginalized as a result of having changed their religion. Baptism
cut them off from companionship and employment in one community but
failed to procure their integration into another, for it could not compensate
for their foreign origins, lack of employable skills, and unfamiliarity with
English ways. Even when worshipping, ironically, some remained a group
apart, banding together to create prayer groups of their own because they
felt uncomfortable in gentile churches and chapels. The earliest such group
was the Beni [B'nai] Abraham, whose forty-one founding members first
met at the Jews' Chapel at Palestine Place in 1813. It functioned as both

a prayer group and a mutual aid society. In 1835 its name was changed to the Episcopal Jews' Chapel Abrahamic Society, and its objects were enlarged to include some missionary work, although it remained essentially a mutual aid group. Similar associations sprang up later in the century, including the Rev. C. Schwartz's Hebrew-Christian Union (later the Hebrew-Christian Alliance) in 1865 and the Rev. Henry Aaron Stern's Hebrew-Christian Prayer Union in 1882. These two groups, while continuing to bring recent converts together for prayer and religious instruction and to perform for them benevolent and supportive functions, also forged a new theological perspective known as Hebrew-Christianity. It celebrated the Jewish past and the Jewish element in Christianity and rationalized the segregation of Jewish converts from other Christians by assigning them a critical and distinctive role in the redemption of mankind. Because the Jews were the first chosen of God, the Hebrew Christians reasoned, their conversion to Christianity was particularly desirable. Indeed, it was critical, for the Jews were the testing ground for the mettle of Christian evangelization—unconverted, they represented a living denial of the need of all men for Jesus. And who could best bring them to see the error of their ways if not those who had once held the very same views? Thus, they concluded, Jewish converts should remain a distinctive presence within the body of Christian believers, for they had a message—in their eyes a Jewish message—to bring to their fellow Jews that gentile Christians were incapable of delivering.[34]

It is difficult to know the extent to which members of these groups shared the theological outlook of their leaders. It may be that they were attracted primarily by the fellowship and assistance they offered and only peripherally, if at all, by their distinctive theology, however successful that theology was in explaining their marginal position in English society. It is also difficult to know how popular these Hebrew Christian groups were among Jews converted by the missionary societies. Stern's Hebrew Christian Prayer Union claimed 143 members in 1883 and 600 in 1890; in the late 1890s, the Hebrew Guild of Intercession maintained it had 1,700–1,800 members throughout London, while the congregation of baptized Jews that met in the Rev. Michael Rosenthal's mission hall in Commercial Road was said to have 300 communicants.[35] But these claims, like others made by missionary groups, were probably grossly inflated, and there is no reason to accept them at face value. Some converts, once they were able to get along without missionary assistance, undoubtedly preferred to broaden their range of acquaintances, and, insofar as they remained attached to Christian practice, attended worship in mainstream gentile congregations. In general, the more anglicized the convert, the less likely he or she was to identify with a Hebrew Christian group. Thus, the children of such converts rarely remained members once they reached maturity, for unlike their parents they were both English and Christian from the start. Hebrew Christianity was then very much a one-generation phenomenon, although it never died out completely, since there were always new converts to replace those who drifted away.

A further consequence of the marginality of converts such as these was
the disproportionate number who, rather than making their way in the
world on their own, became employees of the missionary societies that
were responsible for their conversion or became clergymen and then devoted their careers to missionary activity. Those without much education
or with limited ambition frequently found employment as tract distributors, colporteurs, translators, clerks, teachers, interpreters, printers, binders, scripture readers, cooks, watchmen, and superintendents. These positions, a critic and former employee of the London Society wrote in 1858,
were the "minor prizes" held out to poor Jews as "a tempting reward for
their apostacy." The richest prize, he noted, was the opportunity of becoming a missionary to the Jews and a clergyman of the Church of England—
an opportunity that a striking number of converts of foreign birth exploited
in the Victorian period. Moses Margoliouth estimated in 1851 that there
were more than forty Church of England clergymen of Jewish origin. In
an address to the tenth annual meeting of the British Society two year later,
the Rev. Baptist Noel stated that there were fifty Anglican clergymen and
twenty dissenting ministers who were born Jews. By the 1870s, the Rev.
Albert Augustus Isaacs estimated, there were about 100 former Jews
among the clergy of the established church.[36]

Not all of these former Jews were employed as missionaries; some, probably a minority, were engaged in more-conventional clerical activity. But
most of those who were ordained as clergymen ended up in one kind of
missionary work or another. This is not surprising. The missionary societies needed converts in order to carry out their work both at home and
abroad. Without them they could not operate their far-flung networks of
stations in Central and Eastern Europe and the Near East and their scattered outposts in Asia and the Indian subcontinent, as well, of course, as
their missions in London and other British cities. Gentile agents were usually ignorant of Jewish languages and habits and generally incapable of establishing the initial contacts that might lead to further involvement with
the missionary societies. They were also insufficiently familiar with the
original text of the Hebrew Bible to be able to confound Jewish objections
to its christological exposition. Jewish agents, on the other hand, could
more easily establish rapport with potential inquirers, not only because
they were themselves Jewish, but also because they had once been in the
same position as the objects of their attention. Thus converts with a good
Hebrew education and the potential for becoming clergymen were taken
under the wing of the missionary societies, coddled and comforted, their
future painted in the most glowing terms. They were tutored in English,
provided with a secular education, sent to theological colleges to prepare
for ordination, and virtually guaranteed respectable, if not highly remunerative, employment, in one of the scores of domestic and foreign mission-

ary stations that were opened in the Victorian period. After his baptism in April 1838, Moses Margoliouth was given instruction in English, Latin, and Greek, and in January 1840 he was sent to Trinity College, Dublin. In 1843, he became instructor of Hebrew, German, and English at the Liverpool Institution for Inquiring Jews and from 1844 held various curacies in Ireland and England. At the same time, he devoted himself to various literary projects (such as a Hebrew Christian monthly magazine and a Hebrew translation of the New Testament) to advance the missionary enterprise. Isaac Edward Salkinson, whose exposure to secular learning before his arrival and baptism in London in 1849 was sporadic, was educated at the British Society school there and then sent to the Presbyterian theological college in Edinburgh. He was ordained a Presbyterian minister and served a Glasgow congregation until 1862, when he was appointed head teacher at a school for missionaries in London. The managers of the British Society were greatly impressed by his learning and expected great things from Salkinson, so in the mid-1870s they sent him to do missionary work in Central Europe, first in Pressburg, then in Vienna, where he remained until his death, in 1883.[37]

Becoming a clergyman and entering the missionary field offered converts more than the opportunity for an otherwise unobtainable education and the prospect of comfortable employment. It also helped them to resolve the question of their ambiguous position in society. As clergymen in the employ of missionary organizations, their status and prospects were more or less fixed. Their immediate associates were persons like themselves or evangelical clergymen and lay benefactors with a commitment to Jewish mission. Their foreign origins and Jewish birth, which in other fields would have been obstacles to their success, were in the missionary world distinct assets. By remaining there, they isolated themselves from the difficulties of social integration that other occupations and activities would have presented; at the same time they guaranteed themselves respectable employment.

This preference for missionary work over other kinds of clerical employment may, in fact, reflect an explicit awareness that immigrant origins were a disadvantage in competing for more conventional posts—curacies, vicarages, and the like. Here the experience of Henry Aaron Stern is relevant. Stern, a native of Hesse Cassel who was baptized in London in 1840, devoted almost twenty-five years of his life to missionary work in difficult physical conditions in the Near East and Africa, at one time suffering imprisonment for several years in Ethiopia. He returned to London in 1868, his health broken, unable to continue his work in the field. He tried to find a suburban or country parish where his duties would not be exacting and where he might be in easy reach of medical care. His adventures abroad were well known, and many prominent persons, some with a considerable amount of church patronage at their disposal, pledged to help him. In the end, none of them did anything practical to find him a position. "Letters exist," his biographer wrote, "indicating how persons who volunteered 'to do anything in their power' professed to be powerless when it suited their convenience." The implication is that a missionary of immigrant Jewish origin, however strong his Christian faith, was not quite a gentleman and thus not a suitable candidate for appointment to a country vicarage.[38]

It is surely relevant that the three clergymen of immigrant Jewish background who succeeded in obtaining preferment in the Victorian church hierarchy made their careers outside Britain in ways that deviated from the usual patterns of church advancement. Michael Solomon Alexander became the first Anglican Bishop in Jerusalem in 1841, serving there until his death four years later, but his responsibilities, whatever his title, were those of a common missionary and little more. Isaac Hellmuth (b. 1820), a native of Warsaw, came to England in 1841 and was baptized soon thereafter in Liverpool by Henry Samuel Joseph. The young man settled in Canada a few years later, was ordained there, and advanced steadily up the ecclesiastical ladder, ending as Bishop of Huron from 1870 to 1883. But when he returned to England that year, the former bishop had to be content with a country living of no particular distinction. The third Anglican bishop of Jewish descent in the Victorian era—the Lithuanian-born, *yeshivah*-educated Samuel Isaac Joseph Schereschewsky (d. 1906)—never even set foot in Britain. Schereschewsky studied at the universities of Frankfurt and Breslau, emigrated to the United States, where he was baptized, studied for the ministry at the General Theological Seminary of the Episcopal church, and then sailed to China to do missionary work (among the Chinese, not the Jews). He prepared translations of the Book of Common Prayer and the Hebrew and Christian Bibles into Mandarin and was elevated to the Anglican bishopric of Shanghai.[39]

Anthony Trollope's portrait of the Rev. Joseph Emilius, "the fashionable foreign ci-devant Jew preacher," in *The Eustace Diamonds* (1873) and *Phineas Redux* (1874) suggests how unwilling respectable Victorians were to embrace upstart clergymen of Jewish birth as their social equals. The Hungarian-born Emilius achieves rapid fame one season as an eloquent Mayfair preacher. Yet, despite his pulpit success, he is not considered a gentleman. He is, rather, "a greasy, fawning, pawing, creeping, black-browed rascal." There is an "oily pretence at earnestness in his manner" that tells those who are themselves gentlefolk that he is not fit to associate with them. When the elderly Duke of Omnium hears that Lady Eustace, in a moment of weakness, has agreed to marry Emilius, the Duke asks Lady Glencora Palliser whether Emilius is a gentleman. "About as like a gentleman as you're like an archbishop," she replies.[40] Their marriage soon turns sour, in part because Emilius draws too freely on his wife's substantial income; Lady Eustace runs away from him after only twelve months of marriage, and not long after it is discovered that Emilius had been married to a Jewish woman in Bohemia before he came to England. If that is not enough to condemn him, it is also universally believed that he is responsible for the murder of Mr. Bonteen, a Liberal politician and friend of Lady Eustace, who was helping her uncover her husband's bigamous past.

The disproportionate number of converted immigrants who chose missionary careers may also have been due, to some degree, to the emotional turbulence that frequently accompanied their change of faith. Unlike converts from middle-class families long settled in England, these immigrants were raised in observant Jewish homes suffused with traditional attitudes and prejudices, homes in which conversion was regarded with unreserved horror as an act of treachery and rebellion. Even if they were personally alienated from Jewish practice before their baptism, their upbringing was such that it was unlikely that they could have shrugged off the powerful sentiments regarding apostasy that they had absorbed since childhood. To be sure, we have no evidence that they experienced guilt and remorse at the time of their conversion or in the years that followed, and yet it is impossible to believe that the past had no claims on them and that they were able to pass effortlessly from Judaism to Christianity without a thought of the world they had left behind. (If they were able to do so, then they were a most unusual group indeed.) If, then, apostasy did leave them with a sense of having betrayed those who had once been closest to them—especially their parents—then it is possible that entering the missionary field helped them assuage their guilt, for by doing so they were reassuring themselves that they had acted correctly. By becoming missionaries, they were declaring, in effect, that they were so convinced of the truth of their new faith—and the correctness of their decision—that they were not content merely to enjoy it themselves but were obliged to carry its message to their former brethren. The more Jews they themselves brought into the fold, the more they felt reassured that they had not erred, for now others also testified to the correctness of their change of faith by following in their footsteps.

Although a number of converts went on to become public advocates for their new faith, none developed into virulent antisemites, viciously slandering the Jewish people, as frequently happened in the Russian and Austro-Hungarian empires at this time. There some of the most bitter and dangerous public opponents of the Jews emerged from the ranks of recent converts: Jacob Brafman (d. 1877), forger of *The Book of the Kahal* (1869), a description of alleged Jewish machinations to dominate Russian society; Semyon Efron Litvinov (b. 1836), regular contributor to the antisemitic press of St. Petersburg in the 1880s and specialist in defaming rabbinic literature; Aaron Israel Breiman (Brimanus), author of the scurrilous *Der Judenspiegel* and Hebrew tutor to the antisemitic ultramontanist priest August Rohling, a professor at the German University of Prague who became notorious for his defense of the blood libel in the early 1880s. Renegades such as these did not exist in Britain, in much the same way that the radical antisemitism they peddled was also largely absent. Missionaries of Jewish background attacked the Jewish understanding of scripture as misguided and perverse and declared rabbinic customs to be foolish superstition, but they did not engage in wholesale defamation of the Jewish people, branding them a blight or a cancer destroying gentile society from within.

Indeed, the very opposite was the case. A surprising number of converts became public champions of Jewish interests and devotees of Jewish scholarship and modern Hebrew letters, even though they were no longer connected with the Jewish community in any real sense. When news of the Damascus blood libel reached London in 1840, Michael Solomon Alexander, then Professor of Hebrew and Rabbinical Literature at King's College, London, and the Rev. Alexander McCaul, author of the anti-rabbinic polemic *The Old Paths* (1836) and missionary for the London Society, organized a meeting of Jewish converts to protest the events in Damascus. Led by Alexander, fifty-seven of them signed a statement declaring that they had never heard of a Jewish practice of killing Christians or using Christian blood for ritual purposes.

A decade later Moses Margoliouth offered enthusiastic support for full Jewish emancipation in his three-volume *History of the Jews in Great Britain* (1851) and in his *Anglo-Hebrews: Their Past Wrongs and Present Grievances* (1856). In the latter work, the author condemned the harsh mistreatment of the Jews in medieval England, argued that contemporary Jews were entitled not only to an acknowledgment of the wrongs done to their ancestors but also to reparations for what they had lost, and condemned the London Society for opposing parliamentary attempts to remove the remaining legal obstacles to full Jewish participation in English society. Margoliouth was also an accomplished Hebrew scholar who attempted (but failed) to establish a society for promoting the study of Hebrew literature and reprinting scarce Hebrew works. His nephew, George Margoliouth (1853–1952), also a convert and Church of England minister, was a more-distinguished Hebraist; from 1891 to 1914 he was in charge of the Hebrew, Syriac, and Ethiopic manuscripts at the British Museum. Another nephew, Samuel David Margoliouth (1858–1940), also an orientalist, was a fellow of New College, Oxford, from 1880 and Laudian Professor of Arabic from 1889 until his retirement in 1937. The persecution of the Jews in Germany in the 1930s "haunted him like a passion," the classicist Gilbert Murray wrote in the *Dictionary of National Biography*, and "he worked for them as he had worked before for the Assyrians and Armenians."[41]

How different these converts were from the much larger number of converts who left Judaism for pragmatic reasons without the assistance of missionary organizations! The latter were hardly eager to parade their Jewish antecedents and did not step forward to denounce intolerance toward Jews in England or abroad. In this instance, the behavior of the young Disraeli was typical: he remained silent during the emancipation debates in the House of Commons during his first ten years there, speaking publicly in favor of emancipation only in 1847. (The mature Disraeli's flaunting of his

Jewishness is another matter altogether.) The majority of converts, unlike those gathered into the fold by missionaries, had already detached themselves from exclusively Jewish circles and abandoned Jewish worship and ritual some time before they formally accepted Christianity. Their Jewish interests were minimal or nonexistent. Not so those converts who joined the employ of the missionary societies. They were plucked from the very bosom of Jewry in the sense that they were taken into the church without having undergone significant acculturation or integration beforehand. Once made Christians, they exploited their former Jewishness (and, in the case of Salkinson, Alexander, the Margoliouths, and others, their knowledge of Hebrew and Jewish texts); it became the basis for their claim to employment and other special treatment. They thus remained attached to their people, if not to its religion, while most converts were quite content, if not eager, to let their origins be forgotten.

The arrival of several hundred thousand Jewish immigrants from Eastern Europe between 1870 and 1914 significantly altered the scope of missionary activity in England.[42] The newcomers settled in large manufacturing centers—Leeds, Manchester, Birmingham, Liverpool, and, above all, London—where they crowded together in generally squalid neighborhoods. The poverty and overcrowding of these immigrant "ghettos," their alien sounds and smells, their un-English appearance, focused unprecedented public attention, mostly unsympathetic, on Jews in general and on the new arrivals in particular. But for missionaries and their supporters, the emergence of densely populated, unassimilated, poverty-stricken immigrant quarters offered undreamed-of opportunities for bringing Jews in their very own backyard—rather than the teeming masses in Eastern Europe—to the light of Christianity. (It should be recalled that as English Jews became increasingly prosperous and respectable over the course of the century, they became increasingly inaccessible to missionary efforts to reach them. Thus the arrival of the immigrants was something of a godsend, so to speak, for the conversionists.)

Advocates of the missionary idea responded vigorously to the challenge. Before the onset of mass immigration, the London Society and the British Society were the only major conversionist organizations and the bulk of their funds and energies were directed toward work in larger and more-impoverished communities abroad. After 1870 they expanded the scope of their activities in London and other cities and devised new techniques and strategies to establish contact with the newcomers, but now they no longer had the field to themselves. Beginning in the 1870s and continuing until the outbreak of World War I, the number of domestic missions proliferated. At least a dozen new groups entered the field in London alone before the turn of the century. By 1914, over twice that number were operating there, in addition to which at least two dozen Anglican parishes, mostly in the East End, were receiving grants from the London Society or from two newly established missionary funds to support work among local Jews.[43]

The new missions were modest operations in comparison to their predecessors. Usually conducted by their founders, most of them confined their work to immigrant neighborhoods rather than seeking to evangelize Jews worldwide. Much of what they did differed little from previous missionary activity; like the London Society and the British Society, they distributed tracts and copies of the New Testament, held open-air meetings, provided material relief, sent preachers to small towns and villages, operated charity schools and vocational training schemes, etc. Yet they also developed a number of new programs—medical clinics, reading rooms, adult language classes, country holidays for children—whose ability to attract poor Jews (though not necessarily convert them) seriously worried the Jewish communal establishment.

The most effective of the new techniques was the provision of free medical care. Although missionaries in Africa and Asia had used medical care to win heathen souls since early in the century, this technique was not employed in Jewish work in England until 1880, when the Rev. John Wilkinson, a former missionary for the British Society and founder of the Mildmay Mission to the Jews, opened a free clinic at the mission in Philpot Street in the East End. Other conversionist groups soon followed suit. By 1912, there were seven medical missions in the East End, one in Soho, and one in Notting Hill. The number of Jews receiving free medical care at the missionary dispensaries was remarkable. In 1911, the Barbican Mission in Whitechapel Road recorded nearly 14,000 visits; the Mildmay Mission, 24,000 visits; the two dispensaries of the British Society (the Gilead Medical Mission in the East End and the Wingate McCheyne Memorial Mission in Soho), 9,000 visits; the East End Mission to the Jews in Lemon Street, 10,000 visits. In the same year doctors at the parochial dispensary for Jews at All Saints Church, Mile End New Town, treated 1,300 patients. The method of operation was similar at all the missions. Before patients were permitted to see a doctor, they were required to sit through a Christian service that included prayers, hymns, and a sermon, usually delivered in Yiddish. At some missions the doors were locked before the service began, so it was impossible to leave early.[44]

The success of the medical missions in attracting thousands of Jews to their premises was due above all to the fact that they provided care without charge. To the Jewish poor, this was a great boon, particularly since there were no comparable institutions supported by the Jewish community. (The Jewish Board of Guardians in London closed its medical department in 1873 and stopped giving medical relief of any kind in 1879. The Jewish Provident Dispensary in Leman Street, which was opened in 1897 to counter the influence of the medical missions, met with severe financial difficulties and was forced to close its doors after a few years of operation.[45]) The success of the medical missions rested on more than this, however. Patients were treated courteously and not required to wait hours before being seen, as was the case in other dispensaries serving the poor.

Yiddish-speaking doctors listened to complaints about their aches and pains with sympathy, conversed with them at leisure about their families and their personal affairs, and encouraged them to come again. As a committee of Jewish notables investigating missionary activity in 1912 concluded, "No general hospital, no public dispensary could be carried on under such conditions, if its objects were merely the care of the body." Perhaps because they took a personal interest in their patients and understood that "there is such a thing as curing by sympathy," as one witness told the committee, the doctors at the medical missions acquired a reputation among immigrant Jews for being particularly skilled practitioners, able to cure where others failed. The journalist Ralph L. Finn recalled that in his youth, in the 1920s and 1930s, some of the most devout Jews in the East End "worshipped" the doctors at the Catholic mission in Goolden Street.[46]

The thousands of Jews who sought care at medical missions seem generally to have been unaffected by the prayers and sermons they were forced to hear. Orthodox Jewish women came to the Catholic medical mission, Finn remembered, and "sang—or pretended to sing, or mouthed Yiddish words to—religious hymns; they looked at the forbidden pictures and images all around and they bore the illuminated texts, the figurines, the oil paintings and the prayers with fortitude." They and other patients viewed these attempts at proselytization as the price they had to pay to receive free medical care. They thought they would be fools to refuse something being offered for so very little and smiled at the credulity of those who were trying to win their souls. They sat politely and heard the sermons but did not really listen to them, or did not understand them, or chose not to understand them. Whatever the case, they left with no greater interest in changing their religion than when they arrived.[47]

In addition to the medical clinics, other mission programs were successful in attracting immigrants and their children. Free reading rooms provided books and newspapers, including conversionist literature, in Hebrew, Yiddish, Russian, and English. At the same time they also offered escape and shelter from the noise and crowds of the immigrant quarter. "Comfortably warmed in winter, well-ventilated in summer, liberally supplied with chairs and tables, provided with all sorts of Jewish periodical literature," a correspondent wrote to the *Jewish Chronicle* in 1904, "they form an attractive rendezvous for foreign Jews in leisure moments"— particularly for poor, unmarried men living in squalid lodgings. They were staffed by learned apostates, who welcomed and assisted new readers and were prepared to debate the merits of Judaism and Christianity with those whose curiosity was aroused by the conversionist literature scattered about.[48] Other programs also targeted specific segments of the immigrant community. Children were enticed to attend teas, lantern lectures, and holiday outings; mothers to attend sewing classes; newly arrived immigrants to attend English language lessons. Homes for orphans, the disabled, and the elderly were established, as were schools for youths wishing to learn a trade. In every case, the missions were successful in attracting Jews to their portals to the extent that they were able to meet needs that the Jewish community was either unable or unwilling to service.

A striking example of this can be be seen in the case of abandoned wives. Many immigrants sailed to the United States in search of better opportunities after having lived in England sufficiently long to save money for the fare. Most married men who made the journey left their families behind. When they obtained work, they sent money home, and, after a further period of time, they sent steamship tickets so their wives and children could join them. However, there were a striking number of husbands who took advantage of their initial separation to desert their families. The Jewish Board of Guardians generally refused to assist abandoned wives, believing that to support them would encourage the practice by offering a premium for wife desertion. As a consequence, many abandoned women went to the missionaries for assistance, in some especially desperate cases turning over to them their children to be raised as Christians in orphans' homes.[49]

The case of the Aaronsohn family dramatically illustrates the circumstances that could lead Jews to take such a step. Joseph Aaronsohn first made contact with the London Society in December 1891. His wife was in the Hoxton Lunatic Asylum at the time, and he was unable to take care of their two children, ages seven months and two and a half years. He wanted them to be put in one of the homes for Jewish children operated by the London Society, but his request was rejected because they were too young. Some time after his wife returned home, he sailed to the United States, leaving his family without any means of support. In June 1892, his wife turned to the London Society, which despatched a visitor to report on her condition: "The misery I found her in is inexpressible. Destitute of the means to obtain the most necessaries of her daily life, the children on the brink of death from sickness and want of food, without any friend to counsel or to advize, she, poor woman, is nearly as she was a few months ago, i.e., insane." The visitor gave her ten shillings, adding in his report, however, "But what is this trifle for such a heap of wretchedness?" In this case, the London Society declined to take advantage of her desperate situation and instead shamed the Jewish Board of Guardians into providing her with assistance.[50]

Yet, however successful the missions were as social service agencies, they were failures when it came to the actual business of making Jews into Christians. On this point, both Jewish and Christian observers (with the exception of those who operated or supported the missions) were in agreement. The Jewish committee surveying missionary activity in 1912 concluded that "the number of genuine conversions to be credited to missionary activity is extremely small," noting that the societies themselves were careful to avoid issuing precise statistics about the number of converts they had made. Charles Booth, in his survey of social conditions in East London, noted that despite the considerable material inducements offered, the number of converts was "infinitesimal," a fact, he added, "that throws an interesting side-light on the moral tenacity of the Jewish race." Or, as the Rev. Dimsdale, vicar of Christchurch, St. George's East, told the interviewer for the Booth study, conversionist work among the Jews was "quite hopeless"—it was "simply bribery" and none too effective at that.[51]

The few Jews converted by missionaries in the decades before World War I were overwhelmingly foreign-born, as was largely the case in earlier periods. The lay preacher and communal worker Oswald John Simon wrote tauntingly to the Rev. Aaron Emanuel Suffrin, a former Jew, in 1887, "You only get your converts now from countries like Germany, Russia, and Poland, where Jews are still degraded and oppressed, and not permitted to breathe free air." A "Jewish-Christian Observer," writing in a German conversionist periodical the following year, made essentially the same point: upper- and middle-class Jews, as well as poor Jews who had been settled in England for many years, were beyond the reach of missionaries.[52] Their rootedness in English and/or Anglo-Jewish society removed the likelihood that they would seek support or comfort from missionary agencies or respond to conversionist overtures. However, newly arrived immigrants without family and friends who faced starvation and were unable to obtain relief from Jewish social welfare agencies were very likely to turn to missionary groups. As a result, a few eventually became Christians. In the words of the Rev. M. Wolkenberg of Liverpool, a former Jew who superintended the work of the London Society in the North of England, "very rarely, if ever, is a Jew baptized, who has not been previously fed, lodged, clothed, and provided with pocket money. . . ."[53]

A noticeable number of those who took instruction in Christianity and even of those who actually changed their religion were patently insincere. Oswald John Simon, after interviewing the Jewish men living at the London Society establishment at Palestine Place in 1897, claimed that all the men he saw admitted residing there and being baptized because they had no other means of subsistence. (Simon also claimed that they were all willing to return to Judaism if he could offer them the same physical maintenance.[54]) Simon, like many in the Jewish community who doubted the possibility of Jews coming to an honest profession of Christianity, was predisposed to discover this kind of insincerity. But missionaries as well testified to its apparent growth at this time and repeatedly stressed the difficulty of weeding out the unscrupulous and the merely hungry from the true inquirers. When Adolf Brown (né Braun), age twenty-nine, a native of Poland, asked the London Society for aid and instruction in Christianity in September 1894, claiming that he had come to think a great deal about it from reading the Old and New testaments, the missionary interviewing him noted on his application that he knew little Hebrew, only a few stock Old Testament references, and virtually nothing of the New Testament. A few months later, when Berthold Beckhover, age eighteen, a native of Germany who had spent the previous two years in the United States, asked the London Society to admit him to the Rev. J. M. Eppstein's Wanderers' Home for Enquiring and Relieving Jews in Bristol, it was noted that he was "a regular heathen as regards knowledge of Judaism or Christianity." Eppstein was not eager to take Beckhover because he did not know him personally, and the last Jew sent to him by the London office was, in his words, "an out-and-out rascal" who "ran away on Christmas day after enjoying a good dinner and taking with him his Christmas presents."[55] That individual was undoubtedly one of the small number of Jews who supported themselves by converting over and over again in various towns, on each occasion receiving substantial help from private individuals or missionary agencies.[56]

After World War I, Christian efforts to evangelize the Jews weakened. The number of missions operating in the East End of London and other initially immigrant neighborhoods slowly declined; new strategies and techniques for bringing Christianity to the Jewish poor failed to materialize. The spiritual commitment and evangelical fervor that had sustained missionary work in the previous century were fading. Consequently, conversionist activity ceased to enjoy broad middle-class support and eventually became the hobbyhorse of dotty eccentrics. At the same time, the Jewish population that had provided the clientele for missionary activities—impoverished, unacculturated, recent immigrants—began to shrink. Passage of the Aliens Bill in 1905 slowed the influx of newcomers from Eastern Europe, as did the outbreak of World War I and later the closing of the Soviet Union's borders. In addition, even before the war, the more-prosperous and more-anglicized elements were beginning to move out of the immigrant ghettos and settle in middle-class residential areas that, while still Jewish, were not overwhelmingly so. This migration to new neighborhoods became even more pronounced in the 1920s and 1930s. At the same time those Jews who remained behind were also becoming increasingly anglicized and, if not prosperous, at least somewhat more comfortable. In short, with every decade, there were fewer and fewer poor, unanglicized Jews to respond to missionary offers of material assistance and spiritual comfort. However, as the children and grandchildren of the immigrants followed earlier generations of English Jews in the pursuit of material prosperity and social integration, they also began to contribute, although slowly at first, to the ranks of assimilated Jews who left their community of origins behind and merged into the English mainstream.

6

From World War I to
World War II

The influx of new arrivals from Eastern Europe permanently altered the character of the Jewish community in England. In 1870, before the first wave of emigration broke, there were only 60,000 Jews in Great Britain; at the outbreak of World War I, there were over a quarter of a million, most of whom were immigrants or the children of immigrants. The newcomers shattered the calm of Anglo-Jewish life, disrupting comfortable patterns, challenging established authority, acting as a creative, if unwelcome, leaven. By virtue of their numbers, they gave the community an over-whelmingly foreign-born and lower-class cast that was to disappear only in the middle decades of the twentieth century. Untouched by bourgeois standards of decorum and respectability, they injected vitality into the somnolent religious atmosphere that had become characteristic of the an-glicized community. Like their more numerous counterparts in the United States, they gave a warm reception to radical political causes—socialism, anarchism, Zionism—that in the eyes of the communal elite threatened to undermine Jewish status. Most critically, they ensured the survival of a vi-brant community for several more generations. For without this infusion of new blood, the small, increasingly secularized, native-born community, left to its own devices, would have dwindled considerably, as drift, defec-tion, and indifference took their toll.[1]

Adult immigrants from Eastern Europe, even after having been in Britain for several decades, had relatively little contact with gentile Englishmen (outside of purely instrumental contacts in the marketplace). This was be-cause they came to England in sufficiently large numbers and settled in sufficiently dense and compact communities—Whitechapel in London, the Leylands in Leeds, Red Bank and Strangeways in Manchester—that they had few needs that could not be satisfied among their own people. Cut off from the surrounding population by ethnicity, religion, language, and culture, they lived in a milieu shaped as much by their experience in East-ern Europe as by their new surroundings. These newcomers to the Anglo-Jewish community were obviously not candidates for absorption into the

English mainstream. Those few who became Christians through the efforts of missionaries were unable to merge into gentile circles, as we have seen, for baptism, whatever its import for their future salvation, was incapable of curing their poverty and erasing their foreign accent, manners, and deportment. Now, however, they were foreigners in a double sense, for their apostasy put them outside the pale of the Jewish community as well.

To say that the immigrants remained largely immune to the seductions of assimilation does not mean, however, that they were all pious guardians of Jewish custom and ritual, despite the popular myth to the contrary. To be sure, the religion they brought with them to England was a traditional Judaism not yet harmonized with Western notions of decorum, reason, and piety. Similarly, the religious institutions they established in their immigrant quarters—synagogues, elementary schools, advanced academies, study circles, ritual baths—were patterned after institutions in the towns and villages of Eastern Europe. But the hold of this form of Judaism and its institutions on their loyalties was not as universally strong as is sometimes imagined. Clearly some immigrants were as fervent in their observance of Jewish law as their ancestors had been a century earlier. Many more acknowledged the authority of traditional Judaism and observed the major festivals and dietary rules in a traditional fashion but failed to do so in a manner fully consistent with the requirements of Jewish law. Rumanian-born Maurice Samuel (1895–1972), who grew up in Manchester in the years before World War I, wrote many years later that the religious life of his family—which was in no way atypical—would have seemed "grotesquely eclectic or haphazard" to a traditional Jew. They ate only kosher foods but did not keep separate sets of dishes and utensils for meat and milk; they went to synagogue on the major festivals but stayed away on Friday evenings and Saturdays. Yet they fasted on Yom Kippur and the Ninth of Av, recited psalms on solemn and critical occasions (like births and serious illnesses), and rigidly observed traditional rites of mourning. His father, he recalled, "having lapsed into average piety from a higher standard in Rumania," no longer put on phylacteries and prayer shawl at home for weekday morning prayers although he still abstained from working and smoking on the Sabbath.[2] Perhaps a majority of immigrants were even more casual in their attitude toward traditional religious obligations. Most did not regularly attend Sabbath or festival services. On the first day of Passover in 1903, for example, according to a newspaper census of religious worship in London, only a quarter or so of the adult immigrant population attended synagogue. (Attendance on Rosh Ha-Shanah and Yom Kippur was, of course, much higher.) In the provinces the situation was not much different. In Sheffield, the majority of the members of the orthodox immigrant congregation worked on the Sabbath, most at their stalls in the market, and came to the synagogue only on Rosh Ha-Shanah and Yom Kippur and to say *kaddish* for deceased parents.[3] In addition, a small minority of radicals rejected Judaism altogether as a matter of principle and publicly mocked those who remained faithful to it. In short, the immigrant generation was not monolithically traditional in its religious outlook.

The breakdown of traditional practice and belief was not entirely a product of social and psychological dislocation engendered by migration and resettlement in a foreign land. Most immigrants were exposed to secularist critiques of traditional faith and practice before they left their homes in Eastern Europe, and some had already started to relax their observance of religious practices before emigrating. For others, settling in a country where communal religious standards were less rigorous offered an opportunity to abandon observances that seemed increasingly burdensome. There they could adopt a more-flexible attitude toward ritual and prayer without having to suffer social sanctions for flouting communal norms. As Harry S. Lewis (1861–1947), a resident of Toynbee Hall, noted in 1903, "It is a common saying amongst the foreign Jews that England is a 'freie Medinah'—a country where the restrictions of orthodoxy cease to apply. . . ." Or, in the words of Rabbi Samuel Jacob Rabbinowitz (1857–1921) of Liverpool, "Some . . . of our foreign ignoramuses think that in England one may do anything, that in England there is no God at all, that as soon as one crosses the Russian border everything becomes anarchic, that one is free and excused from everything."[4]

Hyperbole aside, Rabbinowitz's observation was on target. Many immigrants associated religious fundamentalism with life in the old country and, once settled in their new homes, adjusted their behavior to fit their new circumstances. To many of them—and even more to their children— punctilious piety was the hallmark of "the greener" (a term of reproach for freshly arrived newcomers unfamiliar with English or Anglo-Jewish ways). Native Jews living in areas of immigrant settlement—shopkeepers, porters, costermongers, bookmakers, small traders—were notoriously lax and by example reinforced the association between anglicization and a casual attitude toward religious matters. Ralph L. Finn, who grew up in Broughton Street in the East End during World War I and just after, recalled in his two volumes of memoirs that the English Jews in his neighborhood were very much "cockneyfied"—they ate pork and jellied eels, drank beer, went to synagogue only once or twice a year, did not send their children to afternoon Hebrew classes, and in general "were so incredibly naive about their own religion that you could tell them anything and get away with it."[5]

The relaxation of religious standards within the immigrant community, however, had little immediate impact on its ethnic cohesion. The immigrants were too much a foreign colony to sustain much leakage into the host society. So they remained apart, their sense of belonging to a separate people intact, despite their weakening attachment to the Jewish religion. Most of their children retained a clear sense of ethnic distinctiveness as well, seeing themselves as part of a well-defined group. If they remained in the immigrant neighborhoods in which their parents had first settled, they continued to live in largely Jewish surroundings. Ralph Finn had no real contact with non-Jewish boys until he left the Jews' Free School and entered the Davenant Foundation School in the Whitechapel Road. The novelist and dramatist Bernard Kops (b. 1926) recalled in his memoirs that in his youth in Stepney Green his whole world had been Jewish and that he began mixing with non-Jews only during World War II. At school and in the streets Jewish and gentile children occasionally played together but by the time they reached their teens such mixing tended to stop. "Adult standards had begun to prevail," the novelist Willy Goldman (b. 1911) wrote in his memoir of growing up in the East End. He and his friends associated from then on "with our own sort of people and in our own choice of places." There were "gentile" billiard halls and "Jewish" billiard halls, "gentile" dance halls and "Jewish" dance halls. Social intimacy between gentiles and Jews living in predominantly Jewish neighborhoods—and even those living in more-suburban surroundings—was not common. Most second-generation English Jews, like their counterparts in the United States, married within their own community and drew their close friends from within its boundaries as well.[6]

Although most second-generation Jews remained within the communal fold, they did not maintain the same emotional attachment to traditional religious observance that their parents had. Sons and daughters educated in both state and Jewish schools were exposed to anglicizing influences that weakened the hold of Old World attachments. Fluent in English, even if Yiddish remained the language of their homes, and familiar with life outside the workshops, tenements, and markets of the immigrant quarter, they became enthusiastic consumers of English popular culture. By the mid-1920s, for example, so many East End Jews were traveling by train to the Derby that the Southern Railway began printing its schedule for service to Epsom in Yiddish. Leeds Jews were equally enthusiastic about horse racing. "You need only be at any Leeds station when a racing 'special' is about to leave to realise this," the *Leeds Mercury* noted in 1925. For such Jews, the appeal of cinemas, dance halls, football stadiums, racetracks, billiard parlors, boxing arenas, theatres, libraries, political clubs, and gambling dens easily outstripped that of the synagogue and the religious life it represented. A governor of the Stepney Jewish Schools remarked in 1929: "In the past children used to learn a little Hebrew at home. Now they care for none of these things in the family circle—pictures, races, dances, recreation, anything but the old ways and the old faith." Selig Brodetsky (1888–1954), mathematician and Zionist leader, made much the same point the year before: "The road in which I live in Leeds, leading to and from the famous Headingley ground, is crowded every Saturday by *minyonim* if not by *millionim* of wandering Jews, upon whom the 'packele' of the Torah seems to sit very lightly indeed."[7] The same scene occurred in every large city where Jews lived in substantial numbers.

Observers of Jewish life in the interwar years repeatedly lamented the spread of religious ignorance and indifference among the offspring of the immigrant generation. "The average young Jewish boy or girl after leaving school and coming out into the world is drifting away more perceptibly than ever before from Jewish influence," a social worker wrote to the *Jewish Chronicle* in 1929. Brodetsky noted that "thousands of boys" and "tens of thousands of girls" were growing up in complete ignorance of "Jewish learning, life, and thought" and sinking naturally into "the ways of thought and life that surround them." Their Jewishness was, at best, "a thin thread of sentimental attachment, based almost always upon filial loyalty" to their people and "a meaningless, because unintelligent, pride in being Jews." A participant at a conference of Jewish preachers in London in 1927 singled out the lack of Sabbath observance as the great blot on the religious landscape of East End Jewry. A generation before Sabbath observance had been the rule and not the exception in the immigrant quarter. Now a market flourished on Saturdays along the Whitechapel Road, one of the area's principal thoroughfares. Two years earlier, at a similar gathering, Rabbi B. M. Michelson, an official of the United Synagogue, had sounded the same note: blatant disregard of the Sabbath was widespread in the East End—crowds of shoppers filled the streets, hundreds of children queued up at the doors of the cinemas. Many youth who did attend synagogue with their fathers did so primarily out of a sense of obligation and a desire to escape parental displeasure if they did otherwise. In his memoirs, the radical political activist Joe Jacobs (1913–1977) recalled that an East End comrade in the workers movement regularly attended synagogue with his father and younger brother right up to the time when he became a full-time functionary in the Young Communist League. Like other young men who acted similarly, "he did not wish to meet his father's wrath and upset his mother."[8]

Communal and parental efforts to provide the new generation with a sound Jewish education—and thereby enable them to participate in Jewish religious life—were a massive failure. Immigrant parents struggling to survive in a harsh economic climate wanted their children to acquire skills that would enable them to succeed. This, along with their own diminishing commitment to religious observance (however strong their sense of ethnic solidarity), meant that they assigned far less importance to their children's Jewish education than to their secular education. Most children who received some Jewish education—and many did not—were enrolled in afternoon and Sunday classes. But whether these classes were modern or traditional in character, they were notably unsuccessful in instilling religious knowledge and commitment. They tended to utilize primitive methods of instruction and to be taught by persons with few qualifications for teaching the young. Their charges sensed, moreover, that what they were learning was of little utility in the workaday world and was not a matter of high priority with their parents.[9]

The *hadarim* (traditional one-room schools for teaching the elementary

texts of Judaism), to which many immigrants sent their children four after-
noons a week and on Sundays, were particularly unsuccessful in arousing
a commitment to religious learning and observance and earned the contempt of most English-born youth who attended them. They met in
shabby, poorly ventilated, uncomfortable quarters—cellar kitchens, dis-
used workshops, or more frequently the cramped dwellings of the teachers
(*melamdim*). The latter were usually pious immigrants, ignorant of the English language and of the popular culture of their anglicized students, who
were unable to find more remunerative work in trade or industry. They
employed brutal teaching methods that did more to alienate their pupils
from Judaism than act as conduits for its transmission. The novelist Willy
Goldman, who attended *heder* in the East End of London in the 1920s, described the typical *melamed* as "a bearded, unkempt, smelly old man in his
dotage, [who] mumbled at you for hours on end out of a large book. You
had to repeat his mumbles after him. When you mumbled wrong or took
a slight rest from mumbling you received a clout across the ear. It was calculated that being mumbled at for several years would by some mysterious
process turn you into an enlightened and pious Jew." Hebrew classes
taught in this fashion were, in Ralph Finn's words, "a joke." He and his
friends regarded *heder* as "a necessary evil" and "a source of resentment,"
a place where they could behave in ways that they would not have risked
at school, pulling outrageous pranks, mercilessly taunting the teacher, ne-
glecting their work. Goldman, writing in 1940, believed that this system
of after-school education was responsible for "the large-scale reduction in
piety amongst the new generation of adult Jews to-day," for it had created
a permanent association in their minds between religious observance and
"memories of stuffy cellars, perpetual beatings, and a brutal curbing of our
childish instincts."[10] He was, in part, correct, although the *hadarim* alone
were obviously not responsible for the advance of religious indifference.

Many parents failed to provide their children with Jewish education of
any kind. In the late-1920s in Manchester and Salford, for example, only
1,500 children out of a school-age population of 5,500 were receiving any
organized Hebrew instruction. For the country as a whole the number receiving any Jewish education at the time was only 14,000—out of a school-
age population that was at least several times that size. Parents failed to
make provision for the Jewish education of their offspring either because
they could not afford the expense or because they themselves were indifferent or even actively hostile to religious practices. Bernard Kops's father,
a frequently unemployed leather worker, was fond of announcing that religion was "a lot of tommy rot" and a luxury that poor people could not
afford. His mother, who was more sympathetic to Judaism—she lit candles
on Friday evenings, for example—sent Bernard to *heder* once or twice, but,
as he wrote, "the Hebrew symbols were meaningless to me, and the call
of the streets was stronger than the call of God." When the Hebrew teacher
showed up at their door, asking where the truant was and whether his

parents were not concerned about his Hebrew education and bar mitzvah, his father replied: "Would that butter his bread? A poor boy can't afford to be religious." Mark Strong, the central character in Alexander Baron's autobiographical novel, *With Hope, Farewell* (1952), is completely ignorant of Hebrew and Jewish lore because his English-born parents never bother "with all the queer religious things and holidays that he had seen and heard of in other Jewish homes." His father, a high-class ladies' tailor with a workshop in his Hackney home, reasons: "I teach my boys the difference between right and wrong. What should I fill their heads up with religion for?"[11]

Among second-generation Jews who became alienated from Jewish observance there was a small minority who abandoned their ethnic roots as well and either drifted or plunged, the circumstances varying from case to case, into non-Jewish circles. As in earlier periods of Anglo-Jewish history, the commonest form their disengagement took was intermarriage. Although no records of mixed marriage were kept, it is possible to gain some idea of the extent of such unions in another way. In 1929, according to the registrar-general, there was a total of 1,581 marriages performed under Jewish auspices in London and the five Home Counties. Allowing a small deduction for those that took place in Southend, it is reasonable to estimate 1,570 as the figure for Greater London, which yields a marriage rate of 15.0 persons per 1,000 of population. In the same year, the marriage rate for the County of London, where the proportion of persons in marriageable age groups was slightly less than in the Jewish population, was 19.1 persons per 1,000 of population. One plausible explanation for the gap between the two figures is that a small minority of Jews who were marrying were choosing to do so without benefit of a Jewish ceremony. Since it is unlikely that many marriages between Jews took place without a religious ceremony, these persons were probably marrying Christians. The figure for Jewish marriages includes, of course, unions between Jews from well-established families as well. However, since these families were in the minority in the London community, the gap between the Jewish and general rates also reveals, however imprecisely, something about the extent of intermarriage among the offspring of the East European immigrants.[12]

Further evidence of the extent of intermarriage among this generation comes from a study of Jewish soldiers in the British army who were patients in the neurosis wards of Sutton Emergency Hospital during the years 1944 and 1945. Only one of the fifty men studied was the product of a mixed marriage. However, of the 160 marriages contracted by the patients and their siblings—most of whom we can assume were second-generation English Jews of East European origin—twenty-eight were to non-Jews, an incidence of approximately 17 percent. Although the sample was small and the objection might be raised that there could be a connection between exogamous marriage and neurosis (of which there is no indication), its findings do corroborate the evidence from 1929: intermarriage, if not threatening the fabric of the community before the end of World War II, was not infrequent either. (In fifteen of the twenty-one mixed marriages that had produced children at the time, the children were being raised as Christians.[13])

Religious leaders and other contemporary observers frequently noted that intermarriage was no longer confined exclusively to the older sections of the community but was making inroads among families of more recent settlement as well. The Rev. M. L. Perlzweig told a B'nai B'rith meeting in 1931 that the problem of intermarriage was as acute in the East End as in the West End. In an essay on East London Jewry written for *The New Survey of London Life & Labour* in 1934, Henrietta Adler (1868–1950), daughter of the late-Victorian chief rabbi and a prominent communal worker in her own right, reported that her informants believed that religious indifference was producing an increase in intermarriage. Joe Jacobs, who (unlike Adler) was not an outsider in the East End, came to much the same conclusion: parental opposition was becoming increasingly ineffective and "many" mixed marriages were taking place. Toward the end of World War II, a meeting between the London Bet Din (ecclesiastical court) and representatives of the Board of Deputies was convened to discuss intermarriage and conversion. Dayan I. Abramsky remarked that the number of intermarriages before the war was already disquieting and that their increase during the war was due to the dispersal of young Jews in the armed forces.[14]

When the children of families of recent settlement intermarried, they were rarely moved to do so by conscious or programmatic motives to bury their Jewish roots and blend into the mainstream. Rather, intermarriage came about as a natural consequence of intimate social contacts with gentiles, which, while hardly the rule for those living in predominantly Jewish neighborhoods, were not altogether absent either. English-born youth who spent their Saturday nights in dance halls, cinemas, and cafes outside immigrant areas occasionally met and fell in love with persons who were not Jewish. This is what happened, for example, to the East End garment worker Alec, the central figure in *Jew Boy* (1935), a proletarian novel by Simon Blumenfeld (b. 1907). Those who worked in factories and offices with a mixed or largely gentile work force also risked falling in love with young people from outside their community. Similarly, those who drifted into unsavory or criminal ways of living, such as gambling, bookmaking, and prostitution, were also more likely to establish close ties to non-Jews than those employed in "Jewish" trades like tailoring and cabinetmaking. Many of the 200 or so gambling dens (*spielers*) that dotted the East End of London in the interwar period, for example, attracted a mixed clientele. In Willy Goldman's novel of East End Jewry in the mid-1930s, *A Start in Life* (1947), young Yasha Gompers, son of a Petticoat Lane stall holder, starts going with a gentile girl whom he meets at a billiard hall cum gambling den. She herself comes from a respectable Yorkshire working-class background but in London has taken up with a gang of small-time Jewish hoodlums. The oral memoirs of Arthur Harding (b. 1886), a well-known figure in the East End underworld, testify repeatedly to the close links that frequently developed between Jewish and non-Jewish criminals. In the 1920s, for example, Jewish and Italian gangs worked together offering "protection" to racecourse bookmakers. In his memoirs, Harding cited at least a dozen instances of Jewish-gentile marriages in the East End underworld.[15]

In general, Jews who found employment outside "ghetto" trades or who moved to more attractive residential neighborhoods were more likely to intermarry than those who remained behind in familiar surroundings. In the interwar period substantial numbers of men and women from the second generation were entering occupations that brought them into intensive, daily contact with the larger world. The retiring headmaster of the Jews' Free School in London noted in 1930: "Fifty years ago, a boy, however clever in his work at school, would become a tailor, a furrier or a cabinet-maker. To-day many of my boys have become accountants, architects, chemists, and dentists. Others go into drawing offices or become mechanical or motor engineers. The field has enormously enlarged."[16] Young women as well found employment—as teachers, sales clerks, secretaries—in surroundings far removed from the immigrant neighborhoods of their parents. Lacking strong religious commitments that would prevent them from entering into intimate relationships with non-Jews, some of these young people inevitably married persons outside their own community. Parents who strongly opposed intermarriage and were keenly aware that the entry of the younger generation into new occupations increased its probability often took steps to keep their children in "Jewish" trades. Joe Jacobs recalled that his future father-in-law, an East End waistcoat maker, cut short the entertainment career of his eldest daughter, Becky, for this reason. Becky was a budding dancer and singer on the variety stage—she appeared under the name Betty Moore—but when her father heard that a female cousin, a violinist in a band, had run off with a gentile while on tour in Buxton, Derbyshire, he decided that no daughter of his was going on tour unaccompanied. So Becky gave up her career on the stage and went into her father's workshop. In Orthodox families some fathers kept their sons from pursuing professional careers because they felt that such employment would result in their rapid assimilation. In the prewar period, Polish-born Henry Bloomstein, a processor of rabbit down, was so determined that his sons not become doctors or lawyers that he removed them from school at an early age. To the dismay of the headmaster of the Cowper Street Grammar School, he pulled out one of his most talented sons at age fourteen, although the boy was at the top of his class. Similar episodes occurred in other Orthodox families.[17]

Equally potent in diluting the ethnicity of Jews of East European descent was the removal of the more-prosperous elements of the community to middle- and lower middle-class neighborhoods whose ambience and population were less markedly Jewish. Before World War I, the number of East European Jews sufficiently prosperous to move away from the immigrant "ghettos" was quite small. The war, however, with its demand for shirts, coats, trousers, boots, and other items of apparel, brought prosperity to considerable numbers of small factory owners. Riding "the crest of the khaki boom,"[18] they launched an exodus from the old immigrant neighborhoods that continued unabated throughout the interwar years and beyond, fueled by both material prosperity and occupational diversification. (German bombing raids during World War II greatly accelerated the process, of course.) The population of the borough of Stepney, for example, dropped from a peak of 299,000 in 1901 to 225,000 in 1931. While not attributable to Jewish dispersion alone, the decrease would hardly have been as dramatic without it. The Jewish school-age population in the East End dropped even more markedly. By the early 1930s seven of the eleven elementary schools in Jewish areas had been put to other uses, while enrollment at the Jews' Free School, which was full to overflowing at the turn of the century, fell from 3,500 to 1,700. One further striking indicator of residential dispersion during this period is the decline in the population of the immigrant quarters relative to areas of secondary and tertiary settlement. In London, for example, 90 percent of the Jewish population lived in the eastern districts in 1889 but only 60 percent by the early 1930s.[19]

As was the case with previous waves of suburbanization among English Jews, the newly prosperous tended to cluster together rather than scatter at random, so that some new areas of settlement became disproportionately Jewish in their makeup—Stoke Newington and Stamford Hill in London, Chapeltown in Leeds, Cheetham Hill in Manchester, to cite a few examples. Yet not all of those who joined the exodus took up residence among their fellow Jews. In London, the dispersion by the mid-1930s had reached Finchley and Hornsey to the north, Ealing and Richmond to the west, and Croydon, Surbiton, and Kingston to the south. Those who moved to suburbs such as these, even if they went to the effort of joining a synagogue, were bound to interact more frequently with the non-Jewish population than if they had remained behind in the old neighborhood or settled in a new neighborhood overwhelmingly Jewish in complexion. As a writer in *The Times* remarked in 1924, "Whatever the strength of his Judaism the middle-class Jew who settles outside the largely Jewish areas is bound to see more of the Gentile, and I think it would be rather an exception to find a Jewish family established for more than a few years in London outside the Jewish areas of East London and a few smaller settlements who had not Gentile friends as well as acquaintances." Those who remained in the East End, the writer added, had no inducement and little opportunity to make friends outside their own community.[20]

It would be wrong to infer that all those who moved to suburban districts did so in order to shake off their inherited Jewishness and blend into the surrounding population. Were this true, those who moved away would have chosen districts that were less distinctively Jewish in their makeup. Their aim, rather, was to move to healthier and more socially desirable areas and not to non-Jewish surroundings *per se*.[21] The Lakarins, in Charles Landstone's *Blue Tiger Yard* (1927), having prospered in the manufacture of "khaki tunics, army boots, service caps, [and] swagger canes" and subsequently in real estate speculation, move to Highbury New Park in 1917 because "residence in the East End no longer engendered any respect" and because Mrs. Lakarin wants to catch a real English Jew (rather than the son of a recent immigrant) as a husband for her daughter and knows that "no decent English Jew will come to Blue Tiger Yard." Once settled in their new surroundings, the Lakarins continue to mix largely with other Jews. Daughter Becky, for example, is sent to an expensive Jewish boarding school in Brighton to learn how "to do her hair in the latest fashion and to dance the latest dances."[22]

Like the fictional Lakarins, most second-generation English Jews of East European origin remained within the communal fold. Still, the fact that many of them were now living in districts that were less markedly Jewish meant that their intercourse with the gentile world was more extensive than before. Zena Marenbon's memoirs of growing up in Liverpool in the 1920s are instructive on this point. Marenbon's maternal grandparents were pious and mostly unchanged in their "old country" ways: they spoke Yiddish to each other; the grandfather kept his head covered; the grandmother wore a *shaitel* (wig). His reputation as a Talmudist was such that traditional Jews from as far away as Manchester and Southport traveled to his home in Fairfield to study with him. Marenbon's own parents, however, while hardly in flight from their Jewishness, were decidely less observant. For example, they celebrated the Sabbath with a festive Friday evening meal but kept their store open—it was in a gentile district—on Saturdays. The family moved from the rooms above their store to better housing in a nicer, though still gentile, neighborhood when Marenbon was a young girl, and she started at the Vale House School for Girls. At the time she was the only Jewish girl in the school, and most of her friends in her early teen years were not Jewish. When she was asked for the first time to a Saturday night party to which both boys and girls were invited, her parents were not keen on her going and told her, "It's time you started mixing in a Jewish circle." They feared what in fact actually happened: her first boyfriend was a Roman Catholic. Knowing their reaction in advance, she kept the entire matter a secret from them. Yet it was their decision to live in a largely gentile neighborhood and to enroll her in an exclusively gentile school that prepared the way for the kind of social mixing that they were now telling her to abandon.[23]

Residential dispersion and occupational diversification were the two most important avenues by which the children—and eventually grandchildren—of East European immigrants were brought into more intensive contact with the larger society. For a much smaller number of the second generation there were as well two other paths "out of the ghetto"—the world of radical politics and the world of literature and art. Both were spheres of activity that stood outside the common run of everyday experience and above the usual divisions separating the mass of Jews from their fellow citizens. They were realms in which Jews and gentiles mixed more or less freely and intimately because the nature of the activity in which they were engaged was self-professedly universal, rendering irrelevant, in theory, the background and inheritance of the participants. Involvement in either sphere did not require Jews to abandon their religion in any formal sense, although most had ceased to be practicing Jews beforehand, nor did it inevitably lead to social estrangement from kith and kin and eventual intermarriage, although such was frequently the outcome. But without exception, immersion of this kind diluted feelings of Jewish solidarity and cohesion, in much the same way that it had in earlier periods of English Jewish history.

The career of the painter Mark Gertler (1891–1939) illustrates how absorption into artistic and literary circles eroded links to the Jewish community. Gertler was born in Spitalfields and was educated at local schools, where he received some rudimentary drawing lessons. He left school at age fourteen, intent on becoming an artist, and refused to take the clerkship his father had found for him in a timber firm. His family could not understand his determination to become a painter and was not supportive initially, never having heard of anyone studying to become a professional artist. In Gilbert Cannan's thinly disguised fictional account of Gertler's early years, *Mendel* (1916), Mendel's family cannot comprehend what the hero means when he first announces that he wants to be an artist. "An artist? Nobody knew quite what that meant. Golda [Mendel's mother] thought it meant painting pictures, but she could not imagine a man devoting all his time to it—a child's pastime." When Mendel repeats that he is going to be an artist, his brother replies, "But you've got to make your money like everybody else." Alive and sensitive to cultural currents outside the East End, Mendel suffers terribly from the cramped and restricted life of his "ghetto" surroundings—"the dreadful monotony of the home, of the talk, of the squabbles: human life forced to be as dull as that of the God who no longer interfered in human life."[24]

Gertler's family eventually agreed to give him a chance, and he enrolled in art classes at the Regent Street Polytechnic, but after a year and a half their money ran out. At age sixteen, Gertler was force to take a job with a manufacturer of stained glass (although he continued to study painting at night). He then applied, successfully, to the Jewish Educational Aid Society for a grant, and in the fall of 1908 started at the Slade School of Fine Art, where he studied until February 1912. He was an immediate success there both artistically and socially. His romantic good looks, conversational gifts, vitality, charm, and talent as an artist won him many friends among students, although he had never mixed in non-Jewish society before enrolling at the Polytechnic. He fell in love with a fellow student, Dora Carrington, but she preferred Lytton Strachey (who, for his part, preferred men). Just after acquiring his first studio (in Commercial Street in the East End) Gertler wrote appreciatively to William Rothenstein, who was supervising his progress for the Jewish Educational Aid Society: "Just one other thing that makes me so happy, that is my nice friends amongst the upper class. They are so much nicer than the rough 'east ends' I am used to."[25]

Through the friends he made at the Slade and the attention his work attracted in the art world, Gertler became an intimate of social circles far removed from those in which he had grown up. In 1913, for example, he was taken up by the well-connected art patron and civil servant Edward Marsh, through whom he met the writer Gilbert Cannan. The latter introduced him to Lady Ottoline Morrell and her salon, where he eventually met members of the Bloomsbury set. She became a lifelong friend and patron, offering Gertler the hospitality of her Oxfordshire home, Garsington Manor, whenever he wished. He stayed there for many weeks at a time every summer between 1917 and 1928, when she sold the house. Similarly, his friendship with Gilbert Cannan and frequent visits to the latter's converted mill house at Cholesbury, Buckinghamshire, in 1914 and 1915 brought Gertler into contact with a little circle of writers that had gathered there—John Middleton Murry, Katherine Mansfield, and D. H. Lawrence. Lawrence liked Gertler enormously and later drew on him as a model for the sculptor Loerke in *Women in Love* (1921).[26]

As Gertler's circle of well-born and culturally distinguished friends expanded, the character of life in the Jewish East End increasingly repelled him. The surroundings in which he had been raised now appeared to him narrow and sordid. When he was about to leave the East End in January 1915 and take a studio in Hampstead, he wrote to Dora Carrington that he was "immensely relieved" to be leaving the district and his parents. He had felt "stifled by everything here in the East End, worried by the sordidness of my family, their aimlessness, their poverty, and their general wretchedness." In Hampstead, he imagined, he would be "free and detached," belonging to no parents. Echoing a fantasy common to many Jewish writers and artists seeking to rise above their Jewish origins, he wrote: "I shall be neither Jew nor Christian and shall belong to no class. I shall be just myself and be able to work out things according to my own tastes."[27]

As Gertler distanced himself from the world of immigrant Jewry, he did not move correspondingly closer to well-to-do West End Jewish circles, among whom he had found patrons in his early years. Their milieu was as distasteful to him as that of the immigrants. They were, in his view, boors and philistines, patronizing and condescending. If Gilbert Cannan's fictional account of Gertler's early years is to be believed, Gertler had good reason to feel that way. In the novel, Mendel Kuhler's patrons, the

Birnbaums and Fleischmanns, begin inviting the artist to their country homes after he achieves some success—but they put him up in a servant's bedroom or a gardener's cottage since they cannot forget his East End origins. *"The worst kind of person is the rich English Jew*!!!*,"* Gertler wrote in 1913 to Dorothy Brett, a fellow Slade student and daughter of Lord Esher, after having received a letter from "one lady of that class" condemning a picture of his. "She said she had been and seen my 'New English' picture [that is, one exhibited at the New English Art Club] and that she thinks my eyes *must be wrong* to paint like that, and that I would do her a great favour if I would—at her expense—see an oculist!"[28]

Yet for all his distaste for West End "philistinism" and East End "sordidness," Gertler could not pretend that he had achieved Olympian detachment, becoming "neither Jew nor Christian." He remained close to his parents, with whom he continued to converse in Yiddish, his siblings, and their children, visiting them frequently. Though he himself had lost all interest in religion, he still took pleasure in joining his religiously observant parents for Friday evening meals and watching his mother light the Sabbath candles. When his father died in 1917, Gertler described Jewish mourning customs to Dora Carrington and explained that he too would be keeping them up to some extent "for the sake of my mother and also because I somehow want to. I shall not shave, probably for a week, and shall be going down to my people every day for that time to mourn with them."[29] Indeed, his desire to please his mother was such that he once became engaged to a Jewish woman whom he did not love largely because he felt that life with her would both give him a secure place among his family and please his mother. (He broke the engagement not long after, realizing that it had been made for the wrong reasons.) When, at age forty, he decided to marry Marjorie Hodgkinson, he was very anxious about his family's reaction (his four siblings had all married Jews), and though he intended to go ahead with the marriage, he considered their feelings in choosing the kind of ceremony he and Marjorie would have. A very pious Roman Catholic aunt of hers insisted that they be married in a Catholic church and that any children be raised as Catholics. Gertler was himself willing to have a church ceremony but feared that his family would never forgive him; and bringing up their children as Roman Catholics was out of the question. As he wrote to a close friend, "I couldn't hurt my mother to that extent." In the end, he and Marjorie were married by the British consul in Paris.[30]

The dilemma facing Gertler was common to most artists and writers from working-class backgrounds, Jewish or otherwise, catapulted by success into social circles radically different from those in which they had been raised. But for Jewish writers and artists the gap between their former and current circumstances had an additional dimension—their success separated them from family members not only in terms of culture, status, and wealth but also in matters of religion, ethnicity, and (in many cases) language. Literary and artistic success brought in its wake integration into wealthy gentile circles, not wealthy Jewish circles. (In Central Europe, where Jews played a critical role in cultural life at this time, as both producers and consumers, the situation was fundamentally different. There, many Jewish writers and artists continued to mix in largely Jewish circles even after having achieved public recognition.) If Gertler and other children of the immigrant quarter had been able to leave their former selves and all their previous attachments behind them as they journeyed outward and upward, then their full integration into gentile circles would not have posed any emotional problems for them. But most neither could nor wanted to do so. Gertler himself recognized that the distance he had traveled since his youth was a source of inner turmoil, and at one point he even suggested that his life would have been more stable emotionally if he had never left the unpretentious Jewish milieu in which he had grown up. He wrote to a friend in 1919 that coming into contact with his family was always "*most* distressing"—even though he loved them—and that the reason for this was that he had become "so very different." Yet, he continued, he felt there was "some ghastly link" between him and them: "A link which one cannot shake off altogether, and so one feels it would have been better either not to have changed from them at all, or having changed, the link should automatically have broken itself; but no a sort of link *does* persist in remaining."[31]

While immersion in cultural, intellectual, or scientific activity usually resulted in a weakening of Jewish attachments and, not infrequently, full estrangement from the community, few in the second generation drifted away in this fashion—largely because the number of Jews who moved outside the usual range of Jewish occupations, let alone studied at university or devoted themselves to the arts, was quite small, certainly by comparison to what was happening in the United States. One cannot speak of London Jewish intellectuals, for example, in the way one can of Berlin or New York Jewish intellectuals. The offspring of the immigrant generation in Britain left no *collective* mark on cultural or intellectual life. There were, of course, artists and writers among the second generation who received recognition outside their own community—Mark Gertler, David Bomberg, Isaac Rosenberg, Louis Golding, to name the most prominent—but they were in every way exceptional. An apologetic survey of Jewish contributions to British scientific and artistic life issued by the Board of Deputies in 1938 to combat domestic antisemitism included a mere handful of names from this generation.[32]

The relative absence of intellectual and cultural creativity in what was now the largest part of Anglo-Jewry was not at all remarkable in one sense, for English Jews at no time in their history rivaled their counterparts in other westernized communities in scholarly or cultural activity. By comparison with communities on the Continent, that in England had always been intellectually and culturally impoverished, producing few artists, writers, scientists, or even students of Jewish history and literature. Indeed, the most-learned practitioners of Jewish scholarship in England in the nineteenth and early twentieth centuries were foreign-born, the products of communities with richer intellectual resources and traditions. The readership in rabbinics at Cambridge, for example, was allowed to lapse in the 1920s because English Jews would not contribute the few hundred pounds needed each year to support it. Gertler's indictment of Anglo-Jewry for philistinism was not the result of personal pique alone; others more intimately involved in communal life were saying similar things. Selig Brodetsky charged that the much-vaunted Jewish passion for study at school and university was nothing but a rush to enter the professions rather than a reflection of a genuine love of learning. The Jewish community, he thought, admired financial success primarily and acknowledged the achievements of learned Jews only if they first received recognition at the hands of the non-Jewish world. "But Jewish scholars whose learning or whose circumstances are incompatible with such external recognition," he wrote in 1928, "languish in poverty, and suffer the contempt of their financial 'betters.' "[33]

The disinclination of English Jews to pursue cultural and intellectual interests, both Jewish and general, was a long-standing one. In earlier periods, it was due to some extent to the fact that Anglo-Jewry was a new community on the periphery of the settled Jewish world without well-established traditions of piety and scholarship. Jews who emigrated to England were usually young adults in search of better economic opportunities, persons without a firm stake in their native communities and thus more likely to be unlearned than learned. In addition, because English Jews faced relatively little opposition to their integration into the mainstream of society, they were not forced to defend themselves or their religion in a sustained, systematic, intellectual fashion. There was no persistent public debate in the late-Georgian and Victorian periods about the character of Judaism and its adherents, and so there was no external pressure for Jews to engage in a serious examination of Jewish thought, history, and identity, as was the case in Germany, for example, where *Wissenschaft des Judentums* was a weapon in the battle for Jewish emancipation.

The absence of rabid hostility also meant that at most times there was no pressure for Jews to change their traditional occupational profile and seek new avenues of employment outside commerce and finance. The cultural stigma attached to business enterprise and the pursuit of profit was quite mild by comparison with other countries in Europe, and thus few Jews sought to advance their social standing by taking up occupations that required advanced education, such as law, medicine, literature, the civil service, and the academy. Few English Jews, in other words, received the kind of education that would prepare or incline them to treat intellectual or cultural issues in a serious manner. Moreover, few English Jews viewed mastery of English or European high culture as a passport to social integration. The reference groups in English society for most Jews with social aspirations would not have been impressed by such accomplishments. Propertied Englishmen were usually indifferent to the life of the mind, and thus there was no social benefit to Jews to pursue intellectual and cultural interests. While the upper-class twit of Monty Python fame is undoubtedly a crude, though amusing, caricature, it is important to remember that such a caricature succeeds only because it corresponds in some way, however exaggerated, to reality.

The offspring of the immigrant generation were thus conforming to a well-established pattern of behavior in their relative indifference to literature, science, and the arts. However, this alone does not fully explain the matter. Some attention must also be paid to the absence of educational opportunities that would have permitted the participation of larger numbers of immigrant offspring in these spheres of activity. Advanced secondary and university education in Great Britain was a luxury, available mostly to children from upper middle-class and upper-class homes, the number of students restricted by both a paucity of places and the expense of attendance. Only a minority of children of immigrant parents—those fortunate enough to win scholarships—continued their education past fourteen, the normal age for leaving school. Those who stayed on faced even greater obstacles in obtaining a university degree, for Great Britain lacked inexpensive public universities like those to which second-generation American Jewish students flocked in the interwar years. The result was that few Jews attended university, and even fewer chose careers that took them into scientific, literary, academic, or cultural circles. Moreover, Selig Brodetsky argued, those who did move in this direction were likely to distance themselves from the Jewish community precisely because it seemed so parochial and philistine. The best and the brightest, he wrote in 1928, "leave us, often in sorrow or disgust, but oftenest unconsciously and without any sense of struggle or feeling of loss." In a flight of hyperbole designed to twit the Jewish penchant for claiming as their own even notable converts, he declared that the number of persons of Jewish origin in leadership positions in science, literature, sociology, medicine, and art was "beyond the wildest dreams of self-exaltation that Jewry ever dreamt."[34]

Immersion in radical, primarily communist, politics also worked to weaken communal attachments, although perhaps not to the extent that immersion in high culture did. Young men and women from immigrant neighborhoods who embraced communism because it seemed to offer a remedy for the world's ills were not necessarily intent on shedding their Jewishness. The various communist groups that operated in the East End of London in the interwar period contained conspicuously large numbers of Jews and were thus imperfect channels for integration into the larger society.[35] Membership in the Communist Party brought in its wake a degree of contact with gentiles that was unusual for Jewish workers, as Joe Jacobs's memoirs clearly reveal, but did not usually lead to a severing of

Jewish ties. Although Jacobs visited the homes of gentile comrades—a novel experience for Jews from his milieu—his most sustained and most intimate relationships remained those with other Jews, young men and women whose backgrounds were identical to his. Moreover, after the Third International changed to a popular front policy in 1935, Jewish communists participated in broad communal efforts to repel the incursions of the British Union of Fascists and were thus drawn even more closely into the fabric of East End life.

However, because Marxism offered a view of the world that downplayed ethnic and religious divisions and a vision of the future in which such divisions would be altogether irrelevant, those who flocked to its banner were prepared ideologically to move beyond the confines of the Jewish community if at all possible. In addition, communism offered those who wholeheartedly embraced it more than a political outlook on the world. It gave them an alternative identity—a bracing vision of self-definition—and an alternative social universe. As Raphael Samuel has recalled, "To be a Communist was to have a complete social identity, one which transcended the limits of class, gender and nationality." Jewish communists lived "in a little private world of our own." They maintained "intense neighbourhood networks and little workplace conventicles." They had their regular cafes, went out together on weekend rambles, and took their holidays together. For some, communism functioned like a religion, offering profound answers to ultimate questions, taking the place of a faith lost or never possessed. In his memoirs, the writer Maurice Levinson (b. 1911) described a teenage friend of his, Max Stukey, who was miserable about being Jewish—"It bewildered him to think that an accidental origin of birth should cause him so much unhappiness"—and found relief in becoming a communist. While listening to Harry Pollitt speak, Stukey's face "bore an expression of intense rapture." In communism, he found "something that gave him a strength that compensated for his inability to face realities . . . some sort of peace, a peace that infected his ego with the belief that all men were equal."[36] Whether communists like Stukey eventually severed their ties with Jewish circles depended in large part on nonideological circumstances, but having previously embraced a theoretically universalist outlook they were clearly well prepared to move in that direction.

From the discussion so far, one might infer that social circumstances played a greater role in weakening Jewish ethnic ties than did any conscious will to assimilate. While in general this may be true, to ignore quite-deliberate attempts by some second-generation English Jews to flee their origins would be misleading, although it is difficult to trace those who chose this path precisely because they strove to deflect attention from their flight. At the same time it would also be misleading to assume that those who "defected" and those who "drifted" were two distinct groups. In practice, the dividing line was probably blurred, human behavior of this sort defying neat categorization. What seems reasonable to assume is that in most cases of radical assimilation some degree of intentionality came into play. For example, Jews who married outside their community because their education, occupation, or politics led them in that direction might well have taken further steps to hide their origins once married. In Simon Blumenfeld's *Jew Boy*, the sister of Alec's girlfriend is a former school-teacher, now living in Barnes and married to a gentile, a Mr. Saunders. When Alec and Sarah visit them on a Saturday, Mrs. Saunders expresses satisfaction to herself that Alec is clean and respectable and does not look too much like a Jew. "She didn't want the whole neighbourhood to know she was Jewish." A former colleague who is also invited to dinner that Saturday knows she is Jewish but never mentions it and, in fact, avoids talking about Jews altogether in her presence. "It was tacitly understood that Jews were non-existent as far as Mrs. Saunders was concerned." When the subject arose, "she always turned red, and shut up like a clam." Mr. Saunders never spoke to his wife about her background "because he had discovered early in their married life that she was touchy about those things."[37]

At any period, English Jews who ventured outside their own community risked encountering contempt and derision, but the likelihood of that happening appears to have increased in the interwar years. Before World War I, hostility to Jews in England had been more muted than elsewhere in Europe, although it had always been present to some degree. In the 1920s, 1930s, and 1940s, however, it registered remarkable gains: political agitation, social discrimination, street hooliganism, and other expressions of popular contempt reached unprecedented levels.[38] Antisemitism assumed an unprecedented importance in the lives of English Jews, impinging on everyday routine in new and disturbing ways.

Before World War I, systematic, ideological antisemitism made few inroads into British political life. An eccentric current, closer to the periphery than to the center of political discourse, it exerted little influence on public attitudes and policy toward Jews. The most important outburst of anti-Jewish feeling before the war—the agitation against immigration that culminated with passage of the Aliens Act of 1905—grew out of local social and economic grievances in districts of heavy immigrant settlement rather than from fears about a shadowy Jewish menace threatening the survival of the English nation. The great majority of those who supported immigration restriction showed no ideological fervor for revoking emancipation or halting integration, the ultimate objectives of ideological antisemites elsewhere in Europe. Indeed, many MPs who voted in favor of the bill went out of their way to explain that they harbored no animus against Jews *per se*.[39] (Whether or not that was true is beside the point; that they felt compelled to make such a declaration is what is critical.)

In the postwar years, public discussion about Jewish power and influence became more common, and theories about Jewish conspiracies in particular gained a broader and more respectable hearing than they had enjoyed earlier. The notorious Russian forgery about an alleged Jewish plot for world domination, *The Protocols of the Elders of Zion*, appeared in an English-language version, *The Jewish Peril*, early in 1920. It received serious, though generally negative, attention in the national press, the exception being the *Morning Post*, whose reviewer refused to dismiss it as mere antisemitic propaganda because, if a secret Jewish cabal did exist, it posed a threat to the safety of the nation. The "red scare" that swept England at that same time, in the wake of the Bolshevik revolution and the Russian civil war, also raised troubling questions about the loyalty of Jews, especially those of foreign birth. The disproportionate number of Jews who played a prominent role in the revolution was seen by many on the right as evidence of a natural sympathy between world Jewry and revolutionary communism. Attacks in the conservative press on all kinds of left-wing political activity easily took on an antisemitic tone. Anti-communism, anti-alienism, and antisemitism became hopelessly entangled, each reinforcing the strength of the other.[40]

Although political antisemitism of this variety failed to capture the Tory party and thus remained on the periphery of parliamentary politics, it undoubtedly succeeded in planting doubts in the minds of a broader English public about the character of the Jews in their midst—their patriotism, loyalty, trustworthiness, and morality. A number of radical antisemites—Arnold Leese, Henry Hamilton Beamish, Archibald Maule Ramsay—tried to harness these sentiments to a political campaign against Jews in the interwar years, but they were no more successful than Jew-baiting demagogues in the United States at this time, despite the zeal with which they disseminated their views.[41] In the early 1930s, for example, mostly unknown persons sharing their outlook plastered thousands of small labels decrying Jewish world domination on vending machines, mailboxes, lamp posts, and the walls of shops and public buildings in London and other large cities. Their message was simple and to the point: "The wheat trade of the world is controlled by three Jewish firms." "The peace conference was a Jew conference." "All our troubles, Ireland, India, Egypt, China—Jews behind it every time." "The League of Nations is a plot for world-control by Jews." "The Red Flag is a Jew Flag." One label offered a radical solution: "Nationalise the wealth of the Jew banks. Expel all Jews from the country." (A young man affiliated with Sir Oswald Mosely's New Party was convicted in August 1932 for sticking this last label to a draper's shop in Oxford Street.)[42] Again, while such smear tactics bore no immediate political fruit, they were successful to the extent that they strengthened and sharpened broadly diffused nonideological prejudices about Jews, giving them a focus that they might not have enjoyed otherwise.

The East End campaign of Mosley's British Union of Fascists from 1935 to 1937 took this tradition of political antisemitism one step further. Not content with mere sloganeering, squads of Blackshirt toughs unleashed violent attacks on Jewish property and persons in the most recognizably Jewish district in the country, smashing windows, looting shops, physically

assaulting Jews walking in the streets, desecrating synagogues and ceme-
teries. In one attack in October 1936, for example, a week after a Fascist
procession through the East End was stopped by an anti-Fascist front of
about 100,000 people ("the Battle of Cable Street"), Blackshirts retaliated
by smashing the windows of twenty-nine Jewish shops in Mile End Road
and sixteen Jewish shops in a row in Green Street. In one instance, they
threw a man and a little girl through a shop window while the crowd
chanted "Down with the Yids." Blackshirts frequently picketed Jewish
stores, intimidating potential customers with threats, shouting slogans like
"Buy from people who celebrate Christmas," "Boycott the Jews," and
"Why buy goods from stinking Jews?" This campaign of violence and intimidation was not the first outbreak of anti-Jewish hooliganism in the
interwar period. In earlier acts of vandalism synagogues in Leeds (May
1932) and Liverpool (December 1933) were desecrated; a window of the
Manchester Talmud Torah was smashed in 1932 with a brick plastered with
labels condemning the League of Nations as a tool of world Jewry and attacking Jews for purveying erotic films, threatening the sexual purity of
white women, and fomenting unrest in the British Empire.[43] But the East
End attacks were more vicious, better organized, and more numerous than
anything Jews in Britain had previously encountered. They succeeded in
terrorizing much of the local community and sowing apprehension among
Jews living in districts far removed from the violence.

While politically inspired Fascist attacks were confined largely to the East
End and to the period of the mid- and late 1930s, Jews everywhere throughout the interwar period confronted new levels of verbal abuse, public contempt, and slander. In public meetings and newspaper columns, they were
denounced for their clannishness, sensuality, materialism, aversion to
physical labor, and corrupt business ethics. H. H. Spencer, MP, speaking
at the annual dinner of the Bradford Textile Society in September 1924, attributed a recent epidemic of fraudulent bankruptcies in the textile trade
in the West Riding of Yorkshire chiefly to Russian and Polish Jews, whose
motto seemed to be, in his words, "Where I am getting hold of the stuff
there is my fatherland." In November 1924, an anonymous reader of the
Leeds Mercury blamed Jews for the desecration of the English Sabbath.
"Their advent into England has been the thin end of the wedge which has
split up the general observance of the day of rest and been the means of
lowering the moral tone." An anonymous reader of the *Hull Daily Mail*
wrote in April 1926 that, having been employed by Jews for sixteen years,
he could testify that "they get the very most they can out of you for as
little money as possible." A Jewish housewife, for example, would offer
her charwoman "what an English woman would be ashamed to offer, and
expect far more for it." An anonymous letter writer in the same newspaper
in 1930 complained that Jews did not know what hard work was. They
were never to be seen working on the docks or in the mills in Hull, preferring instead the "light work" of shopkeeping. Grocers in Grimsby com-

plained in 1933 that Jewish shopkeepers were forcing "legitimate" traders out of business by cutting prices in order to attract customers to their shops. "Small wonder that there has been trouble in Germany," one grocer grumbled.[44] Similar complaints were heard in both London and the provinces throughout the remainder of the decade and until the very end of World War II.[45]

Popular complaints about Jews' "vices"—their cunning, crafty ways, grasping nature, and clannish solidarity—were voiced in earlier periods of English Jewish history; there was little that was new in all this. What was novel was the sheer volume of such accusations. Most Jews (except those who knew little English and never ventured out of the old immigrant neighborhoods) would have had the unpleasant experience of hearing or reading them at one time or another. The hostility, moreover, went beyond mere verbal abuse: it assumed concrete form in unprecedented levels of discrimination in education, employment, and social life. In the decades before World War I, acculturated Jews seeking integration into the larger society found relatively few obstacles in their path, while those recently arrived from Eastern Europe were insufficiently anglicized even to find themselves in situations where they might face social ostracism or job discrimination at the hands of gentiles. Their children, however, by virtue of their English education and attraction to English values and tastes, looked to the world outside the immigrant quarter to satisfy their needs. In part— and only in part—because they were more numerous than any previous group of English Jews abandoning the "ghetto," there was greater resistance to their integration than there had been to earlier efforts. (Precisely the same thing occurred in the United States, where there was widespread discrimination against Jews in housing, employment, education, and social life from the 1920s through the 1950s.)

Anti-Jewish discrimination in the interwar period was not systematic, poisoning every Jewish contact with the larger society, but it was common enough that few Jews could have avoided it altogether or been unaware of its existence. Some masonic lodges and many fashionable golf, tennis, and motor clubs introduced bans on Jewish members. A young Jewish dentist in Leeds told a journalist in 1925, "No matter how much a Jew is Anglicised he is ostracised by certain clubs." Jews living in Hampstead and Finchley complained bitterly of their inability to join the best lawn tennis clubs.[46] Occupational discrimination became a problem for many young men and women seeking employment in fields outside the usual range of immigrant trades. Newspapers carried advertisements for jobs indicating that Jewish applicants were not wanted. An advertisement for a typist in the London *Daily Telegraph*, for example, specified "No Jewesses," while one in the *British Medical Journal* said "No Jews or men of colour." A young Jewish woman seeking work as a clerk or shop assistant wrote to the *Yorkshire Evening Post* in 1925 complaining that at a number of job interviews she was told that the firms never employed Jews and had no intention of doing so. Jewish teachers in particular experienced difficulty in finding positions. A Jewish reader of the *Leeds Mercury* wrote an angry letter to the editor in 1925 attacking the local school administration as antisemitic and advising Jewish youth "to avoid teaching as they would the plague." Ralph Finn, who joined the teaching staff of a school near the West Ham docks in the mid-1930s, charitably characterized his colleagues as "not very partial to Jews," all of whom they believed to be fat and wealthy—although Finn himself was slim and poor. In the medical profession, Jews routinely faced obstacles in gaining hospital positions and promotions. A deputation of medical students from the London Hospital called on Israel Zangwill in 1918 to complain about both the hostile atmosphere there and their being refused appointments. Leonard Myer, a Harley Street physician, told an interviewer from the *Evening Standard* in 1926 that "none of the plums in the hospitals" was open to Jews. "You may find an anaesthetist here and there, but none of the big jobs can a Jew get."[47]

Admission to public schools and universities also became more difficult as the number of Jewish applicants, now increasingly the offspring of East European immigrants, shot up dramatically. St. Paul's, for example, which had been open to Jewish boys without restriction in the late-Victorian and Edwardian years, imposed an undeclared quota in the interwar period. University College, London, also appears to have restricted Jewish admissions. Ralph Finn, who was a student there in the 1930s, recalled in his memoirs: "You had to be brilliant if you wanted to get into London's favoured college and just happened to be Jewish too. There was no obvious bar but there were some very sinister ones." Those who were admitted encountered an atmosphere where hostility to Jews was openly expressed. Medical and education students at the University of Leeds complained of "a certain amount of antagonism" (which the rabbi of the leading synagogue there attributed to their humble origins, lack of social polish, and clannishness). Finn, who grew up in the East End and received his secondary education at a foundation school with a mixed student population, claimed to have had little firsthand experience of antisemitism before he became a university student in London. He and his fellow Jewish students were the targets of frequent snide remarks and occasional physical beatings. Finn himself was kept off his college football team because he was Jewish—although he was allowed to play for the university team.[48]

Even Jews with limited social horizons were likely to encounter discriminatory practices at some point if they ventured beyond the immigrant quarter: restaurant and hotel owners who advertised that they did not cater to Jews; builders who refused to sell or rent them houses because, as one firm explained, "people buying or renting a house asked to be assured that the estate would be free from Jews"; garage proprietors who refused to rent them cars because insurance companies would not issue short-term policies covering Jews and other allegedly high-risk groups (actors, jockeys, undergraduates, bookmakers, air force officers, minors, senior citizens, and aliens).[49] The last practice in particular received widespread attention in the national press when it was first exposed in 1928 in the *Daily Herald*. An insurance broker in London explained the reason for the ban: Jews "pack the cars to a dangerous capacity and, caring as a rule nothing for their own safety or the safety of the vehicle, dash off without worrying twopence what may happen." A Lloyd's insurance broker offered a similar explanation to readers of the *Daily Express* in 1932. Claiming that insurance industry statistics proved that Jews had more accidents than other drivers, he attributed their recklessness to an innate preference for spectacular amusements. Unlike the English, with their preference for diversions like rugby and cricket, he explained, Jews went in for fast cars, capable of cutting ahead of others on the road. A Yorkshire car rental firm, on the other hand, justified the ban on altogether different grounds. Jews, it told the *Yorkshire Evening News* in 1932, did not have the same steady nerves as Englishmen; they were more excitable, easily losing their heads in dangerous situations.[50]

Discriminatory practices such as these affected a larger number of Jews than those who actually encountered them at first hand. The very knowledge that such bans existed and that they were publicly discussed was alone sufficient to make Jews from diverse backgrounds feel uncomfortable about their origins. At the very minimum it reminded them that they were widely regarded as something other than fully English. In addition, the persecution of Jews in Germany after 1933 and the strife between Jews and Arabs in Palestine further directed public attention to Jewish issues, thereby heightening that sense of discomfort already engendered by domestic concerns. As E. M. Forster wrote in an essay in 1939, "Jew-consciousness is in the air." In this light, it is not surprising that the *Sunday Express*, the first newspaper to reveal the insurance industry ban on one-day car rentals to Jews, asked Israel Mattuck (1883–1954), rabbi of the Liberal synagogue in London, to write on "Why Are Jews So Touchy?" after it received a number of letters from Jews protesting its coverage of the ban. Mattuck explained that Jews were sensitive because others had made them so: "A most healthy body becomes sensitive through many blows." Some had become so sensitive that they even objected to being called Jews, "blaming the accident of their birth for a misfortune they find it hard to escape."[51]

A poignant example of the discomfort created by the growth of antisemitism in the interwar period appeared in the same newspaper in 1931. Under the heading "Because I am a Jew, I am afraid," a Mr. Samuelson confessed his fear that he would not be able to equip his children psychologically to face the hostility of the gentile world. From early childhood, he explained, a Jew becomes conscious that real, though often undefinable, barriers mark him off from his fellows. When his eight-year-old daughter reported to him that a school friend had told her that "all Jews have big noses," he recognized with a shock that she had begun to struggle with the problem of "differentness" and that behind her little nervous laugh was "a subconscious resentment that she should be singled out for derision." In whatever circles a Jew might move in adult life, he continued, his friends and acquaintances "will never accept him with unrestricted completeness." As a consequence, no matter how proud a Jew might feel about his people's history and contributions to civilization, he will still suffer from feeling different.[52]

In the opening section of his autobiographical novel, *With Hope, Farewell*, Alexander Baron powerfully described the torment experienced by acculturated Jews like Samuelson in the face of rising levels of contempt and hostility. Joe and Clara Strong—English-born, religiously unobservant—take rooms for their summer holiday in 1928 at a seaside boardinghouse with a gentile clientele. Clara Strong feels out of place, uncomfortable, ill at ease. She worries at length about making the correct impression. Sitting at the breakfast table the first morning, she becomes annoyed by "the unnatural loudness" of her husband's voice and notes that while she shrinks and whispers in the midst of strangers he talks at the top of his voice, behavior that always infuriates her. She then spots another family, the Munceys, with two boys the same ages as their own and suggests to her husband that they should approach them, but he advises her to let the Munceys make the first move: "You know what they'll say otherwise. Pushing ourselves in." She continues to study the guests at nearby tables, becoming increasingly self-conscious, unsure of the reception they will meet with if they extend themselves. "It was always hard to tell what they [gentiles] were thinking. When you were suspicious they turned out all right. When you thought everything was fine, they suddenly said something." Later, at the beach, her worst fears are realized. The Munceys, who do not realize the Strongs are Jewish, make disparaging remarks about Jews overrunning Bournemouth. When the Strongs reveal that they are Jewish, the Munceys clumsily apologize—they were referring to "foreign" Jews, ever so many of their friends are Jewish, the Strongs don't behave like Jews—but the damage is done. "It was like broken bones grating inside Clara. The more they said the worse they made it. She wanted to leave them, abruptly, to leave the boarding-house and to flee to the sanctuary of her own home."[53]

All Jews who moved outside the boundaries of their own community were potential victims of gentile hostility, but some were more at risk than others. In general, those with the most extensive social and occupational contacts in the larger society—which meant, in practice, Jews whose families had been settled in England for several generations—were the most likely to suffer rejection or humiliation at gentile hands. Such persons were also more psychologically vulnerable to antisemitism, be it the parlor or the political variety, since their ties to the Jewish group were weaker and less extensive than those of second-generation English Jews. If rejected or humiliated, they could not take refuge in their community of origins, find-

ing there the confidence necessary to withstand or ignore gentile contempt. (Less-acculturated Jews assumed, as a matter of course, that most
gentiles were antisemitic in one way or another and were not surprised
when experience confirmed this assumption.) In addition, by virtue of
their assimilation to English norms and their integration, however incomplete, into English circles, Jews descended from earlier migratory waves
were more psychologically dependent on their standing in gentile society
than Jews whose roots in England went back only one generation. Their
own self-esteem was entangled with the larger question of the public image
of Jews in general. For such Jews, antisemitism was more devastating than
it was for those less dependent on gentile goodwill. In response, many
disassociated themselves from the Jewish community, certainly to a far
greater extent than had been the case among the older community before
World War I, when anti-Jewish feeling was less acute.

While its incidence cannot be gauged statistically, defection from the
older Jewish community in the interwar period was sufficiently common
to elicit frequent public comment. When a daughter of the solicitor Sir
George Lewis (1868–1927) was married in a Roman Catholic Church in
1928, the *Yorkshire Herald* noted that recently "quite a number of Jews prominent in the legal world have changed their faith" and that after the death
of the bride's father a year earlier the question arose as to whether he, too,
had converted. Two years earlier, when the engagement of a daughter
of Albert H. Jessel to a non-Jew was announced, a columnist in the
Jewish Chronicle lamented that this was "a story that now grows old and
day by day is becoming more general." In this case, however, the community took much greater notice of her defection because her father had been
a prominent communal worker. The conclusion being drawn, the writer
added, was that parentage and upbringing were unable to ensure "a resistance to the tendency to drift, through marriage, that today is everywhere
rife and rampant in Jewry."[54]

There were few wealthy or cultured Jewish families that remained
immune to intermarriage in this period. Franklins, Jessels, Cohens,
Rothschilds, Salamans, Faudel-Phillipses, Magnuses, Henriqueses, Montefiores, Spielmans—families that were communal pillars in the decades
before World War I—all experienced the loss of younger members through
intermarriage. Prominent Jews who sanctioned such marriages or who
themselves intermarried came under fire in the *Jewish Chronicle* for setting a bad example for Jews of all ranks. In 1931, when Rufus Isaacs
(1860–1936) married his deceased wife's secretary, the newspaper attacked
him for having done "a distinct disservice to his people" by giving "the
cachet of his great and illustrious name to Jewish intermarriage and rendered it just so much more usual and . . . 'respectable.'" When Peggy
Behrens, a granddaughter of the first Lord Rothschild, married a member
of the Church of England in 1924, a columnist described the union as "a
step which amounted to a renunciation of allegiance to Judaism." He con-

demned those Jews who attended the church ceremony for setting a bad example while praising three of the bride's Rothschild relatives, including her grandmother, for staying away. In his opinion, the entire episode was symbolic of "the assimilative tendency that is rife among us."[55]

The spread of drift and defection within the older community was, however, more than a response to the rise of "Jew-consciousness" in the 1920s and 1930s. It was also a consequence of the successful social integration of Jews from long-established families and of the erosion of ethnic and religious loyalties that accompanied such integration. Many of these Jews, unlike the offspring of more recent arrivals, mixed more frequently with gentiles than with their fellow Jews. Ruth Sebag-Montefiore (b. 1916), daughter of the literary critic Laurie Magnus (1872–1933), recalled in a family history that although her parents took an active part in communal affairs, their friends were almost exclusively non-Jews, drawn largely from the worlds of literature and education. Her own situation was similar, so she grew up feeling a sense of detachment from other Jews. When she and her sister Pamela attended religious school classes for a short time at the Reform synagogue in Upper Berkeley Street, they felt they did not belong. "The other children were strange, the teachers were strange and the subject was strange." At services as well, she felt she was worshipping for the most part among strangers. Those families who lived most of the year in the country and sent their children to boarding schools were even more cut off from Jewish circles than families like the Magnuses in London. Robert Henriques (1905–1967), novelist, biographer, army officer, and farmer, served as president of the Anglo-Jewish Association and as a member of the Board of Deputies but raised his children at a home "deep in the Cotswold countryside" where they were, in his daughter's words, "brought up as any well-to-do unreligious English country children were brought up." That children raised in circumstances like these married outside the community should not be surprising. A columnist in the *Jewish Chronicle* made the same point in 1924 in response to a notice in *The Times* about a dinner dance given by a prominent Jewish couple in honor of their two daughters. The writer noted that the obvious purpose of the event was finding husbands for the daughters but that the names of only four members of the Jewish community appeared on the guest list. "What chance have the two young ladies in question of becoming the wives of Jews," he asked, "if they are thus thrust into social intercourse with non-Jews?"[56]

Most members of the older community "thrust into social intercourse with non-Jews" were not exposed to practices or experiences on the domestic scene that might have acted as a counterweight to the attractions of participation in the larger society, for by the interwar period the religious and charitable commitments of the older families were a shadow of what they had been at the height of the Victorian period. Synagogue attendance was infrequent; home observance half-hearted and erratic at best; religious education almost nonexistent. In the Henriques home in the Cotswolds, "there was the odd, amazing and somewhat hilarious emotional outburst about twice a year . . . when candles were lit on a Friday night and dusty prayer books suddenly produced." In the Magnus home in London, Ruth Sebag-Montefiore wrote, Passover seders "consisted of a few prayers read by our father in the drawing room and that was that" (in contrast to those of her maternal grandparents, "who had full-blooded affairs with the entire service, the Grace and all the traditional foods"). Friday evening services "were also watered down and were apt to be performed perfunctorily, as if between inverted commas, like something alien to the normal pattern of family life." Some families still assembled in force for festive Friday evening meals—like the fictional March family in C. P. Snow's *The Conscience of the Rich* (1958), which was based on a branch of the Cohen clan whom Snow knew well in the interwar period—but the blessings and customs at the dinner table marking the entry of the Sabbath were no longer observed.[57]

For Mr. March and his children, as for most Jews whose roots in England went back several generations, Jewish concerns were becoming "something alien"—or at least peripheral—to their central interests. In Snow's words, "the Marches were secure, they were part of the country, they lived almost exactly the lives of other wealthy men." They and their real counterparts had become so rooted in the life of the larger society that they tended to have little attachment to what they regarded as the parochial issues of English Jewish life. Thus veteran leaders frequently complained of the problem of recruiting younger professional and business men to take an active role in the management of communal affairs. When Redcliffe Salaman spoke to the medical historian Charles Singer (1876–1960), son of a well-known London rabbi, about helping to organize non-Orthodox students at Oxford, where he was then teaching, Singer said that he had no interest, "that he was not there to look after Jewish affairs, but to lecture on the history of medicine." Rabbi Walter Levine, speaking at the Conference of Jewish Preachers in London in 1923, lamented that young men no longer thought it an honor to be invited to serve on a synagogue or charity board, as had been the case several decades earlier, remarking that "those who have grown grey in the service of the community oft times experience the greatest difficulty in inducing young people to take upon themselves offices of trust and responsibility." In his view, those young persons who were apathetic to Jewish concerns believed that their standing in the world depended on the extent to which they could distance themselves from their people.[58] The take-over of communal institutions by the children and grandchildren of Russian and Polish Jews in the years after World War II was as much the outcome of disinterest in maintaining control by the offspring of the old notability as it was of the newly acquired wealth and education of the newcomers.

The indifference of the young to Jewish issues stemmed, in part, from their involvement in circles and concerns outside the community and, in part, as Levine argued, from the desire, born of that involvement and fueled by growing antisemitism, to reduce even further the differences still separating them from their gentile friends and associates. Those raised in homes devoid of intense Jewish commitments felt that their Jewishness was a vestigial attachment, more burdensome than benign, hardly worth the effort of cultivating. Whether or not they themselves had been victims of blatant antisemitism, they were still reminded by the "Jew-consciousness" of the age that others viewed them as somehow different. In Snow's novel, young rebellious Charles March, who is based on Richard Cohen (b. 1907), a physician and distinguished civil servant who was a lifetime friend of the author, explains to the gentile narrator how his Jewishness has weighed heavily on him all his life: "I haven't enjoyed being a Jew. Since I was a child, I haven't been allowed to forget—that other people see me through different eyes. They label me with a difference I can't accept." The suffering he has endured is essentially psychological, for his family's wealth and status have shielded him from overt hostility: others make him feel like a stranger. "It isn't their fault. It's simply a fact. But it's a fact that interferes with your spirits and nags at you. Sometimes it torments you— particularly when you're young." Mark Strong, whose parents come from a very different stratum of the older community, offers the same complaint in Alexander Baron's novel: "Always, as far back as he could remember, he had wanted to be the same as other boys; he had no other ambition; always this word 'Jew' sprang up like barbed wire between himself and the world." His Jewishness, however, means little to him—his family observes no rituals; he has received no Jewish education—but this, to his wonder, makes no difference to others. "As soon as they heard, it was as if you had diphtheria. The others. That was how he had come to think of them now. Yet all he wanted of life was to be one of 'the others.'"[59]

Those Jews who wanted to shed their attachments to the Jewish group were generally successful in doing so. Despite the increase in antisemitism in the interwar period, English society remained sufficiently tolerant to absorb those Jews from the older community who wished to forget or put aside their origins and blend unobtrusively into the mainstream. There was no reactionary backlash seeking to halt the mounting influx, as there was in Germany, Austria, and even the United States. In this respect, interwar Britain differed little from Georgian and Victorian Britain: converted Jews, intermarried Jews, and indifferent Jews alike were able to make a place for themselves in settings outside the social boundaries of Jewry without much ado.

Jewish families long settled in England also displayed increasing toleration toward younger members who wished to intermarry and by doing so leave the community in which they had been raised, for intermarriage was no longer the rare, almost unthinkable event it had been a half century earlier. Some wealthy patriarchs still took legal steps to prevent their children from leaving the community by threatening to disinherit them if they converted or intermarried.[60] But many parents who would have preferred their children to marry within the community were now willing to accept, however reluctantly, that this would not be so. When Adrian Franklin announced his intention in 1930 to marry a Miss Redwood-White, his father, Sir Leonard (1862–1944), a Liberal MP and prominent communal worker, was distraught—as his sister-in-law wrote to her daughter Helen Bentwich in Jerusalem, "Uncle Leonard . . . feels it awfully keenly"—but offered no real opposition. (His mother, Laura, on the other hand, was "delighted" and "enthusiastic" about the match.) When Katherine March tells her father that she is engaged to a non-Jew, his immediate response is that he wishes she had never been born. What she is proposing to do, he tells her, is something he will never get over. "You never gave a moment's thought to the fact that you'd make me a reproach for the rest of my life." Yet, in the end, like Leonard Franklin and others who still felt a loyalty to the Jewish community, March loves his daughter more than his principles and family pride, and he and his other children accompany the couple to the registry office to marry.[61] This was a story repeated many times within the older community in the years before World War II and even more frequently afterward.

Conclusion

In the half-century since the start of World War II, drift and defection have continued to thin the ranks of English Jewry. Like other Britons, Jews have become increasingly indifferent to religious practices and beliefs, disinclined to attend worship services or devote time or energy to religious institutions. At the same time they have also taken advantage of the loosening of the British social system that has occurred since the end of the war, moving more extensively than before into professional, cultural, and social spheres outside the traditional boundaries of the community. As in earlier periods, the result has been a weakening of ethnic solidarity, resulting in high rates of disaffiliation through conversion, intermarriage, and simple nonparticipation.[1] In this, there is nothing particularly new. The paths leading to full absorption into the larger society have been the same as before the war: attendance at university, occupational diversification, immersion in general cultural or political movements, and residential dispersion. But the number of Jews with the desire and wherewithal to pursue such opportunities has been vastly greater than in the interwar years, when most Jews entering the work force or marrying were the children, not the grandchildren, of Yiddish-speaking immigrants with few financial resources. Those drifting away from communal affiliation in recent decades have been raised and educated in very different surroundings for the most part. They have come to expect fulfillment on a broader social and cultural plane than did their parents, which means, in practice, outside the informal boundaries of the community.

What is most remarkable about disaffiliation in the postwar period is its dramatic impact on the size of the British Jewish community. The Research Unit of the Board of Deputies, which has been studying demographic trends in the community since its establishment in 1965, has found that the Jewish population has suffered an absolute decline in numbers since the early 1950s, when it peaked at 430,000. (At one time it was thought that the size of the postwar community was 450,000, the figure that communal officials consistently supplied to the *American Jewish Year Book*. The Research Unit now believes that even its initial estimate of 430,000 may have been too high.) Since its zenith a few years after the war, the population has declined steadily, so that in the late 1980s it stood around 330,000. If the estimate for the early 1950s is correct, the population has fallen 25 percent in just over thirty years.[2]

There is little disagreement among contemporary observers about the causes of the decline—a fall in the birthrate, a rise in intermarriage, and, to a lesser extent, an increase in emigration.[3] While it is not possible to measure the extent to which each has contributed to the decline in the size of the community, there is abundant evidence of a massive defection of young people in recent decades. The Research Unit has compared figures for synagogue marriages in the early 1980s with communal circumcision records of two and three decades earlier and has concluded that only half of the Jewish men born in the late 1950s and early 1960s who statistically would have been expected to marry under synagogue auspices in the early 1980s actually did so. In fact, the number of synagogue marriages per 1,000 Jews has been steadily declining since 1900. In the first two decades of this century, the annual marriage rate was 9.0 per 1,000, slightly higher than the 8.0 per 1,000 in the general population. By the period 1971–1975, the rate had fallen dramatically to 4.3 marriages per 1,000, while that of the general population had remained more or less constant, at 8.1;[4] and in the period 1980–1984, with only 1,169 synagogue marriages annually, the rate had sunk to 3.5 per 1,000.[5]

Of course, it would be wrong to infer that this decline is the outcome of a skyrocketing number of intermarriages alone. Clearly, other factors have contributed to this trend, including emigration, alternatives to conventional marriage, nonmarriage, and postponement of marriage. It is also likely that some Jewish couples have chosen to be married in civil ceremonies because they object to any kind of religious ceremony, however liberal or nontraditional, or because they are indifferent to religion altogether and do not want to bear the cost of a synagogue service. There is at present no adequate research indicating the precise extent to which each of these factors has contributed to the declining number of synagogue marriages. Yet, given everything else that is known about the state of Jewish practice, identity, and belief in Britain today, it would not be unreasonable to attribute primary responsibility for this change to widespread intermarriage. This is the view of most observers of the contemporary Anglo-Jewish scene.

The contraction of the Jewish population in recent decades has become a major issue of concern for communal leaders. Expressions of alarm surface repeatedly in public forums, committee meetings, and the pages of the *Jewish Chronicle*. This sense of alarm is justified, for there is little prospect that the situation can be reversed. No vast reservoir of traditional Jewish life remains anywhere in Europe; thus there is no possibility that some future immigration will compensate for the losses currently being sustained—as was the case in the past. (The 50,000 German and Austrian Jews who found refuge in Britain in the 1930s and remained there after the war have not served as a significant demographic reinforcement to counter the impact of widespread disaffiliation. In most cases their own commitment to Jewish practice and continuity before their emigration was as weak, if not weaker, than that of most native English Jews.[6]) Before World War II, the damage inflicted by conversion and intermarriage was in large part hidden from view. The size of the community never declined; indeed, the opposite was true: it was always growing. But this growth was due as much, perhaps more, to the arrival of Jews from somewhere else as it was to natural increase. In every period immigration nourished and replenished a community already experiencing serious losses, making up for those being absorbed body and soul into the larger society. This was already the case in the eighteenth century. One only has to ask what the fate of English Jewry would have been had there been no immigration beyond the initial Sephardi settlement to realize the truth of this proposition. Similarly, it is difficult to imagine that the contemporary community would be the size it is—however reduced that might be!—had there not been mass emigration from Eastern Europe.

This is not to say that in earlier periods contemporaries were blind to instances of drift and defection. They were aware—and gave voice to this awareness, as we have seen—that there were ambitious and indifferent Jews in every generation who converted or intermarried. It was perfectly clear to them, for example, that there were prominent families, once pillars of the Anglo-Jewish establishment, who had ceased to have any connection with Judaism. What Jewish leaders were not able to grasp, however, was the cumulative impact of such defections, as well as the less-noticeable growth of religious indifference, over several generations. In the absence of dramatic waves of conversion, such as were common in Germany, they could not apprehend the long-term demographic toll drift and defection were exacting, particularly when that toll was being masked by the arrival of successive groups of newcomers from abroad. Moreover, except for some in the Zionist camp, it would have been unthinkable to them that legal emancipation and social toleration might in their own way challenge Jewish solidarity and continuity. Most English Jews in the Victorian period and in this century have believed that integration into the fabric of English life is compatible with loyalty to Judaism and group survival. Believing this, they were not ideologically predisposed to undertake a sober assessment of the way English Jewry was really faring.

Of course, there were decades when leakage was not extensive and there was no apparent cause for concern. (I say "apparent" because it is clear in retrospect that some key elements in the maintenance of group loyalty— for example, religious education—were already beginning to weaken.) In the Victorian period, well-to-do families long resident in England were able to preserve their Jewish attachments over several generations. In the first half of the twentieth century, the immigrants and their children remained for the most part within the social boundaries of the community. Yet, as we have seen, neither group was able to transmit successfully its sense of identity to succeeding generations. Eventually both experienced the withdrawal of substantial numbers of young men and women, their interests, ambitions, energies, hopes having been transferred elsewhere. While English Jewry were immune for the most part to the periodic flareups of baptismal fever that gripped other communities, there is no evidence that they were more successful *in the long term* than they were in stemming leakage and ultimately demographic decline.

In drawing up a balance sheet of the causes of drift and defection, however, it is clear that overt hostility to Jewish aspirations did not play the decisive role in eroding Jewish loyalties in England that it did elsewhere.[7] In Germany, for example, tens of thousands of young Jews, both before and after emancipation, embraced Christianity to advance their careers and social standing. For most of the modern period, their Jewishness was a considerable barrier to extensive participation in critical sectors of the larger society. It prohibited them from playing a prominent part in the political life of the state; it blocked their entry into the judiciary, the diplomatic corps, the academy, the military, and the higher reaches of the civil service; it encumbered their social relations, preventing their acceptance into certain circles and organizations and introducing a note of unpleasantness into routine contacts with neighbors, tradesmen, schoolmates, and state officials. Those who became Christians believed that nothing less than formal renunciation of their Jewishness would allow them to play the larger role in state and society they so ardently desired.

In England, Jewishness was not the impediment to social success or occupational mobility that it was in Germany or elsewhere in Europe. To be sure, before the mid-Victorian period, when the last legal barriers to Jewish participation in public life were removed, there were some ambitious persons, already distant from Jewish belief and practice, who joined the Church of England to make their mark outside the community of their birth. But those who made their way to the baptismal font for this reason were never as numerous, neither before nor after emancipation, as those who drifted away from the community and intermarried without changing their religion. Moreover, even those Jews who formally left Judaism usually did so only after they had already achieved a significant degree of integration—after, in fact, most of their friends and associates had ceased to be Jewish. Conversion for them was not an entry ticket into a world from which they had been excluded previously but an acknowledgment of the distance they had already traveled. Most Jews who achieved this level of integration, especially after emancipation, did not choose to convert. But having moved away from the social life of the community, they substantially increased the likelihood that they or their children would intermarry. In the end, the demographic consequences were the same as if they had actually converted.

Yet the question still remains why so many Jews with feet in both worlds were unable to transmit their sense of Jewishness, however they defined it, to succeeding generations. For it is clear that the Jewish commitments of acculturated families who took an active part in the social, cultural, and political life of the larger society weakened with each generation. The balance struck by those who first entered into the life of the country failed to hold. Religious commitments declined; Jewish concerns appeared increasingly parochial; newer, broader, fields of activity seemed ever more attractive and rewarding.

Some of this decline was the outcome of a more general process of secularization at work throughout the Western world in general and requires no further comment. Some was due to the failure of the Jewish community to develop institutions or programs to counteract the erosion of ethnic and religious loyalties that came in the wake of successful social integration. The level of Jewish education, for example, was consistently low (although it may not have been any worse than that prevailing in other Western Jewish communities). Relatively few English Jews of any rank received a Jewish education sufficiently rich or intensive to compete with the influence of secular cultural currents to which they were constantly exposed, whether at school or on the street corner. To cite one further example, English Jews never developed an extensive network of voluntary social organizations capable of reinforcing sentiments of ethnic solidarity. There was no counterpart to the rich nexus of nonreligious, extrasynagogal organizations—city and country clubs, fraternities and sororities, community centers, youth organizations, fraternal orders—that have dotted the American Jewish landscape since the years following the Civil War. The absence of such institutions is not difficult to explain. For most of the period under discussion, there were too few Jews in England, at least outside of London, to sustain such an associational network. More to the point, however, is the fact that Jews were able to gain access to gentile social organizations without great difficulty (the interwar period is something of an exception) and thus had no need to create alternative social institutions of their own, unlike American Jews, who faced extensive discrimination from the 1870s until a generation ago. It should also be remembered that there was no precedent for or tradition of this kind of alternative ethnic network in England, which, in comparison to the United States, received few immigrants from abroad.

An even more profound reason for the failure of English Jewish families to perpetuate their Jewishness for more than a few generations was the nature of English culture—or, to be more specific, the culture of the property-owning social strata into which most Jews were absorbed—which was inhospitable to diversity. It was ruthlessly genteel, monolithic, and exclusive and did not include alternative modes of being authentically English. The very notion would have been beyond comprehension. Jews willing to accept the social and cultural standards of the dominant strata were tolerated and accepted, but their origins were never completely forgotten. To be a Jew was to be regarded as different—a basic fact no amount of acculturation could alter. Even the most English of English Jews, despite their rootedness in their surroundings and their mastery of its cultural nuances, were seen as different in some essential respect.

Many Jews, especially those who continued to practice their faith and take part in community affairs, could live comfortably with this kind of subtly qualified toleration. Their sense of self-worth was not linked exclusively to their reception in gentile circles, while acceptance of their Jewishness, along with active participation in the life of the community, compensated for whatever slights and rebuffs came their way outside its boundaries. But many others could not accept with equanimity their distance, however slight, from circles of which they thought they were an integral part. In need of a less-qualified sense of belonging, they allowed their Jewish attachments, the source of their discomfort, to wither and eventually die. In most cases this process of disengagement was gradual and unprogrammatic, to some extent even unconscious, extending over more than one generation. Few English Jews set out, map in hand, on the road to radical assimilation. Most who left the community were the children and grandchildren of persons who had initiated a process whose end was perhaps more extreme than they could have foreseen or desired.

Jews were not the only minority in England to suffer leakage as a result of an ambiguous social position in recent centuries. The history of Nonconformity reveals similar patterns to those found within the Jewish community.[8] In the seventeenth and eighteenth centuries, both legal disabilities and social and religious prejudice weighed heavily on Protestants who dissented from the Church of England. Prosperous Nonconformists eager to make their mark outside the constricted world of chapel society commonly joined the established church. Doing so allowed them to escape onerous legal disabilities and enhance their social standing. In Quaker circles, where leakage was a constant feature in the eighteenth and nineteenth centuries, it was a common saying that "a carriage and pair does not long continue to drive to a meeting house."[9] As one historian of English religion recently noted, "the severe difficulties involved in maintaining a Nonconformist family tradition over several generations were so common that they are taken for granted in the history and literature of Nonconformity."[10]

The removal of civil disabilities in the nineteenth century failed to stem the flow from chapel to church. Affluent, outward-looking Nonconformists increasingly abandoned the material austerity of earlier generations and moved more regularly in the world. As they began to mix socially with Anglicans, they discovered that a certain amount of mild contempt and social snobbery regarding Nonconformity remained even after legal barriers to full participation in state and society had fallen. The feeling lingered that Nonconformists were not really gentlefolk and that Nonconformity and high social status were not really compatible. Writers, for example, continued to portray them in unflattering terms—as ranting, narrow-minded, emotionally stunted, physically unattractive hypocrites. Nonconformists who were educated at a public school or at university or who later achieved worldly positions were exposed to such attitudes and frequently moved over to the Church of England as a result. Like so many Jews who drifted from their community, they found their ambiguous social status in Anglican circles psychologically intolerable. Since Nonconformist religious tradition mattered little to them, wealth and comfort having eroded whatever piety they had inherited, nothing remained to restrain them from effacing the last mark of their sectarian origins.

The parallel case of Nonconformist apostasy highlights the difficulty of perpetuating minority group identity once legal and social barriers to sources of power and prestige erode. In societies in which Jews lived more or less within the social boundaries of their own communities—Tsarist Russia, interwar Poland, the German states before unification—there was little threat to Jewish cohesion and continuity. Mob violence, bureaucratic harassment, legal discrimination, and social exclusion took their toll—in lives, property, and emotional distress—but never posed even a potential threat to the perpetuation of Judaism or the solidarity of the Jewish group. However, in the more liberal states of the West—and in England, in particular—where Jews were able to make careers, cultivate interests, and find companionship in largely gentile spheres, Jewry as a body suffered irreparable damage. In their own benign way, legal toleration and social acceptance challenged group continuity more effectively than did overt persecution in the period before World War II.

This is not to say that toleration *per se* is inimical to the perpetuation of Jewish life. To argue thus would be absurd. Rather, it was toleration as it was in fact practiced in England and other liberal states—a toleration that was qualified, hedged around with reservations, and thus ultimately ambiguous—that threatened communal cohesion. The toleration that made possible the successful integration of English Jews was hostile to the notion of cultural diversity. Circles and institutions quite willing to tolerate Jews as intimate associates were not willing to endorse the perpetuation of a separate Jewish culture or to see any value in the customs or beliefs of the Jewish religion. Their unshakable faith in the superiority of their own way of life seduced those Jews eager to join them into believing that this was really so. The stigma of Jewishness, however slight, however muted, persisted, continuing to work its corrosive effect on Jews whose faith and ethnicity were already receding. To expect that it might have been otherwise would be unduly utopian, for no Western society has ever developed the kind of cultural pluralism that might have discouraged the radical assimilation that we have been discussing. Whether the influx of Asian, African, and Carribean immigrants into England in the years after World War II will ultimately lead to a shift in attitudes toward cultural diversity remains to be seen. At the moment there is no reason to be sanguine that it will.

Notes

ABBREVIATIONS

C-F	Sir Thomas Colyer-Fergusson Collection, newspaper clippings, Jewish Museum, Woburn House, London
C-F (g)	Sir Thomas Colyer-Fergusson Collection, genealogical charts, Jewish Museum, Woburn House, London
CMJC	Church Mission to the Jews Collection, Bodleian Library, Oxford
DNB	*Dictionary of National Biography*
EJ	*Encyclopaedia Judaica*
JC	*Jewish Chronicle*
JHSE	Jewish Historical Society of England
LSPCJ	London Society for Promoting Christianity among the Jews
MiscJHSE	*Miscellanies of the Jewish Historical Society of England*
TJHSE	*Transactions of the Jewish Historical Society of England*

Introduction

1. See, for example, Arthur Ruppin, *The Jews of Today*, translated by Margery Bentwich (New York: Henry Holt and Co., 1913); Ruppin, *Ha-sotsiyologiyah shel ha-yehudim* [The Sociology of the Jews], 2d ed., 2 vols. in 3 (Tel Aviv: A. I. Stibel, 1932–34); Jacob Lestschinsky, "Ha-shemad be-aratsot shonot" [Apostasy in Different Lands], *Ha-olam* 5 (1911), nos. 1, 4, 5, 6, 8–12; Felix A. Theilhaber, *Der Untergang der deutschen Juden: Eine volkswirtschaftliche Studie*, 2d ed. (Berlin: Jüdischer Verlag, 1921); and various articles from the early twentieth century in the *Zeitschrift für Demographie und Statistik der Juden*, many of whose editors and contributors were Jewish nationalists.

2. Typical of the "diaspora triumphalist" school of historical writing are the following: Marsha L. Rozenblit, *The Jews of Vienna, 1867–1914: Assimilation and Identity* (Albany: State University of New York Press, 1983); Ismar Schorsch, *Jewish Reactions to German Anti-Semitism, 1870–1914* (New York: Columbia University Press, 1972); Deborah Dash Moore, *At Home in America: Second Generation New York Jews* (New York: Columbia University Press, 1981); Naomi W. Cohen, *Encounter with Emancipation: The German Jews in the United States, 1830–1914* (Philadelphia: Jewish Publication Society, 1984).

3. J. F. A. de le Roi, *Judentaufen im 19. Jahrhundert: Ein statistischer Versuch*, Schriften des Institutum Judaicum in Berlin, no. 27 (Leipzig: J. C. Hinrichs Buchhandlung, 1899). A summary of his findings has been reprinted in Paul R. Mendes-Flohr and Jehuda Reinharz, eds., *The Jew in the Modern World: A Documentary History* (New York: Oxford University Press, 1980), p. 539.

4. I include in this group historians like Lucien Wolf, Paul H. Emden, Albert M. Hyamson, Richard D. Barnett, Vivian D. Lipman, and Israel Finestein. I would also argue that Cecil Roth should be considered part of this group, for despite his academic credentials his work on Anglo-Jewish history was similar to that of the

amateurs grouped around the Jewish Historical Society of England. In brief, it lacked the conceptual rigor and critical viewpoint characteristic of professional historical scholarship.

5. Bill Williams, *The Making of Manchester Jewry, 1740–1875* (New York: Holmes & Meier, 1976).

6. This imbalance may also reflect the influence of left-wing political ideology, with its preference for poor Jews rather than rich ones, among academic historians in Great Britain. A number of recent works on the immigrant experience are written from an avowedly radical perspective. See, for example, William J. Fishman, *East End Jewish Radicals, 1875–1914* (London: Gerald Duckworth & Co., 1975); Jerry White, *Rothschild Buildings: Life in an East End Tenement Block, 1887–1920* (London: Routledge & Kegan Paul, 1980); Joseph Buckman, *Immigrants and the Class Struggle: The Jewish Immigrant in Leeds, 1880–1914* (Manchester: Manchester University Press, 1983).

1. Sephardim, 1656–1837

1. The standard accounts of the Marrano colony in sixteenth-century England are Lucien Wolf, "Jews in Tudor England," in his *Essays in Jewish History*, edited by Cecil Roth (London: JHSE, 1934), pp. 71–90; Wolf, "Jews in Elizabethan England," *TJHSE* 11 (1928): 1–91; Edgar R. Samuel, "Portuguese Jews in Jacobean London," *TJHSE* 18 (1958):171–230; Cecil Roth, *A History of the Jews in England*, 3d ed. (Oxford: The Clarendon Press, 1964), chap. 6.

2. The most-recent analysis of the resettlement is David S. Katz, *Philo-Semitism and the Readmission of the Jews to England, 1603–1655* (Oxford: The Clarendon Press, 1982). Katz successfully argues that Cromwell's motives for promoting readmission were primarily religious—i.e., he shared the same millenarian hopes as the divines who championed the return of the Jews—and not pragmatic, as is so often believed.

3. Albert M. Hyamson, *The Sephardim of England: A History of the Spanish and Portuguese Jewish Community, 1492–1951* (London: Methuen & Co., 1951), p. 22; Edgar R. Samuel, "The First Fifty Years," in *Three Centuries of Anglo-Jewish History*, edited by Vivian D. Lipman (London: JHSE, 1961), p. 39.

4. Vivian D. Lipman, "Sephardi and Other Jewish Immigrants in England in the Eighteenth Century," in *Migration and Settlement: Proceedings of the Anglo-American Jewish Historical Conference July 1970* (London: JHSE, 1971), pp. 40–41; A. S. Diamond, "Problems of the London Sephardi Community, 1720–1733—Philip Carteret Webb's Notebooks," *TJHSE* 21 (1968):42.

5. Yosef Hayim Yerushalmi, *From Spanish Court to Italian Ghetto—Isaac Cardoso: A Study in Seventeenth-Century Marranism and Jewish Apologetics* (New York: Columbia University Press, 1971), p. 44.

6. Much of what appears in the older histories of Anglo-Jewry regarding the Mendes da Costa family is untrustworthy. In describing the assimilation of the family into English society, I have utilized the recent work of Norma Perry: "La chute d'une famille sefardie: les Mendes da Costa de Londres," *Dix-huitième Siècle* 13 (1981):11–25; "Anglo-Jewry, the Law, Religious Conviction, and Self-Interest (1655–1753)," *Journal of European Studies* 14 (1984):1–23; "Voltaire and the Sephardi Bankrupt," *TJHSE* 29 (1988):39–52. Information on the economic activity of various members of the family is scattered throughout Gedalia Yogev, *Diamonds and Coral: Anglo-Dutch Jews and Eighteenth-Century Trade* (New York: Holmes & Meier, 1978).

7. Malcolm Brown, "Anglo-Jewish Country Houses from the Resettlement to 1800," *TJHSE* 28 (1984):20–25; "Jewish Country Families," *JC*, 24 May 1889; Daniel

Defoe, *A Tour through the Whole Island of Great Britain*, 2 vols. in 1 (London: J. M. Dent & Sons, 1974), 2:3.

8. F. R. Pryor, ed., *Memoirs of Samuel Hoare by his Daughter Sarah and his Widow Hannah* (London: privately published, 1911), p. 22. On the question of apostasy and the Quaker cousinhood in general, see Jacob M. Price, "The Great Quaker Business Families of Eighteenth-Century London: The Rise and Fall of a Sectarian Patriciate," in *The World of William Penn*, edited by Richard S. Dunn and Mary Maples Dunn (Philadelphia: University of Pennsylvania Press, 1986), esp. pp. 388–389.

9. Perry, "Anglo-Jewry, the Law, Religious Conviction, and Self-Interest," pp. 10, 14–17.

10. Ibid., pp. 13, 17; Todd M. Endelman, *The Jews of Georgian England: Tradition and Change in a Liberal Society, 1714–1830* (Philadelphia: Jewish Publication Society, 1979), pp. 23–24. It was not unusual for members of the same Marrano family to go in different religious directions once they had escaped from the Iberian Peninsula. See, for example, the case of the Gaspar Ribeiro family, discussed in Brian Pullan, *The Jews of Europe and the Inquisition of Venice, 1550–1670* (Oxford: Basil Blackwell, 1983), chap. 13. Pullan comments: "Marrano families were not always cohesive units capable of imposing collective choices upon their members. The richer families—married brothers and their wives, children, and servants—moved themselves and their assets cautiously over long distances, some forging ahead as scouts or pioneers to test the situation in a new centre of operations, others remaining behind to wind up affairs and exact debts in an old one. Discipline and co-operation could be maintained over great distances, but separation was also liable to encourage the habit of acting as an individual and making highly personal choices" (p. 229).

11. *The Proceedings at Large in the Arches Court of Canterbury between Mr. Jacob Mendes da Costa and Mrs. Catharine Da Costa Villa Real* (London, 1734).

12. Paul H. Emden, *Jews of Britain: A Series of Biographies* (London: Sampson Low, Marston & Co., 1943), pp. 16–17; *EJ*, s.v. "Mendes."

13. Catherine da Costa to Joanna Mendes da Costa, 21 June 1731, in *Anglo-Jewish Letters (1158–1917)*, edited by Cecil Roth (London: Soncino Press, 1938), p. 105. On Kitty Villareal, see Myer J. Landa, "Kitty Villareal, the Da Costas, and Samson Gideon," *TJHSE* 13 (1936):275; Emden, *Jews of Britain*, pp. 18–21; Hyamson, *Sephardim of England*, pp. 118–120.

14. The date of the children's baptism is in C-F (g), Villa Real.

15. Hyamson, *Sephardim of England*, pp. 120, 177; Landa, "Kitty Villareal," p. 290. On p. 120, Hyamson states, correctly, that Benjamin da Costa was the son of Joseph da Costa and the brother of Kitty da Costa Villareal Mellish, but on p. 177 he states, quite incorrectly, that he was the son of Anthony da Costa.

16. C-F (g), Da Costa; *DNB*, s.v. "Mendes da Costa, Emanuel"; Edgar Roy Samuel, "Anglo-Jewish Notaries and Scriveners," *TJHSE* 17 (1953):130–131. Both the *DNB* and Samuel state that Emanuel Mendes da Costa married Leah del Prado in 1750; neither indicates whether the marriage service was Jewish or Christian. According to Colyer-Fergusson, on the other hand, who cites the parish register of St. Benet's, Paul's Wharf, they were married in 1747 in what was apparently a Christian service.

17. Brown, "Anglo-Jewish Country Houses," pp. 31–32; Emden, *Jews of Britain*, pp. 151–152.

18. Quoted in James Picciotto, *Sketches of Anglo-Jewish History*, edited by Israel Finestein (London: Soncino Press, 1956), p. 296.

19. Emden, *Jews of Britain*, p. 151; Brown, "Anglo-Jewish Country Houses," pp. 32–33; C-F (g), Lousada and Ximenes.

20. The best survey of Joseph Salvador's life is Maurice Woolf, "Joseph Salvador, 1716–1786," *TJHSE* 21 (1968):104–137.

21. C-F (g), Salvador; Hilda F. Finberg, "Jewish Residents in Eighteenth-Century Twickenham," *TJHSE* 16 (1952):131. Finberg suggests that the young widow Salvador was perhaps frightened into being baptized by the Gordon Riots then raging in London. However, she provides no evidence that the inhabitants of Twickenham were especially alarmed by the looting and violence in London, nor does she successfully explain why the Salvador family, as Jews, had more to fear than other inhabitants of the village. She also confuses Francis Salvador (d. 1754), Joseph's father, with Francis Salvador (1746–1776), Joseph's nephew and son-in-law. A daughter of the former married the diamond and coral merchant Moses Franco (d. 1756), not a daughter of the latter.

22. [Henry Lemoine], "Authentic Memoirs of Baron Ephraim Lopes Pereira D'Aguilar," *The New Wonderful Museum and Extraordinary Magazine* 1 (1803):142–143, 147–148; Picciotto, *Sketches of Anglo-Jewish History*, pp. 92–93.

23. Isaak Markus Jost, *Geschichte der Israeliten seit der Zeit der Maccabaer bis auf unsere Tage*, 9 vols. (Berlin: Schlesinger, 1820–1828), 9:24 [my emphasis].

24. Redcliffe N. Salaman, "The Jewish Fellows of the Royal Society," *MiscJHSE* 5 (1948):148. For the extent of Jewish integration into English society in this period, see Endelman, *The Jews of Georgian England*, chap. 8.

25. The classic account of the legal status of Jews and Judaism in England is H. S. Q. Henriques, *The Jews and the English Law* (London: J. Jacobs, The Bibliophile Press, 1908).

26. Hyamson, *Sephardim of England*, pp. 33, 63. One notable exception to this tendency to romanticize the Marrano experience and thus ignore its impact on Jewish behavior in England is the recent work of Norma Perry, cited above in n. 6.

27. Yosef Hayim Yerushalmi, "Professing Jews in Post-Expulsion Spain," in *Salo Wittmayer Baron Jubilee Volume*, edited by Saul Lieberman and Arthur Hyman, 3 vols. (Jerusalem: American Academy for Jewish Research, 1974), 2:1023–1058; Yerushalmi, "Anusim ha-hozrim le-yahadut be-meah ha-shevah-esreh: haskalatam ha-yehudit ve-hachsharatam ha-nafshit" [Marranos Returning to Judaism in the Seventeenth Century: Their Jewish Knowledge and Psychological Preparation], *Proceedings of the Fifth World Congress of Jewish Studies* (Jerusalem, 1972), 2:201–209; Yerushalmi, *From Spanish Court to Italian Ghetto*, pp. 276–299.

28. Yosef Hayim Yerushalmi, *The Re-education of Marranos in the Seventeenth Century*, Rabbi Louis Feinberg Memorial Lecture in Judaic Studies, no. 3 (Cincinnati: Judaic Studies Program, University of Cincinnati, 1980), p. 7.

29. Ibid; Yerushalmi, *From Spanish Court to Italian Ghetto*, pp. 197–206.

30. Lucien Wolf, ed. and trans., *Jews in the Canary Islands, being a Calendar of Jewish Cases Extracted from the Records of the Canariote Inquisition in the Collection of the Marquess of Bute* (London: JHSE, 1926), p. 205.

31. Pullan, *The Jews of Europe and the Inquisition of Venice*, p. xiv. Pullan discusses the phenomenon of former Marranos living on the frontier between Judaism and Christianity in chapter 12.

32. Yosef Kaplan, "The Social Functions of the *Herem* in the Portuguese Jewish Community of Amsterdam in the Seventeenth Century," in *Dutch Jewish History: Proceedings of the Symposium on the History of the Jews in the Netherlands, November 28-December 3, 1982, Tel Aviv-Jerusalem*, edited by Jozeph Michman and Tirtsah Levie (Jerusalem: The Institute for Research on Dutch Jewry, Hebrew University of Jerusalem, 1984), p. 117. Kaplan emphasizes that not all New Christians who fled the Inquisition "rejoined the Jewish community body and soul." In seventeenth-century Amsterdam, he writes, there were former conversos "whose Jewish identity and whose relation to religious values were rather problematical." Such persons

were not limited in their social contacts to the Jewish community and enjoyed extensive relations with the Dutch population. Thus, communal leaders were unable to impose religious discipline on them, for excommunication (*herem*) could not bring about their social isolation (pp. 117–120). See also his more recent article "The Travels of Portuguese Jews from Amsterdam to the 'Lands of Idolatry' (1644–1724)," in *Jews and Conversos: Studies in Society and the Inquisition*, edited by Yosef Kaplan (Jerusalem: World Union of Jewish Studies, The Magnes Press, The Hebrew University, 1985), pp. 197–224. Kaplan discusses the impact of the converso experience on the genesis of heterodox opinions within the Amsterdam community in the seventeenth century in his study of Orobio de Castro, *Mi-natsrut le-yahadut: hayyav u-fealo shel ha-anus Yitshak Orobio de Castro* [From Christianity to Judaism: The Life and Work of Isaac Orobio de Castro] (Jerusalem: The Magnes Press, The Hebrew University, 1982), pp. 140–142.

33. Katz, *Philo-Semitism and the Readmission of the Jews to England*, p. 3.

34. Stephen Alexander Fortune, *Merchants and Jews: The Struggle for British West Indian Commerce, 1650–1750* (Gainesville: University of Florida Press, 1984), pp. 11, 43, 61, 113, 155, 164.

35. The best account of Gideon's life and work is still Lucy Sutherland, "Samson Gideon: Eighteenth Century Jewish Financier," *TJHSE* 17 (1953):79–90.

36. *Town and Country Magazine*, April 1786, clipping in C-F, Gideon.

37. Hyamson, *Sephardim of England*, pp. 132–133; *The Gentleman's Magazine*, vol. 65, pt. 1 (1795), p. 99.

38. Bernard Susser, "The Jews of Devon and Cornwall from the Middle Ages until the Early Twentieth Century," Ph.D. diss., University of Exeter, 1977, p. 57; Picciotto, *Sketches of Anglo-Jewish History*, pp. 296–298; Geoffrey Alderman, *The Jewish Community in British Politics* (Oxford: The Clarendon Press, 1983), p. 12; C-F (g), Lopes and Franco. Ralph Franco's father, Abraham, died in 1799, and his mother, a sister of Menasseh Masseh Lopes, had him and his sisters baptized a few years later. He was twelve at the time.

39. Richard Barnett, "Dr. Jacob de Castro Sarmento and Sephardim in Medical Practice in 18th-Century London," *TJHSE* 27 (1982):84–114. The letter is quoted in full in Hyamson, *Sephardim of England*, p. 108.

40. Isaac D'Israeli, "A Biographical Sketch of the Jewish Socrates," *The Monthly Magazine*, vol. 6, pt. 2 (July 1798):36; D'Israeli, *The Genius of Judaism* (London: Edward Moxon, 1833), especially chap. 6 and pp. 133, 146, 159–164; D'Israeli, *Curiosities of Literature*, 4 vols. in 3, 14th ed. (New York: A. C. Armstrong and Son, 1881), 1:177–192. For D'Israeli's biography, see James Ogden, *Isaac D'Israeli* (Oxford: The Clarendon Press, 1969).

41. Benajmin Disraeli to Sarah Brydges Willyams, 28 February 1853, quoted in Benjamin Jaffee, "A Reassessment of Benjamin Disraeli's Jewish Aspects," *TJHSE* 27 (1982):116.

42. The account of Isaac D'Israeli's break with Bevis Marks comes from Picciotto, *Sketches of Anglo-Jewish History*, pp. 287–292. D'Israeli's letter to the synagogue of 3 December 1813 is printed in full on pp. 289–290.

43. On dissatisfaction with the state of religious services at the Sephardi synagogue, see Todd M. Endelman, "The Checkered Career of 'Jew' King: A Study in Anglo-Jewish Social History," *AJS Review* 7–8 (1983):97; Picciotto, *Sketches of Anglo-Jewish History*, pp. 192, 261.

44. Jaffee, "Benjamin Disraeli's Jewish Aspects," p. 116.

45. W. F. Monypenny and G. E. Buckle, *The Life of Benjamin Disraeli, Earl of Beaconsfield*, rev. ed., 2 vols. (London: John Murray, 1929), 1:27; Robert Southey to C. W. W. Wynn, 30 May 1830, in *Selections from the Letters of Robert Southey*, edited by J. W. Warter, 4 vols. (London: Longman, Brown, Green, and Longmans, 1856),

4:177; Edward Jones, in *The Standard*, 28 April 1887, quoted in Jaffee, "Benjamin Disraeli's Jewish Aspects," p. 116.

46. C-F (g), Basevi; Hyamson, *Sephardim of England*, p. 246; Edward Jamilly, "Anglo-Jewish Architects and Architecture in the 18th and 19th Centuries," *TJHSE* 18 (1958):133. According to Colyer-Ferguson, Joshua Basevi was himself baptized after resigning from the synagogue, unlike his brother-in-law Isaac D'Israeli. Joshua's brother Jacob/James (1784–1861) married outside the Jewish community in 1811, that is, several years before Joshua's departure from Bevis Marks.

47. Picciotto, *Sketches of Anglo-Jewish History*, p. 187.

48. Robert Blake, *Disraeli*, Anchor Books ed. (Garden City, NY: Doubleday & Co., 1968), p. 3.

49. C-F (g), Furtado; *The Gentleman's Magazine*, vol. 70, pt. 2 (1800), p. 648, and vol. 71, pt. 1 (1801), p. 573; Picciotto, *Sketches of Anglo-Jewish History*, pp. 195–196; Samuel, "Notaries and Scriveners," pp. 132–135. Furtado's letter of resignation to the *mahamad* is printed in full in Samuel.

50. C-F (g), Lindo; applications for admission to the schools of the London Society for Promoting Christianity among the Jews, Dep. CMJ c. 114/1, CMJC; Samuel, "Notaries and Scriveners," pp. 146–147; baptismal register, Catholic Apostolic Church, Parliament Court, Old Artillery Ground, Bishopsgate, 1829–1840, RG4/4375, Public Record Office, London; Mary Denney to the *mahamad*, 20 May 1829, MS 295 (43), Archives of the Spanish and Portuguese Synagogue, London.

51. For a fuller discussion of the different circumstances in which rich and poor Jews encountered non-Jews, see Endelman, *The Jews of Georgian England*, pp. 267–269.

2. Ashkenazim, 1690–1837

1. For a fuller discussion of the growth of the Jewish population of Georgian England, see Todd M. Endelman, *The Jews of Georgian England: Tradition and Change in a Liberal Society, 1714–1830* (Philadelphia: Jewish Publication Society, 1979), pp. 170–173.

2. Ibid., chap. 5.

3. For Rothschild's activities in Manchester, see Bill Williams, *The Making of Manchester Jewry, 1740–1875* (Manchester: Manchester University Press, 1976), pp. 17–22.

4. Hart's family background and communal activities are discussed in Cecil Roth, *The Great Synagogue, London, 1690–1940* (London: Edward Goldston & Son, 1950), pp. 33–35, 48–52. The portrait of Hart is reproduced in Roth, plate 8, facing p. 46, and in *EJ*, s.v., "Hart."

5. Rachel Daiches-Dubin, "Eighteenth Century Anglo-Jewry in and around Richmond, Surrey," *TJHSE* 18 (1958):145–146; Malcom Brown, "Anglo-Jewish Country Houses from the Resettlement to 1800," *TJHSE* 28 (1984):25–26; Endelman, *The Jews of Georgian England*, p. 126.

6. Quoted in James Picciotto, *Sketches of Anglo-Jewish History*, edited by Israel Finestein (London: Soncino Press, 1956), p. 90.

7. Brown, "Anglo-Jewish Country Houses," pp. 26–29; Daiches-Dubin, "Richmond, Surrey," pp. 150–152; Horace Walpole to William Wentworth, Earl of Strafford, 11 November 1774, *The Yale Edition of Horace Walpole's Correspondence*, edited by W. S. Lewis, 48 vols. in 49 (New Haven: Yale University Press, 1937–1983), 35:350; Thomas Pitt to Mr. Hardinge, 3 June 1789, quoted in John Nichols, *Illustrations of the Literary History of the Eighteenth Century*, 8 vols. (London: Nichols, Son, and Bentley, 1817–58), 6:113.

8. Brown, "Anglo-Jewish Country Houses," p. 27; Abigail Franks to Naphtali

Franks, 4 January 1747, in *The Lee M. Friedman Collection of American Jewish Colonial Correspondence: Letters of the Franks Family (1733–1748)*, edited by Leo Hershkowitz and Isidore S. Meyer, Studies in American Jewish History, no. 5 (Waltham, MA: American Jewish Historical Society, 1968), p. 135.

9. Roth, *The Great Synagogue*, pp. 64, 88, 99, 100, 131, 299; Moses Franks, Teddington, to David Franks, Philadelphia, 8 May 1775, Tench Coxe MSS, reel 41, box 1, Historical Society of Pennsylvania, Philadelphia.

10. Daiches-Dubin, "Richmond, Surrey," pp. 152, 160.

11. Paul H. Emden, *Jews of Britain: A Series of Biographies* (London: Sampson Low, Marston & Co., 1943), p. 60; [William Granger], "Authentic Memoirs of Mrs. Levy," *The New Wonderful Museum and Extraordinary Magazine* 1 (1803):400–401; Roth, *The Great Synagogue*, p. 167.

12. Levi Alexander [and Henry Lemoine], *Memoirs of the Life and Commercial Connections of the late Benjamin Goldsmid, Esq., of Roehampton* (London, 1808), pp. 51, 101; Daiches-Duben, "Richmond, Surrey," pp. 160–163; Edmund Nelson, quoted in Emden, *Jews of Britain*, p. 96; John Francis, *Chronicles and Characters of the Stock Exchange* (Boston: W. Crosby and H. P. Nichols, 1850), p. 60.

13. John Coakley Lettsom to Rev. J. Plumptre, 15 May 1810, in *Memoirs of the Life and Writings of the late John Coakley Lettsom*, edited by Thomas Joseph Pettigrew, 3 vols. (London: Longman, Hurst, Rees, Orme, and Brown, 1817), 2:153; Alexander, *Memoirs of Benjamin Goldsmid*, p. 111; Paul H. Emden, "The Brothers Goldsmid and the Financing of the Napoleonic Wars", *TJHSE* 14 (1940):232–233; *The Commercial Habits of the Jews* (London, 1809), pp. 15–17.

14. *The Universal Magazine* 9 (1808):454.

15. *The Monthly Repository* 3 (1808):279. Benjamin Goldsmid's widow, Jessie Salomons Goldsmid, was baptized in 1812 at St. Vedast's, Foster Lane, London. C-F (g), Salomons. Their eldest son may have been baptized before his father's death. An obituary in the May issue of *The Universal Magazine* 9 (1808):452–454 noted that his eldest son, age nineteen, had "recently" converted.

16. For a fuller discussion of the growth of religious laxity among well-to-do English Jews at this time, see Endelman, *The Jews of Georgian England*, chap. 4.

17. Gedalia Yogev, *Diamonds and Coral: Anglo-Dutch Jews and Eighteenth-Century Trade* (New York: Holmes & Meier, 1978), chap. 12; Walter J. Fischel, "The Activities of a Jewish Merchant House in Bengal (1786–1798)," *Revue des Etudes Juives* 123 (1964): 493–497; C-F (g), Salomons.

18. Horace Walpole to William Mason, 11 October 1778, *Horace Walpole's Correspondence*, 28:447; *The Commercial Habits of the Jews*, p. 53.

19. *Reasons Offered to the Consideration of Parliament for Preventing the Growth of Judaism* (London, n.d.), pp. 8–9 [the edition that I used, in the library of the Jewish Theological Seminary, New York, is undated; Cecil Roth, *Magna Bibliotheca Anglo-Judaica: A Bibliographical Guide to Anglo-Jewish History*, rev. ed. (London: JHSE, 1937), p. 214, lists editions from 1738 and 1753]; Thomas Witherby, *An Attempt to Remove Prejudices Concerning the Jewish Nation by Way of Dialogue* (London, 1804), p. 2; *The British Jew to His Fellow Countrymen*, 2d ed. (London: James Ridgway, 1833), pp. 28–29. For a full discussion of Jewish images at this time, see Endelman, *The Jews of Georgian England*, chap. 3.

20. Lawrence Stone and Jeanne C. Fawtier Stone, *An Open Elite? England, 1540–1880*, abridged ed. (Oxford: Oxford University Press, 1986), p. 290.

21. Nathaniel Wraxall, *The Historical and the Posthumous Memoirs of Sir Nathaniel William Wraxall, 1772–1784*, edited by Henry B. Wheatley, 5 vols. (London: Bickers & Son, 1884), 5:121; *The Annual Register for 1806* (London, 1807), p. 458; Alfred Rubens, "Portrait of Anglo-Jewry, 1656–1836," *TJHSE* 19 (1960):25; Roth, *The Great Synagogue*, pp. 162–163.

22. On the subject of Disraeli's resolution of his Jewish identity, see Todd M. Endelman, "Disraeli's Jewishness Reconsidered," *Modern Judaism* 5 (1985):109–123.

23. Osbert Wyndham Hewett, *Strawberry Fair: A Biography of Frances, Countess Waldegrave, 1821–1879* (London: John Murray, 1956), pp. 1–4, 6–9; Emden, *Jews of Britain*, pp. 504–507; Picciotto, *Sketches of Anglo-Jewish History*, pp. 222–224. It is not clear whether Braham ever formally embraced Christianity. According to Wyndham Hewett, he converted as a young man, but according to Picciotto (1830–1897), who often relied on oral testimony preserved by previous generations, "It is not believed that he ever formally adopted any kind of Christianity, but there was nothing visible of Judaism with him in his latter days except the ineffaceable stamp imprinted by nature on his countenance" (p. 224). John Mewburn Levien, whose grandfather John Levien (a son-in-law of Braham's patron Abraham Goldsmid) himself knew Braham, maintained that he had been baptized (*Six Sovereigns of Song* [London: Novello and Co., n.d.], p. 17). In an 1826 essay, "The Religion of Actors," Charles Lamb referred to Braham as "a new convert" (Charles and Mary Lamb, *Miscellaneous Prose*, edited by E. V. Lucas [New York: The Macmillan Co., 1913], p. 338). Thus, even if Braham never formally became a Christian, some of his contemporaries certainly thought he had. For further discussion concerning his possible baptism, see Mollie Sands, "John Braham, Singer," *TJHSE* 20 (1964):210.

24. Edgar Roy Samuel, "Anglo-Jewish Notaries and Scriveners," *TJHSE* 17 (1953):145.

25. The best account of Schomberg's life and thought is Edgar R. Samuel, "Dr. Meyer Schomberg's Attack on the Jews of London," *TJHSE* 20 (1964):83–111. This article includes a translation of Schomberg's *Emunat omen*. See also C-F (g), Schomberg, and Betsy C. Corner and Christopher C. Booth, eds., *Chain of Friendship: Selected Letters of Dr. John Fothergill of London, 1735–1780* (Cambridge: Harvard University Press, 1971), introduction.

26. C-F (g), Gompertz; Emden, *Jews of Britain*, pp. 167–171.

27. David Woolf Marks and Albert Lowy, *Memoir of Sir Francis Henry Goldsmid, Bart., Q.C., M.P.* (London: C. Kegan Paul & Co., 1879), p. 5. Marks and Lowy claimed that the low level of education was not due to Jewish indifference to "the advantages of intellectual culture" but to the absence of career choices outside the world of commerce. Parents gave their sons the minimum training they needed for carrying on business, to which "oppressive legislation" had confined Anglo-Jewry: "Why, said they, should we educate talent which must need rust from want of a field for their exercise? Why should we subject the genius and the fully developed powers of our sons to bitter disappointment, and to the forlorn hope of struggling for bread?" Marks and Lowy's claim has an apologetic ring to it. While it is true that civil disabilities hampered the movement of Jews into public life and the professions, discrimination alone was not the sole or even the major cause of the neglect of learning within Anglo-Jewry. (After all, complaints about anti-intellectualism in Anglo-Jewish life persist well into the twentieth century, long after the disappearance of civil disabilities.) Moreover, there is no evidence that English Jews were eager to abandon Jewish trades to enter less lucrative and unfamiliar occupations, the claims of early champions of Jewish emancipation to the contrary. See, for example, *The British Jew to His Fellow Countrymen*, pp. 13, 20.

28. On Hurwitz/Bernard, see Haim Lieberman, *Ohel Rahal* [The Tent of Rabbi Haim Lieberman] (New York: n.p., 1979–80), pp. 483–488; Israel Zinberg, *A History of Jewish Literature*, translated and edited by Bernard Martin, 12 vols. (New York: Ktav Publishing House, 1978), 11:18–20; "Life of Dr. Bernard," in Hermann Hedwig Bernard, *The Book of Job, as Expounded to his Cambridge Pupils*, edited by Frank Chase,

2d ed. (London: Charles Higham, 1884), pp. lxxxix-ciii; S. Levy, "English Students of Maimonides," *MiscJHSE* 4 (1942):75–76.

29. Quoted in Zinberg, *History of Jewish Literature*, 11:20.

30. For Palgrave's Jewish connections, see Lewis Edwards, "A Remarkable Family: The Palgraves," in *Remember the Days: Essays on Anglo-Jewish History Presented to Cecil Roth*, edited by John M. Shaftesley (London: JHSE, 1966), pp. 304–308; Benjamin Braude, "The Heine-Disraeli Syndrome among the Palgraves of Victorian England," in *Jewish Apostasy in the Modern World: Converts and Missionaries in Historical Perspective*, edited by Todd M. Endelman (New York: Holmes & Meier, 1987), pp. 108–141.

31. Quoted in Braude, "The Heine-Disraeli Syndrome," p. 114.

32. C-F (g), Abrahams, Joseph, Hyman, Solomon. Further information on Myer Solomon can be found in Arthur Barnett, *The Western Synagogue through Two Centuries (1761–1961)* (London: Vallentine, Mitchell, 1961), pp. 151–155.

33. The letter appears in Moses Margoliouth, *The History of the Jews in Great Britain*, 3 vols. (London: Richard Bentley, 1851), 3:78–86, and is also reprinted in Cecil Roth, ed., *Anglo-Jewish Letters (1158–1917)* (London: Soncino Press, 1938), pp. 281–286. See also the comments of David W. Marks at the dedication of the new synagogue in January 1842, quoted in Lloyd P. Gartner, "Emancipation, Social Change and Communal Reconstruction in Anglo-Jewry, 1789–1881," *Proceedings of the American Academy for Jewish Research* 54 (1987): 97.

34. Michael A. Meyer, *The Origins of the Modern Jew: Jewish Identity and European Culture in Germany, 1749–1824* (Detroit: Wayne State University Press, 1967), p. 135; Meyer, *Response to Modernity: A History of the Reform Movement in Judaism* (New York: Oxford University Press, 1988), pp. 90 and 131.

35. William Cooper, *A Sermon Preached at the Jews' Chapel, Spitalfields, on Friday, May 6, 1814* (London: LSPCJ, 1814), p. 6.

36. *The Dictionary of Welsh Biography down to 1940*, s.v., "Phillips, Samuel Levi"; applications for admission to the schools of the London Society for Promoting Christianity among the Jews, Dep. CMJ c. 114/1–2, and certificates of marriage in book of baptisms, Dep. CMJ c. 249/1, CMJC; Bernard Susser, "The Jews of Devon and Cornwall from the Middle Ages until the Early Twentieth Century," Ph.D. diss., University of Exeter, 1977, pp. 299–300, 341; Eric Lipson, "The Brights of Market Place," *Transactions of the Hunter Archaeological Society* 6 (1947):117–118.

37. Naomi W. Cohen, *Encounter with Emancipation: The German Jews in the United States, 1830–1914* (Philadelphia: Jewish Publication Society, 1984), p. 42.

38. The widespread absorption of German Jewish peddlers and shopkeepers into rural and small-town society in nineteenth-century America has not yet received the scholarly attention it warrants. One typical story is that of the paternal grandfather of Arthur Schlesinger, Jr.: Bernhard Schlesinger (b. 1846), the son of a small-town horse dealer in East Prussia, emigrated to the United States in 1860. He settled first in Newark, New Jersey, where he joined an older brother who had arrived earlier and was manufacturing knapsacks for the Union Army. In 1865, seeking greener fields, he settled in Xenia, Ohio, the county seat of a rural community, with a population of 7,000–8,000. He first worked as a clerk in a clothing store and then owned his own not very successful drygoods business. In 1873, he married a gentile woman, who, while not herself a churchgoer, raised their children as Christians, since she believed that "in a community so strongly devout her children should do as their playmates did." Bernhard himself was an agnostic, maintaining "a hands-off attitude" in regard to his children's religious upbringing. Arthur Schlesinger, Sr., *In Retrospect: The History of a Historian* (New York: Harcourt, Brace & World, 1963), p. 12.

39. Evidence regarding the social integration of the Jewish poor can be found in Endelman, *The Jews of Georgian England*, pp. 223–224, 267–268.

40. Applications for admission to the schools of the London Society for Promoting Christianity among the Jews, Dep. CMJ c. 114/2, CMJC.

41. *Old Bailey Sessions Papers; or, The Whole Proceedings upon the King's Commission of Oyer and Terminer and Gaol Delivery for the City of London and also the Gaol Delivery for the County of Middlesex* 21 (1781):327–332; 24 (1783):117; 25 (1785):269–274; 41 (1798):13–16; 67 (1824):57.

42. Endelman, *The Jews of Georgian England*, chap. 6.

43. This point is developed more fully in Todd M. Endelman, "Liberalism, Laissez-Faire, and Anglo-Jewry, 1700–1905," *Contemporary Jewry* 5 (1980):2–12.

3. Native Jews in the Victorian Age

1. Vivian D. Lipman, "The Structure of London Jewry in the Mid-Nineteenth Century," in *Essays Presented to Chief Rabbi Israel Brodie on the Occasion of his Seventieth Birthday*, edited by H. J. Zimmels, J. Rabbinowitz, and Israel Finestein, 2 vols. (London: Soncino Press, 1967), 1:255–258. See also Lipman's discussion of economic mobility in his *Social History of the Jews in England, 1850–1950* (London: Watts & Co., 1954), pp. 29–32.

2. D. W. Marks, *The Jews of Modern Times: Two Lectures Delivered at the Philosophical Institution, Edinburgh* (London: P. Vallentine, n.d. [ca. 1872]), p. 50; Lipman, *Social History of the Jews in England*, pp. 75–78.

3. M. C. N. Salbstein, *The Emancipation of the Jews in Britain: The Question of the Admission of the Jews to Parliament, 1828–1860* (Rutherford, NJ: Fairleigh Dickinson University Press, 1982), p. 241; *The Jewish Year Book* 1 (1896):100–114; 2 (1897):114; 3 (1898):142; 7 (1902):224; 8 (1903):242; 11 (1906):255, 266, and 269. See also Table A.1, "Professing Jews Elected to Parliament," in Geoffrey Alderman, *The Jewish Community in British Politics* (Oxford: The Clarendon Press, 1983), pp. 174–175.

4. *The Man of the World*, 2 March 1889. The most reliable guide to the integration of the Rothschilds into English society is Richard Davis, *The English Rothschilds* (Chapel Hill: University of North Carolina Press, 1983).

5. Leopold de Rothschild to Lionel and Charlotte de Rothschild, n.d., R Fam C/5/231, Rothschild Archives, London.

6. Almeric Fitzroy, *Memoirs*, 3d ed., 2 vols. (London: Hutchinson & Co., 1925), 1:97, 102; Wilfred Scawen Blunt, *My Diaries, Being a Personal Narrative of Events, 1888–1914*, 2 vols. (London: Martin Secker, n.d.), 2:314. On the Jews in Edward's circle, see Cecil Roth, "The Court Jews of Edwardian England," in *Essays and Portraits in Anglo-Jewish History* (Philadelphia: Jewish Publication Society, 1962), pp. 282–294.

7. T. H. S. Escott, *Society in London*, rev. ed. (London: Chatto and Windus, 1886), pp. 44, 158–159; obituary of Clarissa Bischoffsheim, *JC*, 20 October 1922; letter of the pseudonymous "X", *JC*, 12 October 1877; E. C. F. Collier, ed., *A Victorian Diarist: Extracts from the Journals of Mary, Lady Monkswell* (London: John Murray, 1944), pp. 43–44, 110, 116–117, 152, 173–174, 207–208; Lucy Cohen, *Some Recollections of Claude Goldsmid Montefiore, 1858–1938* (London: Faber and Faber, 1940) p. 31. The *Jewish Chronicle* editorial regarding the defection of Sir George Faudel-Phillips's children is in C-F, Phillips; it was not dated but presumably appeared shortly after Faudel-Phillips's death.

8. Escott, *Society in London*, p. 44; M. Simon, "Anti-Semitism in England," *The Jewish Review* 2 (1911):299.

9. Stephen McKenna, *While I Remember* (New York: George H. Doran Co., 1921), p. 85; Beatrice Webb, *My Apprenticeship* (Harmondsworth: Penguin, 1971), p. 71.

To highlight the relatively open character of English society, Webb recounted the following anecdote: "I once asked a multi-millionaire of foreign extraction . . . why he had settled in England rather than in Paris, Berlin or Vienna. 'Because in England there is complete social equality,' was his rapid retort: an answer that was explained, perhaps verified, by a subsequent announcement that King Edward and his *entourage* had honoured by his presence the millionaire's palatial country residence" (p. 72).

10. George Douglas Campbell, Duke of Argyll, *Autobiography and Memoirs*, 2 vols. (New York: E. P. Dutton and Co., 1906), 1:279; Dorothy Nevill, *Under Five Reigns*, edited by Ralph Nevill (London: Methuen, 1910), pp. 140–141.

11. Stephen McKenna noted in his memoirs: "By the end of the South African war London had become a cosmopolitan place of entertainment with more money, a greater zest for pleasure, a larger proportion of sycophants and a weaker control by any recognized group of social leaders than any other European capital" (*While I Remember*, p. 86). See also the comparative study of Jose Harris and Pat Thane, "British and European Bankers, 1880–1914: An 'Aristocratic Bourgeoisie'?" in *The Power of the Past: Essays for Eric Hobsbawm*, edited by Pat Thane, Geoffrey Crossick, and Roderick Floud (Cambridge: Cambridge University Press, 1984), pp. 215–234.

12. The education of middle-class Jewish youth in the nineteenth and early twentieth centuries (as distinct from the education of the Jewish poor in charity schools maintained by the community) would be a fruitful topic for research. In the absence of any systematic survey, the following are useful: Steven Singer, "Jewish Education in the Mid-Nineteenth Century: A Study of the Early Victorian London Community," *Jewish Quarterly Review* 77 (1987):163–178; Joseph Polack, *Jewish Boys and Girls at Public Schools* (London: Central Committee for Jewish Education, [1923]); Charles H. L. Emanuel, "The Jewish House at Harrow: Recollections of the Eighties," *JC*, 23 September 1938, pp. 58–59; Alexander Carlebach, "The Rev. Dr. Joseph Chotzner," *TJHSE* 21 (1968):261–273; A. I. Polack, "Clifton and Anglo-Jewry," in *Centenary Essays on Clifton College*, edited by N. G. L. Hammond (n.p.: The Council of Clifton College, 1962), pp. 51–71; Robert Henriques, *Sir Robert Waley Cohen, 1877–1952* (London: Secker & Warburg, 1966), pp. 39–40. In addition, almost all the biographies and memoirs cited in this chapter contain material on the education of the children of the Anglo-Jewish middle class.

13. Hermann Gollancz, *Sermons and Addresses*, 1st ser. (London: Unwin Brothers, 1909), p. 262.

14. Davis, *The English Rothschilds*, pp. 56–57, 105–107; Lucy Cohen, *Arthur Cohen: A Memoir by His Daughter for His Descendants* (London: Bickers & Son, 1919), p. 13; *JC*, 6 November 1914; Cecil Roth, "The Vicissitudes of the First Oxford Jewish Graduate," *The Oxford Magazine*, new ser., 3 (1962–1963):230–232. In regard to Davis, it should be noted that being banned from lectures was not really much of a punishment. Before the universities were reformed in the mid-Victorian period, students rarely attended lectures, depending instead on private tutors to prepare them for examinations. On the entry of Jews into the ancient universities in general, see Cecil Roth, "The Jews in the English Universities," *MiscJHSE* 4 (1942):102–115; Raphael Loewe, "The Evolution of Jewish Student Feeding Arrangements in Oxford and Cambridge," in *Studies in the Cultural Life of the Jews in England*, edited by Dov Noy and Issachar Ben-Ami, Hebrew University Folklore Research Center Studies, no. 5 (Jerusalem: Magnes Press, Hebrew University, 1975), pp. 165–184; and Davis, *The Rothschilds*, chap. 4.

15. Alan Haig, *The Victorian Clergy* (London: Croom Helm, 1984), pp. 30–31.

16. Hannah Rothschild to Charlotte von Rothschild, 22 November 1841, R Fam C/1/14; Leopold de Rothschild to Lionel and Charlotte de Rothschild, n.d., R Fam C/5/32, Rothschild Archive, London.

17. Redcliffe N. Salaman, *Whither Lucien Wolf's Anglo-Jewish Community?*, The Lucien Wolf Memorial Lecture, 1953 (London: JHSE, 1954), p. 17; Israel Rubinowitz to Herbert Bentwich, 17 December 1906, A100/7aleph/20, Herbert Bentwich Collection, CZA; Rose Henriques, unpublished biography of Basil Henriques, chap. 8, Basil Henriques Papers, AJ/195, Anglo-Jewish Archives, London; Loewe, "Jewish Student Feeding Arrangements," p. 169.

18. Davis, *The English Rothschilds*, p. 143. Davis notes that the second generation of Rothschild men in England—Lionel, Anthony, and Mayer—were not quite accepted into English society, but that Lionel's sons—Nathaniel, Leopold, and Alfred—were very much a part of it, largely because of contacts they made at Cambridge.

19. *Correspondence between Mr. Oswald John Simon and the Dean of Litchfield, Rev. George Margoliouth, and Rev. A. E. Suffrin, on Parochial Missions to the Jews* (London: The Jewish World, 1887), pp. 15–16, 25; Lily Montagu, quoted in *The First Fifty Years: A Record of Liberal Judaism in England, 1900–1950* (London: The Liberal Jewish Synagogue, 1950), p. 4; Diana Hopkinson, *Family Inheritance: A Life of Eva Hubback* (London: Staples Press, 1954), pp. 60–61.

20. Cecil Roth, "The Collapse of English Jewry," *Jewish Monthly* 1 (July 1947):11; *Jewish World*, 15 July 1892.

21. Louisa de Rothschild, *Lady de Rothschild: Extracts from Her Notebooks*, edited by Constance Battersea (London: Arthur L. Humphreys, 1912), p. 4; Constance Battersea, *Reminiscences* (London: Macmillan, 1922), pp. 21–22; Lucy Cohen, *Lady de Rothschild and Her Daughters, 1821–1931* (London: John Murray, 1935), pp. 67 and 109. Richard Davis notes that in the Rothschild homes in general the Sabbath and other major holidays were observed. During Lionel's lifetime (d. 1879), the whole family gathered for the Passover seder at his house in Piccadilly (*The English Rothschilds*, p. 161).

22. Herbert Samuel, *Memoirs* (London: Cresset Press, 1945), pp. 4, 18; Edwin Samuel, *A Lifetime in Jerusalem: The Memoirs of the Second Viscount Samuel* (London: Vallentine, Mitchell, 1970), pp. 15, 306, 311; Adelaide Franklin to Herbert and Beatrice Samuel, 27 January 1898, B/6/39, Herbert Samuel Papers, House of Lords Record Office, London.

23. Cohen, *Claude Goldsmid Montefiore*, p. 29; Leonard A. Montefiore, *Essays and Letters* (London: privately published, 1881), pp. xxi–xxii; Monk Gibbon, *Netta* (London: Routledge and Kegan Paul, 1960), p. 11; Diana Hopkinson, *The Incense-Tree: An Autobiography* (London: Routledge and Kegan Paul, 1968), p. 5.

24. Rose Henriques, biography of Basil Henriques, chap. 1; Basil L. Q. Henriques, *The Indiscretions of a Warden* (London: Methuen, 1937), pp. 9, 11–14.

25. Basil Henriques, *Indiscretions*, p. 9; David Henriques to Basil Henriques, 1911, quoted in Rose Henriques, biography of Basil Henriques, chap. 8; Hannah F. Cohen, *Changing Faces: A Memoir of Louisa Lady Cohen* (London: Martin Hopkinson, 1937), p. 238.

26. Hannah Cohen, *Changing Faces*, pp. 103–104; Basil Henriques, *Indiscretions*, p. 13; Lucy Cohen, *Lady Louisa de Rothschild*, pp. 109–110. Marion Kaplan's work on Jewish women in imperial Germany has shown that there too women played a dominant role in the maintenance and transmission of Judaism in the home—in contrast to the situation before the onset of modernization. Marion A. Kaplan, "Priestess and Hausfrau: Women and Tradition in the German-Jewish Family," in *The Jewish Family: Myths and Reality*, edited by Steven M. Cohen and Paula E. Hyman (New York: Holmes & Meier, 1986), pp. 67–73.

27. On the development of Reform Judaism in England, see Stephen Sharot, "Reform and Liberal Judaism in London, 1840–1940," *Jewish Social Studies* 41 (1979):211–228; Michael Leigh, "Reform Judaism in Britain, 1840–1970," in *Reform*

Judaism: Essays on Reform Judaism in Britain, ed. Dow Marmur (London: Reform Synagogues of Great Britain, 1973), pp. 3–50; Robert Liberles, "The Origins of the Jewish Reform Movement in England," *AJS Review* 1 (1976):121–150; Jakob J. Petuchowski, "Karaite Tendencies in an Early Reform Haggadah: A Study in Comparative Liturgy," *Hebrew Union College Annual* 31 (1960):223–249; Steven Singer, "Jewish Religious Thought in Early Victorian London," *AJS Review* 10 (1985): 181–210; Michael A. Meyer, *Response to Modernity: A History of the Reform Movement in Judaism* (New York: Oxford University Press, 1988), pp. 171–180.

28. Escott, *Society in London*, pp. 80–81; Hugh McLeod, *Class and Religion in the Late Victorian City* (London: Croom Helm, 1974), p. 222. McLeod's work, to which I am considerably indebted, cogently describes the place of religion in the lives of late Victorian Londoners.

29. McLeod, *Class and Religion*, p. 152.

30. Lucy Cohen, *Arthur Cohen*, pp. 24, 150; Israel Finestein, "Arthur Cohen, Q.C., 1829–1914," in *Remember the Days: Essays on Anglo-Jewish History Presented to Cecil Roth*, edited by John M. Shaftesley (London: JHSE, 1966), p. 294.

31. Percy Edwin Spielmann, *The Early History of the Spielmann Family and of Marion Harry Alexander Spielmann (1858–1948)* (Reading: privately printed, 1951), p. 57. Marion Spielmann returned home immediately after his conversation with Adler and set down his memory of it. His son included it in full in the above family history, pp. 53–61.

32. It is interesting to note, by way of comparison, that in Germany at this time Jewish banking families played almost no role in Jewish community life or even in Jewish philanthropy, with a few notable exceptions. "They were an exclusive, closely-knit group of families, marrying among themselves, keeping to themselves, and mostly caring only for themselves. Their social contacts and aspirations turned toward the ruling aristocracy and a good number succeeded in being absorbed in its ranks." Avraham Barkai, "The German Jews at the Start of Industrialization: Structural Change and Mobility, 1835–1860," in *Revolution and Evolution: 1848 in German-Jewish History*, edited by Werner E. Mosse, Arnold Paucker, and Reinhard Rürup (Tubingen: J. C. B. Mohr, 1981), p. 141.

33. One reason Orthodox institutions like the United Synagogue and the Chief Rabbinate enjoyed the support of wealthy Jews who were not themselves observant is that they could lay claim to being the Jewish equivalents of the Church of England and the Archbishop of Canterbury. The conservative nature of Orthodoxy paralleled the conservative nature of the established church, the liberal nature of Reform that of Nonconformity.

34. Henriques, *Sir Robert Waley Cohen*, p. 179.

35. *JC*, 6 November 1914.

36. Hermann Adler to Henry de Worms, 3 May 1886, Correspondence of the Chief Rabbi, vol. 27 (18 October 1885–6 May 1886), Office of the Chief Rabbi, London; *JC*, 7 May 1886, 16 January 1903; R. T. Davidson to F. N. Pickford, 21 December 1908, R. T. Davidson Papers, vol. 147, f. 205, Lambeth Palace Library, London.

37. Davis, *The English Rothschilds*, pp. 59–61; Cecil Roth, *The Magnificent Rothschilds* (London: Robert Hale, 1939), p. 39; Robert Henrey, *A Century Between* (London: William Heinemann, 1937), pp. 11–12, 21–22, 68–71; Anthony de Rothschild to his brothers, 11 and 17 July 1839, XI 103/0/38 and XI 103/0/40*, Rothschild Archive, London. It is not clear whether Hannah formally converted before marrying FitzRoy. Richard Davis of Washington University, St. Louis, who has examined much of the family correspondence in the Rothschild Archive in London, informs me that he has never seen any reference to her baptism and that he suspects she just quietly went to church. Personal communication, 9 November 1982.

38. Lucy Cohen, *Lady de Rothschild*, pp. 153–156, 181–183, 280–281.

39. Chaim Bermant, *The Cousinhood* (London: Macmillan, 1971), p. 155.

40. Davis, *The English Rothschilds*, p. 164.

41. In an undated letter to Leopold de Rothschild some time before his marriage to Constance, Flower wrote: "It was charming at Brighton. I never saw so many people to laugh at in all my life. It ought to be called the New Jerusalem I think—for every other name in the list of visitors is Hebraic and every face bears the type of the race Cainlike upon it" (D Fam C/1/1, Rothschild Archive, London).

42. In addition to family opposition, Jewish public opinion also openly criticized the match. The *Jewish Chronicle*, 5 October 1877, feared that intermarriage at the top of the communal hierarchy would set a bad example: "The rabbinical query is on every lip: 'If the flame seized on the cedars, how will fare the hyssop on the wall; if the leviathan is brought up with a hook, how will the minnows escape?'" The newspaper correctly saw that matches such as this resulted from the successful social integration of the Rothschilds: "May it not be presumed that if opportunities had been as freely afforded for intercourse with high merit in Jewish ranks as it was with that in other circles that racial feeling and religious considerations would have inclined the balance in a direction as gratifying to the community as it is now distressing?" Hannah's intermarriage, moreover, could still rouse passions a decade later. Following a ceremonial visit of hers to a Hebrew school in Edinburgh in October 1888, an indignant reader wrote to the *Jewish Standard*, a short-lived, London-based weekly that championed traditional Judaism, on 2 November 1888, attacking the school for allowing Hannah to visit and treating her as an honored guest. Judaism teaches that intermarriage is wrong, he emphasized, and no exceptions, even for Rothschilds, should be made.

43. Robert Rhodes James, *Rosebery: A Biography of Archibald Philip, Fifth Earl of Rosebery* (London: Weidenfeld and Nicholson, 1963), pp. 79–85, 225; Bermant, *The Cousinhood*, p. 162; Davis, *The English Rothschilds*, pp. 164–173.

44. *JC*, 7 July 1933; Paul H. Emden, *Jews of Britain: A Series of Biographies* (London: Sampson Low, Marston & Co., 1943), p. 537; George Edward Cokayne, *The Complete Peerage*, 13 vols. in 14 (London: St. Catherine Press, 1910–1959), 4:229–230.

45. On the growth of Jewish neighborhoods outside areas of primary settlement, see Vivian D. Lipman, "Social Topography of a London Congregation: The Bayswater Synagogue, 1863–1963," *Jewish Journal of Sociology* 6 (1964):69–74; Lipman, "The Rise of Jewish Suburbia," *TJHSE* 21 (1968):78–103; Zoe Josephs, ed., *Birmingham Jewry, 1749–1914* (Birmingham: Birmingham Jewish History Research Group, 1980), pp. 16–19.

46. Lewis S. Benjamin, "The Passing of the English Jew," *The Nineteenth Century* 72 (1912):493–494; Julia Frankau [Frank Danby], *Dr. Phillips: A Maida Vale Idyll* (London: Vizetelly & Co., 1887), pp. 168, 192.

47. John Mills, *The British Jews*, 2d ed. (London: Houlston and Wright, 1862), pp. 324–325; Frankau, *Dr. Phillips*, p. 168; Chaim Weizmann to Vera Khatzman, 14 April and 8 September 1905, *The Letters and Papers of Chaim Weizmann*, ser. A, vol. 4, edited by Camillo Dresner and Barnet Litvinoff (London: Oxford University Press, 1973), pp. 77, 141–142.

48. *The Jewish Standard*, 15 June 1888; Simeon Singer, *The Literary Remains of the Rev. Simeon Singer*, edited by Israel Abrahams, 3 vols. (London: George Routledge and Sons, 1908), 1:107; Leonard Merrick, *Violet Moses*, 3 vols. (London: Richard Bentley and Son, 1891), 2:235. To some extent, cardplaying symbolized the dividing line between upper middle-class Jewry and middle-class Jewry. Maida Vale Jews played cards; Bayswater Jews did not. See Merrick, *Violet Moses*, 2:264; Olga Somech Phillips, *Solomon J. Solomon: A Memoir of Peace and War* (London: Herbert Joseph [1933]), p. 25.

49. Benjamin, "The Passing of the English Jew," p. 494; Amy Levy, *Reuben Sachs: A Sketch* (London: Macmillan, 1888), p. 103; Frankau, *Dr. Phillips*, pp. 9, 165.

50. Lipman, *Social History of the Jews in England*, pp. 36–37; [Charlotte Montefiore], *A Few Words to the Jews*, 2d ed. (London: John Chapman, 1855), p. 88; "A Few Words on the Sabbath," *Jewish Sabbath Journal*, 3 February 1855; Mills, *The British Jews*, p. 174. The attempt by Lipman to deny the implications of the low synagogue attendance that he himself presents is curious and can only be attributed to an inability to admit that the community was not as attached to Judaism as he would like to imagine it was. This kind of filiopietism is characteristic of the old school of Anglo-Jewish historiography.

51. These figures are drawn from appendices 1 and 4 in Lipman, "The Rise of Jewish Suburbia." For the number of persons in attendance at each synagogue in London, see Richard Mudie-Smith, ed., *The Religious Life of London* (London: Hodder and Stoughton, 1904), p. 265.

52. Norman Bentwich to Herbert Bentwich, 21 April 1897, A100/57, Herbert Bentwich Collection, Central Zionist Archives, Jerusalem.

53. Gollancz, *Sermons*, 1st ser., pp. 92–93; *Jewish Society*, 7 March 1890; Salaman, *Lucien Wolf's Anglo-Jewish Community*, p. 10.

54. *JC*, 1 August 1884; album of newspaper clippings, 1872–1893, A100/39, Herbert Bentwich Collection, Central Zionist Archives, Jerusalem; G. J. Emanuel, *The Mission of Israel*, sermon, 23 January 1897, Birmingham Synagogue (n.p.: privately published, n.d.), p. 3.

55. Singer, *Literary Remains*, 1:14; *Jewish Standard*, 8 June 1888; *JC*, 15 November 1901. One of the bleakest pictures of the state of Anglo-Judaism was drawn by Samuel Daiches (1878–1949), rabbi of the Sunderland synagogue, in a sermon of 1907: "The whole hopelessness and lifelessness of the present state of Judaism here is vividly brought before me, and nothing seems to be left but despair. A gloomy landscape. Devastated fields. Trees outrooted. A leaden sky. Thunder and lightning. A sweeping storm. No life. No sunshine. The end seems to be near. . . ." *Judaism in England: Congregation and Minister* (Sunderland: privately published, 1907), p. 4.

56. Hermann Adler, *The Jews during the Victorian Era: A Sermon Preached at the North London Synagogue, June 26, 1897* (London: Alfred J. Isaacs & Sons, [1897]), pp. 9–11; Singer, *Literary Remains*, 1: 147–148.

57. On Jewish images in Victorian novels and on the Victorian stage, see Anne Aresty Naman, *The Jew in the Victorian Novel: Some Relationships between Prejudice and Art* (New York: AMS Press, 1980); Montagu Frank Modder, *The Jew in the Literature of England* (Philadelphia: Jewish Publication Society, 1961), chaps. 8–14; M. J. Landa, *The Jew in Drama* (London: P. S. King & Son, 1926), chaps. 12–16.

58. M. Lissack, *Jewish Perseverance, or, The Jew at Home and Abroad: An Autobiography* (London: Hamilton, Adams, & Co., 1851), p. ix; E. Lawrence Levy, *Birmingham Jewry, 1870, Then; and 1929, Now* (Birmingham: Birmingham Jewish Literary Association, n.d.), p. 52.

59. Jawaharlal Nehru, *Jawaharlal Nehru: An Autobiography* (London: John Lane, Bodley Head, 1936), p. 18; Charles de Rothschild to Hugh Birrell, quoted in Miriam Rothschild, *Dear Lord Rothschild: Birds, Butterflies and History* (Philadelphia: Balaban Publishers, 1983), p. 90; John Carswell, *The Exile: A Life of Ivy Litvinov* (London: Faber and Faber, 1983), p. 35. Litvinov incorporated her mother's views about the social burden of Jewishness into her short story "Call It Love," first published in 1969 in *The New Yorker* and recently republished in a collection of her stories, *She Knew She Was Right* (London: Virago Press, 1988).

60. Merrick, *Violet Moses*, 1:151; Leonard Woolf, *The Wise Virgins: A Story of*

Words, Opinions and a Few Emotions (New York: Harcourt Brace Jovanovich, 1979), pp. 9, 123, 195; Virginia Stephen to Leonard Woolf, 1 May 1912, *The Letters of Virginia Woolf*, edited by Nigel Nicolson, 6 vols. (London: The Hogarth Press, 1975–1979), 1:496; Virginia Woolf to Ethel Smyth, 2 August 1930, *Letters*, 4:195–196. Woolf was never able to accept her in-laws' Jewishness. After Leonard's mother, brother Herbert, sister Bella, and Bella's husband came to tea at Monks House, Rodmell, Virginia wrote to Ethel Smyth, 28 September 1930, "here they are, dressed, like all Jews, as if for high tea in a hotel lounge, never mixing with the country, talking nasally, talking incessantly, but requiring at intervals the assurance that I think it really jolly to have them." With the exception of Leonard, she continued, all of her mother-in-law's nine children "might well have been drowned without the world wagging one ounce the worse" (*Letters*, 4:222–223).

61. MS diary of J. L. Mallet, entry for 24 June 1830, quoted in Pierro Sraffa, ed., *The Works and Correspondence of David Ricardo*, 11 vols. (Cambridge: Cambridge University Press, 1951–1955, 1973), 10:16; Joseph L. Ricardo to Horace Wilkinson, 12 November 1895, C-F (g), Ricardo; Francis Espinasse, *Literary Recollections and Sketches* (London: Hodder and Stoughton, 1893), p. 19; Lewis Edwards, "A Remarkable Family: The Palgraves," in *Remember the Days: Essays on Anglo-Jewish History Presented to Cecil Roth*, edited by John M. Shaftesley (London: JHSE, 1966), p. 306; Arthur Schomberg to Israel Solomons, 8 June 1904, C-F (g), Schomberg.

62. Victor Rousseau Emanuel, *The Selmans* (New York: The Dial Press, 1925), p. 16. Although the novel was written in the 1920s, it describes events and attitudes at the turn of the century.

63. Victoria Sackville-West, *The Edwardians* (London: The Hogarth Press, 1930), p. 129; Rothschild, *Dear Lord Rothschild*, pp. 26–27; Frances Evelyn Greville, Countess of Warwick, *Discretions* (New York: Charles Scribner's Sons, 1931), p. 43. Sackville-West's novel is set in the years 1905–1906 and draws upon the snobbery the author imbibed as a child from her parents, Lord and Lady Sackville, while she was growing up at Knole, her family's magnificent country home. Both Sackville-West and her husband, Sir Harold Nicolson, disliked Jews, according to their son Nigel. *Portrait of a Marriage* (New York: Atheneum, 1973), p. 230.

64. Colin Holmes, *Anti-Semitism in British Society, 1876–1939* (New York: Holmes & Meier, 1979), part 1.

65. *JC*, 25 August 1911; Morris Joseph, "Anti-Semitic Tendencies in England," *JC*, 4 July 1913.

66. *JC*, 12 April 1907; *DNB*, q.v., "Samuel Phillips"; *The Times*, 17 October 1854; Samuel Phillips, *Caleb Stukeley* (London: Nathaniel Cooke, 1854); *DNB*, q.v., "Julius Salter Elias"; R. J. Minney, *Viscount Southwood* (London: Odhams Press, 1954), pp. 20–21. Minney fails to mention Elias's Jewish origins—no doubt intentionally, since the biography was commissioned by the directors of Odhams, who were probably reluctant to broadcast the firm's Jewish associations in the antisemitic atmosphere of the time.

67. Singer, *Literary Remains*, 1:254–255; Gollancz, *Sermons*, 1st ser., pp. 190–191; Gollancz, *Sermons and Addresses*, 2d ser. (London: Chapman & Hall, 1916), p. 108; F. L. Cohen, "Jews in the Army and Militia," *JC*, 22 April 1904 and 23 March 1900.

68. Merrick, *Violet Moses*, 2:79, 139; Frankau, *Dr. Phillips*, pp. 112–113.

69. C-F, Cohen; Gollancz, *Sermons*, 2d ser., pp. 96–97.

70. Walter G. Yates to Herbert Samuel, 25 January 1896, B/6/10, and 30 June 1896, B/6/13, Herbert Samuel Papers, House of Lords Record Office, London; Kingsley Martin, *Harold Laski (1893–1950): A Biographical Memoir* (London: Victor Gollancz, 1953), pp. 14–17, 54–55.

71. C-F, Halford, Henry, and Magnus.

72. Sigismund David Waley, *Edwin Montagu: A Memoir and an Account of His Visits to India* (New York: Asia Publishing House, 1964), pp. 5, 7–8, 11, 24.

73. Ibid., pp. 47–48, 58; H. H. Asquith, *Letters to Venetia Stanley,* edited by Michael Brock and Eleanor Brock (Oxford: Oxford University Press, 1982), pp. 6, 576, 604. The editors of the Stanley-Asquith correspondence suggest that Venetia's initial reluctance to convert was related to the social antisemitism of the period: "Venetia's circle was not free of anti-Semitism, and in 1912 this flight from Christianity to Judaism, largely for financial motives, would have represented a painful defiance of convention even for a free-thinking Stanley." They attribute her change of mind in 1915 to the relaxation of social standards during the war; in that atmosphere, they write, "it no longer seemed impossible for a Stanley to embrace the Jewish faith" (pp. 6, 351).

74. *Jewish Society,* 31 January, 18 June, 25 June, 13 August 1890.

75. Singer, *Literary Remains,* 1: 156; Morris Joseph, *The Jewish Spirit* (London [1910]), p. 3.

76. C-F, Lee; Evelyn Sharp, *Hertha Ayrton, 1854–1923: A Memoir* (London: Edward Arnold & Co., 1926), pp. 24–26; Hester Burton, *Barbara Bodichon, 1827–1891* (London: John Murray, 1949), pp. 207–209; Sheila R. Herstein, *A Mid-Victorian Feminist, Barbara Leigh Smith Bodichon* (New Haven: Yale University Press, 1985), pp. 184–188. Through Bodichon, Marks met George Eliot, whose house she frequently visited. When *Daniel Deronda* appeared in 1876, many thought that Marks was the inspiration for the character of Mirah.

77. I have drawn on the following sources in describing Franklin's rebellion: Hugh Franklin Papers, box 226, Fawcett Library, City of London Polytechnic, folder 1 (autobiographical notes, 1911; notes for paper entitled "Religion," 21 February 1909), folder 4 (Victor Duval to Arthur L. Franklin, 13 January 1911); Helen Bentwich, *If I Forget Thee: Some Chapters of Autobiography, 1912–1920* (London: Paul Elek Books, 1973), pp. 4, 10–11; C-F (g) Franklin; Arthur Ellis Franklin, ed., *Records of the Franklin Family and Collaterals,* 2d ed. (London: George Routledge & Sons, 1935), pp. 83–84; copy of an entry of marriage, Hugh Arthur Franklin and Elsie Constance Tuke, 16 May 1923, General Register Office, London.

78. Jeffrey Cox, *The English Churches in a Secular Society: Lambeth, 1870–1930* (New York: Oxford University Press, 1982), pp. 232–233, 238–240.

79. Vincent Alan McClelland, *English Roman Catholics and Higher Education, 1830–1903* (Oxford: The Clarendon Press, 1973), pp. 5, 20, 206, 208, 378, 381, 408.

80. Phillips, *Solomon,* pp. 56–57; Norman Bentwich, *My Seventy-Seven Years: An Account of My Life and Times, 1883–1960* (Philadelphia: Jewish Publication Society, 1961), pp. 7–8.

81. Benjamin, "The Passing of the English Jew," p. 496.

4. German Immigrants in the Victorian Age

1. The most reliable estimate of the German Jewish exodus is in Avraham Barkai, "German-Jewish Migrations in the Nineteenth Century, 1830–1910," *Leo Baeck Institute Year Book* 30 (1985):306–310.

2. C. C. Aronsfeld estimates that of the 250,000 Jews who left Germany between 1830 and 1930 only "a very few thousand" chose Britain. "German Jews in Victorian England," *Leo Baeck Institute Year Book* 7 (1962): 312. Aronsfeld's essay, which is essentially a survey of prominent Victorians of German Jewish origins, is the only treatment of the topic, aside from paragraphs here and there in Bill Williams, *The Making of Manchester Jewry, 1740–1875* (Manchester: Manchester University Press, 1976).

3. A. R. Rollin, "The Jewish Contribution to the British Textile Industry: Builders of Bradford," *TJHSE* 17 (1953):47, 49; Robert Speaight, *William Rothenstein: The Portrait of an Artist in His Time* (London: Eyre & Spottiswoode, 1962), pp. 1–3; Ernest Jones, *The Life and Work of Sigmund Freud*, 3 vols. (New York: Basic Books, 1953), 1:13; Jacob Behrens, *Sir Jacob Behrens, 1806–1889* (n.p.: privately published, [ca. 1925]).

4. Felix Semon, *The Autobiography of Sir Felix Semon*, edited by Henry C. Semon and Thomas A. McIntyre (London: Jarrolds, 1926); J. M. Cohen, *The Life of Ludwig Mond* (London: Methuen, 1956).

5. Williams, *The Making of Manchester Jewry*, pp. 93, 168–169; Rosemary Ashton, *Little Germany: Exile and Asylum in Victorian England* (Oxford: Oxford University Press, 1986), p. 207; *The Christian Reformer*, new ser., 9 (1853):596–597.

6. J. B. Priestley, *English Journey* (London: William Heinemann, 1934), p. 160; Oswald E. Stroud, ed., *The Story of the Stroud Family* (Bradford: privately published, [ca. 1974]), p. 83; Zoë Josephs, *Birmingham Jewry, 1749–1914* (Birmingham: Birmingham Jewish History Research Group, 1980), pp. 23–24; Williams, *The Making of Manchester Jewry*, pp. 169, 260, 412n95; Ashton, *Little Germany*, p. 164.

7. *JC*, 23 March 1900; Alexander Behr, "Isidore Gerstenberg (1821–1876)— Founder of the Council of Foreign Bondholders," *TJHSE* 17 (1953):208–209.

8. Stanley Chapman, *The Rise of Merchant Banking* (London: Unwin Hyman, 1984), pp. 45, 50, 54, 136.

9. Behrens, *Sir Jacob Behrens*, pp. 20–21; Semon, *Autobiography*, pp. 31–32, 60; Jones, *Sigmund Freud*, 1:13, 24, 178–179.

10. Behrens, *Sir Jacob Behrens*, pp. 11–13; J. M. Cohen, *The Life of Ludwig Mond* (London: Methuen, 1956), pp. 16, 62.

11. Cecily Sidgwick [Mrs. Andrew Dean], *Isaac Eller's Money* (London: T. Fisher Unwin, 1889), pp. 46, 110.

12. Bernard Susser, ed., "Statistical Accounts of All the Congregations in the British Empire," 5606/1845, MS 104, Office of the Chief Rabbi, London, printed in *Provincial Jewry in Victorian Britain*, edited by Aubrey Newman (London: JHSE, 1975); *JC*, 8 and 15 April 1859, 11 August 1865, 21 and 28 October 1870, 6 October 1871; Chaim Weizmann, *Trial and Error* (New York: Harper & Brothers, 1949), p. 115; Stroud, *The Stroud Family*, pp. 26–27.

13. Behrens, *Behrens*, pp. 91, 93–94; *JC*, 21 March and 4 April 1913.

14. Cohen, *Mond*, pp. 189, 247; Jean Goodman, *The Mond Legacy: A Family Saga* (London: Weidenfeld and Nicolson, 1982), pp. 30, 31, 34, 39, 68, 69, 75; Hector Bolitho, *Alfred Mond, First Lord Melchett* (London: Martin Secker, 1933), pp. 44, 92, 358.

15. Semon, *Autobiography*, pp. 33–34; Henry C. Semon to S. Levy, 21 October 1926, AJ/151/1/B/14, Cecil Roth Papers, Anglo-Jewish Archives, London.

16. Solomon Marcus Schiller-Szinessy, *Harmony and Dis-Harmony between Judaism and Christianity: Two Sermons Preached on the Sabbaths Shemot & Va-eira 5619 (December 25th, 1858, and January 1st, 1859) at the Manchester Synagogue of British Jews* (Manchester [1859]), p. 9; Williams, *Manchester Jewry*, pp. 82–83, 93; *The Christian Reformer*, new ser., 9 (1853):596–597; Malwida von Meysenbug, *Memoiren einer Idealisten*, 10th ed., 3 vols. (Berlin: Schuster and Loeffler, 1906), 2:38–39; Cross Street Chapel, Manchester, *Proceedings on the Occasion of the Bi-Centenary of the Chapel, June 24–25th 1894* (Manchester, 1894), p. 67.

17. C. C. Aronsfeld, "German Jews in Nottingham," *AJR Information*, December 1955, p. 8; Roy A. Church, *Economic and Social Change in a Midland Town: Victorian Nottingham, 1815–1900* (London: Frank Cass & Co., 1966), pp. 76–77, 182; register of births and baptisms, High Pavement Chapel, Nottingham, 1828–1837, RG4/2674, Public Record Office, London; High Pavement Chapel, Nottingham, *A Biographical*

Catalogue of Portraits ([Nottingham], n. d.), p. 28; William Blazeby, *My Year's Ministry at the Old High Pavement Chapel, Nottingham* (London, [ca. 1906]), p. 8.

18. John Seed, "Unitarianism, Political Economy and the Antinomies of Liberal Culture in Manchester, 1830–50," *Social History* 7 (1982):1–25; Margaret J. Shaen, ed., *Memorials of Two Sisters: Susanna and Catherine Winkworth* (London: Longmans, Green, and Co., 1908), p. 26.

19. Rosslyn Hill Chapel, list of members, 1 January 1875, RNC 38.189; subscriptions, 1886–1896, RNC 38.154; minutes, 1907–1922, RNC 38.132, Dr. Williams's Library, London; Cecily Sidgwick to Cecil Roth, 16 October 1926, AJ/151/1/A/4/54, Anglo-Jewish Archives, London; Frederic Whyte, *William Heinemann: A Memoir* (London: Jonathan Cape, 1928), pp. 30, 38–39.

20. John Carswell, *The Exile: A Life of Ivy Litvinov* (London: Faber and Faber, 1983), pp. 21–23; *DNB*, 1922–1930, s.v. "Sonnenschein, Edward Adolf"; F. A. Mumby and Frances H. S. Stallybrass, *From Swan Sonnenschein to George Allen & Unwin Ltd.* (London: George Allen & Unwin, 1955), pp. 13–15, 36; *The Ethical Message*, special number, A Souvenir of the Ethical Church, vol. 2, nos. 7–8 (1917), pp. 30–31; Susan Budd, *Varieties of Unbelief: Atheists and Agnostics in English Society, 1850–1960* (London: Heinemann, 1977), p. 205.

21. There is no social history of the Ethical Culture movement in the United States, but contemporary observers frequently remarked on the overwhelmingly Jewish makeup of the societies. Waldo Frank, for example, wrote in 1919: "The main adherence of these Societies in New York and other American cities was among the prosperous Jews who had shown themselves most apt to run the American race. Religious memories haunted these people. Most of them had been brought up in the Jewish church. They turned to Adler to give them a semblance of creed: one which would still the stirring of the Past, bring them no preoccupation to conflict with their affairs and, on the contrary, fit them the more aptly and the more politely for the life of respectable material dominion which America afforded." *Our America* (New York: Boni and Liveright, 1919), p. 87.

22. Budd, *Varieties of Unbelief*, pp. 36, 84–85, 110; Horace L. Friess, *Felix Adler and Ethical Culture: Memories and Studies*, edited by Fannia Weingartner (New York: Columbia University Press, 1981), p. 114.

23. See, for example, Theodor Lessing, *Der jüdische Selbsthass* (Berlin: Jüdischer Verlag, 1930); Peter Loewenberg, "Antisemitismus und jüdischer Selbsthass," *Geschichte und Gesellschaft* 5 (1979): 455–475; and Sander L. Gilman, *Jewish Self-Hatred: Anti-Semitism and the Hidden Language of the Jews* (Baltimore: Johns Hopkins University Press, 1986).

24. A. S. Diamond, "A Sketch of Leeds Jewry in the 19th Century," in Newman, *Provincial Jewry in Victorian Britain*; *JC*, 11 August 1865.

25. Williams, *The Making of Manchester Jewry*, p. 262; *JC*, 8 April 1859; Michael A. Meyer, *Response to Modernity: A History of the Reform Movement in Judaism* (New York: Oxford University Press, 1988), p. 131.

26. *JC*, 23 March 1900; Bernard Homa, *A Fortress in Anglo-Jewry: The Story of the Machzike Hadath* (London: Shapiro, Vallentine & Co., 1953), pp. 10–11, 70.

27. Humbert Wolfe, *Now a Stranger* (London: Cassell and Co., 1933); Wolfe, *The Upward Anguish* (London: Cassell and Co., 1938). See also Norman Bentwich, "Humbert Wolfe: Poet and Civil Servant," *Menorah Journal* 31 (1943):34–45.

28. Speaight, *William Rothenstein*, pp. 5–6.

29. John Rothenstein, *Summer's Lease: Autobiography, 1901–1938* (New York: Holt, Rinehart and Winston, 1965), pp. 9, 30, 37, 123; Speaight, *William Rothenstein*, pp. 151, 405–406, 410.

30. Frankau family tree and biographical notes, in possession of John Howard Frankau, Avening, Tetbury, Gloucestershire; Paul J. Jacobi, "The Geiger Family,"

mimeographed (Jerusalem, November 1984), unpaginated; Aryeh Newman, "From Exile to Exit: The Frankau Family Connection," *The Jewish Quarterly* 34/4 (1987):49–50; Adolph Frankau & Co., *100 Years in the Service of Smokers: Adolph Frankau of London Celebrate Their Centenary* (London, 1947), unpaginated; Rosslyn Hill Chapel, list of members, 1 January 1875, RNC 38.189, and minute book, 1907–1922, RNC 38.132, Dr. Williams's Library, London; Thomas Carlyle, *Reminiscences*, edited by Charles Eliot Norton (London: J. M. Dent & Sons, 1972), p. 127n1; *Jewish Encyclopedia*, s.v. "Neuberg, Joseph"; Hester Burton, *Barbara Bodichon, 1827–1891* (London: John Murray, 1949), p. 93. I am especially grateful to Aryeh Newman of the Hebrew University of Jerusalem for providing me with copies of the Frankau family tree and biographical notes and for sharing with me the fruits of his own research on the Frankaus.

31. Jacobi, "The Geiger Family"; Newman, "From Exile to Exit," pp. 49–50; C-F (g), Davis; Gilbert Frankau, *Gilbert Frankau's Self-Portrait: A Novel of His Own Life* (London: Hutchinson & Co., 1940), pp. 16, 24; Louis Hyman, *The Jews of Ireland from Earliest Times to the Year 1910* (London: JHSE; Jerusalem: Israel Universities Press, 1972), pp. 134–135; Eliza Aria, *My Sentimental Self* (London: Chapman & Hall, 1922), pp. 3–4, 9–11, 13–14; Marie Belloc Lowndes, *The Merry Wives of Westminster* (London: Macmillan, 1946), p. 59.

32. Gilbert Frankau, *Self-Portrait*, pp. 16, 24, 97; JC, 24 March 1916; register of marriages, 1842–1889, and wardens' minutes, February 1882–September 1893, West London Synagogue of British Jews.

33. Gilbert Frankau, *Self-Portrait*, p. 18; Lowndes, *The Merry Wives of Westminster*, pp. 57–60.

34. Julia Frankau [Frank Danby], *Dr. Phillips: A Maida Vale Idyll* (London: Vizetelly & Co., 1887), pp. 5, 15, 168.

35. Ibid., p. 61; Julia Frankau, *The Sphinx's Lawyer* (New York: Frederick A. Stokes, 1906), p. 245.

36. Julia Frankau, *Dr. Phillips*, 2d ed. (London: Vizetelly & Co., 1887), p. 3.

37. Hyman, *The Jews of Ireland*, pp. 134–135; *The Jewish Encyclopedia*, s.v. "Davis, James"; *The Universal Jewish Encyclopedia*, s.v. "Davis, James"; JC, 12 April 1907; Aria, *My Sentimental Self*, pp. 7, 15–20; George Moore, *Confessions of a Young Man*, edited by Susan Dick (Montreal: McGill-Queen's University Press, 1972), p. 184.

38. Aria, *My Sentimental Self*, pp. 27–30, 37; JC, 18 September 1931; Observer, 11 February 1923.

39. M. C. Bradbrook, "Queenie Leavis: The Dynamics of Rejection," *The Cambridge Review*, 20 November 1981, pp. 56–57; Aryeh Newman, "Jewish Identity: Cambridge 1941–44," *The Cambridge Review*, p. 176; idem, personal communication, 8 June 1983.

40. DNB, 1951–1960, s.v. "Frankau, Gilbert"; obituary of Gilbert Frankau, *The Times*, 5 November 1952; Gilbert Frankau, "As a Jew I Am Not against Hitler," *Daily Express*, 9 May 1933.

41. Pamela Frankau, *Pen to Paper: A Novelist's Notebook* (London: Heinemann, 1961), pp. 202, 203, 208.

42. E. H. W. Meyerstein, *Of My Early Life (1889–1915)*, edited by Rowland Watson (London: Neville Spearman, 1957), pp. 17–19; Meyerstein, *Some Letters of E. H. W. Meyerstein*, edited by Rowland Watson (London: Neville Spearman, 1959), pp. 240–241. For further evidence that it was more difficult to be a "half breed" than a self-acknowledged Jew at a boarding school, see the memoirs of the literary agent David Higham, *Literary Gent* (London: Jonathan Cape, 1978), p. 20.

43. Meyerstein, *Some Letters*, pp. 131, 138, 241–243.

44. Fredric Warburg, *An Occupation for Gentlemen* (Boston: Houghton Mifflin,

1960), pp. 31–32; David Farrer, *The Warburgs: The Story of a Family* (New York: Stein and Day, 1975), pp. 226–227.

45. Warburg, *An Occupation for Gentlemen*, p.32.

46. Ibid., pp. 30, 32–33.

47. Albert Rutherston to William Rothenstein, 2 April 1916, William Rothenstein Papers, BMS ENG 1148 (1296), Houghton Library, Harvard University. Sir Thomas Colyer-Fergusson clipped scores of change-of-name notices from *The Times*. They can be found throughout the volumes of newspaper clippings he kept, arranged alphabetically by family name. See also the changes of name recorded in *Merchant Taylors' School Register, 1561–1934*, edited by Mrs. E. P. Hart, 2 vols. (London: The Merchant Taylors' Company, 1936) and *Charterhouse Register, 1872–1931*, 3d ed., 2 vols. (Guildford: The Old Carthusian Club, 1932). In Somerset Maugham's short story "The Alien Corn," the rabidly assimilationist Sir Adolphus Blank (whose father's name was originally Bleikogel) breaks off relations with his uncle Ferdinand Rabenstein over the latter's refusal to anglicize his name during World War I.

48. Priestley, *English Journey*, pp. 160–161; Stephen Spender, *World Within World* (London: Hamish Hamilton, 1951), p. 13.

5. The Fruits of Missionary Labors

1. Anonymous appeal for funds, Manchester, undated [ca. 1903], Dep. CMJ d. 38/5, CMJC.

2. The authoritative account of the millenarian background to the resettlement is David S. Katz, *Philo-Semitism and the Readmission of the Jews to England, 1603–1655* (Oxford: Clarendon Press, 1982).

3. *Gentleman's Magazine* 29 (1759): 269–270. On the persistence of conversionist sentiment between the Resettlement and the French Revolution in general, see Todd M. Endelman, *The Jews of Georgian England: Tradition and Change in a Liberal Society, 1714–1830* (Philadelphia: Jewish Publication Society, 1979), pp. 57–65.

4. James Picciotto, *Sketches of Anglo-Jewish History*, edited by Israel Finestein (London: Soncino Press, 1956), p. 136.

5. Endelman, *The Jews of Georgian England*, pp. 65–69.

6. Joseph Samuel C. F. Frey, *Narrative of the Rev. Joseph Samuel C. F. Frey*, 4th ed. (New York, 1817), pp. 50, 62, 71.

7. The story of Frey's break with the London Missionary Society and the establishment of the London Society for Promoting Christianity among the Jews is told in Endelman, *The Jews of Georgian England*, pp. 71–72; R. H. Martin, "United Conversionist Activities among the Jews in Great Britain, 1795–1815: Pan-Evangelicalism and the London Society for Promoting Christianity amongst the Jews," *Church History* 46 (1977):442–444; and Robert Michael Smith, "The London Jews' Society and Patterns of Jewish Conversion in England, 1801–1859," *Jewish Social Studies* 43 (1981): 276.

8. Memoir from Joseph Samuel C. F. Frey to the Committee for Jewish Affairs, London Missionary Society, 19 October 1807, Archives of the Council for World Mission, School of Oriental and African Studies, University of London.

9. Smith, "The London Jews' Society," p. 279.

10. On the early years of the London Society, see Martin, "United Conversionist Activities," pp. 444–447; Smith, "The London Jews' Society," pp. 276–279; and Mel Scult, *Millennial Expectations and Jewish Liberties: A Study of the Efforts to Convert the Jews in Britain up to the Mid Nineteenth Century* (Leiden: E. J. Brill, 1978), chap. 6.

11. Frey, *Narrative*, p. 130.

12. Endelman, *The Jews of Georgian England*, pp. 75–76; William Carus, ed., *Mem-*

oirs of the Life of the Rev. Charles Simeon (London: Hatchard and Son, 1847), p. 656; Susan Edith Ruskin, "The Making of London's East End Jewish Community, 1830–1880: The Convergence of the Immigrant, the Missionary, and the Anglo-Jewish Elite" (B.A. honors thesis, Harvard University, 1979), p. 48.

13. B. R. Goakman, *The London Society Examined and the Pretensions of the Converted Jew Investigated* (London, 1816), p. 19.

14. Ridley Herschell, *Conversion of Mr. and Mrs. Levi* (New York, 1852), pp. 12–16.

15. Yisrael Cohen, *Yitshak Eduard Zalkinson: hayyav u-mifalo ha-sifruti* [Isaac Edward Salkinson: His Life and Literary Activity] (Tel Aviv: Mesilah, 1942); Shmuel Leib Tsitron, *Mei-ahorei ha-pargod: mumarim, bogedim, mitkahshim* [From Behind the Screen: Converts, Traitors, Deniers], 2 vols. (Vilna: Tsevi Mats, 1923–25), vol. 2, chap. 2.

16. Goakman, *The London Society Examined*, p. 25; Bat Yisrael [pseud.], *Letter to Mr. Frey by a Daughter of Israel* (London, 1810), p. 6; M. Sailman, *The Mystery Unfolded* (London, 1817), p. 7.

17. Reports on home mission work, 1851–1853, entry for 16 December 1851, Dep. CMJ d. 11, CMJC. So strong was the association between poverty and conversion that the witness to a baptism in Manchester in 1845 stressed that the convert was "in respectable circumstances, not needing pecuniary assistance." Bill Williams, *The Making of Manchester Jewry, 1740–1875* (Manchester: Manchester University Press, 1976), p. 149.

18. *Voice of Jacob*, 12 September 1845; M. Lissack, *Jewish Perseverance, or, The Jew at Home and Abroad: An Autobiography* (London: Hamilton, Adams, & Co., 1851), pp. 191–192, 197–202, 205, 214–215.

19. Reports on home mission work, 1851–1853, entries for 16 December 1851, 18 June 1853, 10 September 1851, 8 March 1852, Dep. CMJ d. 11, CMJC.

20. On Jewish charities in London before 1859 and the origins of the Board of Guardians, see Vivian D. Lipman, *A Century of Social Service, 1859–1959: The Jewish Board of Guardians* (London: Routledge and Kegan Paul, 1959), pp. 13–31.

21. Goakman, *The London Society Examined*, pp. 42–43, 50.

22. Thomas Witherby, *The Wisdom of the Calvinistic Methodists Displayed* (London, 1810), p. 17, quoted in Martin, "United Conversionist Activities," p. 451.

23. Endelman, *The Jews of Georgian England*, pp. 241–243; Harvey W. Meirovich, "Ashkenazic Reactions to the Conversionists, 1800–1850," *TJHSE* 26 (1979):12–14; Smith, "The London Jews' Society," p. 282.

24. Ruskin, "London's East End Jewish Community," pp. 49–50.

25. Certificates of application for admission to the schools of the LSPCJ, Dep. CMJ c. 114/1, 116/1, CMJC.

26. Lissack, *Jewish Perseverance*, p. 213; Ruskin, "London's East End Jewish Community," pp. 50–53.

27. John Dunlop, ed., *Memories of Gospel Triumphs among the Jews during the Victorian Era* (London: S. W. Partridge & Co.; John Snow & Co., 1894), pp. 280–281; Moses Margoliouth, *The Fundamental Principles of Modern Judaism Investigated* (London: B. Wertheim, 1843), pp. i–vi; Albert Augustus Isaacs, *Biography of the Rev. Henry Aaron Stern, D.D.* (London: James Nisbet, 1886), pp. 14–18, 21.

28. Williams, *The Making of Manchester Jewry*, p. 149; *JC*, 15 September 1848, 15 February 1850.

29. Lissack, *Jewish Perseverance*, pp. 197–198; Ruskin, "London's East End Jewish Community," pp. 65–67; Margoliouth, *Fundamental Principles*, p. 210.

30. *JC*, 27 July 1860; Israel Finestein, "Some Conversionists in Hull in the Nineteenth Century," *The Gates of Zion* 11 (1957): 10; Emden, *Jews of Britain*, pp. 351–354.

31. Bernard Susser, "The Jews of Devon and Cornwall from the Middle Ages

until the Early Twentieth Century," Ph.D. diss., University of Exeter, 1977, pp. 348–349; *EJ*, s.v. "Alexander, Michael Solomon"; Muriel W. Corey, *From Rabbi to Bishop: The Biography of the Right Reverend Michael Solomon Alexander, Bishop in Jerusalem* (London: Church Missions to Jews, n.d.). Corey describes in some detail the inner torment that Alexander experienced as he made his way slowly and fitfully from Judaism to Christianity. She also provides the fullest account of his relations with his in-laws and other Plymouth Jews as he struggled with his religious beliefs. Her account, however, should not be accepted uncritically; it is very much a hagiographic, partisan rendering of Alexander's conversion and later career.

32. Moses Margoliouth, *The History of the Jews in Great Britain*, 3 vols. (London: Richard Bentley, 1851), 3:128–131; Henry Samuel Joseph, *Reasons for Renouncing Judaism and Embracing Christianity* (Norwich, 1830); Cecil Roth, *The Rise of Provincial Jewry: The Early History of the Jewish Communities in the English Countryside, 1740–1840* (London: The Jewish Monthly, 1950), p. 30. According to Roth, "the late Professor [David W.] Marks used to recount how, while on a visit to Strassburg many years later [that is, after 1830], he witnessed Nathan Joseph's death-bed return to the religion of his fathers."

33. Margoliouth, *Fundamental Principles*, p. 193; Endelman, *The Jews of Georgian England*, p. 286; Jonas Abraham Davis, *Autobiography of Jonas Abraham Davis, Convert from Judaism to Christianity* (Knoxville, 1850), pp. 101–105; Margoliouth, *The Jews in Great Britain*, 1:97.

34. The history of Hebrew Christian groups in Great Britain and the United States is treated uncritically in Hugh J. Schonfield, *The History of Jewish Christianity from the First to the Twentieth Century* (London: Duckworth, 1936), and more satisfactorily in B. Z. Sobel, *Hebrew Christianity: The Thirteenth Tribe* (New York: John Wiley & Sons, 1974).

35. Schonfield, *Jewish Christianity*, pp. 219–220; report on districts 7 and 8, file A39, pp. 41–42, Charles Booth Collection, Manuscript Room, British Library of Political and Economic Science, London School of Economics.

36. *JC*, 19 February 1858; Margoliouth, *The Jews in Great Britain*, 2:229; Dunlop, *Memories of Gospel Triumphs*, p. 226; Isaacs, *Henry Aaron Stern*, p. 433.

37. Margoliouth, *Fundamental Principles*, p. ix; *DNB*, s.v. "Margoliouth, Moses"; Cohen, *Zalkinson*, pp. 20–23.

38. Isaacs, *Henry Aaron Stern*, pp. 399–400.

39. Patrick Irwin, "Bishop Alexander and the Jews of Jerusalem," in W. J. Sheils, ed., *Persecution and Toleration: Papers Read at the Twenty-Second Summer Meeting and the Twenty-Third Winter Meeting of the Ecclesiastical History Society* (Oxford: Basil Blackwell, 1984), pp. 317–327; *Short Memoirs of Jewish Converts*, 1st ser., 2d ed. (London: LSPCJ, 1907), pp. 6–7; Helen Alpert-Levin, "A Jewish Hero of Christian Missions," in Henry Einspruch, ed., *When Jews Face Christ* (Baltimore: The Mediator, 1931), pp. 69–78.

40. Anthony Trollope, *The Eustace Diamonds*, chaps. 66 and 80.

41. Corey, *From Rabbi to Bishop*, p. 43; Margoliouth, *The Jews in Great Britain*, vol. 2, chaps. 16–17, vol. 3, chaps. 1–2; Moses Margoliouth, *The Anglo-Hebrews: Their Past Wrongs and Present Grievances—Two Epistles* (London: L. Booth, 1856); *DNB*, s.v. "Margoliouth, Moses"; *EJ*, s.v. "Margoliouth, Moses"; *DNB*, 1931–1940, s.v. "Margoliouth, David Samuel."

42. Lloyd Gartner estimates that about 120,000 Jews settled in Great Britain during this period. (*The Jewish Immigrant in England, 1870–1914*, 2d ed. [London: Simon Publications, 1979], p. 49.) However, many more Jews passed through England on their way to the United States, some remaining there for several months to several years. In addition, over 50,000 Jews returned to their countries of origin, usually

with the encouragement of Jewish communal agencies. Thus, the number of immigrants who lived in England during this period was greater than the number who settled there permanently, although it is impossible to know how much greater.

43. The proliferation of missionary societies is treated in Michael D. Sherman, "Christian Missions to the Jews in East London, 1870–1914" (M.A. thesis, Yeshiva University, 1983), chap. 1. The confidential report of a committee appointed by the Board of Deputies in 1912 to investigate missionary activity and recommend Jewish responses lists nine major organizations and describes in detail the scope of their work. The report is available at the archives of the Board of Deputies of British Jews, London. I am grateful to Rabbi Sherman for making a copy available to me.

44. Report of Mission Committee, undated [late 1912 or early 1913], pp. 14–15, 27–28, Board of Deputies of British Jews, Woburn House, London.

45. The reluctance of communal notables to provide free medical care to the Jewish poor is discussed in Sherman, "Christian Missions to the Jews," pp. 32–42.

46. Simeon Singer, *Conversionist Activity and Its Perils* (London: Jewish Chronicle, 1903), p. 4; Report of Mission Committee, p. 15; Ralph L. Finn, *Spring in Aldgate* (London: Robert Hale, 1968), p. 78.

47. Finn, *Spring in Aldgate*, p. 78; Singer, *Conversionist Activity*, p. 5; Report of Mission Committee, p. 11; Jewish-Christian Observer, "Das Evangelium unter den Juden in England," *Nathanael* 4 (1888):110–11.

48. Singer, *Conversionist Activity*, p. 4; Report of Mission Committee, p. 8; *JC*, 14 and 16 October 1904, 5 July 1895.

49. Report of Mission Committee, pp. 9–10, 18.

50. Letters of inquiry from Jews to the London mission, Dep. CMJ c. 107, CMJC. The report on the Aaronsohn case noted: "They [Jewish leaders] complain that missionaries bother themselves with poor Jews, which business is none of theirs, but belongs to the Jewish Board of Guardians, who are ever watching their poor and ever ready to relieve them. Unfortunately, however, this is a mere boast and an obvious falsehood." See also, in the same file, the case of Lina Weissfeldt, whose husband left her to find work in Australia.

51. Report of Mission Committee, pp. 4–5; Charles Booth, ed., *Life and Labour of the People of London*, vol. 1, *East London* (London: Williams and Norgate, 1889), pp. 575–576; interview with the Rev. Dimsdale, Christchurch, St. George's East, file B197, Charles Booth Collection, Manuscript Room, British Library of Political and Economic Science, London School of Economics.

52. *Correspondence between Mr. Oswald John Simon and the Dean of Lichfield, Rev. George Margoliouth, and Rev. A. E. Suffrin, on Parochial Missions to the Jews* (London: The Jewish World, 1887), p. 25; "Das Evangelium unter den Juden in England," *Nathanael* 4 (1888):107. In the 1890s, in order to reach Jews who were otherwise outside the scope of their usual activity, a number of conversionist groups established what they called "postal missions" to the Jews. They mailed—unsolicited—tracts, church newspapers, and the New Testament to prominent West End Jews. For a brief account of some of these "postal missions" and of the reaction of Jews who received such literature, see Sherman, "Christian Missions to the Jews," pp. 18–20.

53. M. Wolkenberg to W. Fleming, 14 August 1897, Frederick Temple Papers, vol. 4, ff. 105–107, Lambeth Palace Library, London.

54. Oswald John Simon to Frederick Temple, 5 August 1897, Frederick Temple Papers, vol. 4, ff. 70–75, Lambeth Palace Library, London.

55. Letters of inquiry from Jews to the London mission, Dep. CMJ c. 107, CMJC.

56. For a report on such a case in Manchester, see Walter Tomlinson, *Bye-Ways of Manchester Life* (Manchester: Butterworth and Nodal, 1887), p. 47. See also the testimony of A. Hornstein, a convert who returned to Judaism, in *JC*, 22 September 1893.

6. From World War I to World War II

1. The current chief rabbi, Immanuel Jakobovits, makes this same point in his introduction to Lloyd Gartner, *The Jewish Immigrant in England, 1870–1914*, 2d ed. (London: Simon Publications, 1979), p. 1.

2. Maurice Samuel, *The Gentleman and the Jew: Twenty-Five Centuries of Conflict in Manners and Morals* (New York: Behrman House, 1977), pp. 14–15; Samuel, *Little Did I Know: Recollections and Reflections* (New York: Alfred A. Knopf, 1963), p. 66.

3. Lloyd Gartner, *The Jewish Immigrant in England*, p. 197; Solomon Fisch, *Yeriot Shlomo: pirkei hayyim, divrei hagut, derashot, ve-hidushei torah* [The Pages of Solomon: Memoirs, Studies, Addresses, and Novellae], with introduction by Harold Fisch (Jerusalem, privately published, 1983), pp. 13–14.

4. Harry S. Lewis, "East End Judaism: The Possibilities of Reform," *JC*, 20 February 1903; Samuel Jacob Rabbinowitz, *Menuhat shabbat* [Sabbath Rest] (Liverpool, 1919), p. 25, quoted in Gartner, *The Jewish Immigrant in England*, p. 193.

5. Ralph L. Finn, *No Tears in Aldgate* (London: Robert Hale, 1963), pp. 17–18; Finn, *Grief Forgotten: The Tale of an East End Jewish Boyhood*, Futura Books ed. (London: Macdonald & Co., 1985), pp. 17–18, 29. See also the description of the native Jewish porters working in the Spitalfields produce market in the interwar years in Alexander Baron, *With Hope, Farewell* (London: Jonathan Cape, 1952), p. 48: "the many Jewish porters there . . . are only distinguished from their Gentile workmates by the fact that they are burlier, their Cockney accent more pronounced, their language more obscene, and their capacity for beer greater."

6. Finn, *No Tears in Aldgate*, p. 76; Bernard Kops, *The World Is a Wedding* (New York: Coward-McCann, 1963), p. 91; William Goldman, *East End My Cradle* (London: Art & Educational Publishers, 1947), p. 64. The world described by Alexander Hartog (b. 1922), an East End mantle presser, in his oral memoir was entirely Jewish; see *Born to Sing*, edited by Clive Murphy (London: Dennis Dobson, 1978).

7. *Leeds Mercury*, 6 March 1925; *East London Observer*, 15 June 1929; Selig Brodetsky and Herbert M. J. Loewe, *The Intellectual Level of Anglo-Jewish Life* (London: Independent Order of B'nai Brith, First Lodge of England, 1928), p. 5. Harry Blacker, the well-known cartoonist Nero, recalled how his generation of East End Jews became aware of the glittering attractions of metropolitan life outside the immigrant neighborhood: "The first generation stemming from the early settlers were born and nurtured in the quarter, where they slowly assumed the characteristics of the native environment, at the same time, through education and contact, becoming more and more aware of life outside the narrow limits of their neighbourhood. Visits to the West End of town, when funds permitted, revealed a facet of living which, whilst foreign to their strict upbringing, held for them a strange fascination. The bright lights, theatres, cinemas, restaurants lavish with red plush banquettes and parchment-shaded chandeliers, all were eloquent of the dolce vita, an unattainable dream to the dwellers in the Mittel East." *Just Like It Was: Memoirs of the Mittel East* (London: Vallentine, Mitchell, 1974), p. 109.

8. *JC*, 15 March 1929; Brodetsky and Loewe, *The Intellectual Level of Anglo-Jewish Life*, pp. 6–7; Harris Cohen, "The Sabbath Problem," *Papers Read at the Third Conference of Anglo-Jewish Preachers, July 12th, 13th, and 14th, 5687–1927* ([London, 1927]), pp. 32–33; *The Times*, 16 July 1925; Joe Jacobs, *Out of the Ghetto: My Youth in the East End—Communism and Fascism, 1913–1939* (London: privately published, 1978), pp. 24 and 190. Military service during World War I very likely contributed to the growth of religious laxity at this time. In the army young Jews mixed with gentiles (for the first time, in many cases), learned new habits and ways, and were far removed from the influence of the immigrant community. Arthur Barnett, Jewish chaplain with the British army in France, believed that "the effect of war on the

Jewish soldier will have been to make him less Jewish in life and outlook. Men who before had lived a fairly Jewish life, will now, after these years of de-Judaising tendencies and influences, find it difficult to recover their faded Jewish consciousness. Army life has produced a sort of Jewish anaesthesia" (*JC*, 28 February 1919). For further evidence about the irreligiosity of East End Jewish youth in the 1920s and 1930s, see David Cesarani, "The East London of Simon Blumenfeld's *Jew Boy*," *London Journal* 13 (1987–1988):46–53.

9. There is no good account of Jewish education in interwar Britain. Some useful information can be found in Henrietta Adler, "Jewish Life and Labour in East London," *The New Survey of London Life & Labour*, vol. 6 (London: P. S. King & Son, 1934), pp. 276–277. In general, the most accessible sources for reconstructing the tenor of everyday life in Jewish neighborhoods at that time are the several dozen memoirs and autobiographical novels about the period that have appeared since the 1940s. There is no bibliography of such materials but many of them are cited in the notes to this chapter.

10. Goldman, *East End My Cradle*, pp. 13, 16; Finn, *No Tears in Aldgate*, pp. 62–63. See also the description of the *heder* in Cyril Spector, *Volla Volla Jew Boy* (London: Centerprise Trust, 1988), p. 20.

11. *Manchester Guardian*, 9 January and 17 July 1929; Kops, *The World Is a Wedding*, pp. 15–16, 18–19; Baron, *With Hope, Farewell*, p. 28.

12. Adler, "Jewish Life and Labour in East London," p. 298.

13. Eliot Slater, "A Note on Jewish-Christian Intermarriage," *Eugenics Review* 39 (1947–48):19–21.

14. *JC*, 27 February 1931; Adler, "Jewish Life and Labour in East London," p. 280; Joe Jacobs, *Out of the Ghetto*, p. 58; A. G. Brotman, notes on meeting at the London Bet Din, 14 June 1945, E2/53, Archives of the Board of Deputies of British Jews, London. There was general agreement at the meeting that conversion to Christianity was not a problem.

15. Simon Blumenfeld, *Jew Boy* (London: Lawrence & Wishart, 1986); Jacobs, *Out of the Ghetto*, p. 59; *Penang Gazette*, 5 February 1930; William Goldman, *A Start in Life* (London: The Fortune Press, n.d. [1947]); Raphael Samuel, *East End Underworld: Chapters in the Life of Arthur Harding* (London: Routledge & Kegan Paul), pp. 131–132, 179, 185.

16. *London Evening Standard*, 1 September 1930.

17. Jacobs, *Out of the Ghetto*, p. 121; John Cooper, "Two East End Jewish Families: The Bloomsteins and the Isenbergs," in *The Jewish East End, 1840–1939*, edited by Aubrey Newman (London: Jewish Historical Society of England, 1981), p. 68.

18. The phrase appears in Charles Landstone's novel about an East End family that makes a fortune during World War I and moves to Highbury New Park. *Blue Tiger Yard* (London: Faber & Gwyer, 1927), pp. 8–9.

19. Adler, "Jewish Life and Labour in East London," pp. 269–271.

20. Ibid., pp. 274–275; *The Times*, 8 December 1924. A contemporary novelist noted that as soon as Jews of immigrant origins made money they moved into better neighborhoods and ceased to be as observant as they had been previously: "you can positively tell from their addresses, afterwards, what degree of Orthodoxy they've retained. Just ask a man where he lives, and you know to what extent he's a Jew. . . ." Woolfe Summerfield [Ben Mowshay], *Fraudem Bear: The Story of a Modern Jew* (London: Hurst & Blackett [1928]), p. 233.

21. On this point see the discussion of residential dispersion in Ernest Krausz, *Leeds Jewry: Its History and Social Structure* (Cambridge: W. Heffer and Sons, 1964), pp. 22–26.

22. Landstone, *Blue Tiger Yard*, pp. 65–68.

23. Zena Marenbon, *Don't Blow Out the Candle: A Liverpool Childhood, 1921–1931* (London: Hart-Davis, MacGibbon, 1973), pp. 22, 86–89, 110, 113–114.

24. John Woodeson, *Mark Gertler: Biography of a Painter, 1891–1939* (London: Sidgwick & Jackson, 1972), chap. 3; Gilbert Cannan, *Mendel: A Story of Youth* (London: T. Fisher Unwin, 1916), pp. 45, 57–58.

25. Woodeson, *Mark Gertler*, chaps. 3–10; Mark Gertler to William Rothenstein, n.d., Sir William Rothenstein Papers, *60M-181 bMS Eng 1148 (566), Houghton Library, Harvard University.

26. Charles Spencer, "Anglo-Jewish Artists: The Migrant Generations," in *The Immigrant Generations: Jewish Artists in Britain, 1900–1945*, The Jewish Museum, New York, May 24-September 15, 1983 (New York: The Jewish Museum, 1982), p.34; Joseph Cohen, *Journey to the Trenches: The Life of Isaac Rosenberg, 1890–1918* (New York: Basic Books, 1975), pp. 113–114; Woodeson, *Mark Gertler*, chaps. 11, 15, 18, 30, 34.

27. Mark Gertler, *Selected Letters*, edited by Noel Carrington (London: Rupert Hart-Davis, 1965), pp. 80–81.

28. Cannan, *Mendel*, p. 115; Gertler, *Selected Letters*, p. 54.

29. Quoted in Woodeson, *Mark Gertler*, p. 240.

30. Woodeson, *Mark Gertler*, pp. 293–294; Gertler, *Selected Letters*, pp. 232–233.

31. Quoted in Woodeson, *Mark Gertler*, p. 250.

32. Sidney Salomon, *The Jews of Britain*, 2d ed. (London: Jarrolds, 1938).

33. Brodetsky and Loewe, *The Intellectual Level of Anglo-Jewish Life*, pp. 7–8, 15.

34. Ibid., p. 9.

35. There are at present no adequate accounts of Jewish involvement in left-wing politics in interwar Britain. Henry Srebrnik's forthcoming work on the Jewish Communist movement in East London should allow us to be more precise about the extent of Jewish participation in the Stepney Communist Party at this time.

36. Raphael Samuel, "The Lost World of British Communism," *New Left Review* 154 (1985):11; Maurice Levinson, *The Trouble with Yesterday* (London: Peter Davies, 1946), pp. 65, 68–69. See also the comments of Raphael Samuel in "Jews and Socialism: The End of a Beautiful Friendship?—The Jacob Sonntag Memorial Symposium," *The Jewish Quarterly* 35/2 (1988):8–9.

37. Blumenfeld, *Jew Boy*, pp. 131–132, 139–140.

38. The standard accounts of antisemitism in interwar Britain emphasize political rather than social or popular forms of Jew-hatred. See, for example, Colin Holmes, *Anti-Semitism in British Society, 1876–1939* (New York: Holmes & Meier, 1979); Gisela C. Lebzelter, *Political Anti-Semitism in England, 1918–1939* (New York: Holmes & Meier, 1978).

39. John A. Garrard, *The English and Immigration: A Comparative Study of the Jewish Influx, 1880–1910* (London: Oxford University Press, 1971); Bernard Gainer, *The Alien Invasion: The Origins of the Aliens Act of 1905* (New York: Crane, Russak & Co., 1972).

40. Sharman Kadish, "Jewish Bolshevism and the 'Red Scare' in Britain," *The Jewish Quarterly* 34/4 (1987):13–14.

41. The views and activities of interwar ideological antisemites are well treated in Holmes, *Anti-Semitism in British Society*, chaps. 9 and 10; Lebzelter, *Political Anti-Semitism*, chaps. 3–5; Richard Thurlow, *Fascism in Britain: A History, 1918–1985* (Oxford: Basil Blackwell, 1987), chaps. 3–5; Kenneth Lunn and Richard C. Thurlow, eds., *British Fascism: Essays on the Radical Right in Inter-War Britain* (London: Croom Helm, 1980), chaps. 3, 4, 7.

42. *London Sunday Express*, 14 June 1931; *Manchester Guardian*, 18 August 1932; *Manchester Daily Express*, 21 November 1932; *Manchester Daily Dispatch*, 17 February 1933; *London Star*, 12 June 1933. The British Union of Fascists used the same

technique—plastering shops, cars, lamp posts, mailboxes, etc., with labels smearing Jews *en bloc*—later in the decade. See Lebzelter, *Political Anti-Semitism*, p. 40.

43. Lebzelter, *Political Anti-Semitism*, pp. 37–43.

44. *Bristol Times & Mirror*, 18 September 1924; *Leeds Mercury*, 28 November 1924; *Hull Daily Mail*, 30 April 1926 and 18 March 1930; *The Grocer*, 16 September 1933. Further examples of this kind of nonideological anti-Jewish feeling can be found in Lebzelter, *Political Anti-Semitism*, pp. 30–33. The following letter from a resident of Stamford Hill is typical of complaints made at the time about Jewish price-cutting: "I should like to see something done to stop Jews in this country opening up shops everywhere with their unfair 'cut price' methods of trading, for they are a curse to the fair Gentile tradesman, whom the Jews go right out to ruin. To make things worse, the Jewish public boycott the Gentile shopkeeper as much as they possibly can, for they don't spend a penny with a Gentile tradesman if they can help it. That's the reason why Hitler doesn't want them." *Hackney Gazette*, 29 September 1933.

45. For the vitality of such themes up through the war years, see Todd M. Endelman, "Anti-Semitism in War-Time Britain—Evidence from the Victor Gollancz Collection," *Michael* 10 (1986):75–95; Aaron L. Goldman, "The Resurgence of Antisemitism in Britain during World War II," *Jewish Social Studies* 46 (1984):37–50; Tony Kushner, *The Persistence of Prejudice: Antisemitism in British Society during the Second World War* (Manchester: Manchester University Press, 1989).

46. *Yorkshire Post*, 9 May 1924 and 10 September 1925; *Manchester Empire News*, 11 May 1924; *Belfast Telegraph*, 10 November 1926; *Birmingham Mail*, 11 November 1926; *Newcastle Daily Journal*, 11 November 1926; *London Daily Mirror*, 11 November 1926; *London Evening Standard*, 11 November 1926; *London Daily Mail*, 13 November 1926; *London Sunday Express*, 6 May 1928; *London Daily News*, 7 May 1928; *London Daily Herald*, 7 May 1928; *Manchester Daily Express*, 27 September 1932; *London Daily Sketch*, 18 and 20 December 1933.

47. Lebzelter, *Political Anti-Semitism*, p. 32; *Yorkshire Evening Post*, 27 April 1925; *Leeds Mercury*, 12 September 1925; Finn, *No Tears in Aldgate*, pp. 180, 183; Israel Zangwill to Nina Salaman, 4 May 1918, A120/51/1, Israel Zangwill Collection, Central Zionist Archives, Jerusalem; *London Evening Standard*, 11 November 1926. See also the evidence in Hartog, *Born to Sing*, p. 39.

48. Norman Bentwich, *My Seventy-Seven Years: An Account of My Life and Times, 1883–1960* (Philadelphia: Jewish Publication Society, 1961); Finn, *Grief Forgotten*, pp. 170–172; *Yorkshire Post*, 9 October 1925.

49. *Portsmouth Evening News*, 8 December 1931; *Yorkshire Evening Post*, 10 September 1925; *Manchester Daily Express*, 27 September 1932; Lebzelter, *Political Anti-Semitism*, p. 32.

50. *London Daily Herald*, 18 June 1928; *London Daily Express*, 20 June 1932; *Yorkshire Evening News*, 8 November 1932. Jews encountered difficulty in securing fire and burglary insurance as well. See the *London Daily Express*, 17, 18, 20, 21, and 22 June 1932; *Manchester Daily Express*, 27 September 1932; Lebzelter, *Political Anti-Semitism*, p. 32.

51. E. M. Forster, *Two Cheers for Democracy* (London: Edward Arnold, 1951), p. 25; Israel Mattuck, "Why Are Jews So Touchy?" *London Sunday Express*, 24 June 1928.

52. *London Daily Express*, 17 March 1931.

53. Baron, *With Hope, Farewell*, pp. 13, 15, 20.

54. *Yorkshire Herald*, 2 November 1928; *JC*, 28 May 1926.

55. *JC*, 14 August 1931, 11 July 1924.

56. Ruth Sebag-Montefiore, *A Family Patchwork: Five Generations of an Anglo-Jewish Family* (London: Weidenfeld and Nicolson, 1987), pp. 14–15, 48; Robert Henriques,

From a Biography of Myself: A Posthumous Selection of the Autobiographical Writings of Robert Henriques (London: Secker & Warburg, 1969), p. xx; *JC*, 11 July 1924.

57. Henriques, *From a Biography of Myself*, p. xx; Sebag-Montefiore, *Family Patchwork*, p. 48; C. P. Snow, *The Conscience of the Rich* (London: Macmillian, 1958); Chaim Bermant, *The Cousinhood* (London: Macmillan, 1971), pp. 190–192.

58. Snow, *Conscience of the Rich*, p. 48; Israel Zangwill to Nina Salaman, 15 December 1919, A120/51/2, and Nina Salaman to Israel Zangwill, 18 December 1919, A120/51/3, Israel Zangwill Papers, Central Zionist Archives, Jerusalem; *JC*, 13 July 1923.

59. Snow, *Conscience of the Rich*, p. 40; Baron, *With Hope, Farewell*, p. 28.

60. For examples of well-to-do Jews who attempted to prevent their children from abandoning Judaism by threatening to disinherit them, see C-F, Emanuel, Gubbay, Henry, Marks, and Tuck; *Yorkshire Evening Press*, 12 December 1928 (Solomon Phillips); *London Evening Standard*, 15 January 1931 (Maximilian Hahn); *Manchester Guardian*, 17 October 1932 (Herbert Bentwich).

61. Caroline Franklin to Helen Bentwich, 7 February 1930, A255/464, Norman Bentwich Collection, Central Zionist Archives, Jerusalem; Snow, *Conscience of the Rich*, pp. 160, 179, 186.

Conclusion

1. On the state of British Jewry in the postwar period, see Maurice Freedman, ed., *A Minority in Britain: Social Studies of the Anglo-Jewish Community* (London: Vallentine, Mitchell, 1955); Julius Gould and Shaul Esh, eds., *Jewish Life in Modern Britain* (London: Routledge and Kegan Paul, 1964); Julius Gould, *Tzurot mishtanot ba-hevrah ha-briytit ve-hashpaatan al ha-kibbutz ha-yehudi* [The Changing Structure of British Society and Its Impact on the Jewish Community] (Jerusalem: Institute for Contemporary Jewry, Hebrew University, 1966/67); Sonia L. Lipman and Vivian D. Lipman, eds., *Jewish Life in Britain, 1962–1977* (New York: K. G. Saur, 1981); Stanley Waterman and Barry Kosmin, *British Jewry in the Eighties: A Statistical and Geographical Study* (London: Board of Deputies of British Jews, 1986); Geoffrey Alderman, "Tadmit u-metsiyyut be-yahadut britanyah ka-yom" [Image and Reality in Contemporary Anglo-Jewry], *Gesher* 116 (Summer 1987):23–31. Chaim Bermant's more anecdotal account *Troubled Eden: An Anatomy of British Jewry* (New York: Basic Books, 1970) can also be read with profit.

2. Waterman and Kosmin, *British Jewry in the Eighties*, p. 7. Many communal officials were reluctant to admit that Anglo-Jewry was shrinking, preferring instead to cite the older (and now discredited) estimate and denounce the findings of the Research Unit. For an interesting discussion of their motives, see Alderman, "Tadmit u-metsiyyut be-yahadut britanyah ka-yom," pp. 23–24.

3. The Research Unit of the Board of Deputies has estimated that in 1970 about 44,000 British-born Jews were living in Israel, the United States, Australia, Canada, Rhodesia, and South Africa—that is, about twelve percent of the resident British Jewish population at that time. Since young families were disproportionately represented in those who settled abroad, the loss is even greater: it was not just that of the migrants themselves but also of their offspring. Waterman and Kosmin, *British Jewry in the Eighties*, pp. 16–18.

4. S. J. Prais, "Polarization or Decline? A Discussion of Some Statistical Findings on the Community," in Lipman and Lipman, *Jewish Life in Britain*, p. 5.

5. Waterman and Kosmin, *British Jewry in the Eighties*, p. 12.

6. Despite its subtitle, the only study of the settlement of Jewish refugees from Central Europe in the 1930s—Marion Berghahn, *German-Jewish Refugees in England: The Ambiguities of Assimilation* (London: Macmillan, 1984)—does not include a satis-

factory treatment of the Jewish commitments of the refugees and their offspring.

7. For a comparative perspective, see Todd M. Endelman, "The Social and Political Context of Conversion in Germany and England, 1870–1914," in *Jewish Apostasy in the Modern World*, edited by Todd M. Endelman (New York: Holmes & Meier, 1987); Endelman, "Conversion as a Response to Antisemitism in Modern Jewish History," in *Living with Antisemitism: Modern Jewish Responses*, edited by Jehuda Reinharz (Hanover: University Press of New England, 1987).

8. On leakage from the Nonconformist churches, see Jeffrey Cox, *The English Churches in a Secular Society: Lambeth, 1870–1930* (New York: Oxford University Press, 1982), pp. 133–135, 229–242; Jacob M. Price, "The Great Quaker Business Families of Eighteenth-Century London: The Rise and Fall of a Sectarian Patriciate," in *The World of William Penn*, edited by Richard S. Dunn and Mary Maples Dunn (Philadelphia: University of Pennsylvania Press, 1986), pp. 363–399; John Seed, "Gentlemen Dissenters: The Social and Political Meanings of Rational Dissent in the 1770s and 1780s," *The Historical Journal* 28 (1985): 315; Hugh McLeod, *Religion and the People of Western Europe, 1789–1970* (Oxford: Oxford University Press, 1981), p. 69; Robert Roberts, *The Classic Slum: Salford Life in the First Quarter of the Century* (Harmondsworth, Middlesex: Penguin Books, 1974), pp. 173–174.

9. T. A. B. Corley, *Quaker Enterprise in Biscuits: Huntley and Palmers of Reading, 1822–1972* (London: Hutchinson & Co., 1972), p. 7. The poet and essayist Anna Letitia Barbauld (1743–1825) applied this saying to Dissent in general. She thought "it would be difficult to find an instance of families who for three generations have kept their carriage and continued Dissenters." *The Works of Anna Letitia Barbauld*, 2 vols. (London: Longman, Hurst, Rees, Orme, Brown, and Green, 1825), 2:314. A similar epigram is attributed to Ralph Waldo Emerson, who is said to have remarked that "no dissenter rides in his coach for three generations; he invariably falls onto the Establishment." E. Digby Baltzell, *The Protestant Establishment: Aristocracy and Caste in America* (New York: Random House, 1964), p. 223.

10. Cox, *The English Churches in a Secular Society*, p. 229.

Index